RITUAL AND RELIGIOUS BELIEF

Critical Categories in the Study of Religion

Series Editor: Russell T. McCutcheon, Associate Professor, Department of Religious Studies, University of Alabama

Critical Categories in the Study of Religion aims to present the pivotal articles that best represent the most important trends in how scholars have gone about the task of describing, interpreting, and explaining the position of religion in human life. The series focuses on the development of categories and the terminology of scholarship that make possible knowledge about human beliefs, behaviours, and institutions. Each volume in the series is intended as both an introductory survey of the issues that surround the use of various key terms as well as an opportunity for a thorough retooling of the concept under study, making clear to readers that the cognitive categories of scholarship are themselves historical artefacts that change over time.

Published:
Syncretism in Religion
A Reader
Edited by Anita M. Leopold and Jeppe S. Jensen

Forthcoming:
Defining Hinduism
A Reader
Edited by J. E. Llewellyn

Myths and Mythologies
A Reader
Edited by Jeppe S. Jensen

Religion and Cognition
A Reader
Edited by D. Jason Slone

Readings in the Theory of Religion
Map, Text, Body
Edited by Scott S. Elliott and Matthew Waggoner

Mircea Eliade
A Critical Reader
Edited by Bryan Rennie

Defining Religion
A Reader
Edited by Tim Murphy

What is Religious Studies?
A Reader in Disciplinary Formation
Edited by Stephen J. Sutcliffe

Defining Buddhisms
A Reader
Edited by Karen Derris and Natalie Gummer

RITUAL AND RELIGIOUS BELIEF

A Reader

Edited by

Graham Harvey

LONDON

Published by

Equinox Publishing Ltd.
Unit 6
The Village
101 Amies St.
London
SW11 2JW
www.equinoxpub.com

First published 2005

British Library Cataloguing-in-Publication Data
A catalogue record for this book is available from the British Library.

ISBN   1 904768 17 2   (paperback)

Typeset by ISB Typesetting, Sheffield
www.sheffieldtypesetting.com

Printed and bound in Great Britain by Antony Rowe Ltd, Chippenham,
Wiltshire

CONTENTS

Acknowledgements   vii

Introduction   1
GRAHAM HARVEY

PART I
Exemplifying the Problem

1   MARTIN LUTHER   18
The Sacraments of Holy Baptism and of the Altar

2   REFORM RABBIS IN THE USA   22
The Pittsburgh Conference "Declaration of Principles"

PART II
Surveying the Discussion

3   JONATHAN Z. SMITH   26
To Take Place

PART III
Relating Ritual to Actions and Ideas

4   MAURICE BLOCH   52
Myth

5   STANLEY J. TAMBIAH   61
Malinowski's Demarcations and his Exposition of the Magical Art

6   KIERAN FLANAGAN   78
    Holy and Unholy Rites: Lies and Mistakes in Liturgy

7   IAN READER   87
    Cleaning Floors and Sweeping the Mind:
    Cleaning as a Ritual Process

8   MARGARET J. KING   105
    Instruction and Delight: Theme Parks and Education

9   EDWARD J. SCHIEFFELIN   124
    Problematizing Performance

10 PETER STALLYBRASS AND ALLON WHITE   139
    Introduction

11 GERRIE TER HAAR   163
    Ritual as Communication: A Study of African Christian
    Communities in the Bijlmer District of Amsterdam

12 DAVID I. KERTZER   189
    The Rites of Power

13 SUSAN S. SERED   202
    Ritual Expertise in the Modern World

14 CARLO SEVERI   218
    Memory, Reflexivity and Belief:
    Reflections on the Ritual Use of Language

    PART IV
    Conclusion: Reflecting on our Categories

15 MALCOLM RUEL   242
    Christians as Believers

16 CATHERINE BELL   265
    Ritual Reification

    Index of Names   286

    Index of Subjects   291

ACKNOWLEDGEMENTS

It has been a pleasure and privilege working with Janet Joyce and Val Hall at Equinox again. Thanks also to Russell McCutcheon for the possibility of putting together this collection and contributing to the series "Critical Categories in the Study of Religion."

Tina Welch was exceptionally helpful at a busy time – thanks!

As ever, my chief thanks are to my wife and favourite proofreader, Molly. Any faults that remain in what follows are entirely because I forgot to follow her excellent advice.

I am grateful to the various authors and publishers who have given permission to reprint material in this book.

Part I: Exemplifying the Problem
Martin Luther, "The Sacraments of Holy Baptism and of the Altar" from *Martin Luther's Basic Theological Writings* edited by Timothy F. Lull, 1989. © 1989 Fortress Press. Used with permission of Augsburg Fortress.

Part II: Surveying the Discussion
Jonathan Z. Smith, "To Take Place" from *To Take Place: Toward Theory in Ritual* by Jonathan Z. Smith, 1987. © 1987 The University of Chicago. Used with permission of The University of Chicago Press.

Part III: Relating Ritual to Actions and Ideas
Maurice Bloch, "Myth" from *Prey into Hunter: The Politics of Religious Experience* by Maurice Bloch, 1991. © 1991 Cambridge University Press. Used with permission of Cambridge University Press.

Carlo Severi, "Memory, Reflexivity and Belief: Reflections on the Ritual Use of Language" from *Social Anthropology* 10(1) (2002): 23–40, published by Cambridge University Press. © 2002 European Association of Social Anthropologists. Reproduced with permission.

Part IV: Conclusion: Reflecting on our Categories
Malcolm Ruel, "Christians as Believers" from *Belief, Ritual and the Securing of Life* by Malcolm Ruel, 1997. Used with permission of Brill Academic Publishers.

Catherine Bell, "Ritual Reification" from *Ritual: Perspectives and Dimensions* Catherine Bell. © 1997 Catherine Bell. Used with permission of Oxford University Press.

INTRODUCTION

Graham Harvey

Ritual and belief are often contrasted in religions and wider cultures as well as in academic discourse and theory. So, too, are their various expressions, including ritualizing and believing. The contrast seems simple: doing something is not the same as thinking it. Having ideas is not the same as acting on them. The arrangement of ceremonies or of valued objects is not the same as their meanings. However, a more intimate relationship between ritual and belief may be revealed by the fact that they can both be suspected of being deceitful. Someone might be acting a role, deceiving others; and they might be insincere, ignorant or mistaken, deceiving themselves. What people do and why they do it (their motivations and their sincerity) are linked. Even apart from any suspicions about deceitful behaviour or intentions, we are commonly confronted (in religions, cultures and academia) with other questions about how beliefs and rituals might be related. Are rituals ways of performing beliefs? Are beliefs learnt and taught in rituals? Do rituals require correct belief and sincerity? Do firm beliefs lead to rich and profound rituals? Are rituals more satisfying if people know what is happening in them? Alternatively, if people fully understood whatever a ritual might convey, would they need to bother going through the actions at all? In all these and other questions, the contrast seems to require us to understand that rituals are outer, physical, bodily actions while beliefs are inner, metaphysical, spiritual ideas. Rituals are more-or-less public, communal and corporate, while beliefs are more-or-less private, individual and exclusive. In fact, however, this is a dubious distinction. Beliefs are far from a private matter in any religion: rituals may well be most suspect precisely because beliefs are also more-or-less public, communal and corporate. Certainly this too is a common cause of debate. By various names in particular religions, and probably in all religious cultures, beliefs are talked about, taught and

1

examined in public. Beliefs, ideas, worldviews or knowledges are not left inside people's heads or hearts but are, by virtue of being more-or-less publicly debated, a matter of performance and other actions. Discussion or teaching of belief (or ideas, worldviews or knowledges) is not only an idea but an activity.

In fact, even the idea that beliefs might be located in the heart or head already shows that they are in some respects embodied. Admittedly these metaphors are different from those ways of talking that might relate ritual or ritualizing to more visible and public bodily activities: dance, movement, gesture. Nonetheless, the question of whether someone wearing a mask or a costume is sincere and knowledgeable, or whether they truly embody the divine or an ancestor, point to something behind the mask, within the actor's body, hidden from view but open to question. The interior state of a ritualist's motivations, intentions and devotion is often of public concern. It is possible to ask whether particular priests are moral people. It is possible to debate whether all priests should be moral. The distinction between an actor or entertainer and a ritualist or priest is important to many religious people. The reason why this, or any of the preceding issues, are of interest to religious people is that they are uncertain. Appearances can be deceptive and different types of action (if we agree that belief and ritual are types of action) can be confused with other ways of doing or being.

This much, and more, is true in various specific and local ways in different religions and religious cultures worldwide. Similarly, academics have not only engaged with these religious debates but have also brought their own concerns to bear on the question of ritual and religious belief. They have sought to clarify and even codify what makes one sort of action a "ritual" while another is not. How can "ritual" be defined so that it does not include other performances? Is football a ritual? Are politics ritualized? Is there a difference between rituals and etiquette? Is shaking hands different to laying on hands? If any of these actions are rituals, are they similar to or different from *religious* rituals? Then there are questions about the relationship between rituals (whatever kinds of actions these might be understood to be) and beliefs. How are rituals related to the performance or public expression of beliefs? Are myths half way between interior beliefs and public rituals? Do myths convey beliefs more adequately than rituals? Are doctrines part of ritual behaviour (as public discourse) or of belief? Even the definition of "religion" is affected by the question of ritual and belief: does "religion" refer to institutional, public religion and, if so, how does it relate to "spirituality"? How did "spirituality" come to be popularly applied to interior, sincere, personal and experiential religiosity when it can label "regular practice of defined actions" in more traditional contexts and literatures?

It seems likely that every academic discipline in the humanities and social sciences may have a particular interest in some aspect or other of the question of ritual and religious belief. Even before they talk to each other, or raid each other's books for inspiration, scholars of a particular background and training may see matters in particular ways. Some may privilege questions of interiority but find rituals more interesting than belief. That is, they may ask what ritual performances reveal about cognition, individuation or the interiorization of culture. Others may privilege questions of performance but find beliefs more interesting than rituals. They may ask how ideas are shared, communicated and generate communal experience. The possibilities seem endless and in continuous flux—partly, of course, because academics interested in rituals and beliefs regularly read outside of their disciplinary boundaries.

The following readings engage with these and other questions in a quest to understand the breadth of academic reflection on ritual and ritualizing as they relate to belief and other ideas. Before surveying these readings and then introducing each one, there is another issue that needs consideration. The history of academia is entangled with the history of the West, of Europe and its globalization or colonialism. Academics have been moulded by the kind of debates of importance to religious Europeans, and that means, by and large, Christians. It is no exaggeration to say that a specific religious conflict (between Protestant and the Roman Catholic Christians) generated a particular understanding of ritual and belief that has had considerable impact far beyond Christianity and Europe. It is not hard, for example, to discern Martin Luther's privileging of belief (understood as individual and inner faith) over action in the Cartesian privileging of mind over matter. More will be said about this below because the first reading, by way of exemplifying the problem, is a piece by Luther. The point now is to note that because of the trajectory given impetus by the Lutheran Reformation and its consequences in the Enlightenment, a considerable portion of academic writing about ritual has been skewed by a denigration of performance and a privileging of ideas. It can be hard to read Buddhist texts about "mindfulness" without being distracted by the rumours and ramifications of modernity's individualist ideology. It can be hard to see veneration of masks or statues without being tempted by words such as "idolatry" or "fetishism" into thinking that materiality must be separated from true religion. The contemporary preference for "spirituality" over "religion" is unlikely to be an accident. Modernity has accepted the problematizing of materiality, physicality, display, performance. Its ideologues and proponents in the media, for example, exhort individuals to "look within" and manages to disguise the degree to which people follow trends and fashions.

In short, this debate about ritual and religious belief, and the following readings, are not only of religious interest and should not only be considered by students of religion. The real issues touch the heart and profile the embodiment of modernity at least as much as they engage with traditional religious cultures.

Studying Ritual

While the Parts and essays of this Reader (introduced in the following sections) specifically consider the problematic relationship between ritual and belief, these do not stand alone but benefit from engagement with broader discussions of ritual. A few of these can be briefly introduced here. Articles about "ritual" or "performance" in books that introduce particular academic disciplines or in encyclopedia that support them are a good place to begin a study of ritual (e.g. Zuesse 1987; Grimes 1987, 2000; Schechner 1994b; Alexander 1997; Bell 1998). Some of these authors are among those who have written significant books on ritual (e.g. Bell 1992, 1997; Grimes 1990, 1995; Schechner 1993, 1994a). Other important authors, articles and books include van Gennep (1975 [1909]); Turner (1967; 1991); Staal (1975); Bourdieu (1977; 1997); Goody (1977); Tambiah (1979); Bateson (1972); Geertz (1983); J. Z. Smith (1987); Bloch (1989); E. Turner (1992); De Coppet (1992); Boyer (1993); Humphrey and Laidlaw (1994); Rothenbuhler (1998); Rappaport (1999); Lincoln (2000); and McCauley and Lawson (2002). While this list may be lengthy, it hardly includes any ethnographies that describe and theorize about rituals and ritualizing in particular cultures and communities (e.g. Guss 1989; Brown 1991; Drewal 1992; Viveiros de Castro 1998), but neither does it reach much beyond the disciplines of religious studies, anthropology, performance studies and cultural studies. The list is, in other words, only a selection among many studies of ritual. It is, however, a list devoted to provocative and important works. Sometimes the titles of these books will suggest positions taken, arguments made, and disciplines enhanced. Many of them are cited in the essays that follow or in the survey articles referred to above as good places to begin studying ritual and ritualizing.

Part I

Structurally, there are four main Parts to this book. The first includes two readings that exemplify the problem. Martin Luther's *Small Catechism* contains instructions on the sacraments that illustrate Lutheran Protestant orthodoxy. Even fully Catholic teaching would demonstrate similar tensions between ritual and belief, act and thought, or objects and meanings, precisely because of an understanding that some actions are "sacraments": practices that (somehow) have spiritual meaning or effects. But Luther privileged belief and contributed to a reduction in the number of rituals considered sacramental, or even Christian, in Protestant Christianity.

A second reading comes from a different kind of Reform. The 1885 Pittsburgh Platform of the American Jewish Reform movement is part of the process by which some Jews aligned themselves with the Enlightenment, thereby acculturating Judaism to modernity and its rationalism. The Platform held, among other things, "that Judaism presents the highest conception of the God-idea as taught in our Holy Scriptures and developed and spiritual- ized by the Jewish teachers, in accordance with the moral and philosophical progress of their respective ages." Once God has become an "idea" to be "spiritualized" and made universally relevant, the rituals of traditional Judaism could not continue without challenge. The notion of Judaism as the observance of a particular lifestyle has been replaced by the notion of Judaism as a religion of choice and as one religion in a more-or-less free market of belief-systems (Neusner 2002).

There are, of course, many other examples of the problematic relation- ship between ritual and belief. The Muslim scholar and Imam, Abu Hamid Muhammad al-Ghazālī's *'Ihya 'Ulum al-Din* (translated as *Inner Dimensions of Islamic Worship*, 1983), written around the turn of the twelfth century CE, encourages Muslims to perform religiously required actions with devo- tion, awareness, correct intention and conscious attention. Unlike Luther, al-Ghazālī's stress on inwardness never diminishes the importance of obser- vance. More recently, indigenous peoples have often been confused about the actions and skills of literate Europeans or Euro-Americans. For example, Catherine Bell, in this Reader, cites a Zuni anecdote about the participation of the ethnographer Frank Hamilton Cushing:

> Once they made a White man into a Priest of the Bow
> he was out there with the other Bow priests
> he had black stripes on his body
> the others said their prayers from their hearts
> but he read his from a piece of paper.

This is also discussed by Dennis Tedlock (1983) and John Fulbright (1992). Examples could be multiplied that demonstrate that there may be an ubiquitous human preference for the performance of rituals by those for whom they are "meaningful" and "meant" in some way.

These preferences for the integration of sincerity, understanding, aware- ness, intent and devotion (or true belief) with ritual performances could be traced backwards to earlier religious literatures. Al-Ghazālī's distinction (made in order to insist on their integral unity) can be found in the Qur'an: sura 49:14 castigates a group of Bedouin who made a public confession of the faith without having true faith in their hearts. Luther's distinction (made in order to separate "vain repetition" from salvific faith) can be traced to the insistence in Romans 3:28 that "faith not works saves." At least part of the inspiration of the *Bhagavad-gita* is the idea that Krishna needed to understand the call to arms and the necessity of conflict (a thoroughly ritualized practice). Again, examples could be multiplied by reference to other literatures.

Similarly, we could also trace their resonances and ramifications forward in time. For example, Jean Comaroff writes of how Luther's heirs, Protestant missionaries in Africa, spread their concerns about the "tension between inner and outer verities, the life of the spirit and the sensuous world." Among the Southern Tswana, she continues,

> [d]ress epitomized this conflict. It was a fitting means for showing self-improvement, but it was also the stuff of the flesh. Unless it could be seen to effect reform that was more than skin deep, it remained an exterior overlay or vain deception. The concern with dress revealed what was often a vain effort to fuse the cultivation of the body with the conversion of the spirit. At the same time, the evidence suggests that many Southern Tswana acknowledged the ritual resonance of dress — albeit from a perspective of their own, one that gave voice to a distinct understanding of the colonial encounter. As they read them, the European gestures with clothes were unambiguously embodied and pragmatic (Comaroff 1996, 21–22).

However, this brief encapsulation of what the Southern Tswana understood European costume to mean suggests an opposite move in which ritual and meaning are decoupled, separated and even contrasted. Ritual and belief may not, after all, be integral to one another—they may be separate. A similar possibility may be seen in Jain performance of daily *puja*, morning rituals of veneration to deities in temples. While researching among Jains in Jaipur, Caroline Humphrey and James Laidlaw were regularly given different and sometimes contradictory explanations of the meaning of *puja* (or aspects of its performance). On seeking explanations they were regularly told that *puja* was meaningless or, if it was meaningful, that "anything of any religious value that can be done through *puja* can be done better in other ways" (Humphrey and Laidlaw 1994, vii). This initiated their quest for a theory of ritual which concludes, among other things, that the "pivotal transformation which ritualization effects is to sever the link, which is present in everyday life, between the actors' intentions and the identity of the acts they perform" (Humphrey and Laidlaw 1994, 262). A number of the readings that follow pick up this theme of the meaninglessness of ritual—or, perhaps put more clearly, the separation of ritual from the need for understanding and belief.

Part II

The second Part contains a single and singular reading in which Jonathan Z. Smith surveys the discussion of the relationship between ritual and belief— or ritual and meaning. This essay is taken from his book, *To Take Place: Toward Theory in Ritual* (Smith 1987). While the conclusion to his argument that ritual is, by definition, a mode of "paying attention," the essay is included at this point not to suggest that he conclusively ends the debate of interest here but because of the clarity with which Smith surveys and furthers the debate. The visit of an eighteenth-century Protestant to Rome and a view of western modernity "from outside," by a sociology professor from Delhi, provide a door into Smith's discussion. An interest in the particular places in which rituals "take place" is combined with discussion of the relationship between ritual, superstition, repetitive behaviours, myth and other matters in particular religious texts and actions, and in academic theorizing. Not for the last time among these readings, Smith's essay argues that there is an open-ended dialogue between ritual and everyday life, and between the temporal and spatial nature of ritual and ordinary life. At stake throughout Smith's work is the project of comparison, not least that of comparing religious phenomena. His conclusions are, therefore, of considerable value as a foundation for considering the following readings (some written before Smith's book, some afterwards). What is particularly valuable is Smith's establishment of the view that the problem of ritual and religious belief is central to an understanding of modernity and Western culture in general.

Part III

The bulk of the readings are contained in Part III: "Relating Ritual to Actions and Ideas." In a variety of ways the ten essays in this Part engage either with different ways in which ritual and belief are related, or with different academic approaches to this issue.

Maurice Bloch is included here, like other scholars interested in ritual, not because he has said the last word about the issue that interests him—in this case the relationship between ritual and myth—but because his argument and approach are provocative. It would not be possible to study ritual without considering Bloch's contribution, but neither would it be prudent to consider Bloch's thesis without noting the wider debate to which his argument contributes. Like other scholars, Bloch marshals an array of ethnographic descriptions of particular ceremonies and particular indigenous understandings of such rituals. It might be interesting to attempt to check such data against other scholarly and insiderly views. The interest of this

Reader, however, is with the use to which Bloch and others put the data that they consider relevant. Bloch refers to the view that there is a "direct relation between myth and practice," imputing this view to Bronislaw Malinowski and Edmund Leach and agreeing with Claude Lévi-Strauss that such an approach is misleading, but not entirely so. (For a more comprehensive survey and argument about the "myth and ritual theory"—the claim that myths and rituals necessarily operate together—see Segal 1998.) Bloch posits a place for both myth and ritual in dealing with the "rebounding violence" that he views as challenging all human attempts to build communities and lifestyles that will last into the future. Indeed, they play particular roles in enabling life to continue in the face of experiences that contest it in each present moment.

A quite different demarcation, comparison and debate is significantly presented in Stanley Tambiah's discussion of Malinowski's functionalist understanding of "magic." Distinctions between magic and religion on the one hand, and between religion and science on the other, are commonplace. Malinowski and Tambiah, each in their own way, and drawing distinctly different conclusions, explore these putatively separate kinds of activity. In addition to engaging with what might be particular kinds of ritual, and thereby clarifying what "ritual" itself might mean, this discussion is a key part of Tambiah's contribution to a wider debate about rationality. Once more, we are asked to consider questions of efficacy and pragmatism, and the underlying problem of the relationship between objectivity and subjectivity. It may help to consider this issue in light of the distinction elucidated by Berel Lerner between "instrumental" and "expressive" actions (2000, 116): the former aim to achieve something, the latter to express something. Debates about the rationality of magic and religion are part of Christian, Western, Enlightenment or modern discourses and perspectives on this distinction. For an enlightening argument about the rationality or religiosity of science, see Mary Midgley's admirable *Evolution as a Religion* (2002). In turn, this distinction is enmeshed with that between ritual and belief.

Another particular kind of ritual and another context in which beliefs might be expressed, is labelled "liturgy." There is a vast literature that discusses the liturgies of particular religions, especially Christianity, and even more especially Roman Catholic and "high" Anglican (Episcopalian) liturgy. Kieran Flanagan is a sociologist with interests in Christian liturgy. However, it is not the religious data that determined the inclusion of Flanagan's essay here. Rather, it is his attention to the question of mistakes, "virtuous dissimulation," dissatisfaction, diversity and ambiguity that are important. This contributes to debates that are significant in previous and subsequent readings. It is important that Flanagan situates himself in this arena as a sociologist rather than a theologian because he has different questions and perspectives, especially that he wants to "unmask" that which theologians and other participants may wish to keep concealed or may be unaware of. For all these reasons, Flanagan's essay advances the debate about the nature of ritual, its sub-varieties and its relationships with belief.

The next essay is concerned with another attempt to distinguish everyday actions from ritualized ones, and meaningful from meaningless ritual. Ian Reader's discussion of "Cleaning Floors and Sweeping the Mind: Cleaning as a Ritual Process" is interested in Zen Buddhist and wider Japanese activities. In an interesting conceptualization of the meaningful/meaningless dichotomy, he argues that individuals' desires or thoughts are irrelevant to the specific ritualized tasks set, but that some "inner meaning" is of considerable importance. The fact that temple sweeping is undertaken for longer than is pragmatically useful—in other words, long after the temple is clean—indicates that more is involved than a tidy metaphor. Similarly, the fact that not only monks in temples but also housewives in streets might sweep places, *whether they want to or not*, causes Ian Reader to question the intentionality, individuality and purposefulness of ritual, or these rituals anyway. On the other hand, the genius of Zen is to insist that the religious goal, enlightenment, is "the basic human condition and hence, logically, is a matter of the everyday." Thus everyday sweeping *is* a form of meditation. The question Ian Reader's essay raises most clearly, then, is whether it is possible to distinguish ritual from any other kind of action except when someone explicitly says "this is a ritual."

The next essay entails a quite different contrast and comparison. How do rituals relate to leisure activities? How do ritual spaces (e.g. places of pilgrimage) relate to theme parks? In "Instruction and Delight: Theme Parks and Education," Margaret King argues that the "ancestors of the theme park are venerable, including pilgrimage place, fair, harvest rite, royal pleasure ground, theater, science exposition, history park, world's fair, and museum." If there is little explicit reference to ritual, belief or religion in this essay, the agreed fact that Disneyland is a place of entertainment that inculcates and educates a particular, evolving culture makes it an admirable context for testing similar understandings of ritual. But even the recognition that Disney has established pilgrimage sites, a contemporary form of masking, and a repetitive engagement that might structure the experience of the flow of time, all demonstrate that ritual is to be found in theme parks. King's explicit questioning of the denigration of popular culture by many academics is well aimed. It seems easier to compare and contrast religious rituals with more elite theatrical performances—Greek tragedy and Shakespearean dramas in particular—than to recognize the continuities between Disney and more august pilgrimage venues. A comparison with carnivals and more playful ritualizing is tempting (and with this a reference to Mikhail Bakhtin 1984) but for the fact that Disneyland seems less revolutionary and far more polite than that. Perhaps instead it could illustrate Victor Turner's

(1991) discussion of liminality and *communitas*. If so, maybe this is what theme parks are education for. Without doubt, a consideration of ritual that ignores the possibilities of its links with and severances from entertainment will not be as fruitful as one that considers Disneyland to be an "instructive delight."

A number of the themes and debates already mentioned are admirably taken further in Edward Schieffelin's essay, "Problematizing Performance." The question of the relationship between ritual and "ordinary action," theatre, habit and other repeated and/or repetitive actions or performances is central. Similar questions are raised in disciplines such as performance studies and theatre studies, most clearly in the work of Richard Schechner (e.g. 1994a). In this essay, Schieffelin also engages with expressive issues, not only that of the difference between expressive and instrumental actions, but also, more centrally, the place of ritual in expressing culture by performers in the presence of an audience. He is aware that performances can be repetitive and highly structured while also, at least sometimes, making space for improvisation and play. He draws attention to the "creation of presence," not uniquely in religious ritual but also in theatre and other cultural contexts, in which "modes, social relations, bodily dispositions and states of mind" are altered. Participants in performance (of whatever kind), including but not only performers themselves, construct a world and make themselves. All of this happens in a context that is problematic both for participants (should you take a performance seriously when you know that someone is performing a role?) and for scholars (what is the role of non-performers in a performance?). Schieffelin is at his best in pointing out matters that require more careful consideration and more detailed research.

Peter Stallybrass and Allon White also engage with the distinction between "high" and "low," or "elite" and "popular" culture as they bring notions of carnival and transgression into the foreground. Rituals by which people transit from one phase of life into another are often seen to be about change. But how do cultures change? What role do rituals play in unsettling established norms or even in perceiving dominant hierarchies in the first place? Another comparison, between rituals and literature, is also inherent in this essay and others that follow. Academic vocabularies now use "text" and "read" to speak of performances and ways of dealing with them. Rituals and other performances may be scripted, aiding performers to prepare their roles. Identities may be "written on" bodies or "read from" them as rituals express ideas, passions, visions and other "inner" realities. Towards the end of this essay, Stallybrass and White conclude that Bakhtin's "carnivalesque" can be "analytically powerful in the study of ideological repertoires and cultural practices." If so, once again, there are powerful reasons for applying this argument to the specific question of ritual and religious belief.

Foundational studies of ritual are also invoked in Gerrie ter Haar's discussion of "Ritual as Communication." In particular she makes use of Arnold van Gennep's classic study of rites of passage (1975) in order to examine ritual behaviour in African Christian communities in Amsterdam. The thesis of some of her colleagues in a collaborative research project was that rituals or "ritual behaviour" would be designed by people living in plural societies to differentiate themselves from "others." In contrast, ter Haar found that African Christian communities in southeast Amsterdam geared ritual not to "inter-religious demarcation" but to "intra-religious communication." As with other readings, the precise nature, actions and thoughts of the subjects of ter Haar's ethnography, or the adequacy of her description of them, are not the chief reason for the essay's inclusion here. What contributes to consideration of the central problem of ritual and belief is ter Haar's application not only of van Gennep's tripartite ritual schema but, more interestingly, of Victor Turner's discussion of liminality and *communitas* (V. Turner 1991), including its further development in Edith Turner's "anthropology of experience" (E. Turner 1992). When ter Haar discusses ritual in a pluralist context she not only corrects an over-emphasis on the imagination of "cultures" as discrete and individual entities (seeing them rather as necessarily entangled and engaged), but also enables a closer consideration of the intentions, function and effects of rituals in real life. Indeed, it is the ways in which rituals contribute to the (re-)formation of real life that is most interesting here. More broadly, the essay is instructive in seeing ritual as a communicative act and, therefore, requiring consideration in the light of other ways of communicating.

In the next essay, David Kertzer attends to the expression of political power through symbolic rites. This is, in part, a discussion of the nature of culture, society, power and politics, but it also entails a significant discussion of the role of rituals. Again, rituals may express and communicate matters that are otherwise hidden as ideologies, and they may entail negotiation of different possibilities that present themselves to social actors or participants. As previous essays in this Reader have argued, rituals may create social facts as much as they arise from, make evident, and express them. At the same time, part of the power of rituals is that they may disguise what is really happening. The "convincing world" that rituals seem to establish, as Kertzer's conclusion suggests, may be a confidence trick that diverts our attention away from real power and contingent reality. Meanwhile, therefore, one of the larger and increasingly important questions raised in Kertzer's essay is the role of ritual in change. The common easy association of ritual with "tradition" might itself mask the collusion of both with change and with those forces (personal, environmental or social) that actively construct cultures. (Whether these forces are discrete domains or not is debated by, for example, Ingold 2000 and Hornborg 2000.) As with

Gerrie ter Haar's consideration of pluralist societies, so Kertzer's focus on politics necessarily draws attention to change. The issue is discussed particularly clearly in an important essay by Bruce Lincoln, "On Ritual, Change, and Marked Categories" (2000), and will be considered again later in this volume. Proper attention to the dynamics and processes of change would not only improve understanding of "tradition" (itself never a fixed and static phenomena), but would also enhance appreciation of rituals in relation to other acts and contexts. This is why a view of political rituals is helpful.

Susan Starr Sered's essay, "Ritual Expertise in the Modern World," also explores change, but in a rather different context. Her interest is in changes in women's lives as they are impacted by modernization. Family and community structures, subsistence, education and political participation are all entailed in these impacts. Although this book is not principally concerned with the particular communities that are discussed within the readings—to some extent these are accidents of a scholar's interests, positions and access—there is something significant in the choices researchers and authors make. Sered's interactions with elderly Jewish women, mostly from Middle Eastern communities, now living in Jerusalem and attending day centres, result in a discussion that casts a particularly clear light on important theoretical issues. The essay is invaluable as a focus on the way rituals change, how they enable or impede change, and their entanglement in wider cultural changes—especially with regards to gendered practice. Too many older studies of religions, cultures, rituals and beliefs ignored gender so absolutely that they forgot to mention their ignorance of women. Traditional Jewish texts, like many other traditional religious sources of authority, pay little attention to the activities of women, and academics have followed this trend by writing as if men's activities were everything. In doing so they could hardly be said to present a valid interpretation of *men's* practices let alone those of the ignored and marginalized women. Sered redresses this balance and proffers a useful model for further consideration of the gendered nature of rituals and their motivations, implications and performances.

The question of change and tradition is also raised in Carlo Severi's discussion of "Memory, Reflexivity and Belief" in relation to "oral" rather than literate cultures. He begins with a clear statement of claims and counter-claims made about the stability or instability of the transmission of traditional cultural knowledge. These have often been considered in relation to narratives and other discursive modes of communication. Severi's interest is in ritual actions. Apart from the question of change, Severi also deals with rituals as communicative practices, social interactions, constructive and reflexive behaviours and more. In relation to Humphrey and Laidlaw's consideration of the "archetypal actions of ritual" (1994), Severi argues that

Ritual is not to be seen as the static illustration of a traditional "truth," but rather as the result of a number of particular inferences, of individual acts of interpretation, involving doubt, disbelief and uncertainty. The acts performed during a rite regularly appear to demand a commitment from the actor, even when the actor does not understand them.

If so, the relationship between belief and ritual is an important and complex one. The use of language in ritual, and the interrelationship of language and ritual, are the chief interest in Severi's essay, making these thoughts about change and reflexivity into comments about discourse and performance. While he is most interested in Amazonian shamanic discourse and ritual, his conclusions are significant for the consideration of the wider phenomena of religious language. In many religions the question may be asked, "are we supposed to understand what is being said or done in this ritual?" This becomes especially clear when Severi draws some general conclusions from the special case that generates his discussion. This essay, therefore, aids an examination of ritual and religious belief in the context of broader reflection on communication and language.

Part IV

The final part of this Reader contains two essays that serve as a conclusion by "reflecting on our categories," namely ritual and belief. The first is Malcolm Ruel's "Christians as Believers" and the second is Catherine Bell's "Ritual Reification." They are not intended as a conclusion in the sense of answering all the questions, or putting everybody else right, or ending an argument. Rather, they provide clear statements about critical issues that require further debate in relation to issues underlying or made visible throughout the previous readings. They end this book without ending the debate because they are provocative. Although they are only briefly introduced here, as programmatic definitional meditations of the meaning and use of "belief" and "ritual," they deserve to be at the heart and head of any consideration and presentation about ritual and its relation to belief.

Beyond Initiation

In surveying a debate that touches not only questions of how ritual and belief may be defined, related, researched and understood, but also how modernity and indigeneity, religions and religion, culture, action and thought may be considered, the chapters of this book remain initiatory. They do not propose a single resolution of the problem—the editor remains undecided about some of the relationships and distinctions suggested or supported. There is more work to be done and the job of this kind of anthology is to encourage its readers to engage more fully with the issues, to participate actively in the debate. Each chapter contains references that are worth following up. Most chapters come from books that enhance these arguments. Each chapter also makes its claims based on evidence drawn from particular contexts and therefore permit, if they do not require, attempts to test their theses against other data. Is what one author says about Jewish observances relevant or enlightening when applied to Yoruba rituals? Is there anything to be gained from bringing studies of Christian liturgies into conversation with Amazonian shamanic discourses? This is not to encourage the kind of comparison that seeks the unification of all religions or cultures in one grand narrative. It does not suggest that a comparison will result in seeing that x is the same as y. The point is more straightforward: to attempt to see x and y more clearly. This may establish that a conclusion about the ritual behaviour of one is completely different to that of the other. More importantly, since the project, exercise or purpose of academic study and debate is not to collect facts that might win a pub or trivia quiz but to raise and debate questions, comparison of the effectiveness of an argument in different contexts may greatly enhance the value of the debate. Anything else really would be vain repetition and deceit.

Finally, at stake throughout the following chapters is the large question of how "religion" is to be approached, researched, understood and debated. The nature of ritual and its relationship with belief(s) is at the heart of a particular understanding of religion—a Protestant Christian and a modern(ist) definition that privileges beliefs and believing. The export of this particular notion and its implicit (and sometimes explicit) polemic against rituals has led to many religions around the world appearing similar. Arguably, however, this is a result of diverse communities and their religious authorities bowing to a strongly supported ideology. For example, among the many "modernizing" cultural changes instituted at Meiji in Japan was a suppression of a host of rituals and material expressions of a traditional religious culture that were now considered superstitious, primitive and improper (Reader 1991). Rather than challenging Western understandings of "religion" as parochial, particular and limited, Meiji modernization submitted. A similar story took place in many other contexts. The study of ritual and its relationship with other forms of behaviour and with beliefs, ideas and ideologies is of considerable importance in understanding the world. The very idea that "belief" is an inner affirmation or affiliation that should take precedence over all outward behaviour is itself among the most invidious and pernicious of the doctrines of a particular culture that pretends to universality. In its place, within a particular religion, there could be no objection to such an idea. The problem is that the supposedly different project of academia has often adopted this understanding of ritual and belief uncritically. It has acquiesced to the implication that religion (a matter of private and personal beliefs sometimes contaminated by ritualization) is separate from politics, economics and a variety of other allegedly autonomous aspects of life. Part of the motivation behind this collection of readings is not only to reveal this problem but also to recognize some of the possibilities for critiquing it in the quest for a richer understanding of those behaviours called religions and cultures.

References

Alexander, Bobby C. 1997. "Ritual and Current Studies of Ritual: Overview." In *Anthropology of Religion: A Handbook*, ed. Stephen D. Glazier, 139–60. Westport: Greenwood Press.

Al-Ghazālī, Abu Hamid Muhammad. 1983. *Inner Dimensions of Islamic Worship*. Leicester: The Islamic Foundation.

Bakhtin, Mikhail. 1984. *Rabelais and his World*. Bloomington: Indiana University Press.

Bateson, Gregory. 1972. "A Theory of Play and Fantasy." In *Steps to an Ecology of Mind*, 177–93. New York: Ballantine.

Bell, Catherine. 1992. *Ritual Theory, Ritual Practice*. New York: Oxford University Press.

—1997. *Ritual: Perspectives and Dimensions*. Oxford: Oxford University Press.

—1998. "Performance." In *Critical Terms for Religious Studies*, ed. Mark C. Taylor, 205–44. Chicago: University of Chicago Press.

Bloch, Maurice. 1989. *Ritual, History, and Power*. London: Athlone Press.

Bourdieu, Pierre. 1977. *Outline of a Theory of Practice*. Cambridge: Cambridge University Press.

—1997. *Language and Symbolic Power*. Oxford: Oxford University Press.

Boyer, Pascal, ed. 1993. *Cognitive Aspects of Ritual Symbolism*. Cambridge: Cambridge University Press.

Brown, Karen McCarthy. 1991. *Moma Lola: A Vodou Priestess in Brooklyn*. Berkeley: University of California Press.

Comaroff, Jean. 1996. "The Empire's Old Clothes: Fashioning the Colonial Subject." In *Cross-Cultural Consumption: Global Markets, Local Realities*, ed. David Howes, 19–38. London: Routledge.

De Coppet, Daniel. 1992. *Understanding Rituals*. London: Routledge.

Drewal, Margaret T. 1992. *Yoruba Ritual*. Bloomington, IN: Indiana University Press.

Fulbright, John. 1992. "Hopi and Zuni Prayer-Sticks: Magic, Symbolic Texts, Barter or Self-Sacrifice?" *Religion* 22: 221–34.

Geertz, Clifford. 1983. *Local Knowledges*. New York: Basic Books.

Goody, Jack. 1977. "Against 'Ritual': Loosely Structured Thoughts on a Loosely Defined Topic." In *Secular Ritual*, ed. Sally Moore and Barbara Myerhoff, 25–35. Assen: Van Gorcum.

Grimes, Ronald L. 1987. "Ritual Studies." *Encyclopedia of Religion* 12: 422–25.

—1990. *Ritual Criticism*. Columbia: University of South Carolina Press.

—1995. *Beginnings in Ritual Studies*. Columbia: University of South Carolina Press.

—2000. "Ritual." In *Guide to the Study of Religion*, ed. Willi Braun and Russell T. McCutcheon, 259–70. London: Cassell.

Guss, David M. 1989. *To Weave and Sing: Art, Symbol, and Narrative in the South American Rain Forest*. Berkeley: University of California Press.

Hornborg, Alf. 2000. "From Animal Masters to Ecosystem Services: Exchange, Personhood, and Ecological Practice." In *Negotiating Nature: Culture, Power, and Environmental Argument*, ed. Alf Hornborg and Gísli Pálsson, 133–52. Lund: Lund University Press.

Humphrey, Caroline, and James Laidlaw. 1994. *The Archetypal Actions of Ritual*. Oxford: Clarendon.

Ingold, Tim. 2000. *The Perception of the Environment: Essays in Livelihood, Dwelling and Skill*. London: Routledge.

Lerner, Berel D. 2000. "Magic, Religion and Secularity among the Azande and Nuer." In *Indigenous Religions: A Companion*, ed. Graham Harvey, 113–24. London: Continuum.

Lincoln, Bruce. 2000. "On Ritual, Change, and Marked Categories." *Journal of the American Academy of Religion* 68(3): 487–510.

McCauley, Robert, and Thomas Lawson. 2002. *Bringing Ritual to Mind: Psychological Foundations of Cultural Forms*. Cambridge: Cambridge University Press.

Midgley, Mary. 2002. *Evolution as a Religion*. London: Routledge.

Neusner, Jacob. 2002. *Judaism: An Introduction*. London: Penguin.

Rappaport, Roy A. 1999. *Ritual and Religion in the Making of Humanity*. Cambridge: Cambridge University Press.

Reader, Ian. 1991. *Religion in Contemporary Japan*. Basingstoke: Macmillan.

Rothenbuhler, Eric W. 1998. *Ritual Communication*. London: Sage.

Schechner, Richard. 1993. *The Future of Ritual*. London: Routledge.

—1994a. *Performance Theory*. London: Routledge.

—1994b. "Ritual and Performance." In *Companion Encyclopedia of Anthropology*, ed. Tim Ingold, 613–47. London: Routledge.

Segal, Robert A. 1998. *The Myth and Ritual Theory*. Oxford: Blackwell.

Smith, Jonathan Z. 1987. *To Take Place: Toward Theory in Ritual*. Chicago: University of Chicago Press.

Staal, Fritz. 1975. "The Meaninglessness of Ritual." *Numen* 26(1): 2–22.

Tambiah, Stanley J. 1979. "A Performative Approach to Ritual." *Proceedings of the British Academy* 65: 113–69.

Tedlock, Dennis. 1983. *The Spoken Word and the Work of Interpretation*. Philadelphia: University of Pennsylvania Press.

Turner, Edith. 1992. *Experiencing Ritual: A New Interpretation of African Healing*. Philadelphia: University of Pennsylvania Press.

Turner, Victor. 1967. *The Forest of Symbols: Aspects of Ndembu Ritual*. Ithaca, NY: Cornell University Press.

—1991. *The Ritual Process: Structure and Anti-Structure*. Ithaca, NY: Cornell University Press.

Van Gennep, Arnold. 1975 [1909]. *The Rites of Passage*. Chicago: University of Chicago Press.

Viveiros de Castro, Eduardo. 1998. "Cosmological Deixis and Amerinidan Perspectivism." *Journal of the Royal Anthropological Institute* n.s. 4(3): 469–88.

Zuesse, Evan M. 1987. "Ritual." *Encyclopedia of Religion* 12: 405–22.

Part I

Exemplifying the Problem

THE SACRAMENTS OF HOLY BAPTISM AND OF THE ALTAR

Martin Luther

Editor's Introduction

Martin Luther (1483–1546) was a Christian priest in Wittenberg, Germany, whose protest against what he saw as abuses by the Church evolved into a life-long attempt to reform Christianity and the assertion of his own leading role within Protestantism. In the following extracts from his *Short Catechism* (1529), Luther sets out questions and answers that aim to establish correct understanding of the nature of sacraments of "Holy Baptism" and the "rite of the Altar" (elsewhere known as the Mass, Communion or Eucharist). This is intended to enhance firm belief and also to root out false beliefs and inappropriate practices. The first questions and answers about each sacrament deal with descriptive matters: what does this mean and what scriptural authority is there for it? Luther's reforming, Protestant, argument and polemic come after that. They insist that all material forms and acts (water, bread, wine, immersion, eating or drinking) are signs, signals or signifiers. They require acts of God, acts of grace, and "truly believing hearts" to give them meaning. Or rather, God and faith give acts and objects positive meaning. Without faith and God's grace, rituals are empty of meaning (e.g. mere washing) at best and idolatrous at worst. A secular version of such a polemic might agree that ritual without correct understanding, sincerity and/or intent is mere vain repetition.

Whether Luther intended it or not, these sacramental dialogues are evidence of rising trends that would become the culture of western modernity. Locating the effectiveness of sacraments in "truly believing hearts" created a new individualism. Luther took this position not primarily because his reading of the Bible demanded it—that realization followed rather than initiated his protest—but rather because he sought to reform what he saw as ecclesiastical abuses. However, in enshrining inward "faith" as solely effective and necessary for salvation he firmly established the autonomy of individuals over against any social context, even that of the Church. Nonetheless, the tension between individual faith and its public dissemination, celebration and expression is clear in the need to write Catechisms and in the proliferation of denominational or sectarian diversity in Protestantism. The relationship between ritual and belief cannot easily be controlled. Continuous effort has to be made to inculcate faith, individuate people and otherwise police the boundary between materiality and spirituality, acts and meanings and so on. The modern debate about ritual and belief begins.

ℰᏗ ℭᏒ

The Sacrament of Holy Baptism

in the plain form in which the head of the family shall teach it to his household[1]

First

What is Baptism?

Answer: Baptism is not merely water, but it is water used according to God's command and connected with God's Word.

What is this Word of God?

Answer: As recorded in Matthew 28:19, our Lord Christ said, "Go therefore and make disciples of all nations, baptizing them in the name of the Father and of the Son and of the Holy Spirit."

Second

What gifts or benefits does Baptism bestow?

Answer: It effects forgiveness of sins, delivers from death and the devil, and grants eternal salvation to all who believe, as the Word and promise of God declare.

What is this Word and promise of God?

Answer: As recorded in Mark 16:16, our Lord Christ said, "He who believes and is baptized will be saved; but he who does not believe will be condemned."

Third

How can water produce such great effects?

Answer: It is not the water that produces these effects, but the Word of God connected with the water, and our faith which relies on the Word of God connected with the water. For, without the Word of God, that water is merely water and no Baptism. But when connected with the Word of God it is a Baptism, that is, a gracious water of life and a washing of regeneration in the Holy Spirit, as St. Paul wrote to Titus (3:5–8), "He saved us by the washing of regeneration and renewal in the Holy Spirit, which he poured out upon us richly through Jesus Christ our Saviour, so that we might be justified by his grace and become heirs in hope of eternal life. The saying is sure."

Fourth

What does such baptizing with water signify?

Answer: It signifies that the old Adam in us, together with all sins and evil lusts, should be drowned by daily sorrow and repentance and be put to death, and that the new man should come forth daily and rise up, cleansed and righteous, to live forever in God's presence.

Where is this written?

Answer: In Romans 6:4, St. Paul wrote, "We were buried therefore with him by baptism into death, so that as Christ was raised from the dead by the glory of the Father, we too might walk in newness of life."

[...]

The Sacrament of the Altar

in the plain form in which the head of the family shall teach it to his household[2]

What is the Sacrament of the Altar?

Answer: Instituted by Christ himself, it is the true body and blood of our Lord Jesus Christ, under the bread and wine, given to us Christians to eat and drink.

Where is this written?

Answer: The holy evangelists Matthew, Mark, and Luke, and also St. Paul, write thus: "Our Lord Jesus Christ, on the night when he was betrayed, took bread, and when he had given thanks, he broke it, and gave it to the disciples and said, 'Take, eat; this is my body which is given for you. Do this in remembrance of me.' In the same way also he took the cup, after supper, and when he had given thanks he gave it to them, saying, Drink of it, all of you. This cup is the new covenant in my blood, which is poured out for many for the forgiveness of sins. Do this, as often as you drink it, in remembrance of me."[3]

What is the benefit of such eating and drinking?

Answer: We are told in the words "for you" and "for the forgiveness of sins." By these words the forgiveness of sins, life, and salvation are given to us in the sacrament, for where there is forgiveness of sins, there are also life and salvation.

How can bodily eating and drinking produce such great effects?

Answer: The eating and drinking do not in themselves produce them, but the words "for you" and "for the forgiveness of sins." These words, when accompanied by the bodily eating and drinking, are the chief thing in the sacrament, and he who believes these words has what they say and declare: the forgiveness of sins.

Who, then, receives this sacrament worthily?

Answer: Fasting and bodily preparation are a good external discipline, but he is truly worthy and well prepared who believes these words: "for you" and "for the forgiveness of sins." On the other hand, he who does not believe these words, or doubts them, is unworthy and unprepared, for the words "for you" require truly believing hearts.

Notes

1. Latin title: How, in a very Plain Form, Schoolmasters Should Teach the Sacrament of Baptism to their Pupils.
2. Latin title: How, in a very Plain Form, Schoolmasters Should Teach the Sacrament of the Altar to their Pupils.
3. A conflation of texts from 1 Cor. 11:23–25; Matt. 26:26–28; Mark 14:22–24; Luke 22:19, 20. Cf. *Large Catechism, Sacrament of the Altar*, 3.

THE PITTSBURGH CONFERENCE "DECLARATION OF PRINCIPLES"

Reform Rabbis in the USA

Editor's Introduction

This "declaration of principles" is often known as the Pittsburgh Platform. It was adopted by a conference of American Reform Jewish rabbis gathered in that city in 1885, but it was also preceded by extensive debate between its framer, Kaufmann Kohler, and other rabbis, especially Alexander Kohut. It was also preceded by a similar conference in Philadelphia in 1869 and others in Germany in the 1840s. The purpose of all this debate, and especially of this Platform, was to demarcate Reform Judaism between the poles of traditional and radical Jewish movements and identities. The more traditional wing, represented by Orthodoxy, stressed the continuing validity of Torah-observant lifestyles. Indeed, it continued to define itself in debates about observance. This is not to say that the Orthodox cannot or do not articulate beliefs, but that the central concern of traditional rabbinic Judaism is observance of Torah (not just a reference to the biblical text but to the entirety of how Jews are taught to live). The more radical wing, represented in the nineteenth century by The Society for Ethical Culture, rejected any notion of Jewish distinctiveness in lifestyle or in ideology. All Jews in Europe and America had been affected by the Enlightenment. Of particular importance for understanding the Pittsburgh conference and the larger question of the relationship of ritual and belief is that Jews had to make choices. Even to remain entirely traditional, to concern oneself with observance and not to pay much attention to creeds and beliefs, was to choose. All Jews were therefore faced in a new way with a question of the relevance and meaning of rituals and other practices. The Orthodox as much as progressive Jews sought to understand the reasons for doing what they decided to do. It is arguable that the freedom and necessity of choice made Judaism a "religion" whereas before the Enlightenment it had remained a lifestyle. But this would be to capitulate to a Protestant understanding that religion is about belief. It is in this dangerous and creative territory that the following Principles were accepted. It is important to note not only that further conferences debated these and other "principles" but also that Reform Judaism reversed its opposition to ritual and, increasingly through the twentieth century, found and expressed good reasons to reintroduce rituals, observances that this foundational document rejects.

The text is included here precisely because these contested formulations of what it means to be Jewish in modernity clearly express a contrast between ritual and religious belief.

℘ ℭ

1. We recognize in every religion an attempt to grasp the Infinite, and in every mode, source or book of revelation held sacred in any religious system the consciousness of the indwelling of God in man. We hold that Judaism presents the highest conception of the God-idea as taught in our Holy Scriptures and developed and spiritualized by the Jewish teachers, in accordance with the moral and philosophical progress of their respective ages. We maintain that Judaism preserved and defended, midst continual struggles and trials and under enforced isolation, this God-idea as the central religious truth for the human race.

2. We recognize in the Bible the record of the consecration of the Jewish people to its mission as the priest of the one God, and value it as the most potent instrument of religious and moral instruction. We hold that the modern discoveries of scientific researches in the domain of nature and history are not antagonistic to the doctrines of Judaism, the Bible reflecting the primitive ideas of its own age, and at times clothing its conception of divine Providence and Justice dealing with men in miraculous narratives.

3. We recognize in the Mosaic legislation a system of training the Jewish people for its mission during its national life in Palestine, and today we accept as binding only its moral laws, and maintain only such ceremonies as elevate and sanctify our lives, but reject all such as are not adapted to the views and habits of modern civilization.

4. We hold that all such Mosaic and rabbinical laws as regulate diet, priestly purity, and dress originated in ages and under the influence of ideas entirely foreign to our present mental and spiritual state. They fail to impress

the modern Jew with a spirit of priestly holiness; their observance in our days is apt rather to obstruct than to further modern spiritual elevation.

5. We recognize, in the modern era of universal culture of heart and intellect, the approaching of the realization of Israel's great Messianic hope for the establishment of the kingdom of truth, justice, and peace among all men. We consider ourselves no longer a nation, but a religious community, and therefore expect neither a return to Palestine, nor a sacrificial worship under the sons of Aaron, nor the restoration of any of the laws concerning the Jewish state.

6. We recognize in Judaism a progressive religion, ever striving to be in accord with the postulates of reason. We are convinced of the utmost necessity of preserving the historical identity with our great past. Christianity and Islam, being daughter religions of Judaism, we appreciate their providential mission, to aid in the spreading of monotheistic and moral truth. We acknowledge that the spirit of broad humanity of our age is our ally in the fulfillment of our mission, and therefore we extend the hand of fellowship to all who cooperate with us in the establishment of the reign of truth and righteousness among men.

7. We reassert the doctrine of Judaism that the soul is immortal, grounding the belief on the divine nature of human spirit, which forever finds bliss in righteousness and misery in wickedness. We reject, as ideas not rooted in Judaism, the beliefs both in bodily resurrection and in Gehenna and Eden (Hell and Paradise) as abodes for everlasting punishment and reward.

8. In full accordance with the spirit of the Mosaic legislation, which strives to regulate the relations between rich and poor, we deem it our duty to participate in the great task of modern times, to solve, on the basis of justice and righteousness, the problems presented by the contrasts and evils of the present organization of society.

Part II

SURVEYING THE DISCUSSION

TO TAKE PLACE

Jonathan Z. Smith

Editor's Introduction

Jonathan Z. Smith is Robert O. Anderson Distinguished Service Professor of the Humanities at the University of Chicago. He is an historian of religions whose research interests include ritual theory, Hellenistic religions, Maori new religious movements in the nineteenth century, and the religiously motivated violence of Jonestown, Guyana. All of his publications are rewarding for those interested in the questions of what religion is or religions are. In the book from which the following extract is drawn and in a number of other publications (notably *Drudgery Divine: On the Comparison of Early Christianities and the Religions of Late Antiquity*, 1990), Smith demonstrates that a Protestant anti-Catholic polemic is rife and unacknowledged (and perhaps unconscious) in many academic debates. This is particularly clear with reference to the problem of ritual and religious belief. Or, rather, it becomes clear precisely when the relationship between ritual and belief is seen to be a problem.

The following extract is the conclusion to Smith's book, also called *To Take Place*, in which he draws together various threads of his evidence and arguments and presents some conclusions. Interesting as these conclusions are, it is as initial statements and building blocks that they are most useful here. This is not counter to Smith's purpose; after all, he subtitles his book, *Toward Theory in Ritual*. This can be read not only as his intention to contribute to a theory but also as his aim to contest existing theories of ritual. His opening pages introduce a Protestant who, in visiting Rome, claimed to see Paganism in every Catholic activity there, and an Indian sociologist who sees the influence of the Protestant Reformer Zwingli pervading the culture of the West's modernity. We might agree with Smith that Zwingli only expressed particularly clearly a problem with which other Christian thinkers had

26

struggled. Nonetheless, the notion that the modern world is fully manifest in the wedge driven between symbol and reality is powerful and important. Its ramifications can be seen in the comparable separation of meaning and act, belief and ritual, mind and body, spiritual and material, action and intention, and consciousness and matter. These are the subject matters of a host of academic disciplines and publications. If they are indeed entangled in an inner-Christian polemic it may be of immense value to trace the threads and see if they result in an illuminating tapestry or an uncomfortable blindfold. Issues are raised here that resonate throughout the remaining readings and essays.

References

Smith, Jonathan Z. 1990. *Drudgery Divine: On the Comparison of Early Christianities and the Religions of Late Antiquity*. Chicago: University of Chicago Press.

℘ ℭ

Nothing shall have taken place but place.
Stéphane Mallarmé

I

Between 1724 and 1725, Conyers Middleton, D.D., English divine and recently appointed University Librarian at Cambridge, undertook a journey to Italy, most especially to Rome. It was a curious sort of a trip, one that might be described as a reverse pilgrimage. For Middleton insists that he went to Rome, not out of "any Motive of Devotion":

> My Zeal was not that of visiting the Holy Thresholds of the Apostles or kissing the Feet of their Successor: I knew that their Ecclesiastical Antiquiaries were mostly fabulous or legendary; supported by Fictions and Impostures, too gross to employ the Attention of a Man of Sense.[1]

Rather than wishing to gaze at "ridiculous Fictions of this Kind," Middleton hoped to encounter the "genuine Remains and venerable Reliques of Pagan Rome; the authentick Monuments of Antiquity." He keenly anticipated his "Joy at viewing the very Place and Scene of these important [ancient] Events ... treading on that ground ... [where the] Great Heroes of Antiquity had been personally engaged."[2] He thrilled at the thought of standing before "those very Walles where Cicero and his Friends had held their Philosophical Disputations."[3] Some 1300 years after Egeria, this Christian pilgrim was about to undertake an opposite sort of journey, filled with the same emotions at encountering the associative conjunction of textual and topographical *loci*, but now in terms of the "very Place and Scene" of a pre-Christian, non-Christian "Pagan" past.

Unlike Egeria, Middleton was not delighted by the contemporary ceremonial world he encountered. He was annoyed, troubled, and, finally, repelled by it. It presented itself to him as static, interfering in his communion with the antique past.

Middleton had vowed, before traveling to Rome, "to lose as little Time as possible in taking notice of the Fopperies and ridiculous Ceremonies of the present Religion of the Place." But this would not prove possible. "I soon found myself mistaken; for the whole Form and outward Dress of their Worship seemed so grossly idolatrous and extravagent."[4] To his surprise, although he was not unaware of other authors who had claimed the same,[5] "all these Ceremonies appeared plainly to have been copied from the Ritual of Primitive Paganism."[6] His beloved past was alive in contemporary Roman Catholic ritual, but distorted, as in a fun-house mirror. He scoffs at the priest who presides "with many ridiculous Motions and Crossings."[7] He observes votive objects that belong "in the Cabinets of the Curious."[8] In what might appear to us to be all but a grotesque parody of the sort of locative enthusiasm typified by figures like Egeria, he observes that some Catholic ceremonies "called to his Mind" a passage in a classical text, where "the same Ceremony was described, as transacted in the same Form and Manner, and in the same Place ... where I now saw it before my eyes."[9] The rituals were performed in "the same Temples, at the same Altars, sometimes [before] the same Images, and always with the same Ceremonies."[10] He compares, often at considerable length, parallels in eleven ceremonial categories,[11] all of which he has been "a Witness to myself."[12]

What had occurred, Middleton believes, was a process of linguistic sleight of hand. He returns to this theme insistently. The present ritual activities are but "verbal Translations of the old Originals of Heathenism."[13] "By a Change only of Name they have found the means to return to the Thing."[14] They have "changed the Name rather than the Object of their Worship."[15] But what stands revealed after the disguise has been penetrated is not the cool rationalism of his beloved Cicero (a quote from whose *De natura deorum* prefaces the work),[16] but the "superstitious man" caricatured by Theophrastus. There was, as the title of his published diatribe states, "an Exact Conformity between Popery and Paganism."

Middleton was far from an original thinker. In many respects, this makes him a more precious witness, for it allows us to perceive what is typical and characteristic in his work. He is an already late representative of a change in the Christian imagination at least as profound and far-reaching as that of the fourth century, considered in the previous chapter. It is a change that made possible, for the first time, the western imagination of religion (as opposed to religions) and gave rise to those three classic works which stand at the origin of our present academic enterprise: John Spencer's *De legibus Hebraeorum et earum rationibus* (1685); David Hume's dissertation *The Natural History of Religion* (written between 1749 and 1751, published in 1757); and Charles de Brosses's *Du Culte des Dieux fétiches, ou Paralléle de l'ancienne Religion de l'Egypte avec la Religion actuelle de Nigritie* (1760). It is an enterprise that was influenced as much by the novelties of exploration as by the polemics of theological disputation: an affair, jointly, of humanists, reformers, and philosophes. It marked the study of religion as, essentially, a Protestant exercise, a heritage that continues to haunt theorists of religion even to the present day.

Claude Lévi-Strauss has written: "Anthropology is the science of culture as seen from the outside," that "anthropology, whenever it is practiced by members of the culture it endeavors to study, loses its specific nature and becomes rather akin to archaeology, history and philology."[17] He makes an important point. And so it is well, from time to time, for those concerned with aspects of western civilization to learn about generalities concerning the West that are made from the outside—an endeavor in reverse anthropology. The particular work I have in mind is that by J. P. Singh Uberoi, a professor of sociology at the University of Delhi.

Uberoi is part of a lengthy tradition of those both within and outside the West who identify its unique characteristics with the enterprise of (modern) science. Likewise, he stands within a dominant intellectual tradition (from Max Weber through Robert K. Merton) in locating the source of modern western science in relation to the Protestant tradition. Where he differs is in where he places the generating issue. Writing from the perspective of what he terms an Indian "semaisiological world-view" (a tradition he traces back to Pāṇini), he insists that the decisive moment was the debate over "the question of liturgy, i.e. the mode of presence of divinity in Christian ritual,"[18] and that it was Zwingli who established the crucial distinction that was to give rise to a distinctive western world view.

> Zwingli insisted that in the utterance "This is my body" (*Hoc est corpus meum*) the existential word "is" (*est*) was to be understood, not in a real, literal and corporeal sense, but only in a symbolical, historical or social sense (*significat, symbolum est* or *figura est*). ... Dualism or double monism was fixed in the world-view and the life-world of the modern age, which was thereby ushered in. ... By stating the issue and forcing it in terms of dualism, or more properly double monism, Zwingli

29

had discovered or invented the modern concept of time in which every event was either spiritual and mental or corporeal and material but no event was or could be both at once. ... Spirit, word and sign had finally parted company for man at Marburg in 1529; and myth or ritual ... was no longer literally *and* symbolically real and true. ... Zwingli was the chief architect of the new schism and ... Europe and the world followed Zwingli in the event. Zwingli, the reformer of Zurich, was in his system of thought the first philosopher ... of the modern world.[19]

Matters were, of course, more complex than Uberoi's analysis suggests, as the history of eucharistic controversies makes plain,[20] but there is no doubt that he has focused attention on a major revolution in thought: ritual is not "real"; rather, it is a matter of "signification" for Zwingli,[21] or of "metonymy" for Theodore Beza.[22] A wedge was decisively driven between symbol and reality; there was no necessary connection between them.

There was an implication in this position, already faced in disputation by Beza: Does such an understanding of eucharistic presence imply that ritual is "something ineffectual, as if a thing were represented to us by a picture or a *mere* memorial or figure?"[23] Beza's answer was clearly negative, but to no avail. Despite what may have been the intentions of the Reformers, a new language was brought into being with respect to ritual. Rather than some rituals being "idolatrous," that is, false, one could speak of all rituals as being "only" or "merely symbolic." Thus, the position of Zwingli and others could be described in a 1585 polemic as being that of "the Symbolists, Figurists, and Significatists who are of [the] opinion that the Faithfull at the Lord's Supper doe receive nothing but naked and bare Signes."[24] Ritual could be perceived as a matter of surface rather than depth; of outward representation rather than inward transformation. It was a matter of "bare ceremoniousnesse" (1583); "it is onlie a ceremonie" (1693), a "mere ceremony" (1759).

As such, ritual was to be classed with superstition (shallow, unreasoning action) or with habit (a customary, repetitive, thoughtless action). "Let vs not come to y^r. Chirche by vse & custome as the Oxe to his Stalle" (1526). Although this language might be directed by Protestant authors against "Jewish" or "Pharasaic ritualism,"[25] its polemic object was, in fact, always Roman Catholicism. It was Catholicism that could be described as having "Rytes superstycyouse" (1538), "a vayne supersticious ceremoniall Masse" (1545), "superstiousness of Beades" (1548), "papistical superstitions" (1547); the host was an example of "supersticious worshippyng" (1561), of "paganick rites and foolish observances" (1573).

It is this controversy literature concerning what will be termed "paganopapism" (a term apparently introduced into English by John Corbet in 1667)[26] out of which Middleton came. Of greater significance to our topic, it is this same (often ugly) controversy literature that decisively established the valences of ritual as expressed in theories of religion up to our own time. It was a literature that sometimes took the form of learned treatises (Pierre Mussard, *Les conformitez des cérémonies modernes avec les anciennes* [1667] was, perhaps, the most influential example of the genre);[27] but it could be fulminated against in versified sermons:

> And what are Ceremonies? are all vaine? are all
> superstitious?
> God forbid.
> Many are tolerable. A few necessary.
> Most are ridiculous. And some abominable.[28]

or ridiculed in bald-faced doggerel:

> Natural Religion was easy first and plain,
> Tales made it Mystery, Offrings made it Gain;
> Sacrifices and Shows were at length prepar'd,
> The Priests ate Roast-meat and the People star'd.[29]

No matter what the format, the matter and message remained the same. In Erasmus's blunt formulation, "To place the whole of religion in external ceremonies is sublime stupidity."[30]

I insist on this point, in part, because the usual histories of the study of religion conceal it. They speak as if the correlation of myth and ritual was commonplace, as if the major task of rectification was to disabuse the notion that myths were false or that they were lies. Not so! The history of the imagination of the categories myth and ritual was sharply divergent. To say myth was false was to recognize it as having content; to declare ritual to be "empty" was to deny the same.

The study of myth was conceived, from the beginning, as the study of belief, an enterprise of a "hermeneutic of recovery" in that the study welcomes the foreign if only to show, by some allegorizing or rationalizing procedure, that it is, in fact, the "same." The *logos spermatikos* turned out to be fecund beyond the wildest erotic fantasies of the old Church Fathers. Utilizing the same methods the Fathers had employed on the Greco-Roman fables, the sages of the Enlightenment insisted that in even the most "savage corruptions" one could find "signs of truth." It was only a matter of decoding, of decipherment.[31] It was an enterprise of recovering "remnants," "remainders," "reminders," "seeds," "sparks," "traces," and "footprints."[32] It was a rare figure, such as the always-provocative Charles de Brosses, who would protest on behalf of both the "primitive" and the "ancient" that "their religion is never allegorical."[33] For most, the study of myth was an exercise in cultural appropriation.

How different the attitudes at the beginnings of the study of ritual! It is a difference signaled by the earliest instance of the English use of the word reported by the *Oxford English Dictionary:* "contayning no manner of Doctrine ... but onely certayn ritual Decrees to no purpose" (1570). Here, there is no question of beliefs, no problem of the endless subtlety of words, but rather, nonsense. Ritual, lacking speech, resisted decipherment. The "other," with respect to ritual, remained sheerly "other"—there could be no penetration behind the masks, no getting beneath the gestures. The study of ritual was born as an exercise in the "hermeneutic of suspicion," an explanatory endeavor designed to explain away. That which was "other" remained obdurately so and, hence, was perceived to be bereft of all value. The "other" displayed in ritual could not be appropriated as could myth and was therefore shown the reverse face of imperialism: subjection or, more likely, extirpation.

The Protestant insistence on the "emptiness" of ritual has had a number of additional consequences that persist. Perhaps the most significant affects the mode of the academic presentation of rituals. If exegesis has been held to be the proper mode for studying the linguistically rich myths, then description becomes the proper mode for the linguistically impoverished rituals. The scholar can be "hot" with respect to his or her interpretation of myth, while remaining more or less "cool" with regard to ritual—except for certain selective and highly condensed moments, such as in examining sacrifice.

On the other hand, attempts could be made, especially in the beginning of this century, to "save the phenomenon." Most prominent has been the largely failed enterprise of providing ritual with a verbal text, the conjoining of myth to ritual, with the former serving as a libretto for the latter. Almost as common, in some circles, has been the imposition of a Romantic (and equally Protestant) theory of origination on ritual. Its first instance, it was declared, was some awe-filled, spontaneous, dramatic moment of "seizure" that subsequently became "depleted" by repetition.[34] Common to both these attempts, however, is the insistence that ritual once had meaning, but has, somehow, lost it—through historical processes of becoming separated from its text (so that ritual becomes a mere "survival"), or through routinizing processes of impoverishment.

More recently, especially in contemporary American theory, there has been an attempt to invert the valences. Priority is given to the categories of action and experience at the expense of rationality and language. It is as if the Faustian proposal were accepted, substituting "in the beginning was the deed" for "in the beginning was the word." In such proposals, the old dualistic problems return, merely in reversed guise.

I shall want more to argue forcefully against such attempts to "restore" ritual than to quarrel with the older formulations of its emptiness. Though I reject the evaluation, I find a shrewd recognition of a characteristic of ritual in the Reformation formulations. That is to say, I shall use their initial perception concerning ritual to argue a quite different conclusion in terms of the test cases we have considered in the previous chapters. What is required is a rectification of the old theory of the emptiness of ritual, not its outright rejection; a repositioning of the theory that will take its start from thinking about ritual itself and, only then, go on to consider hybrid forms such as myth/ritual.

II

Ritual is, first and foremost, a mode of paying attention. It is a process for marking interest. It is the recognition of this fundamental characteristic of ritual that most sharply distinguishes our understanding from that of the Reformers, with their all too easy equation of ritual with blind and thoughtless habit. It is this characteristic, as well, that explains the role of place as a fundamental component of ritual: place directs attention.

Such a preliminary understanding of ritual and its relation to place is best illustrated by the case of built ritual environments—most especially, crafted constructions such as temples. When one enters a temple, one enters marked-off space (the usual example, the Greek *temenos*, derived from *temno*, "to cut") in which, at least in principle, nothing is accidental; everything, at least potentially, demands attention. The temple serves as a focusing lens, establishing the possibility of significance by directing attention, by requiring the perception of difference. Within the temple, the ordinary (which to any outside eye or ear remains wholly ordinary) becomes significant, becomes "sacred," simply by being there. A ritual object or action becomes sacred by having attention focused on it in a highly marked way. From such a point of view, there is nothing that is inherently sacred or profane. These are not substantive categories, but rather situational ones. Sacrality is, above all, a category of emplacement.[35]

This understanding of emplacement is insistently testified to by ancient stories and debates concerning ritual. It is present in the defense of the status of the Song of Songs attributed to Akiva, that "he who sings it like a secular song or pronounces a verse in a banquet house ... brings evil into the world" (*b. Sanhedrin* 101a; cf. Tosefta *Sanhedrin* 12.10 and parallels). The issue, here, is not the content of this collection of erotic ditties, but their place. When chanted in the Temple (or its surrogate), they are, perforce, sacred; when chanted in a tavern, they are not. It is not their symbolism or their meaning that is determinitive; the songs are sacred or profane sheerly by virtue of their location. A sacred text is one that is used in a sacred place—nothing more is required.

The same point recurs in other traditions. As a part of the extensive Egyptian section in book 2 of his *Histories,* Herodotus narrates the tale of Amasis. Amasis was a "mere private person" who was elevated to king but despised because of his "ordinary" origins. He had a golden footpan in which he and his guests used to wash their feet. This was melted down and remolded into the statue of a god, which was then reverenced by the people. Amasis called a public assembly and drew the parallel as to:

> how the image had been made of the footpan, in which they formerly had been used to washing their feet and to deposit all manner of dirt, yet now it was greatly reverenced. And truly it has gone with me [Amasis] as with the footpan. If I were formerly a private citizen, I have now come to be your king, and therefore I bid you to do honor and reverence to me.[36]

This is a sophisticated story concerning the arbitrariness of place and of placement and replacement. It comes out of the complex ideology of archaic kingship that foreshadows the kinds of distinctions later, western political thought will make between the king as divine with respect to office and human with respect to person. For example, in the twelfth century Christian writing attributed to the Norman Anonymous:

> We thus have to recognize in the king a twin person. ... One through which, by the condition of nature, he conformed with other men; another through which, by the eminence of [his] deification and by the power of the sacrament [of consecration], he excelled all others. Concerning one personality he was, by nature, an individual man; concerning his other personality, he was, by grace, a *Christus*, that is a God-man (*Deus-homo*).[37]

Note in this text that sacrality is conferred "by virtue of the sacrament." We do well to remember that long before "the Sacred" appeared in discourse as a substantive (a usage that does not antedate Durkheim),[38] it was primarily employed in verbal forms, most especially with the sense of making an individual a king or bishop (as in the obsolete English verbs *to sacrate* or *to sacre*), or in adjectival forms denoting the result of the process of sacration.[39] Ritual is not an expression of or a response to "the Sacred"; rather, something or someone is made sacred by ritual (the primary sense of *sacrificium*).

In the examples just given, divine and human, sacred and profane, are transitive categories; they serve as maps and labels, not substances; they are distinctions of office, indices of difference. The same point is made in the *topos* found independently in both Israelitic and Latin literatures of the carpenter who fashions a sacred object out of one part of a log and a common household utensil out of the other.[40] Or the reverse, the melting down of a statue of a deity in order to fashion a commonplace vessel: Tertullian scoffs, "Saturn into a cooking pot; Minerva into a washbasin."[41] Although such exempla are frequently used in antiritualistic polemics (especially against so-called idolatry),[42] this should not be allowed to obscure their witness. The *sacra* are sacred solely because they are used in a sacred place; there is no inherent difference between a sacred vessel and an ordinary one.

In theoretical terms, this understanding of sacrality is most congruent with that of Durkheim, who is largely responsible for the widespread use, in religious studies, of the nominative "the Sacred." The linchpin of Durkheim's argument, in *Elementary Forms*, occurs in a few pages of book 2, chapter 1, section 3.[43] The issue is the *tjurunga* and its markings.

> In themselves, the tjurunga are objects of wood and stone, like all others; they are distinguished from profane things of the same kind by only one particularity: this is that the totemic mark is drawn or engraved on them. Thus it is this mark, and this mark alone, which confers on them their sacred character.[44]

It is the nature of these "marks" that most interests Durkheim and provides him with his key argument. The marks are non-representational, that is to say, not natural. Hence, they are to be derived from social rather than sensory experience. This latter is Durkheim's persistent claim, and here he comes close to developing an adequate linguistic model that would have decisively advanced his work. Although the Australians are capable of depicting natural objects with reasonable accuracy (in, for example, their rock paintings), they do not do so when marking their *tjurungas*. These marks:

> consist essentially of geometric designs ... having only a conventional meaning. The connection between the sign and the things signified [*entre la figure et la chose figurée*] is so indirect and remote that it cannot be seen except when it is pointed out. Only the members of the clan can say what meaning is attached to such and such combinations of lines. ... The meaning of the figures thus obtained is so arbitrary that a single design may have two different meanings for the men of two different totems.[45]

Unfortunately, Durkheim did not further develop this linguistic analogy for the sacred, turning instead to the unnecessarily mystifying notion of *mana*, and the social covariation of the alternation of ceremonial and ordinary life, to explain the duality sacred/profane.[46] It remained for Claude Lévi-Strauss to develop the linguistic analogy with respect to even *mana* itself.

Lévi-Strauss takes up the Durkheimian agenda in the context of writing on Marcel Mauss, Durkheim's closest collaborator.[47]

Conceptions of the *mana* type are so frequent and so widespread that we should ask ourselves if we are not in the presence of a universal and permanent form of thought which, far from being characteristic of only certain civilizations or alleged "stages" of thought. . . will function in a certain situation of the mind in the face of things, one which must appear each time that this situation is given.[48]

To elucidate this "situation," Lévi-Strauss calls attention to the "exceedingly profound remark" of Father Thevanet with respect to the Algonquin (as quoted by Mauss), that *manitou* "particularly refers to all beings which still have no common name, which are not familiar."[49] After giving a set of ethnographic examples, Lévi-Strauss draws the striking conclusion:

Always and everywhere, notions of this [*mana*-]type intervene, somewhat as algebraic symbols, to represent a value of indeterminate signification, in itself empty of meaning and therefore susceptible to the reception of any meaning whatsoever. Thus [*mana*'s] unique function is to make good a discrepancy between the signifier and the signified, or more precisely, to signal the fact that in this circumstance, on this occasion, or in this one of its manifestations, a relationship of inadequacy is established between the signified and the signifier to the detriment of the anterior relation of complimentarity.[50]

Thus, for Lévi-Strauss's argument, the notion of *mana* does not pertain to the realm of "reality" but rather to that of thought; it marks discontinuity rather than continuity by representing, with precision, floating or undecided signification (*signifiant flottant*).[51] *Mana* is neither an ontological nor a substantive category; it is a linguistic one. It has a "semantic function."[52] It possesses a *valeur symbolique zéro*. It is a mark of major difference, like the zero, signifying nothing, devoid of meaning in itself, but filled with differential significance when joined to another number (as in the decimal system). It allows thought to continue despite discontinuity.[53] "It is the function of notions of the *mana*-type to oppose themselves to the absence of signification without allowing, by themselves, any particular signification."[54] In the language of typography, Lévi-Strauss's notion of *mana* might be thought of as an italicizing device; in the language of ritual books, it serves as a rubric. It signals significance without contributing signification.

It is this latter characteristic that most resembles ritual, and it is exemplified by the practices of the Temple in Jerusalem. In chapter 4, where the Temple was compared with the Church of the Holy Sepulchre, the Temple ritual was described in language congruent with that adopted here. The Temple in Jerusalem was the focus of a complex, self-referential system. Its arbitrariness guaranteed its ordering role. Within the Temple, all was system from which nothing could distract. The actions in the Temple consisted of a series of hierarchical and hieratic transactions concerning pure/impure, sacred/profane. These are, above all, matters of difference. The ritual elements in the Temple, it was claimed, functioned much as do phonemes in Roman Jakobson's linguistic theories: as "purely differential and contentless signs" forming a system "composed of elements which are signifiers and yet, at the same time, signify nothing." That is to say, despite ingenius attempts, there is no possibility of decoding the meaning of the causes of impurity—they signify sheer difference. Nor is there any relationship of equivalence between the modes of purification and the forms of impurity—they signify sheer change in status, sheer difference. Within its arbitrarily demarcated boundaries, each transaction was the focus of all transactions; each transaction was capable of endless formal replication. For it is not the terms but the relations that mattered.[55]

Admittedly, there are documentary problems with this description. There are no surviving ritual books from the Israelitic period. What is preserved in the Hebrew Bible is a set of brief descriptions gathered together for other than ritual purposes. Not a single Temple ritual in the Hebrew Bible is capable of being performed fully on the basis of the information contained therein. There are, no doubt, particular historical reasons for this,[56] but the fact remains: in their present form, the largely Priestly documents have already reduced the rituals of the Temple from performances to systems—primarily by mapping modes of emplacement. As we have seen, these maps allow a prescission from place. They could be thought about in abstract topographies; they could be transported to another place; they could be extended to other sorts of social space; they could become sheerly intellectual systems.

In each of these, there is no break with the dynamics of ritual itself. Ritual is, above all, an assertion of difference. Elsewhere, interpreting a set of rituals far removed from Jerusalem, I have written that, among other things, ritual represents the creation of a controlled environment where the variables (the accidents) of ordinary life may be displaced precisely because they are felt to be so overwhelmingly present and powerful. Ritual is a means of performing the way things ought to be in conscious tension to the way things are. Ritual relies for its power on the fact that it is concerned with quite ordinary activities placed within an extraordinary setting, that what it describes and displays is, in principle, possible for every occurrence of these acts. But it also relies for its power on the perceived fact that, in actuality, such possibilities cannot be realized. There is a "gnostic" dimension to ritual. It provides the means for demonstrating that we know what ought to have been done, what ought to have taken place. Nonetheless, by the very fact that it is ritual action rather than everyday action, ritual demonstrates that we know "what is the case." Ritual thus provides an occasion for reflection on and rationalization of the fact that what ought to have been done was not, what ought to have taken place did not. From such a perspective, ritual is not best understood as congruent with something else—a magical imitation of desired ends, a translation of emotions, a symbolic acting out of ideas, a dramatization of a text, or the like. Ritual gains force where incongruency is perceived and thought about.[57] This view accords well with a recent description of Indic sacrificial ritual:

> [The ritual] has nothing to say about the world, its concerns and conflicts. It proposes, on the contrary, a separate, self-contained world ruled exclusively by the comprehensive and exhaustive order of the ritual. It has no meaning outside of its self-contained system of rules to connect it with the mundane order. ... The ritual is *ardrstārtha*, without visible purpose or meaning other than the realization of its perfect order, be it only for the duration of the ritual and within the narrow compass of the ritual enclosure. ... The ritual holds out to man the prospect of a transcendent world he creates himself on condition that he submits to the total rule of the ritual injunction. But at the same time, the open gap between the transcendent order of the ritual and the mundane ambivalence of conflict and interest is all the more obvious.[58]

Ritual is a relationship of difference between "nows"—the now of everyday life and the now of ritual place; the simultaneity, but not the coexistence, of "here" and "there." Here (in the world) blood is a major source of impurity; there (in ritual space) blood removes impurity. Here (in the world) water is the central agent by which impurity is transmitted; there (in ritual) washing with water carries away impurity. Neither the blood nor the water has changed; what has changed is their location. This absolute discrepancy invites thought, but cannot be thought away. One is invited to think of the potentialities of the one "now" in terms of the other; but the one cannot become the other. Ritual precises ambiguities; it neither overcomes nor relaxes them.

Ritual, concerned primarily with difference, is, necessarily, an affair of the relative. It exhibits, in all its forms, what Arnold van Gennep terms the "pivoting of the sacred."[59] As such, ritual is systemic hierarchy par excellence. In ritual, the differences can be extreme, or they can be reduced to micro-distinctions—but they can never be overthrown. The system can never come to rest. This accounts for the definitive characteristics of ritual as described by its two most profound students: Freud and Lévi-Strauss, the former in his brief essay *Zwangshandlungen und Religionsubungen*, the latter in the exasperating and controversial "Finale" to *L'homme nu*.

As is well known, Freud, in his first essay on religion, proposed an analogy between "what are called obsessive acts in neurotics and those of ritual observances." The connection was to be found in the notion of "obsession," in the compulsion to do certain repetitive things and to abstain from others. The things done and the things not done are ordinary, everyday activities that are elaborated and made "rhythmic" by additions and repetitions. Obsessive acts in both individuals and religious rituals are described by Freud as exhibiting an overwhelming concern for:

> little preoccupations, performances, restrictions and arrangements in certain activities of everyday life which have to be carried out always in the same or in a methodically varied way ... elaborated by petty modifications ... [and] little details ... [accompanied by the] tendency to displacement ... [which] turns apparently trivial matters into those of great and urgent import.

In this early essay, the defining characteristic of ritual is "conscientiousness [toward] details."

> The ceremonial appears to be only an exaggeration of an ordinary and justifiable orderliness, but the remarkable conscientiousness with which it is carried out ... gives the ceremonial the character of a sacred rite.[60]

Lévi-Strauss, starting from the analysis of quite different sorts of data, comes to an analogous conclusion. He asks the question that confronts any theorist of ritual: How are the actions in ritual to be distinguished from their close counterparts in everyday life? His answer (like Freud's) is by way of a characterization. "In all cases, ritual makes constant use of two procedures: parcelling out [*morcellement*] and repetition." It is the first procedure that is of most interest to us. Parcelling out is defined as that activity in which:

> within classes of objects and types of gesture, ritual makes infinite distinctions and ascribes discriminatory values to the slightest shade of difference. It has no concern for the general, but on the contrary goes into great detail about the varieties and sub-varieties in all the taxonomic categories.[61]

Parcelling out is the same procedure that Lévi-Strauss elsewhere describes as the processes of "microadjustment" (*micro-péréquation*), which are the central concern and chief characteristic of ritual.[62]

If ritual is concerned with the elaboration of relative difference that is never overcome, myth begins with absolute duality (for our purposes best expressed as the duality of "then" and "now"); its mode is not that of simultaneity, but rather of transformation. In myth, through the devices of narrative and the manipulation of temporal relations, the one becomes the other—often after much conflict and a complex repertoire of relations.

If the Temple ritual may be taken as exemplary of ritual itself, what of the conjoining of myth to ritual with respect to place as we saw in the case of the Aranda (in the first chapter) and the post-Constantinian Christian experience of Palestine (in the fourth)? Typically, these combinations focus neither on the simultaneous modes of difference characteristic of ritual nor on the serial modes of conflict and transformation characteristic of myth. The issue is not diverse forms of differentation but rather of coexistence. Such conjoined instances of myth/ritual are not so much invitations to reflectivity as invitations to reflexivity: an elaboration of memory.

Although the Aranda myths appear to be loose, paratactic constructions, connected only by "then ... then ... then ... ," they presuppose an absolute duality between "then" and "now," between the time of the Dreaming and the present.[63] At the juncture between the two are the mediating processes of transformation described in chapter 1. In the words used there, the transformation of the ancestor is an event that bars, forever, direct access to his particular person. Yet through this very process of metamorphosis, through being displaced from his "self" and being emplaced in an "other"—in an object, person, or mark—the ancestor achieves permanence. He becomes forever accessible, primarily through modes of memorialization.[64] Here, myth/ritual loses ritual's definitive character of sheer differentiation.

Matters, especially those bearing on temporal relations, are, in fact, more complex. Ancestral time—"their" time, "then," the time of the Dreaming—is characterized by a sort of perpetual motion as the ancestors freely transform the featureless landscape (as often by accident as by design) into its present configuration. All is fluidity, all is process and change; everything is indeterminate, everything is exponential, and, to that degree, might be termed historical. Our time—the "now," what *we* might identify as the historical present—is, in fact, characterized by a sort of atemporality from the point of view of the myths. In an inversion of ancestral times, "now" all is determinate and constant; the fluidity of the ancestors has established the forms of the present. The ancestral motion has been permanently frozen in stable memorials. It is not the ancestor, but, paradoxically, his movement, his act of transformation, that remains forever fixed and accessible. In this system, movement is what is most at rest.

How is this paradoxical inversion systemically accomplished? Nancy Munn provides part of the answer when she writes that, since the transformations were effected in Dream-time, but remain visible forever, "they condense within themselves the two forms of temporality"—what we have termed the "then" and the "now"—"and are thus freed from specific historical location."[65] More precisely, the prescission from temporal location results in spatial location. In W. E. H. Stanner's formulation, "a time sequence ... is transposed into a spatial sequence."[66]

In what way does this sense of place differ from that already described as characteristic of pure ritual? All the qualities of attention are present in this form of myth/ritual—all but the arbitrarily demarcated boundaries. Any place can, in principle, be a focus of ancestral presence. Indeed, while some places are forgotten, other places may be newly discovered.

> Change, in Aboriginal religion, can take place through the discovery of sacred objects left by the Dreamtime beings. ... This is often effected through dreams: thus, Aborigines claim that they have met spirit beings in dreams who have described the whereabouts of objects left behind by the beings of the Dreaming. The implication of this is that the "deposit of revelation" is not definitely completed or closed for Aboriginals since traces of the Dreamtime heroes may still be brought to light.[67]

The repertoire is not fixed but remains open. Anything, any place, can potentially become the object of attention; the details of any object or place can be infinitely elaborated in the myth. It is a notion of difference so universalized in its potential that difference disappears. To cite Stanner: "Anything that is symmetrically patterned attracts notice, and the same is true of marked asymetry."[68]

Such a mode of myth/ritual resists the economy of signification, the exercise of the strategy of choice, that is characteristic of ritual.[69] The only economy occurs not with respect to ritual categories but with respect to social ones. Each *tjurunga* is owned by either an individual or a clan—indeed, such ownership is one of the very few forms of personal property recognized by the Aranda.[70] Rather than Lévi-Strauss's concept of "parcelling out" with respect to ritual elements, we find Stanner's use of the same term to describe the social process. "The effect ... is to parcel out, on a kind of distributive plan, all the non-human entities made or recognized by the ancestors."[71]

A different set of dynamics appears to be at work in the case of the Christian conjoining of myth to ritual with respect to a quite particular, indeed, a unique, place. The Christian practice appears, in many respects, to be the inverse of the Aranda.

As was argued in chapter 4, the early Christian ritual was atemporal and paradigmatic. It was contact with the *loca sancta* of now-Christian Palestine in the fourth century that transformed Christian ritual into a celebration of the historical and syntagmatic as well as, in Palestine, the topographic. As we saw, the historical and syntagmatic was continued apart from Palestine and was, through structures of temporality, the means of overcoming the topographic.

Unlike the Aranda, whose mythology was largely developed through encounters with their land, the fourth-century Christians came to Palestine with preexisting lists of loci to be located in the land—onomastika and other concordance materials to both Israelitic and Christian mythic, scriptural traditions. They came, as well, with rituals that had been developed apart from the land, rituals in which topography played no role. The full Christian myth (the life and deeds of Jesus and their connection with a Christian reading of Israelitic narrative), which had previously played but little part in Christian ritual, was now freely projected onto the land. In the formative fourth century, it was the myth—the conjunction of the *locus* in the text with the topographical *locus*—that provided both the meaning of the place and the principles of ritual economy. It was the myth that generated the places which became the objects of memorialization. The ritual was extended to take account of this projection—employing, within Palestine, both spatial and temporal coordinates.

As the nontransferable stational liturgy evolved in Jerusalem, it could be exported (as we saw in the fourth chapter) only by inverting the Aranda model. That is to say, a spatial sequence was transposed into a temporal one—the newly invented Christian year.

Within Palestine, especially within Christian Jerusalem, other sets of transformations can be observed. Some were the creations of Constantinian and early post-Constantinian times; others were Byzantine; others, the creations of the Latin Kingdom of Jerusalem in the eleventh and twelfth centuries, following the Crusades when Christian Jerusalem was reinvented. Regardless of the date, these transformations have a single feature in common: the expansion of the lists, of the repertoire of *topoi* through new narrative.

The most familiar and striking example has already been discussed: the *inventio Crucis* associated with Helena. There is little doubt that, in the East, this narrative rapidly came to overshadow that of the discovery of the Tomb. Or, to put it another way, a contemporary Christian experience displaced the archaic. What was joined together in the West under a single name, the Church of the Holy Sepulchre, was, in Eastern sources, carefully distinguished: the *Anastasis* as the site of the Tomb; the *Martyrium* (with its sense of contemporary witness) as the site of the Crucifixion and the place of the discovery of the Cross. These differing spatial arrangements were replicated on the temporal plane. In the West, both the discovery of the tomb and the discovery of the Cross were celebrated on a single day (September 17; later, May 3). In the East, there were two separate celebrations—closely linked, as were the two churches—but nevertheless distinct: September 13 for the discovery of the Tomb; September 14 for the discovery of the Cross.[72]

Later, in a process described by Anton Baumstark as the development of "concomitant feasts," that is, "feasts immediately following some other feast of higher rank of which they are a kind of echo," a third feast was superimposed on these significant dates, that of the Exaltation of the Cross.[73] This feast represents a second, contemporary overlay placed on the archaic myth. It commemorates the restoration of the relic of the Cross in 627 by Heraclius after it had been removed by the armies of the Sassanian king, Khosrau II.[74] Although the event commemorated is more closely tied to the Helena myth of the discovery of the Cross, later Christian tradition made of the "second" recovery a replication of Constantine's victories and recovery of the site of the Tomb. Khosrau was equated with Lucifer. Demonic forces had, once again, gained possession of a central Christian sign, and once again it was liberated by a pious Christian emperor.[75]

If the Helena myth may be understood as a secondary elaboration out of contemporary Christian experience, to it, at the level of narrative, was added a tertiary elaboration of prehistory: the legend of the wood of the Cross (the Rood Tree).[76] The wood was passed down from Adam, at length becoming an element in Solomon's Temple, before ultimately being fashioned into the Cross. In both the *inventio Crucis* associated with Helena and the prehistoric legend of the *origo Crucis*, the temporal narrative has all but replaced the spatial memorial.

The processes of both condensation and concomitant duplication characteristic of Jerusalemite tradition continued.[77] The Church of the Holy Sepulchre became an immense treasury of relics that conferred even greater density on this holy site.[78] The activities in the narrative of the Passion were further divided, new *topoi* were invented and connected to the Church: the Stone of Unction; the "prison" where Jesus awaited crucifixion.[79]

For the bulk of Christendom, however, especially in the West, such matters became increasingly irrelevant. Through schism and conquest, Jerusalem was lost to Christian experience and became, increasingly, an object of fantasy. If Jerusalem were to be accessible, it was to be gained through participation in a temporal arrangement of events, not a spatial one. It was through narrative, through an orderly progression through the Christian year, by encountering the *loci* of appropriate Scripture, and not by means of procession and pilgrimage, that memorialization occurred.

For this reason, our consideration of the Christian myth/ritual must end, not with the brief recovery of the place by the Crusaders, or with the beginnings of the complex negotiations for rights of access to the place between varieties of Christians and the Muslims, or with the intricate arrangements of article 62 of the Congress of Berlin (1878), which froze the status quo with respect to the Church of the Holy Sepulchre (and the other holy places) and which persists, in its bizarre patchwork, even to this day. Rather, we may make a halt in a distant land, in Paris, in 1535. For there, bringing to conclusion a project begun in a small village thirty miles from Barcelona twelve years earlier, and possibly influenced by a one-month pilgrimage to Jerusalem,[80] Ignatius of Loyola completed his classic manual of devotion, *The Spiritual Exercises*. There, as the first set of exercises for the third week of retreat, he commends, for the contemplation at midnight, meditation on the events of the Passion of Christ spread out over seven days.[81] In each of these, the individual is asked, first, to "call to mind the narrative of the event" and, second, to make a "mental representation of the place."[82] Here, all has been transferred to inner space. All that remains of Jerusalem is an image, the narrative, and a temporal sequence.

Notes

1. C. Middleton, *A Letter from Rome Shewing an Exact Conformity between Popery and Paganism: or, The Religion of the Present Romans to be derived entirely from that of their Heathen Ancestors* (London, 1729), 9. Although the copy I have is of the same date and by the same printer as the first edition, it appears to be a second printing.
2. Ibid., 11.
3. Ibid., 12.
4. Ibid., 13.
5. Ibid., ii (the second, unpaginated page of the Preface).
6. Ibid., 13.
7. Ibid., 16.
8. Ibid., 23.
9. Ibid., 13–14.
10. Ibid., 69–70.
11. Incense and altars (ibid., 15–16); altar boys (16); holy water (16–21); lamps and candles (21–22); votive offerings (22–29); devotion to the saints and their statues (29–43); roadside shrines, altars, and crosses (44–49); pomps and processions (50–52); miracles and relics (52–64); notion of sanctuary (64–65); priesthood (65–67).
12. Ibid., ii.
13. Ibid., 26.
14. Ibid., 31.
15. Ibid., 33; see, further, 36–37.
16. Middleton was later to achieve considerable fame with the publication of his *Life of Cicero* (London, 1741), until it was demonstrated that it was heavily plagiarized from W. Bellenden, *De tribus luminibus Romanorum* (Paris, 1633). The majority of the copies of this work were lost in transit to England. One of the few survivors was deposited at the Cambridge Library, where Middleton was University Librarian. See *Encyclopaedia Britannica*, 11th ed., 3:698, s.v. *Bellenden*.
17. C. Lévi-Strauss, *Structural Anthropology* (New York, 1963–76), 2:55.
18. J. P. S. Uberoi, *Science and Culture* (Delhi, 1978), 25.
19. Uberoi, *Science and Culture*, 31, 28, 33.
20. The question whether the eucharist was to be understood as *figura* or *ueritas* was first raised in strong form in the ninth-century controversy between Paschasius Radbertus and Ratramnus and gained classical formulation in the eleventh-century work of Berengar. It is in a retort to the latter that one finds one of the earliest expressions of the notion of "merely a symbol," in the response of Peter, a deacon of Rome at the Council of Vercelli in 1050: "If up till now we hold only the symbol, when shall we have the thing itself?" (Berengar, *De sacra coena adversus Lanfrancum*, 9, in the edition by A. F. Vischer and F. T. Vischer [Berlin, 1834], 43; in the new, and far from satisfactory, edition by W. H. Beekenkamp [The Hague, 1941], in the series Kerkhistorische Studien, 2, the passage occurs on p. 13, lines 2–3).

For the debate, see the standard treatments by J. R. Geiselmann, *Die Eucharistie-lehre der Vorscholastik* (Paderborn, 1926); A. J. MacDonald, *Berengar and the Reform of Sacramental Doctrine* (New York, 1930), cf. idem, ed., *The Evangelical Doctrine of Holy Communion* (Cambridge, 1930); C. E. Sheedy, *The Eucharistic Controversy of the Eleventh Century* (Washington, D.C., 1947); J. de Montclos, *Lanfranc et Berengar: La controverse eucharistique du XIe siecle* (Louvain, 1971), in the series Spicilegium sacrum Lovaniense, Études et documents, 37; and G. Macy, *The Theologies of the Eucharist in the Early Scholastic Period* (Oxford, 1984). The article by N. M. Haring, "Berengar's Definitions of *Sacramentum* and Their Influence on Mediaeval Sacra-mentology," *Mediaeval Studies* 10 (1948): 109–46, is particularly helpful in showing the wide semantic range of *sacramentum* and Berengar's attempt to stipulate a restric-tive definition. Two recent works review the eucharistic controversies in a manner refreshingly different from the usual histories of dogma: B. Stock, *The Implications of Literacy: Written Language and Models of Interpretation in the Eleventh and Twelfth Centuries* (Princeton, 1983), 241–315; R. Wagner, *Symbols that Stand for Themselves* (Chicago, 1986), 96–125.

21. Among other references, see H. Zwingli, *On the Lord's Supper* 3 (translation in G. W. Bromiley, *Zwingli and Bullinger* [Philadelphia, 1953], 185–238, esp. 233–35). The Marburg debate, on which Uberoi lays so much emphasis, has been reconstructed by W. Köhler, *Das Marburger Religionsgespräch 1529: Versuch einer Rekonstruktion* (Leipzig, 1929), in the series Schriften des Vereins für Reformationsgeschichte, 48:1 (no. 148); pp. 7–38 of Köhler's work has been translated into English by D. J. Ziegler, *Great Debates of the Reformation* (New York, 1969), 71–107, esp. 82–83: "We must take the word 'is' in the Lord's Supper to mean 'signifies' … [Melanchthon agrees] with me that something is only 'signified' by the words." Curiously, the concession by Zwingli that "we have no scriptural passage that says, 'This is the sign [*figura*] of my body'" (Ziegler, *Great Debates*, 80) echoes an early polemic by Theodore of Mop-suestia, "Christ did not say, 'This is the symbol [*symbolon*] of my body and blood,' but rather, 'This is my body and blood'" (*Fragmenta in Mt.* 26.26, Migne, *PG* 66:713).

22. See the texts from Beza cited in the important study by J. Raitt, *The Conversion of the Elements in Reformed Eucharistic Theory with Special Reference to Theodore Beza*, Ph.D. dissertation. University of Chicago (Chicago, 1970), 208–9. Raitt's study of the issue among the Reformers is the most searching to date.

23. Text quoted in ibid., 157.

24. In the following paragraphs, all the dated, but otherwise un identified, quotations, are taken from the *Oxford English Dictionary*, s.vv. *ceremony, custom, rite, ritual, symbol*.

25. For example, Duncan Forbes, *Some Thoughts Concerning Religion Natural and Revealed and the Manner of Understanding Revelation: Tending to Shew that Christianity is, Indeed very Near, as Old as the Creation* (London, 1735), 34, "Almost all the Jewish religious Service consisted in external, emblematical acts, rites and observances which, in themselves, and but for the institution and what was intended to be represented by them, served for no good purpose." (The copy I cite, in Special Collections of the Joseph Regenstein Library of the University of Chicago, is bound together with Mid-dleton's *A Letter from Rome*.) The usual term for empty ritualization is "Pharasaic," as in "The causes of Superstition are … Excesse of Outward and Pharisicall Holinesse" (1625), which allows the combination, "Pharisaically and Papistically" (1655).

26. J. Corbet, *A Discourse of the Religion of England* (London, 1667), 17. On pagano-papism, see H. Pinard de la Boullaye, *L'etude comparee des religions* (Paris, 1922–25), i: 151–56; L. Stephen, *History of English Thought in the Eighteenth Century*, 3d ed. (New York, 1949), 1:253–62; M. T. Hodgen, *Early Anthropology in the Sixteenth and Seventeenth Centuries* (Philadelphia, 1964), 325–30 *et passim*.

27. P. Mussard, *Les conformitez des cérémonies modernes avec les anciennes. Où il est prouvé par des autoritez incontestables que les cérémonies de l'église romaine sont empruntées des pagans* (London [?], 1667). I have not seen the English translation, *Roma antiqua et recens, or the Conformity of antient and modern Ceremonies, shewing from indisputable Testimonies that the Ceremonies of the Church of Rome are borrowed from the Pagans* (London, 1732). It has been charged that Middleton took parts of *A Letter from Rome* from Mussard (Stephen, *History of English Thought*, 1:256 n. 11). I doubt it. (See notes 5 and 16, above.)

28. P. Smart, *A Sermon Preached in the Cathedral Church of Durham, 1628*, 2d ed. (London, 1640), 18.

29. J. Toland, *Letters to Serena* (London, 1704), 130.

30. Erasmus, *Enchiridion militis Christiani* (1503), in J. P. Dolan, *The Essential Erasmus* (New York, 1964), 68.

31. For a profound meditation on the notion of "decipherment," see M. V. David, *Le débat sur les ecritures et l'hieroglyphique aux XVIIᵉ et XVIIIᵉ siècles et l'application de déchiffrement aux écritures mortes* (Paris, 1965).

32. See the study of this terminology and its implications in M. T. Hodgen, *The Doctrine of Survivals: A Chapter in the History of Scientific Method in the Study of Man* (London, 1936).

33. [C. de Brosses], *Du culte des dieux fétiches* ([Geneva], 1760), 267. The first edition, which I cite, was published anonymously, without indication of the author, publisher, or place of publication.

34. See the critique of Adolf Jensen and the presuppositions of the Frobenius School in J. Z. Smith, *Imagining Religion* (Chicago, 1982), 42–44.

35. In the formulations in this and the following three paragraphs, I am relying on, and modifying, my earlier set of statements in ibid., 54–56.

36. Herodotus, 2.172. I have adapted the standard translation by G. Rawlinson, 1st ed. (London, 1858–60).

37. [Norman Anonymous] *De consecratione pontificum et regium* in *Libelli de lite imperatorum et pontificum saeculis XI et XII conscripti*, H. Bömer (Hanover, 1891–97), 3:664, in the series *Monumenta Germaniae historica*. I have followed the English translation by E. H. Kantorowicz, *The King's Two Bodies* (Princeton, 1957), 46.

38. See H. Bouillard, "Le categorie du sacré dans la science des religions," in *Le sacré: Études et recherches*, ed. E. Castelli (Paris, 1974), esp. 33–38.

39. See E. Benveniste, *Le vocabulaire des institutions indo-europeennes* (Paris, 1969), 2:179–207.

40. Isaiah 44.14–17; Horace, *Satires* 1.8.1–3. Compare, Wisdom of Solomon 13.11–14.8; Tertullian, *De idolatria* 8.

41. Tertullian, *Apologia* 13.4.

42. See the use of the Amasis story in Minucius Felix, *Octavius* 22.4; Theophilus, *Ad Autolycum* 1.10. Compare Philo, *De Vita Contemplativa* 7; Justin, *1 Apologia* 9.3; Arnobius, *Adversus nationes* 6.12.

43. E. Durkheim, *Les formes élementaires de la vie religieuse*, 6th ed. (Paris, 1979), 167–80; English translation by J. W. Swain, *The Elementary Forms of the Religious Life* (London, 1915; reprint, New York, 1965), 140–49. On this topic, see the useful article by M. Singer, "Emblems of Identity: A Semiotic Exploration," in *On Symbols in Anthropology*, ed. J. Maquet (Los Angeles, 1982), 73–133, esp. 80–90, which compares Durkheim and Lévi-Strauss.

44. Durkheim, *Les formes élémentaires*, 172; *Elementary Forms*, 144. I am aware, *as was Durkheim* (*Les formes élémentaires*, 168 n. 3; *Elementary Forms*, 140 n. 101) that not all *tjuriinga* are marked. See T. G. H. Strehlow, *Aranda Traditions* (Melbourne, 1947;

reprint, New York, 1968), 57, 73. This has been emphasized by C. Lévi-Strauss (*La pensée sauvage* [Paris, 1962], 318) in attacking Durkheim's formulation. A few counter-examples do not necessarily destroy a theory if they can be explained. Strehlow provides ample explanation. The first example (Strehlow, *Aranda Traditions*, 54–55) represents a native Northern Aranda distinction between the stone *tjurunga talkara*, which is the metamorphized body of the ancestor, and the wooden (always engraved) *tjurunga ititjangariera*, which are thought to be representations of the original *tjurunga talkara*. If these are engraved, "they are not engraved by the hand of man." The second example comes from the outer border of the Aranda-*tjurunga* culture: "[From that point] onwards, sea-shells, known as *pott' irkara* had taken their [the tjurunga's] place as objects of worship" (Strehlow, *Aranda Traditions*, 73).

45. Durkheim, *Les formes élémentaires*, 178–79; *Elementary Forms*, 148–49.
46. See p. 40 [of the original book].
47. C. Lévi-Strauss, "Introduction à l'oeuvre de Marcel Mauss," which serves as a preface to Lévi-Strauss's collection *Sociologie et anthropologie par Marcel Mauss* (Paris, 1950), ix–lii. See Lévi-Strauss's remarks on the relationship between Durkheim and Mauss, p. xli.
48. Lévi-Strauss, "Introduction," xlii–xliii. I have profited from D. Pocock's translation of some paragraphs of this essay in his "Foreword" to the English translation of M. Mauss, A *General Theory of Magic* (London, 1972), 1–6.
49. Lévi-Strauss, "Introduction," xliii. The passage is cited from Tesa, *Studi del Thevenet* (Pisa, 1881), 17 (*non vidi*), in Mauss, *A General Theory of Magic*, 114. Both Thevenet's examples and those provided by Lévi-Strauss refer to new objects introduced by trade and culture contact. See, further, J. Z. Smith, *Map Is Not Territory* (Leiden, 1978), 298–99.
50. Lévi-Strauss, "Introduction," xliv.
51. Ibid., xlvii, xlix.
52. Ibid., xlix.
53. Ibid., i. In his text, Lévi-Strauss uses the analogy of the number zero; in a footnote, he refers to the linguistic notion developed by R. Jakobsen of "un phoneme zéro."
54. Lévi-Strauss, "Introduction," i n. 1.
55. See pp. 85–86 [of the original book].
56. I am much taken with the suggestion by G. G. Porton ("Defining Midrash," in *The Study of Ancient Judaism*, ed. J. Neusner [New York, 1981], 1:64–65) of the existence "during the intertestamental period ... [of] two possible sources of authority, two parallel but possibly conflicting paths ... the priesthood/priestly traditions and the Torah."
57. Smith, *Imagining Religion*, 63.
58. J. C. Heestermann, *The Inner Conflict of Tradition: Essays in Indian Ritual, Kingship and Society* (Chicago, 1985), 3.
59. A. van Gennep, *Les rites de passage* (Paris, 1909), 16; English translation, *The Rites of Passage* (London, 1960), 12.
60. S. Freud, "Zwangshandlungen und Religiosübungen" (1907), in *Gesammelte Werke*, S. Freud (London, 1940–), 7:129–39; English translation, "Obsessive Acts and Religious Practices," in *The Standard Edition of the Complete Psychological Works of Sigmund Freud*, ed. J. Strachey (London, 1953–), 9:117–27.
61. C. Lévi-Strauss, *L'homme nu* (Paris, 1971), 596–603; English translation by J. and D. Weightman, *The Naked Man* (New York, 1981), 667–75.
62. Lévi-Strauss, *La pensée sauvage*, 17.
63. See W. E. H. Stanner (*On Aboriginal Religion* [Sydney, 1966], 14, in the series The Oceania Monographs, 11), who speaks of "the great split of the pristine unity."

64. See pp. 11–12 [of the original book]. There, as well as in what follows, I have been much influenced by N. Munn, "The Transformation of Subjects into Objects in Walbiri and Pitjantjatjara Myth," in *Australian Aboriginal Anthropology*, ed. R. M. Berndt (Nedlands, 1970), 141–63. Though taking a different tack, the question I raise here is that raised by Lévi-Strauss in *La pensée sauvage*, 302–23.

65. I have been influenced in these formulations by, in addition to Munn (see above, note 64), W. E. H. Stanner, "Religion, Totemism, and Symbolism," in *Aboriginal Man in Australia*, ed. R. M. Berndt and C. H. Berndt (Sydney, 1965), 207–37, as reprinted in *Religion in Aboriginal Australia: An Anthology*, ed. M. Charlesworth et al. (Queensland, 1984), esp. 164.

66. Stanner, *Aboriginal Religion*, 11.

67. M. Charlesworth, "Introduction: Change in Aboriginal Religion," in Charlesworth et al., eds., *Religion in Aboriginal Australia*, 113.

68. Stanner, *Aboriginal Religion*, 63.

69. Smith, *Imagining Religion*, 56.

70. Strehlow, *Aranda Traditions*, 120, cf. 84–172.

71. Stanner, *Aboriginal Religion*, 32.

72. See the crisp formulation of this in H. A. Drake, "A Coptic Version of the Discovery of the Holy Sepulchre," *Greek, Roman, and Byzantine Studies* 20 (1979): 384–85.

73. A. Baumstark, *Comparative Liturgy* (London, 1958), 182.

74. See the treatment by A. Frolow, "La vraie croix et les expéditions d'Héraclius en Perse," *Festschrift M. Jugie* (Paris, 1953): 89–105 = *Revue des études byzantines* 11 (1953).

75. On Khosrau = Lucifer, see H. P. L'Orange, *Studies on the Iconography of Cosmic Kingship* (Oslo, 1953), 114–84, in the series Forelesninger av det Instituttet for sammenlignende Kulturforskning, ser. A, 12. Note that in the *Chronicum venetum* (Altinate), edited by H. Simonsfeld, *Monumenta Germaniae historica*, series *Scriptores* (Hanover, 1826–), 14:49–50, Constantine's and Heraclius's campaigns have been combined into a single event.

76. The standard monograph remains W. Meyer, *Die Geschichte der Kreuzholzes vor Christus* (Munich, 1882) in the series Abhandlungen der philosophisch-philologischen Classe der Königlich Bayerischen Akademie der Wissenschaften, 16.2 (1882): 103–60. E. C. Quinn, *The Quest of Seth for the Oil of Life* (Chicago, 1962) is the most recent full treatment.

77. See the important treatment of this in M. Halbwachs, *La topog raphic légendaire des évangiles en Terre sainte* (Paris, 1941). I find most helpful his notions of "concentration" and "doubling" (pp. 185–86).

78. This density is revealed at the level of chapels, not to speak of individual relics. See, among others, the description by C. Deshayes, *Voyage du Levant fait par le commandement du Roy* (Paris, 1624), 392–402, as reproduced in F. A. de Chateaubriand, *Itinéraire de Paris à Jerusalem* (1811). I cite the critical edition by E. Malakis, *Chateaubriand: Itinéraire de Paris à Jerusalem* (Baltimore, 1946), 2:92–97.

> Upon entering the Church, you come to the Stone of Unction on which the body of Our Lord was anointed with myrrh and aloes. ... Some say that it is of the same rock as mount Calvary, others assert that it was brought to this place by Joseph and Nicodemus. ... The Holy Sepulchre is thirty paces from this Stone. ... At the entrance to the door of the Sepulchre, there is a stone about a foot and a half square ... upon this stone was seated the angel when he spoke to the two Marys. ... The first Christians erected before it a little chapel which is called the Chapel of the Angel. Twelve steps from the Holy Sepulchre, turning north, you

come to a large block of gray marble ... placed there to mark the spot where our Lord appeared to the Magdalene in the form of a gardener. Further on is the Chapel of the Apparition where, according to tradition, Our Lord first appeared to the Virgin after his resurrection. ... Continuing your walk around the Church, you find a small vaulted chapel ... the Prison of Our Lord where he was held while the hole was dug for the erecting of the Cross. ... Very near is another chapel ... standing on the very spot [*au même lieu*] where Our Lord was stripped by the soldiers before being nailed to the Cross. ... Leaving this chapel ... going down thirty steps, you come to a chapel ... commonly called the Chapel of St. Helena because she prayed there before bringing about the search for the Cross. You descend eleven more steps to the place where it was discovered, along with the nails, the crown of thorns, and the head of the lance. ... Near the top of this staircase ... is a chapel ... underneath the altar [of which] is a pillar of gray marble. ... It is called the pillar of *Impropere* because Our Lord was forced to sit there in order to be crowned with thorns. Ten paces from this chapel [is the staircase by which you ascend] to Mount Calvary. ... You still see the hole dug in the rock. ... Near this is the place where stood the two crosses of the two thieves.

79. See note 78, above. For the "Stone of Unction," see M. A. Graeve, "The Stone of Unction in Caravaggio's Painting for the Chiesa Nuova," *The Art Bulletin* 40 (1958): 230. Compare A. Millet, *Recherches sur l'iconographie de l'Évangile aux XIVᵉ, XVᵉ et XVIᵉ siècles*, 2d ed. (Paris, 1960), 479. For the "prison," see G. Dalman, *Sacred Sites and Ways: Studies in the Topography of the Gospels* (London, 1935), 336.

80. For the biographical details, see I. Iparraguirre, *Practica de los Ejercicios de San Ignaci de Loyola en Vida de su autor* (Rome, 1946), 34*–40*, in the series Bibliotheca Instituti Historici Societatis Jesus, 3.

81. The scheme is pre-Ignatian. The most immediate influence on Ignatius was the four-teenth-century *Vitae Christi* by Ludolfus of Saxony. See M. I. Bodenstedt, *The Vitae Christi of Ludolphus the Carthusian* (Washington, D.C., 1944), and C. A. Conway, Jr., *The Vitae Christi of Ludolph of Saxony: A Descriptive Analysis* (Salzburg, 1976), in the series Analecta Carthusiana. For earlier exemplars, see the anonymous, thirteenth-century *De meditatione passionis Christi per septem diei horas* (Migne, *PL* 94:561–68), and the popular, late-thirteenth-century Tuscan text, falsely attributed to Bonaventure, *Meditationes vitae Christi*. On the latter, see the study by L. Oliger, "Le meditationes vitae Christi del pseudo-Bonaventura," *Studi Francescani*, n.s. 7 (1921): 143–83; 8 (1922): 18–47; and the translation of the text and reproduction of an illustrated version by I. Ragusa and R. B. Green, *Meditations on a Life of Christ: An Illustrated Manuscript of the Fourteenth Century, Paris, Bibliothèque Nationale, Ms. Ital. 115* (Princeton, 1961), in the series Princeton Monographs in Art and Archaeology. The instructions for medi-tating over a period of a week include the detail "feeling yourself present in those places as if the things were done in your presence" (Ragusa and Green, *Meditations*, 387).

82. Ignatius of Loyola, *Ejercicios espirituales*, 150–51, in the critical edition by J. Calveras, *Sanctii Ignatii de Loyola, Exercitia spiritualia* (Rome, 1969), 250–53, in the series Monumenta historica societatis Jesu, 100. In the enumeration of the convenient edition by J. Roothan (*Los ejercicios espirituales de San Ignacio de Loyola*, 3rd ed. [Zaragoza, 1959], 192–93), the passages appear as numbers 191–92. Although the meditations were designed to produce a mental picture, in the sixteenth century, Jeronimo Nadal was commissioned by the Jesuits to supply illustrations for the Gospels keyed to Ignatius's *Ejercicios* (the *Evangelicae historiae imagines* [Antwerp, 1596]); by the eigh-teenth century, illustrated editions of the *Ejercicios* themselves were common in Europe.

To the passages quoted from the *Ejercicios* should be compared other texts, such as the *Zardino de Oration* 16, a fifteenth-century manual of devotion for young girls, which instructs the girls to mentally "place" the figures of the actors in the Passion narrative in Jerusalem, "taking for this purpose a city that is well-known to you" (quoted in M. Baxandall, *Painting and Experience in Fifteenth Century Italy* [Oxford, 1972], 46).

For a full discussion of Ignatius's "application of the senses," see H. Rahner, *Ignatius the Theologian* (London, 1968), 181–213. Both R. Barthes (*Sade, Fourier, Loyola* [New York, 1976], 39–75) and J. Spence (*The Memory Palace of Matteo Ricci* [New York, 1984], 12–22 *et passim*) have contributed strikingly original views on the Ignatian enterprise of visualization.

Part III

RELATING RITUAL TO ACTIONS AND IDEAS

MYTH

Maurice Bloch

Editor's Introduction

Maurice Bloch is Professor in Anthropology at the London School of Economics. Much of his fieldwork research has been in Madagascar among rice cultivators and shifting agriculturalists. His work blends British and French approaches to anthropology and has been significant in introducing the best of French Marxist theory to Anglophone anthropologists. In his many publications he commonly engages with ideology, ritual and language, but in recent years he has also engaged more with cognitive issues. He is, therefore, well placed to contribute importantly to this debate about ritual and religious belief.

In the following extract from *Prey Into Hunter*, Bloch is particularly interested in myth, myth-making and myth telling. However, after arguing that some earlier scholars misconstrued a "direct relation between myth and practice," Bloch contributes to understanding how they might in fact relate. Following an argument he pursues through the rest of the book, and elsewhere in his writings, he dismisses the notion that myth is an entirely intellectual, speculative exercise, and argues that it is one way in which people review doubts and fears.

Bloch's name is most often associated with the phrase "rebounding violence" which is central to his thesis about cultures and societies and their myths, rituals, religions and politics. The classic studies of ritual by van Gennep (1975) and Victor Turner (1991) detail ways in which particular rites (re-)incorporate people into their societies after aiding or forcing particular changes of state or status. Bloch's work agrees with Bruce Lincoln (1991) and René Girard (1992) that since these societies are often hierarchical, at least, and commonly violent in practice, it would be pointless not to expect and discuss the violence inherent in rituals and myths. More to the point, societies maintain and legitimate themselves by acts of violence against individual members of society or against plants or animals ritually or mythically constituted as a suitable object for the transfer of power. Nonetheless, Bloch suggests that ritual and myth may also seek and instigate alternatives to any status quo.

Whether or not Bloch's thesis is convincing, it is important to engage with his contribution to the question of how myth and ritual are related.

References

Gennep, Arnold van. 1975. *The Rites of Passage*. Chicago: University of Chicago Press.
Girard, René. 1992. *Violence and the Sacred.* Baltimore: Johns Hopkins University Press.
Lincoln, Bruce. 1991. *Emerging from the Chrysalis: Rituals of Women's Initiation*. Oxford: Oxford University Press.
Turner, Victor. 1991. *The Ritual Process: Structure and Anti-Structure*. Ithaca, NY: Cornell University Press.

හ ශ

[T he previous chapter in *Prey Into Hunter*] consisted of a discussion of the way in which it is possible to reverse the predatory implications of rebounding violence by arresting the progression half-way, at the point when native vitality has been abandoned but before restrengthening external vitality has been consumed. This possibility comes to the fore when political circumstances make all forms of social continuation appear hopeless. In many ways this millenarian transformation can be thought of as revolutionary in that it may lead to political upheaval, as it did in Madagascar in 1863. However, in spite of this political radicalism, there is a sense in which the millenarian option is also intellectually conservative. It does not reject the symbolism of conquest in rebounding violence; it merely seeks to abort the sequence. To find a truly radical challenge occurring on a sufficiently regular basis as to be recorded by ethnographers, it is necessary to leave the realm of organized practice for the most part and move to the freer speculation of what has been called myth.[1] It is, however, quite possible that such speculation may hover in the background and occur quite frequently in the minds of the peoples we have so far discussed, but, nonetheless, only rarely achieve the public formulation which would make the recording of this type of thinking likely.

This chapter deals with such radical rejections, but since these occur in the world of imagination, it leads the argument away from the main concern of the book, which is actual practice and the linked experiences it evokes. This final part of the book is therefore perhaps best seen as a sort of appendix, or as a sketchy joint speculation by the author and the subjects of the ethnographies discussed concerning how matters might be if everything was different and the attempt to establish transcendental institutions had not even been attempted.

There was a time when anthropologists saw a direct relation between myth and practice, for example Malinowski (1948) and also Leach (1954). However, Lévi-Strauss has shown quite conclusively how misleading such an approach actually is (1958, chapter 11). He has pointed out how mythology is so often a speculation on practice, exploring all imaginable possibilities in what must remain an intellectual search. Myths often seem simply to review the possible doubts of the participants and explore these with horrified fascination. Myths seem to concentrate on the terrifying or ironic possibilities of the failure of the system (Huntington 1988, 79) or on the impossibility of its teleological implications rather than, as anthropologists used to believe, provide a charter for action.

From what I know of mythology in different parts of the world, such a view seems largely correct and it is unfortunate that the radical difference between the general discourse of mythology and most forms of ritual practice is so often forgotten by anthropologists whose study implicitly homologizes the two different types of data. However, Lévi-Strauss's view also requires a certain amount of qualification. The distinction between myth and ritual is not quite as sharp as he makes out, nor does it correspond exactly with the dividing line between the two phenomena as they are usually understood (Lévi-Strauss 1971, 596–603). In the example of the Ma'Betisek to be discussed below we find that the kind of radical intellectual adventurousness and refusal of distinction which Lévi-Strauss identifies with myth sometimes also spills over into ritual practice. Secondly, we find that there are some myths which do indeed serve as charters for conservative social practices and for rituals which construct rebounding violence.

The anthropologist with experience of fieldwork will also be well aware that even the most speculative myths are not quite the relaxed, curious speculation which Lévi-Strauss seems to suggest. When we look at mythology in context we get the feeling that the intellectual is much more driven, much more anxious and more directed than we would imagine from reading his work. In particular, myths are so often directed to a painful consideration of the problems hidden by the treacherously easy solutions which the rituals of rebounding violence propose.

We have already come across a number of myths and practices in this book which can serve to make these points. In chapter 5 [of *Prey Into Hunter*] it was pointed out that the combination of self-denial and aggression present in Ladakhi marriage was often related to a myth which among other things illustrates bride capture. This is the story of the mythical king and hero Kesar who, after many adventures, regains his bride and lives happily ever after. These final episodes are the events which the rituals of marriage are seen to evoke, but in fact this part of the story is only a little section of the total myth, in which we find that before settling the matter quite so satisfactorily Kesar had a much more uncertain marital career.

In the full story Kesar, himself the product of bizarre unions, first marries a princess by stealth and becomes incorporated into her father's kingdom in contradiction of the rule of virilocality. He next kills an ogre and goes on to live with the ogre's wife and produce a child. Meanwhile, his former wife moves in with a new husband. Finally, after much complication Kesar abandons his second wife and recaptures the first. Such bewildering accounts of behaviour which goes against the morality thought appropriate for more ordinary mortals are in fact typical of myths which Malinowski so misleading considered as "charters" for social institutions. Although one cannot rule out the possibility that they might well be that, they are therefore also much else besides.

In her careful study of this myth, Phylactou shows how the different stages of the story evoke many of the possibilities of marriage permutations that can be envisaged within the Tibetan cultural framework. Not only do we have a story which corresponds fairly closely to an ideal marriage, where the bride is triumphantly taken back to the groom's house, but we also have the opposite, where the groom is incorporated into his wife's house, and also many other variants on the general theme of marriage.

The fact that the Kesar myth dwells on the possibility of the hero's being absorbed in his wife's family is typical of myth. We find again and again in myth the imaginary consideration of worlds without rebounding violence or of worlds where the consumed become the consumers. Thus in Orokaiva mythology we find stories of pigs which, because they have been captured and penetrated by ancestral spirits, can therefore, like initiated humans, hunt, capture and eat both pigs and humans. Such evocations are thus radical fantasies, imagining what would happen if the sequence of rebounding violence was reversed so that it ended with the consumption of humans by pigs. Referring to an analogous myth, Iteanu is thus able to say that: "In the myth initiation is represented as the negative of what it is in the ritual" (Iteanu 1983, 71).

Again, if we turn to Buid ethnography we find similar ideas. The Buid see their relation to predatory spirits, which are themselves sometimes imagined as giant pigs, as pig-like (Gibson 1986, 154). That is, in the images of myth and in the visions of spirit mediums, the horrifying possibility of being consumed by those beings they consume emerges in Buid imagination. In such images we have a truly radical potential challenge to the order established by rebounding violence, even if it remains almost exclusively in the realm of the imaginary.

In order to illustrate such subversive thought I conclude this book with one more example from a stimulating ethnography by Wazir-Jahan Karim of a South East Asian people, the Ma'Betisek (Karim 1981). The Ma'Betisek are an aboriginal group from Malaysia who now live in very precarious conditions, powerless, driven from their land and surrounded by much more powerful neighbours. Karim identifies as the root of Ma'Betisek religious ideas two fundamental and largely incompatible principles, which she denotes by the Ma'Betisek uses of the words *tulah* and *kemali'*. *Tulah* can be translated into English as either "domination" or "curse." The two meanings are linked in that legitimate domination is the result of a successful curse. Thus, if a member of a senior generation feels he has in some way been slighted by a junior, he may curse him. The junior will then, as a result of the curse, lose his rights as a human being. If we envisage this form of cursing within the schema of rebounding violence it means that if a junior refuses to be conquered by his senior, he then loses his right to conquer in turn and thus becomes like a plant or an animal who can be consumed with impunity.

One aspect of the curse of *tulah* which particularly interests Karim and the Ma'Betisek is its significance for defining the food one may eat. Like many Asian and Amerindian peoples the Ma'Betisek consider plants, animals and humans as having been originally so closely linked as to have been almost identical. Thus plants and animals are sometimes seen as descended from humans who, because of overcrowding in villages which existed in the distant past, had to move out to the forest. Sometimes, in a somewhat similar way, plants and animals are believed to have originated from the souls of dead humans (Karim 1981, 45, 67).

In the past therefore plants, animals and humans were continually interacting in a somewhat promiscuous fashion. However, in the end, plants and animals seem to have failed to observe the fundamental rules of mutual co-operation and sharing which common residence should imply and instead they were found to be doing the very opposite. They were secretly killing and eating humans, thereby being guilty of eating their own kind, i.e. cannibalism, since at that time all living forms were undifferentiated and therefore one (Karim 1981, 34). Because of this immoral behaviour towards those one should co-operate with, the elders cursed the plants and animals with the curse of *tulah*. This meant that from then on plants and animals could be exploited and eaten by humans. From having been illegitimate killers and hunters, plants and animals became legitimate prey. Humans, for their part, were henceforth able to kill and consume plants and animals legitimately. Because they had once been food, humans could be eaters: they had changed from prey into hunters. This story, therefore, explains why, for the Ma'Betisek, plants and animals can be consumed by humans and why plants and animals cannot consume humans in return.

As it stands the story follows the pattern of rebounding violence perfectly. Humans, plants and animals share a lot, but are also distinguished by the presence or absence of one critical element, which is rather like the spirit element of the Orokaiva, or the speech element of the Dinka. What makes humans more than plants and animals is that they obey the social rules enforced by elders, especially those prototypical social rules forbidding cannibalism and incest. Because they obey and submit to the transcendental element implied in following these rules, in other words because they allow their native vitality to be regulated, the Ma'Betisek obtain, according to the logic of rebounding violence, the right to consume the vitality, by now external and alien, of those beings which had refused the first conquest. The plants and animals by their failure have become *other* forms of living things who henceforth have to live in *other* places and humans can therefore legitimately feed on them.

But even within this confident formulation of the legitimation of consumption the shadow of doubt is not far away. After all, by explaining why they may consume other living things the Ma'Betisek are also acknowledging the potentially dismaying fact of the initial identity of all forms of life. This inevitably raises the suggestion of questions such as what, for example, would have happened if the plants and animals had not been cursed? Then the hunting, killing and consumption of plants and animals would be both illegitimate and horrifying. It would be a form of cannibalism, the very crime which would justify plants and animals consuming humans.

This possibility seems to be continually envisaged in such cultures as a haunting undeveloped theme in the orchestration of meaning. To keep such eventualities from becoming realities, the Ma'Betisek, like many other South East Asian peoples, seem obsessive about maintaining boundaries between humans and other life forms, by, for example, insisting on the contrast between the raw food of plants and animals and the cooked food of humans and by expressing the fear that any act of over-familiarity on the part of humans towards animals or plants will bring about a cosmic calamity (Needham 1964). However, it is when things go wrong and illness strikes that the fear of the possibility of the reversal of rebounding violence, caused by the near-cannibalism implied in eating plants and animals, really comes to the fore. This is shown by the fact that the Ma'Betisek attribute the cause of all the most serious diseases to a kind of revenge on the part of the plants and animals against the humans. This retaliation is envisaged as taking the form of diseases which result from the attacks of animal and plant spirits avenging themselves for the illegitimate consumption of their species.

In a manner that is similar to the African curers discussed in chapter 3 [of *Prey Into Hunter*], the Ma'Betisek deal with such problems of invasion in one of two ways. The first is akin to the first tack of African diviners, that is, they attempt to expel the invading animal or plant spirit. As noted above, among the Ma'Betisek trouble is attributed to the idea that the curse enacted so long ago, which made plants and animals the legitimate prey of humans, does not hold any more and so the plants and animals have been able to take their revenge. If the curse is weak this means that the differentiation between humans, on the one hand, and plants and animals, on the other, has been breached and so eating plants and animals has become once more cannibalism and is therefore punishable. The image of this state of affairs is all the more horrific as an idea because the original reason for the *tulah* curse which made them eatable was precisely that it was a punishment administered to plants and animals because of their cannibalism. But now, if the curse is not holding, it is the humans who are the cannibals and it would therefore follow that plants and animals would be justified in their spirit attacks on people.

The first Ma'Betisek solution to such a state of affairs is to restore the *status quo* and to drive out the plant and animal spirits yet again, by re-enacting the original curse against them and thereby re-establishing the legitimacy of human consumption. The curse used by qualified elders on such an occasion could not express more clearly the idea that the problem is that the original separation of plants and animals and humans is no longer as clear as it should be and that it must, therefore, be re-established: 'if an animal, *be* an animal; if human, *be* a human; but do not be both human and animal' (Karim 1981, 39, italics added).

This first tack, however, may not always be fully satisfactory, as is shown when the disease persists. Then the Ma'Betisek try a second tack. This is, however, quite unlike the second tack of people like the Dinka who, as we saw, simply re-enact the process of rebounding violence with still greater emphasis through sacrifice. What the Ma'Betisek do on such occasions actually implies the total abandonment of the symbolism of rebounding violence and at the same time the whole attempt to establish a life-transcending social order which differentiates people from other life forms. In a way which must have much to do with their political powerlessness they refuse the whole system on which human societies build their claim to transcendence and thereby conjure up a truly radical rejection of rebounding violence in ritual. They do this by abandoning the principle of *tulah* and by turning instead to their second religious idea, that of *kemali'*.

Kemali' thought occurs much less frequently in practical and political circumstances than does *tulah* thought. As Lévi-Strauss would have predicted, it comes to the fore in certain types of myth which stress the indistinguishable aspects of all living things. *Kemali'* thought emphasizes the continuity between plants, humans and animals, which are all seen as mutually helpful siblings. In this perspective every act of consumption is an illegitimate act of aggression and the fragile basis of *tulah* is negated. By stressing unity, *kemali'* myth inevitably raises the disturbing questions: What if plants and animals were truly our sisters and brothers? What if the extra transcendental element which distinguishes humans from other life forms was a mere illusion?

This doubt, as we have seen, is the source of Ma'Betisek explanations of disease and can sometimes be dealt with by a re-emphasis of *tulah*; however, *kemali'* ideas can also be used for curing. This occurs in shamanistic sessions when, with the help of animal and plant spirit familiars, a kind of temporary peace and community among all living forms is evoked through dance, song and the sharing of food which is half raw, half cooked, thereby symbolizing the lack of differentiation between humans and animals (Karim 1981, 195). It is as if the state of existence in myth as it was before the curse of *tulah* was being reinstated in the present and human beings had abdicated their superiority. This tack brings about respite from disease because, once the siblingship of all species has been established, there is no room for anybody consuming anybody else and it would therefore be unreasonable for the plant and animal spirits to continue their interference with humans.

This solution is achieved, however, at a very great cost. It implies the abandonment of the claim to the superiority of human society; it implies the abandonment of the attempt to transcend process by establishing permanent structures; it implies the abandonment of all forms of consumption. This is the most radical solution of all, though obviously one which cannot be maintained for long. Unlike millenarianism it does not just refuse the second half of rebounding violence, but rejects the whole process. It is a solution which implies a practice that has learnt the implicit lesson of the critical commentary on human existence found in myth, which asks, rather like an anarchist critique of society, what if the consumers were the consumed? But even for such an unassuming group of people as the Ma'Betisek such liberating humility can only be a temporary solution. After all one must eat. The seance finished, the world of *tulah* must be discreetly re-established so that food can once more be obtained, so that society can continue and so that the world of rebounding violence may regain its full potential for conquest of other species and of oneself.

To end here is perhaps to suggest that, given the raw materials of our shared perceptions of the processes of life and with the limited tools of ritualization and metaphor at our disposal, the constructions of rebounding violence, in their many structural forms and contents, are the only way in which the necessary image of society as a transcendental and legitimate order can be constructed. This would also mean, therefore, that we cannot construct cosmologies other than those which offer a toe-hold to the legitimation of domination and violence. But perhaps the Ma'Betisek example shows something quite different. It may show that, when in real trouble, we are able to analyse and criticize the very basis of our ideologies, to begin to demystify ourselves and to search for fundamentally different solutions.

Note

1. There are in fact a whole range of types of linguistic behaviours which have been labelled myth by anthropologists and they have very different sociological implications. Not since Malinowski has a serious attempt been made to try to classify them. It is clearly inappropriate for me to try to do so here and in this discussion I am merely using the word loosely, much in the way it has been used by Lévi-Strauss.

References

Gibson, T. 1986. *Sacrifice and Sharing in the Philippine Highlands.* London School of Economics Monographs in Social Anthropology 57. London: Athlone.

Huntingdon, R. 1988. *Gender and Social Structure in Madagascar.* Bloomington: Indiana University Press.

Iteanu, A. 1983. *La Ronde des échanges. De la circulation aux voleurs chez les Orokaiva.* Cambridge: Cambridge University Press.

Karim, W.-J. 1981. *Ma'Betisek Concepts of Living Things.* London School of Economics Monographs in Social Anthropology 54. London: Athlone.

Leach, E. R. 1954. *Political Systems of Highland Burma.* London: Bell.

Lévi-Strauss, C. 1958. *Anthropologie Structurale.* Paris: Plon.

—1971. *L'Homme nu.* IV. *Mythologiques.* Paris: Plon.

Malinowski, B. 1948. *Magic, Science and Religion.* Glencoe: The Free Press.

Needham, R. 1964. "Blood, Thunder and the Mockery of Animals." *Sociologus* (n.s.) 14: 136–49.

Phylactou, M. 1989. "Household Organisation and Marriage in Ladakh, Indian Himalaya." PhD dissertation, London School of Economics and Political Science.

MALINOWSKI'S DEMARCATIONS AND HIS EXPOSITION OF THE MAGICAL ART

Stanley J. Tambiah

Editor's Introduction

Stanley Tambiah is Emeritus Professor and the Esther and Sidney Rabb Professor of Anthropology at Harvard University. The majority of his research and publications concentrate on Buddhism, especially in its relationship with politics in Thailand and Sri Lanka, and include an insistence on asking difficult questions (for example, about how the non-violent philosophy of Buddhism relates to the political violence of the Sinhalese against the Tamils).

The following extract engages with a rather different controversy: the relationship between magic, religion, science and rationality. In particular, he is interested in the demarcations made between these putatively separate discourses or practices by Bronislaw Malinowski. (Tambiah introduces Malinowski in the first pages of the extract.) These distinctions are commonplace in the study of religions and cultures but Malinowski and Tambiah make significant and distinctive contributions. One particularly important moment is when Tambiah states his preference for "ritual speech" rather than "magical speech." Like others, he considers the "instrumental" and "expressive" purposive of different genres. He notes that the question of how "ritual speech" is different from ordinary speech or whether it might be "an intensification of ordinary speech like poetic diction" is unsettled. He also says that the question of whether magical ritual in the Trobriand Islands was efficacious or not remains open. Like Malinowski, Tambiah wants to know whether ritual was intended to be efficacious and whether, if it was done for that purpose but failed to achieve it, what the Islanders did about it. He remains dissatisfied with claims that rituals might be effective in "creating a change of state in the human actors" even when their putative purpose was something more obviously external, physical or transcendent. While such rationalizations are easy to understand, it is not clear that they actually arise from ethnographic observation, that is, that they were observed or recorded as the views of the Islanders.

Tambiah's chapter is important in its recognition of the lack of clarity in much that passes for ethnography and the theorization that results from it. Decisions about the relationship between magic and other kinds of rituals—if rituals are not in fact always some kind of magic as opposed to science or religion—demand a better understanding of whatever actions and discourses "magic" might properly refer to.

℘ ℃

B ronislaw Kaspar Malinowski,[1] born in Cracow, Poland in 1884, died in New Haven, Connecticut in 1942, is instructive for us as a kind of negation of the Tylor–Frazer points of view (of seeing science, magic, religion in a developmental perspective, and of seeing magic and religion as phenomena that had to be tested against the yardstick of scientific rationality). Interestingly enough, the early part of his career was in the sciences: his doctorate was in physics and mathematics, and it is alleged that during an illness, which prevented his continuing his scientific studies, he read Frazer's *Golden Bough* and was filled with such enthusiasm that he became an anthropologist.

It is intriguing then that, like the Father of American Anthropology, Franz Boas, another emigrant, from Germany this time, who was also first trained as a scientist and at the end of an intellectual odyssey founded the science of culture, Malinowski found his way to London (to the London School of Economics), and thereafter to New Guinea partly at least owing to the constraints and accidents of the First World War, and founded the self-proclaimed school of Functionalism, whose basic point of reference was an anti-Durkheimian individualistic pragmatic psychology.

It is intriguing, but not altogether mystifying in an expatriate who had taken to a new country (he is said to have had an exaggerated respect for England and things English) and a new discipline, that Malinowski *qua* anthropologist rarely referred to his Polish intellectual cultural and political antecedents and how they may have contributed to his "functionalism." And it is somewhat remarkable that Malinowski's British disciples also seemingly evinced little interest in their guru's past, and tended to see his anthropological perspective as cut out of whole cloth.

In recent years, interesting information has surfaced concerning the intellectual influences and contexts to which Malinowski was exposed in Poland quite early in his career, and which helped to shape his later scientific and ideological positions as a professional anthropologist.[2] Malinowski's father, Lucjan, was professor of Slavonic Philology at Cracow University. Malinowski's studies at the same historic Jagellonian University in Cracow were chiefly in physics, mathematics and philosophy, and there he read and was influenced by the writings of Ernst Mach, Richard Avenarius, Wilhelm Wundt and others. Indeed Malinowski's doctoral dissertation, entitled "On the Economy of Thought," was centrally concerned with the ideas of Ernst Mach, who was an exponent of a certain type of positivist scientific methodology.[3]

Some of Mach's ideas that are thought to have influenced Malinowski are as follows: Mach launched "a sustained critique of any philosophy of science which fails to take account of the observer and his position relative to the object of observation, or which fails to take account of the cognitive structure of the human mind in its account of scientific method."[4] Mach's positivism which entailed the "concept of 'field' and holism in the physical sciences" is possibly reflected in Malinowski's insistence that the "empirical ethnographic fact must always be evaluated in the context of the whole."[5] Machian positivism included a biological interpretation of knowledge: "It sees ideas as serving a total organism, and as vindicated by constituting the most 'economical' way of serving the organism's needs ... This leads, in a very natural way to Malinowski's functionalism, and to his holistic attitude to culture."[6]

Evidence provided by Malinowski's daughter[7] shows that Malinowski was developing interests that presaged his later career. After his doctorate in 1908, he studied at Leipzig University until 1910, and there attended courses on Völkerpsychologie taught by Wilhelm Wundt, and worked in economics under Karl Bücher. Indeed by 1908 he had already developed his new interest in anthropology from reading German and English anthropological literature. We should also keep in mind that Malinowski was possibly influenced by the ethnographic and linguistic work of his father and his colleagues.

Between 1910 and 1914 Malinowski studied at the London School of Economics under Seligman and Westermarck, read at the British Museum, and began to make his mark in British anthropology. In 1924 he became Reader at the L.S.E. and in 1927 he rose to the top as Professor of Social Anthropology.

It is interesting that Edmund Leach is one of the few students of Malinowski who have probed Malinowski's philosophical and scientific presuppositions. Being unaware of the details of Malinowski's intellectual antecedents in Cracow, Leach imaginatively surmised that Malinowski's functionalism showed affinity with the philosophy of Pragmatism of William James, which was influential at the time of Malinowski's transplantation to

London.[8] We may view Leach as analogically supplementing and deepening our understanding of Malinowski, even if there is no direct proof of the latter's debt to James.

William James's Pragmatism (which in turn owed much to the ideas of Charles Peirce whose semiotics enjoys high fashion today) had its maximum vogue around 1910, the year Malinowski arrived in London and began his studies there. William James argued that the main function of thought was to satisfy certain interests of the organism, and this criterion constituted a measure of truth. James's Pragmatism, while appreciative of the evidence of directly observable facts, and while recognizing that strict logic cannot lead to or be involved in metaphysical judgments, yet supposed metaphysical judgments to have a psychological basis in reason. Thus he argued that it is reasonable and valid to believe and to embrace whatever thought (and behavior) can be shown to be biologically satisfying to the individual, even though such a consequence cannot be verified by experiment or rational argument. Malinowski's perspective, which constituted the heart of his functionalist position, was that certain kinds of behaviour are entirely reasonable because they are based in psychological or organic needs. His interpretation of magic and religion in particular was formulated from this vantage point. It was a dogma for Malinowski that all human beings were reasonable, that is, sensibly practical individuals, and as Leach has remarked, Malinowski's biggest guns were directed "against notions that might be held to imply that, in the last analysis, the individual is not a personality on his own possessing the capacity for free choice based in reason."[9]

Malinowski left for Australia in 1914 to embark on his fieldwork, and he returned to England in 1920. The circumstances of the First World War that forced him to stay down under, and the details of his adventurous field trips in New Guinea and to the Trobriand Islands, interspersed with trips to Australia to write, to recuperate and to conduct his ardent courtship, have been documented in some detail.[10] I therefore only need to draw attention to the inspiration and legitimation that this experience provided for his anthropological assertions. Unlike the Victorian armchair theorists, Malinowski pioneered the techniques of fieldwork, especially participant observation, that have become the distinguishing badge of the profession. Frazer, ensconced in his study at Trinity College, Cambridge, is alleged to have replied to William James's query about his undoubted personal knowledge of some of the savages about whom he wrote so profusely, "God forbid that I should encounter a savage in the flesh!" By comparison, Malinowski preened like a peacock about his live experience and first-hand observations of the primitives. He once remarked "Rivers is the Rider Haggard of Anthropology: I shall be the Conrad."[11] This comparison with another great expatriate Pole is suggestive. But his vanity also participated in a Frazerian universalist ambition: Malinowski, it is said, jumped from the Trobriand Islands (tiny specks off the New Guinea coast) to humanity at large, of which he too spoke in grandiloquent terms.

Malinowski's Demarcations between Magic, Science, and Religion

Malinowski sharply separated off science from magic. Science was a "profane" activity, while magic grouped with religion belonged to the "sacred" domain. (This demarcation is basically opposed to Tylor's and Frazer's scheme, which grouped magic with science as "pseudo-science.")

Malinowski's characterization of "science" was both simplistic and generous when he actually credited the Trobrianders with the possession of scientific knowledge. It is simplistic when judged in terms of the delineation of science by contemporary philosophers and historians of science as a self-conscious, reflexive, open-ended process of knowledge construction. Said Malinowski with a nourish: "If by science be understood a body of rules and conceptions, based on experience and derived from it by logical inference, embodied in material achievements and in a fixed form of tradition and carried on by some sort of social organization," then even the lowest savage has science however rudimentary. He went so far as to claim that even judged against a more rigorous definition of science—for example, the formulation of explicit rules open to experiment and critique by reason—the Trobrianders possessed sciences, as instanced by the grasp of hydrodynamics in canoe building.

Comparison of Religion and Magic

Malinowski did not address in any significant way in his actual ethnographic works—such as *Argonauts, The Sexual Life of Savages, Coral Gardens and their Magic*—the question of how he would distinguish between religion and magic. I surmise that he did not do so principally because the Trobrianders themselves did not have an indigenous category term for "religion" or its analogue, and Malinowski would therefore have found it difficult to make the demarcation stick. Whereas "magic" and "garden work" (practical activity) were Trobriand categories, there was no local notion that he might have translated as "religion."

But he did try to demarcate religion from magic in his *Magic, Science and Religion and Other Essays* (1948). There he first makes the sacred/profane cut, and lumps religion and magic with the sacred, and science with the profane. The sacred he defined as traditional acts and observances regarded by the natives as sacred and carried out with reverence and awe, and hedged around with prohibitions. Such acts are associated with supernatural forces. The profane he related to arts and crafts (hunting, fishing, tilling, woodwork and so on) which were carried out on the basis of careful empirical observation of natural process and a firm belief in nature's regularity.[12]

While we may declare Malinowski unduly loose in his "demarcation" and comparative use of the concept "science," what makes him unusually interesting is that he, more than any anthropologist up to that time, insisted that a primary issue to address was how, within the confines of a single society or culture, "symbolic" activities like ritual and magic were linked to and interacted with activities of a practical or "pragmatic" character.

In other words, he raised the question how we are to understand man's participation in at least two modes of reality, man's readiness to shift from one context to the other, and also how we are to see them as complementary in relationship. Before we tackle this important topic, let us dispose of Malinowski's general pronouncements on religion.

Every organized religion, says Malinowski (in his famous "Magic, Science and Religion" essay), "must have a dogmatic system backed by mythology, a developed ritual in which man acts on his belief and communes with the powers of the unseen world; there must also be an ethical code of rules which binds the faithful and determines their behaviour towards each other and towards the things they worship."

Although he was capable of this kind of inclusive definition of religion, Malinowski essentially distinguished religion not in the famous Robertson-Smith and Durkheim mode of associating religion with *collective* organizational forms, especially a church and its congregation (and magic with individual self-interested practice) or in the Tylorian modes in terms of animistic beliefs in spiritual beings and the cults associated with them. Instead Malinowski defined religion by function, primarily psychological and secondarily sociological, and in terms of a means (instrumental) and ends (ultimate purposes) distinction.

Religious action was not like magic a means to an end, it was an end in itself and it celebrated ultimate values, such as Providence and Immortality.

The subject matter of every religion is the twin beliefs in Providence and Immortality. The first implies a supernatural agent or essence who is in sympathy with man's destinies and with whom man feels he must communicate. The second deals with the question of continuance after death whether it be reincarnation or some form of after-life. "Religion is rooted in human life"—for the individual it answers to spiritual needs, for society it provides social integration. Again: "Religious development consists primarily in the growing predominance of the ethical principle and in the increasing fusion of the two main factors of all belief, the sense of Providence and the faith in Immortality."

Providence meant for Malinowski the importance attributed to God as the provider for man's biological and psychological needs, and this dependence is manifest in the rules for handling food and the values placed on sacrifice and communion and on exchanges of food gifts. Totemism too expresses man's natural selective interest in nature as provider: as Lévi-Strauss has said, this view comes close to giving a utilitarian explanation by which animals are sacred because they are good to eat. Death and mortuary rites are quintessentially religious: They express the force of emotive attachments and reactions to loved ones, and spring from a spontaneous attitude of horror of death and love for the deceased. Religious acts are in such contexts acts of faith—the belief in immortality is a voice of hope. In religious rites, means and ends are one. Initiation rites and marriage rites are not meant to "cause" the end in question, they are in themselves this transformation, heralding lasting attitudes and stable relationships. (Here one can compliment Malinowski as anticipating the Austinian notion of a "performative" act: more of this later.) Again, once again attempting to illustrate his means–ends relation, he contrasted initiation rites, which are religious because their function is the inculcation and maintenance of collective traditions valued for themselves, with childbirth rites which are magical because they are directed to the practical aim of safe child delivery.

Although Malinowski as a good individualist and pragmatist maintained that society was merely a vehicle for enacting religious beliefs based in individual psychology and reason (such as the notion of immortality), he was well aware of the implications of religious rites as public and collective enactments, and documented the social functions deriving from this public aspect. (He went so far as to say, however, that the public aspect and publicity of ritual are a matter of technique.)

In sum, it is difficult to maintain that Malinowski was an important thinker on religion. His views on it were a mixture of derivative Christian theology and pragmatist considerations akin to the doctrines of William James that however threatened to deteriorate into crude utilitarianism. It has therefore been rightly said that Malinowski's view of religion comes close to Plato's notion of the "noble lie." It is however upon his analysis of Trobriand magic that he expended his imaginative energies, and deployed his linguistic skills and observational powers. It is on the subject of magic that he excelled and scintillated, even though he sometimes overdid the rhetoric and overworked his narrow psychology.

The Sacred and the Profane

Malinowski adopts the Durkheimian dichotomy—sacred versus profane— but his demarcation only bears a superficial resemblance to Durkheim's partition.[13] Malinowski identified the domain of the profane with practical and technical activity (agriculture, canoe building stripped of the ceremonial features), which he associated with the Trobriander's "rational mastery" of his surroundings, and this again, as we have seen before, he over-enthusiastically assimilated to "science."[14] The sacred therefore embraced all those types of thought and action manifest in religion and magic, and which were concerned with metaphysical relations. Thus Malinowski's partitioning would not admit any such proposition as that made by Durkheim in *The Elementary Forms of the Religious Life* that religion (and magic) was the forerunner of science, especially as regards the concept of force and necessary connections between things.

The Disaggregation and Interlacing of Magic and Practical/Technical Activity in Trobriand Life

I consider as one of Malinowski's foremost contributions—and this is related to his demarcation between the sacred and the profane—his descriptions of how the separate strands of magic and practical activity were interlaced to form the braid (or double-helix as I am tempted to say) of Trobriand life. For example, consider this passage from *Coral Gardens*[15] in which Malinowski, using somewhat different language from mine, speaks of ritual and technical sequences as being "parallel":

> The association between technical pursuit and its magical counterpart is, as we know, very close, and to the natives essential. The sequence of technical stages, on the one hand, and of rites and spells, on the other, run parallel. The place of a magical act is strictly determined. There are inaugurative rites such as *yowoto* or *gabu*, there are concluding rites such as *vilamalia* and the last act of *kaytubutala*.

Malinowski's most ample and colourful ethnography relates to the widespread and ramifying role of magical rites in every aspect of Trobriand life, and in my essay *The Magical Power of Words* (which was first delivered as the Malinowski Memorial Lecture at L.S.E. in 1968)[16] I came to the conclusion after a close analysis that indeed an important and problematic question was being posed: how are we to describe and interpret the interlacing of magical and technical acts to form an amalgam or, if you prefer, a total activity, which we may label as Trobriand "yam cultivation" or Trobriand "canoe building," activities that covered long stretches of time and combined multiple modalities?

The issues posed by the Malinowski ethnography constitute puzzles for us even to this day: In almost all societies there are on the one hand rites that are set apart and take place as special enactments removed from the doings of everyday life. Examples are cosmic festivals (e.g. Festival of Lights in India or Visākha Pūjā in Thailand, which commemorates the birth, death and enlightenment of the Buddha); rites of passage such as baptism, or wedding or funeral rites; and rites of affliction such as exorcism ceremonies. These enactments are eminently analyzable in terms of the Van Gennep tripartite scheme of separation, liminality, and (re)-aggregation, which among modern anthropologists Victor Turner above all has brilliantly exploited in his discussion of the ritual process.

But these same societies also conduct all kinds of ritual cycles or intermittent rites that are interlaced with practical activities like agriculture, or crafts, or fishing, and here both kinds of action, technical and magical/religious, constitute amalgams and, though often internally distinguished, in a sense occupy the same space such that a simplistic disaggregation into technical aspects and expressive aspects is not possible.

The Art of Magic

By far the most significant and innovative part of Malinowski's ethnography in *Argonauts, Coral Gardens,* and *The Sexual Life of Savages* speaks to, what in contemporary jargon I would call, a dramatistic and performative view of the magical performance, and a special sensitivity to the role of language in magical acts.

But before I treat this issue, I have to separate the dross (of which there was a generous amount) from the gold, and I also have to argue that the nuggets of gold frequently lie not where Malinowski explicitly said they were (though he implicitly knew deeper truths).

A basic assertion of Malinowski's was that magic serves two functions, one psychological the other sociological, and of these the former was primary and the basic source of inspiration.

But as it turns out his psychological thesis was both naive and easily falsified in terms of his own data. Magic comes into play, he said, whenever primitive man "has to recognize the impotence of his knowledge and of his rational technique." In other words magic is resorted to in those contexts where man's technical control of nature has reached its insufficient limits. Magic is thus directed towards the uncontrollable agencies which affect the success of its practical activities. This is a species of explanation that one may label as "anxiety reduction" and "compensatory action."

In the form it is stated—that magic begins where technology ends—it is easily refuted. Malinowski's famous example was that in the Trobriands lagoon fishing is safe and invites no magic, but deep-sea fishing is dangerous and the uncertain elements of the ocean are not easily controlled, so magical rites are resorted to. But in this comparison Malinowski fails to inform us that unlike the products of lagoon fishing, deep-sea fishing yields shark, which had a high ritual valuation in the Trobriand scheme of things. And therefore there may be other considerations than sheer danger that may have surrounded deep-sea fishing with ritual.

But gardening provides us with an internal test. In Trobriand agriculture the cultivation of yams and taro is surrounded with profuse magic while the cultivation of coconut and mango is not. Trobriand interest in, and control of, yam and taro cultivation techniques was impressive and a matter of great pride, and the good yam and taro gardener enjoyed prestige. So the technical criterion does not yield an answer as to why Trobriand yam gardening is suffused with magic, while coconut gardening is not.

A different kind of answer to this puzzle is suggested by the facts that the Trobrianders lay great stress on the obligations of *urigubu* payments (by which a man has to make annual payments of yams to his sister's husband), and the fulfillment of this obligation is tied to the high social valuation of a good gardener. Moreover, the fact that these gifts of yams were exhibited in yam houses for all to see until they rotted simply underscores the social valuations of generous gifts and conspicuous display which illuminate the social concerns surrounding the magic rather than the technological inadequacies. In other words, we have to look more at the social valuations and social imperatives which indicate which of a society's economic activities are important to it, and to relate that society's rituals and ceremonials to its anticipations and anxieties in the realization of social values rather than to insufficiencies presented by raw nature or by technology. Malinowski himself coined the felicitous expression "anticipatory affirmations of prosperity and plenty" which inspired magical ritual, an expression that throws more light on Trobriand psychology than the thesis of reduction of anxiety caused by technological insufficiency.

Moreover, as our previous case studies have shown, both in early Greece and in seventeenth-century England—as described in the works of Geoffrey Lloyd and Keith Thomas—"magical" explanations and practices (consisting of the attempted manipulation of occult powers and agents for achieving practical benefits) were rejected in favour of "naturalistic" explanations before these latter could provide better practical and technological results. There is also evidence against the reverse implication in Malinowski's hypothesis: that if man developed adequate technical procedures for dealing with a task, then any previous "magical" ritual connected with that task ought automatically to disappear.

Malinowski's discovery of the sociological function of magic is then of far greater import than his psychological theorizing. He saw how the calendar of magical rites inaugurated, marked out, phased out, regulated and carried through to a successful conclusion activities such as gardening, and fishing and canoe building and overseas *kula* expeditions. He saw how the ritual expert and specialist, by conducting imperative ceremonies, actually thereby mobilized manpower and resources and that the rites served as triggering mechanisms for the sustained conduct of practical operations. All these insights were exploited and elaborated by Raymond Firth in his masterly work, *Primitive Polynesian Economy*.

How Does Magic Work?

Malinowski had two specific insights into the internal structure and constitution of Trobriand rites. The first was that they exploited simultaneously both words and acts, both speech and the manipulation of objects and substances, thereby posing the problem of the logic of use of multiple media in ritual for his successors to ponder over. Secondly his so-called "ethnographic theory of the magical word" proposed some illuminating insights which foreshadowed and anticipated in England Austin's "linguistic philosophical" notions of performative force carried by speech acts, that is, how speech acts created both illocutionary and perlocutionary effects by virtue of being conventional acts; and in this country, Kenneth Burke's discussion of the "rhetoric of motives."

For Malinowski there were three elements or constituents of the magical performance: the *formula*, the *rite* and the *condition of the performer*. We may quickly enumerate these as the distinctive features of Trobriand ritual he never tired of expatiating:

(1) The dramatic expression of emotion, the essence of the magical act, through kinesic gestures and movements.

(2) The use of objects and substances, which were "impregnated" with the recited words, and to which through a "rubbing effect" were transferred certain potencies. The techniques by which the power of the spell is transferred to the charmed object he vividly portrayed.[17]

(3) But above all, Malinowski selected the spell as the most critical component of the Trobriand magical system, and dissected its tripartite structure (the foundation [*u'ula*], the body [*tapwana*], and the tip [*dogina*]), and the various powers it radiated as magical word. The components that generated these powers were: phonetic effects including onomatopoeic words; words of an imperative kind that evoked, stated and commanded certain feeling states and certain consequences; constructions that retrospectively referred back to myths of origins and the pedigrees of ancestors, thereby serving as pragmatic charters for present practice; and strings of words that prospectively looked forward to anticipatory effects. He coined the phrases "verbal missile" and the "creative metaphor of speech" to convey the efficacy of magical words. It is pertinent to note that Malinowski in expounding

the creative power of sacred words compared their significance to the binding character of "legal formulas," and comes very close to explaining their efficacy in Austinian terms—that "saying is doing" under the appropriate conventions and conditions.

The Ethnographic Theory of the Magical Word

Malinowski expounded at length his ethnographic theory of the magical word in volume 2 of *The Coral Gardens and their Magic*. He reported that the Trobrianders themselves made a distinction between the language of magic (*megwa la biga*) and the language of ordinary speech (*livala la biga*)—a distinction that brings to mind another we discussed earlier between the road of magic and the road of gardening. He attributed the special character of Trobriand ritual speech to such features as these:

(1) Their intrinsic character such as their being sacred and set apart from ordinary linguistic uses, their containing distinct prosodic features including even "meaningless" words which are supposed to exercise special influence.

(2) The context of native belief, which included the native belief in a world pervaded by sympathetic affinities and powerful forces (*mana*); but more importantly the belief that magical speech, man-made, existed from the very beginning as primeval text coeval with reality, and could be launched as "breath" and transformed into magical missiles by accredited magicians.

(3) The "coefficient of weirdness" that magical speech contained (as compared with the higher "coefficient of intelligibility" of ordinary speech), and this was indexed by strange and archaic grammatical forms, condensed structures, words containing esoteric meanings, and strange mythological and metaphorical references and allusions which have to be laboriously tracked by ethnographic inquiry. (As he said: "Weirdness yields to treatment as soon as we place the spells within their context.")

On the basis of this evidence Malinowski came to the conclusion that there are two crystallizations of language in all societies—the language of technology and science versus the language of "magic and persuasion." In expounding the nature of the latter he drew upon examples from our own contemporary Western world and thereby helped to bring some of the esoteric and mystifying features of magic within the scope of understanding of a modern (Western) man's experience. One example he gave was the language of advertising and the "beauty magic of Helena Rubinstein and Elizabeth Arden." (Trobriand beauty magic by which young men hoped to seduce young women or ambitious men their *kula* partners becomes more comprehensible for contemporary Americans when viewed in terms of the TV advertisements that continually bombard us daily, nay hourly, nay every few minutes: such as that if you use a particular deodorant or soap you might make it with your date and so on.) I ask you therefore: how is it that many of us "moderns" are prepared to accept Madison Avenue advertising labelled as "selling costs" as an essential component of rational economics and of the rational theory of the firm, and not grant a similar compliment to Trobriand *kula* magic? Another example, indicated by Malinowski, is the rhetoric of political speeches and the public orations of politicians. In this country when in 1984 the Presidential race was staged, and in 1985, when President Reagan and Gorbachev were grooming themselves for the arms control meetings in Geneva, we were saturated by the rhetoric of these alleged "great communicators."

A third example is the binding character of "legal formulas" which is "at the very foundation of order and reliability in human relations."[18] It is for these reasons that I say that Malinowski's expositions come close to—even anticipate the notions of performative speech expounded by Austin and other linguistic philosophers—that "saying is doing," when done by the properly accredited persons according to proper conventions under the right conditions.

Pointing to marriage vows Malinowski said that whether they were treated as sacrament or as mere legal contract, they portray "the power of words in establishing a permanent human relation"; the average man he argued must have "a deep belief in the sanctity of legal and sacral words and their creative power" if social order is to exist. There is thus "a very real basis to human belief in the mystic and binding power of words."[19]

The Unsettled Issues

It would be foolish to claim that Malinowski—whatever his superiority to Tylor and Frazer—has explained to us beyond doubt how to construe Trobriand magic, let alone magical ritual elsewhere. One unsettled issue on which he vacillated, and argued on both sides, is the question whether magical speech—or as I prefer to say ritual speech—is a different genre from ordinary speech or is an intensification of ordinary speech like poetic diction. While in certain contexts he argued for their difference he also at other places affirmed its purposive objectives. Magical speech thus "presents significant speech under the guise of esoterica and mysterious forms," it is "but part of the universal, essentially human attitude of all men to all words" (p. 233).

Indeed in characteristic fashion he resorted to an ontogenetic or biographical approach to explain the origins of magical speech, and laid it at the door of infantile experiences. When the child's early cries and babbling evoke the mother's services the child has its first experiences of the power of words. Citing Piaget, Bühler and Stern (p. 233) Malinowski traced the origins to this early experience: "The child actually exercises a quasi-magical influence over its surroundings. He utters a word, and what he needs is done for him by his adult entourage." And he concluded with a flourish—just as when he tried to explain kinship terminology by the same argument—"The development of speech in humanity must have its fundamental principles, being of the same type as the development of speech within the life history of the individual" (p. 232). Thus while Malinowski's origins of magical speech remind us also of Freud's tracing of the child's illusory sense of omnipotence to its infantile wishes and experience, we have to concede that the biographical approach does not decisively settle the problem of the relation of magical speech to ordinary speech.

The second unsettled issue is whether we can unambiguously elucidate the character of the efficacy (or lack of efficacy) of Trobriand magical ritual. Malinowski's answer, when he was pushed to it, was that magic was "objectively" false but that it was "subjectively" true to the actors. But it was also true in the sense of being a "pragmatic" truth, that is in a sense that we may find stated in William James's Pragmatism. It was psychologically true in that it was "reasonable" in terms of addressing certain psychological needs of the individual, and it was sociologically true because its practice raised the optimism and hopes of the human beings, who heard and saw it performed, and because it had multiple positive social consequences. A magician's spell and manipulations may not objectively, causally and directly affect the processes of nature (the garden soil and the plants growing on it could not respond to the magical words and acts), but these words and acts did influence the human witnesses and through them produced consequences by affecting their intentions and their motivations and their expectations. So Malinowski's answer would be that magic was pragmatically effective by creating a change of state in the human actors.

A Digression on Kenneth Burke

Since in my earlier writings I have used some aspects of the linguistic philosophy of Austin, Searle and Grice, and some features of Charles Peirce's semiotics, to expound the performative features of ritual,[20] but have never referred to Kenneth Burke, let me take this opportunity to include him in my pantheon.

Kenneth Burke in his *Rhetoric of Motives* explicitly refers to Malinowski, who may be taken to have anticipated some features of his theory of rhetoric, and Burke himself may be included among those who would wish us to move away from seeing magic as "bad science" to seeing it instead as "rhetorical art."

Burke has stated that the basic function of rhetoric is "the use of words by human agents to form attitudes or to induce actions in other human agents."[21] Magic therefore is "primitive rhetoric," "it is rooted in an essential function of language itself, a function that is wholly realistic, and is actually born anew; the use of language as a symbolic means of inducing coopera-tion in beings that by nature respond to symbols."[22] This attribution of a "real" linguistic function to magic thus appeals to a "reality" of a different kind judged by science to be true or false.

Burke is essentially in accord with Malinowski when he asserts that "The 'pragmatic sanction' for this function of magic lies outside the realm of strictly true-or-false propositions; it falls in an area of deliberation that itself draws upon the resources of rhetoric; it is itself a subject matter belonging to an art that can 'prove opposites'."[23] By "proving opposites" Burke is refer-ring to rhetoric that tries to persuade you to accept the truth of tendentious advocacy; for example, the assertion that U.S. commercial investment in Saudi Arabia is truly good because it will help transform that country's unsavoury feudal structure, whereas the true intent of that speech may be to persuade the American public to approve its country's expansionist policy. The present-day U.S. involvement in El Salvador and Nicaragua can be sub-ject to similar analysis.

But the theory of rhetoric does not completely solve our puzzle about the form and intentions behind Trobriand magical acts. When the chips are down, Burke in effect agrees with Malinowski that though magic may be a false technical act it is a true social act (i.e. it acts upon the human actors rather than upon nature). Burke's formulation reads: "The realistic use of addressed language *to induce action in people* became the magical use of addressed language *to induce motion in things* (things by nature alien to purely linguistic orders of motivation)."[24] This transposition in the use of language implies then that magic, whatever its social efficacy, has an aspect of "distorted" communication.

So it would seem that we cannot yet completely exorcize the ghosts of Tylor and Frazer. Let us therefore for the present leave aside the puzzle posed by magic by virtue of its "duality" or dual structure. On the one hand, it seems to imitate the logic of technical/technological action that seeks to transform nature or the world of natural things and manifestations. On the other hand, its structure is also transparently rhetorical and performative (in that it consists of acts to create effects on human actors according to accepted social conventions). Tylor and Frazer fastened exclusively on the first equa-tion and said it was bad science; Malinowski appreciated the force of the second equation and said that magic was constituted of speech acts in a per-formative and persuasive mode,and that therefore they were pragmatically reasonable. My own feeling is that one of the most fruitful interpretive devel-opments in recent anthropology, a development that has still to be completed and exhausted, is that kind of exegesis begun by Malinowski, and taken further by recourse to Wittgensteinian and Austinian linguistic philosophy, Peircean pragmatics and Burke's theory of rhetoric. The now puzzling duality of magic will disappear only when we succeed in embedding magic in a more ample theory of human life in which the path of ritual action is seen as an indispensable mode for man anywhere and everywhere of relating to and participating in the life of the world.

Notes

1. The following are Malinowski's principal works: *A Diary in the Strict Sense of the Term* (New York: Harcourt, Brace and World, Inc., 1967); *Magic, Science and Religion and Other Essays* (New York: Doubleday Anchor Books, 1954) (Illinois: The Free Press of Glencoe, 1948); *The Foundations of Faith and Morals* (Riddell Memorial Lecture, Durham, 1934–35) (London: Oxford University Press, 1936); *Coral Gardens and their Magic* (London: George Allen and Unwin, 1935) (New York: American Book Co., 1935), 2 vols.; *The Sexual Life of Savages in North West Melanesia* (London: Routledge and Kegan Paul, 1929); *Sex and Repression in Savage Society* (New York: Harcourt, 1927); *The Father in Primitive Psychology* (New York: W. W. Norton & Co., 1927); *Myth in Primitive Psychology* (New York: W. W. Norton & Co., 1926); *Crime and Custom in Savage Society* (London: International Library of Psychology, Philosophy and Scientific Method, 1926); "The Problem of Meaning in Primitive Languages" in *The Meaning of Meaning* by C. K. Ogden and I. A. Richards (London: International Library of Psychology, Philosophy and Scientific Method, 1923); *Argonauts of the Western Pacific* (London: Routledge and Kegan Paul, 1922).
2. Interesting and illuminating facts about Malinowski's biographical, intellectual and cultural antecedents are contained in these two essays that appeared in *Anthropology Today*, January 5, 1985: Ernest Gellner, "'Malinowski Go Home': Reflections on the Malinowski Centenary Conferences" (5–7); and Robert J. Thornton "'Imagine yourself set down...' Mach, Frazer, Conrad, Malinowski and the Role of Imagination in Ethnology" (7–14). For a vivid account of the interpersonal aspects of Malinowski's career, see Helena Wayne (Malinowska): "Bronislaw Malinowski: The Influence of Various Women in his Life and Works," *American Ethnologist*, December 3, 1985: 529–40.
3. Ernst Mach's ideas on this are contained in his *Erkenntnis und Irrtum* (1905), translated as *Knowledge and Error: Sketches on the Psychology of Enquiry* by Thomas J. McCormack and Paul Foulkes (Boston, MA: D. Reidel Publishing Co., 1976).
4. Thornton, "'Imagine yourself set down ...'" 9.
5. *Ibid.*, 9.
6. Gellner, "'Malinowski Go Home'," 7.
7. Wayne, "Bronislaw Malinowski," 531.
8. See Edmund Leach's essay "The Epistemological Background of Malinowski's Empiricism" in *Man and Culture: An Evaluation of the Work of Bronislaw Malinowski*, ed. Raymond Firth (London: Routledge and Kegan Paul, 1957), 119–37. Leach also comments that what W. B. Gallie (in his *Peirce and Pragmatism*, Harmondsworth: Penguin, 1952) says of William James also applies to Malinowski: That he was an individualist, interested in the experiences, perplexities, and satisfactions of individual souls, and "anything claiming to be more-than-individual he distrusted from the depth of his soul."

9. I am however skeptical of Leach's allegation that Malinowski imposed on the Trobriander the conscious distinction between the rational and metaphysical: "He himself found the conceptual distinction between the rational and the metaphysical self-evident; he insisted that it must be self-evident to the Trobriander also" (128). I shall provide the evidence on which Malinowski based the distinction between "magical" acts and "technical" acts as in line with Trobriand conceptions.

10. See Firth, *Man and Culture*, 1–14; *A Diary in the Strict Sense of the Term by Bronislaw Malinowski*, trans. Norbert Gutennan (New York: Harcourt, Brace and World, Inc., 1967); also see Wayne, "Bronislaw Malinowski."

11. Firth, *Man and Culture*, 6.

12. One quickly sees that Malinowski's notion of profane is not exactly Durkheimian. See Emile Durkheim, *The Elementary Forms of the Religious Life*, 52–57, where he sees the sacred and profane worlds as not only separate but antagonistic: "The sacred thing is *par excellence* that which the profane should not touch" (55).

13. Durkheim's discussion contains these assertions: All known religious beliefs presuppose a classification of all things, real and ideal, into two classes or opposed groups—the sacred and the profane. The division of the world into two domains is "the distinctive trait of all religious thought." "Sacred things are those which the interdictions protect and isolate; profane things, those to which these interdictions are applied and which must remain at a distance from the first. Religious beliefs are the representations which express the nature—of sacred things and the relations which they sustain, either with each other or with profane things. Finally, rites are the rules of conduct which prescribe how a man should comport himself in the presence of these sacred objects." *The Elementary Forms of the Religious Life*, 52, 56.

14. Nadel in his critique of Malinowski's notion of science (in Firth, *Man and Culture*) sides with the Durkheim–Mauss view of magic as in some ways being the forerunner of a "theoretical science." But Malinowski would disagree because the essence of magic for him was that it was man-made, not that it represented or stemmed from conceptions of an impersonal collective *mana*-like force, and its protocausal connections. This is part and parcel of his anti-intellectualistic anti-mentalist pragmatic posture.

15. *Coral Gardens and their Magic*, I, 477.

16. See *Man* 3, no. 2 (June 1968): 175–208; also *Culture, Thought and Social Action* (Cambridge, MA: Harvard University Press, 1985), ch. 1.

17. An example is the recitation of the principal spell of Omarakana garden magic over the magical mixture by the magician (*Coral Gardens and their Magic*, II, 216): "He prepares a sort of large receptacle for his voice—a voice trap ... He moves his mouth from one end of the aperture to the other, turns his head, repeating the words over and over again, rubbing them, so to speak, into the substance."

18. *Coral Gardens and their Magic*, II, 234.

19. *Ibid.*, 234–35.

20. See especially my "Form and Meaning of Magical Acts" and "A Performative Approach to Ritual" in *Culture, Thought and Social Action*, chs. 2 and 4.

21. Kenneth Burke, *A Rhetoric of Motives* (Berkeley and Los Angeles: University of California Press, 1969), 41.

22. *Ibid.*, 43.

23. *Ibid.*, 44.

24. *Ibid.*, 42, original emphasis.

HOLY AND UNHOLY RITES:
LIES AND MISTAKES IN LITURGY

Kieran Flanagan

Editor's Introduction

Kieran Flanagan is a Reader in Sociology at the University of Bristol. His publications and research so far have been about various aspects of the sociology of religion, particularly liturgy, ethics and identities, but also the (re)presentation of religions in visual media. He often considers the relationship between sociology and theology—both as academic disciplines and as they manifest themselves in particular religious communities, behaviours and discourses.

In this excerpt from chapter six of his *Sociology and Liturgy* he asks a variety of questions about the authenticity and authentication of liturgical acts, worship rituals, consequent to the possibility of lies and mistakes. This is not a re-visitation to the religious debate about whether a priest must be pious and moral in addition to technically prepared (i.e. "ordained") to minister to the faithful. Rather, it arises from the recognition of changes and continuities in sociological aspects of the liturgy. The elevation or conversion of otherwise ordinary objects and everyday acts into "holy" or religious objects and acts that might legitimately play roles in liturgy is, perhaps, fundamental to ritualization. In theatre, audiences are invited to "suspend their disbelief," and make believe that an actor on a stage is, for the duration of the performance, a Danish prince. In Christian and other religious liturgies, disbelief is rarely encouraged—except accidentally by the disjunction between expectations and performance, tradition and innovation, and so on. Flanagan offers, for example, confusions between liturgy and concerts or carnivals when someone not yet acculturated into Tractarianism on the one hand and evangelicalism on the other observes the respective rites of these distinctive Christian cultures. His argument helpfully alerts us to the dynamics inserted into ritual by ambiguity and various contradictions of participants' expectations and experiences. Handled well, structure can be liberating so that corporate liturgical events can aid individuals to worship in ways that informality may not.

In the remainder of Flanagan's chapter, not reprinted here, he examines these issues, especially the functional ambiguities that operate between the actions and functions of rituals, in more detail. Among other important works, he engages with Roy Rappaport's *Ecology, Meaning and Religion* (1979), the argument of which is greatly enhanced in Rappaport 1999.

References

Rappaport, Roy. 1979. *Ecology, Meaning and Religion*. Richmond: North Atlantic Books.
Rappaport, Roy. 1999. *Ritual and Religion in the Making of Humanity*. Cambridge: Cambridge University Press.

ℰ℧ ℃℞

Profanations are to be expected, for every religious ceremony creates the possibility of a black mass.
          Erving Goffman, "The Nature of Deference and Demeanor."

Since the Second Vatican Council, there has been a tendency amongst theologians and liturgists to give modern culture a benign, undifferentiated "reading," one innocent of the sociological complications such a view poses. A stress on incarnational theology gave a blanket blessing to culture, that was not offset by an awareness of the degree to which it has ambiguous, limited qualities that beg questions of meaning. Theologians seem to have become enchanted with modern culture, precisely at the time when sociologists became disenchanted and began to review its theoretical significance in the light of a growing awareness of post-modernism. A theological failure to specify the use of culture within a particular context partly accounts for the naiveté of many of its contemporary positions and the degree to which it has taken refuge in ideology rather than sociology to shape its presuppositions about religion and society.

Within an inductive approach to liturgy, the implications of a virtuous dissimulation emerge. The actor confronts particular dilemmas in practice that require regulation and disguise, if the social act of worship is to be accomplished in an authentic and intended manner. Some form of collaboration in enactment is required to protect liturgy at its weakest point, where it transforms that which is cultural into the holy, a process as elusive as it is mysterious. To follow Berger, it is to transform that which is implausible into the plausible for believer and non-believer alike. It is in this process that liturgies are prone to generate misunderstandings, and to require a degree of virtuous dissimulation to protect their basis, both for the actor and the definition of the situation sought. Representations of the sacred involve risks in the task of transferring indeterminate meanings into a determinate ritual event. This bears on a point of Niklas Luhmann. He regards religion as effecting a sacralizing task through "ciphering," where the indeterminate is replaced and hidden in a social act that incarnates what it proclaims. The unreal nature of the religious act is disguised.[1] I wish to argue that virtuous dissimulation is a means of understanding this process from a sociological point of view in a way that links the actor to the structure of what he re-produces in the performance of rite. A similar form of transposition that also requires a degree of defence arises in the context of Goffman's notion of "keying," which I mentioned earlier.

If liturgies operated under a sense of a steely Divine gaze, so that dissatisfaction was registered all too clearly, the sociologist would have little to worry about. An altar server, passing the altar, bowing ever so slightly, might hear a loud voice booming out "deeper boy, deeper, or I'll have you up on the second commandment." Unfortunately, there seems to be a Divine reticence about what is liked and disliked in rite.

A certain agnosticism seems have settled into contemporary liturgical life. A degree of liturgical pluralism is now sanctioned (within limits in Catholicism) without any great certainty as to what arrangement "works" best, or what difference all these differences do make. The only difference this climate of liturgical agnosticism over forms of worship has effected is a continued fall in attendance rates at Church in the United Kingdom. Those who have taken diversity of rite the furthest, such as the Anglicans, seem to have lost the most in terms of weekly attendance at Church, which presumably is not the purpose of the experiment.

At some point, a limit to liturgical pluralism has to be stipulated, otherwise the act can become, eventually, an oddly random exercise. Far from generating conditions of plausibility for belief, pluralism has had the unintended effect of increasing levels of implausibility about religion in modern society. Agency and choice are not solutions but problems that can undermine the need to believe.[2] Few theologians, liberal or otherwise, have understood the implications of relativism as it bears on issues of liturgical praxis.[3]

Pluralism generates indifference towards religion in the wider society, but in a way that disguises intense competition within, especially between liturgical forms seeking scarce believers. Liturgies operate in the manner of rituals of the tribe, defending territorial practices against the hostile imputations of their neighbours. Boundary maintenance in rite is less about defence against hostile charges of the wider society (which is usually too indifferent to bother) than against fellow Church members who adhere to a rival form of rite. Breaches in the wall of liturgical practice are to be precluded at all costs. Each form of rite tends to give its rival a fatal test that shows it to be wanting before God. This notion of a liturgical market-place reaches a state of perfection in contemporary English Anglicanism.

In the Church of England, Anglo-Catholic Eucharists and Evangelical assemblies operate in a free and largely unregulated market. There are endless sets of permutations of liturgical form permitted, operating with a variety of veneers, Tractarian, Charismatic or feminist, whose borrowings are barely discernible even to a liturgist. All forms seem to operate with their own set of rules for engagement. No rules for ceremonial enactment are stipulated in the Alternative Service Book (ASB), 1980. A diversity of rite, reflecting accommodation to local circumstances, is not only tolerated, but seems to be enjoined in modern Anglican thoughts on liturgical use. In its response to *Faith in the City*, the Liturgical Commission of the Church of England rejoiced in the new era of flexibility brought to pass by the ASB. It called for liturgies to reflect local cultures to meet the needs of Urban Priority areas. It felt that more engagement and liturgical relevance were required so that congregations would have some sense of affiliation with the rites they had constructed. The Commission indicated that

> the congregation can be involved in both drama and dialogue readings. It might mean changing the visual presentation, removing distractions by putting all lights out apart from a spotlight on the reader, or signalling the fact that a story is being read by using a Jackanory armchair, or that a proclamation (for example Amos?) is being made by using a soapbox.[4]

These suggestions attracted some rather ungrateful comments in the mass media and exposed an ambiguous attitude towards rituals in Anglican liturgical tradition. There is a stereotype in Anglican theology regarding rituals that lingers from the Tractarian period and the debates which followed in the nineteenth century. Adherence to ritual form in liturgical enactment is equated with "ritualism" and the deadening hand of the "spike," who kills the spirit in deadening ceremonials. The Liturgical Commission went to the opposite extreme in striving to establish "living" rituals for local cultures, but without reference to any anthropological thought on the subject.

Most anthropological studies of ritual concentrate on the meanings they fulfil, the belief systems they embody and the functions their orders effect. Ritual forms use complex social arrangements cast in ceremonial form and the more odd and arbitrary these are, the more they are likely to attract anthropological scrutiny. Rituals function to cope with conditions of uncertainty, or unsettlement. Somehow, they manage to render these definite and stable. This accounts for the way many rituals deal with healing, with magic to handle spells, with rites of passage to mark transitions of age, or death, or to cope with the arrival of the stranger with the least social disruption to a settled order. Rituals enable the weak to handle anxiety by domesticating their worries in a social order that harmonizes and heals. They can also serve to communicate qualities of deference, and to confer rights and obligations in an elaborate manner that signifies an event of crucial political importance. The pomp and circumstance of a coronation follows complex rules hallowed in tradition. It is a majestic social means of marking dignity and the right to marshal symbolic forces to rule dutifully in a credible and accepted manner. Deference is secured through the solemn demeanour that characterizes the style of the rite. Regal ceremonies confer properties of grandeur and power on their object of dedication, providing an unmatched means of enhancing a public claim to rule. The social resources of a ritual are used to consecrate objects or actions that would be otherwise insignificant and the manner of dedication secures their credible redefinition.[5]

We are concerned with examining ritual in liturgical use in a way that unmasks its social base, and reveals that which the actors strive to keep concealed. When a form of rite becomes unsecured, deceptive possibilities arise that are peculiar to the style of worship. This unsettlement forces the actors involved in the social construction of rite to look closely at the assumptions governing its enactment. As one young altar server noted, "it is only when things go wrong that things get really interesting." Infelicities and mistakes of a significant kind have to be regulated out lest an unproductive uncertainty emerges. Tacit assumptions over how the rite ought to proceed can be breached by a failure on the part of the liturgical actors to monitor their performance. Desired liturgical outcomes can easily be unsecured. This need to regulate the shape and order of rite points to a distinctive concept in this study: the notion of a "liturgical mistake." This indicates how the autonomous defining qualities of this form of ritual have to be serviced and kept secure in a tactful manner so that tacit assumptions can be protected. These are deemed to be vulnerable and are associated, crucially, with the intended definition of the situation.

Some means of regulation of liturgical performance is required, lest its enactment collapses into a series of unprofitable ambiguities and paradoxes that would estrange even the most curious of sociologists. Failure to regulate a form of rite can give rise to lies and deceptions in its performance. These are believed to be culpable and are of a type which liturgical actors ought to avoid. These mistakes are usually about the detail of the rite and its mismanagement.

Gestures, vestments, symbols, and actions are minutiae in a collective effort, details in the ritual mosaic, that provide a structured means of coping with the holy in a public place. In Catholicism, rubrics or ceremonial guidelines help to keep the detail of rite in its proportionate place, so that the whole of the liturgy always exceeds its parts. If the details of a liturgy are adjusted with careless disregard, the shape of the rite takes on an unfruitful unpredictability that also impairs its claim to be a public order of worship.

Because liturgical forms represent habitual modes of linking with the sacred, forms of rite take on a brand loyalty. They establish orders of trust that elicit a congregational response, an investment on their part that often represents a career in dealing with the holy through the social means. The detail of the rite also services an order of predictability. It confirms a sense of expectation that the use of detail in the rite *can* yield particular qualities of the holy. But such a belief is arbitrary, intuitive and difficult to defend in public. Liturgical details are ambiguous and a scaling of their significance is problematic. Small points of detail can take on disproportionate value, such as the way the bell is rung at mass, or the form of introduction used by the priest, or the way the altar server makes the sign of the cross. These minor elements of style can offer comforting means of identification, points of recognition that give the form of the rite a certainty against which the self can lean to find the uncertain.[6] These cues become part of a liturgical biography of the actor. As David Martin has noted aptly, "the liturgical order belongs to these familiar rhythms and ways of doing things. All the buried selves of innumerable yesterdays are reactivated in the order of worship."[7] A sense of the detail of a rite can make an overwhelming impact, as is indicated in the recollections of the main character in *Sinister Street* serving an Anglo-Catholic high mass for the first time.

> During the Elevation of the Host, as he bowed his head before the wonder of bread and wine made God, his brain reeled in an ecstasy of sublime worship. There was a silence save for the censer tinkling steadily and the low whispered words of the priest and the click of the broken wafer. The candles burned with a supernatural intensity: the boys who lately quarrelled over precedence were hushed as angels: the stillness became fearful; the cold steps burned into Michael's knees and the incense choked him.[8]

Detail moved from one liturgical context for display to another tradition of worship can give rise to profound unsettlement and a sense of threat difficult to articulate. Such an arbitrary action can break a precarious sense of liturgical order. A sense of affiliation with an order of completeness is broken by the inclusion of a point of detail from an alien rite. A deep bow to the altar, or table, of a United Reformed Church could cause as much consternation as a Catholic priest turning up with lace, biretta and maniple to a Eucharistic gathering of liberal theologians. The displacement of detail signals affiliations at odds with the domestic assumptions of a particular congregation as to what ought to happen in the rite. The transplantation of detail to an alien rite generates an ambiguity. At one level, detail ought not to count, and a concern with it might seem obsessive, but at another remove

it might be felt to be of crucial importance, being considered a defining characteristic of a particular style of rite. Detail has an ambiguous relationship
to the form of a rite. Not only does it signal badges of ritual affiliation, it
also secures a relationship between the part of a rite and its whole. In this
latter task, it also has an ambiguous role that needs regulating. It has to be
kept in a proportionate place, lest it becomes promoted to a disproportionate rank that might limit the credibility of the rite and warp its shape.
Because detail poses a potential but uncertain threat to a ritual order, furi-
ous disputes can arise. As Weber noted,

> the greatest conflicts between purely dogmatic views, even within
> rationalistic religions, may be tolerated more easily than innovations in
> symbolism, which threaten the magical efficacy of action....[9]

The structure of rite supplies a context that can contain its detail. This
does not resolve the question of ambiguity that detail gives rise to within
liturgy. Rites are polyvalent in effect and this capacity to generate many
meanings increases the subjectivity of response of those present, as actors or
in the congregation. A mosaic of detail is presented as offering a variety of
cues and passages into the holy, but the price of this availability is that it is
difficult to stipulate which minute aspect counts most. There are theological
rules that try to order and to settle matters of detail. Our concern is with
the way these details, often insignificant, can emerge as ambiguous in the
performance of rite. They take on a disproportionate significance for some
as entry points into the façade of the rite, to find what lies hidden. The
actors and the audience come to rites with a variety of expectations. They
handle the uncertainty it generates with differing procedures. Competitive
assemblies of God operate in a liturgical market through an amplification of
the weaknesses of their rivals, and that which they wish to escape from.[10]
There are incommensurable antinomial elements of meaning and action operating in liturgical forms that can threaten their desired image. Choral even-
song can descend into a concert, and a conceited choir might get a clap after
the canticle from some disedified born-again Christians. An evangelical service might get so convivial in its praise that a displaced "spike" might faint
under the pressure of the joy, overcome less by the Holy Spirit than outrage.

Hostile and reductionist overtones can be imputed to any form of rite by
its rivals. Amplification of undesirable aspects of a particular liturgical style
can give comfort to rivals, thus confirming their worst fears regarding its
"real" basis. Despite their purity of intention, liturgical actors can face charges
of impurity arising from the styles of rite they proclaim. Antinomial facets of
a particular liturgical style can be given a one-sided reductionist reading by
adherents of rival assemblies, which ignores the dilemmas of the actors in its
production. Thus, rites that use beautiful Church music in elaborate ceremonial orders can generate a sense of the glory and wonder of God, but

they can also convey an intrinsic aesthetic quality that appeals to the secular mind. This represents a dilemma of witness and enactment for the actors, but to those of a Puritan cast the whole exercise is deceptive, idolatrous and self-serving. The response of actors to these potential charges of deception and impurity of practice point to procedures governing the production and enactment of liturgical performances.

The social procedures upon which custody of a particular liturgical form is secured involve a degree of disguise of its mechanism of reproduction. If the mechanism intrudes too far into the quest for the sacred, the ritual can fail. As Durkheim has noted, "when a rite serves only to distract, it is no longer a rite."[11] If the liturgy is to "work" in sociological *and* theological terms, the social form of the rite has to produce a sensibility of something greater than the ceremonial mechanism that realizes its basis. This need to affirm through denial points to an antinomial aspect of rite that continues the problem we examined earlier in terms of the concept of innocence and also the need to exercise a virtuous dissimulation.

Any form of rite that denies having some procedures for the management of holy effects deceives. Some means of regulation of rite is required if it is not to lapse into that which it fears and so produce effects it would wish to deny. A charismatic assembly, which denies having a stage-managed form, could find its clapping getting out of hand, producing hysteria rather than ecstasy. We wish to argue that as long as ambiguities are domesticated and contained within a form of the rite, meaningful paradoxes can be handled without damage. The liturgical form operates to enhance a sense of the uncertain, to quicken the spirit to engage with the indeterminate. But if uncertainty becomes attached to the form of the rite itself, focus on the indeterminate switches to the mechanism, and doubt ensues over the nature of the message proclaimed by its enactment. Such doubt disables and subtracts from efforts to deal in a certain manner with the uncertain. The rite never quite manages to escape the form used to produce the holy, and in being so limited it imprisons those present in the purely social. There is an ambiguous quality attached to the use of the social in liturgical forms. Too much attention produces a reductionist effect, but too little can generate an uncertain witness.

There is a necessary ambiguity operating between action and structure as this relationship is conceived in sociological terms. This is apart from the ambiguity of the message proclaimed as it emerges between the manifest and hidden aspects of rite. Actions and structures are mutually implicated in a rite in a way that relates to Anthony Giddens' notion of "structuration." This concept suggests a duality operating that enables an event to occur, but also constrains its enactment.[12] Actions are bound into structures in a way that disguises the ambiguous link between the two. Liturgies handle a sense of contradiction, between the need for rules that will enable them to have a predictable cast, and the affirmation of a sense of play that transcends the requirements for an orderly enactment. As Gilbert Lewis suggests, rituals present constraints that paradoxically free the individual to explore indeterminate meanings and playful effects.[13] Somehow the liturgy binds its form in a way that surpasses the totality of its contradictions and so releases the individual to pray and to worship.

Notes

1. These comments are taken from Garrett Green, "The Sociology of Dogmatics: Nikias Luhmann's Challenge to Theology," *The Journal of the American Academy of Religion* 50, no. 1 (1982): 23–24.
2. Peter L. Berger, *The Heretical Imperative, op. cit.*, 17–31. See also *The Social Reality of Religion*, Chapter 6 and "Secularization and the Problem of Plausibility," *op. cit.*, 131–56.
3. Robin Gill, *Competing Convictions* (London: SCM Press, 1989), 143–45.
4. The Liturgical Commission of the General Synod of the Church of England, *Patterns for Worship* (Church House Publishing, 1989), 10.
5. David Cannadine and Simon Price, eds., *Rituals of Royalty: Power and Ceremonial in Traditional Societies* (Cambridge: Cambridge University Press, 1987).
6. Joseph Gelineau, *The Liturgy Today and Tomorrow*, trans. Dinah Livingstone (London: Darton: Longman & Todd, 1978), 16.
7. David Martin, "Profane Habit and Sacred Usage," *Theology* 82, no. 686 (March 1979), 83–95.
8. Compton Mackenzie, *Sinister Street* (London: Penguin, 1960), 179.
9. Max Weber, *The Sociology of Religion*, trans. Ephraim Fischoff (London: Methuen, 1966), 7.
10. Kieran Flanagan, "Competitive Assemblies of God: Lies and Mistakes in Liturgy," *Research Bulletin* (University of Birmingham: Institute for the Study of Worship and Religious Architecture, 1981), 20–69.
11. Emile Durkheim, *The Elementary Forms of the Religious Life* (London: George Allen & Unwin, 1915), 382.
12. Anthony Giddens, *Central Problems in Social Theory: Action, Structure and Contradiction in Social Analysis* (London: Macmillan, 1979), Chapter 2, "Agency, Structure," 49–95.
13. Gilbert Lewis, *Day of Shining Red: An Essay on Understanding Ritual* (Cambridge: Cambridge University Press, 1980), 38.

References

Berger, Peter. 1973. *The Social Reality of Religion*. London: Penguin.
—1980. *The Heretical Imperative: Contemporary Possibilities of Religious Affirmation*. London: Collins.
Berger, Peter, and Thomas Luckmann. 1996. "Secularisation and Pluralism." *International Yearbook for the Sociology of Religion* 2: 73–84.
Goffman, Erving. 1956. "The Nature of Deference and Demeanour." *American Anthropologist* 58: 473–502.

CLEANING FLOORS AND SWEEPING THE MIND: CLEANING AS A RITUAL PROCESS*

Ian Reader

Editor's Introduction

Ian Reader is Professor in Religious Studies at Lancaster University. His long-term interest in Japanese religions has resulted in a number of significant publications dealing not only with "traditional" religions but also with new movements in and from Japan. While considering the implication of religious violence, pilgrimage, meditation and other issues in relation to Japanese religiosity, he has also contributed invaluably to debates about the meaning of "religion." As noted in the Introduction, these arise particularly because some Japanese leaders and groups have adopted Western, originally Protestant, understandings of the nature of religion, ritual and belief. Others, however, have contested this restructuring as inapplicable and confusing in relation to Japan.

The following reading is generated by the deliberate endowment of cleaning activities with symbolic meaning: sweeping the floor aids the sweeping of the mind. Seemingly mundane and pragmatic pursuits may be considered to be, in themselves, meditation that reaches towards enlightenment. The question, then, is whether there is a distinction between ritual and work, or between ritual and any other everyday activity. Does it aid or obscure understanding to speak of ritual—and even of "religion"? In a number of places Ian Reader refers to the obligatory nature of some activities. Is it purely the authority or tradition of monks or texts that creates a distinction and, perhaps, elevates a mundane act into a spiritual one? Or is that distinction either meaningless or resisted precisely in the insistence that sweeping floors is meditation? Is this resistance, in turn, aided by the formality of some acts of clearly pragmatic and "secular" sweeping (for example when housewives sweep outside their homes)?

If obligation and formality play important roles in this argument and suggest themselves as contributing to an ability to distinguish rituals from other actions, the question of meaning and meaninglessness is also significant here. The familiar notion (whether correct or not) that Zen Buddhism is best expressed in questions that it is impossible to answer, or questions with meaningless answers, joins with various comments throughout this chapter on the pointlessness of some obligatory actions, for example sweeping an already well-swept floor. This notion that ritual is meaningless and pointless in itself will be met in other chapters. For some scholars it almost defines religious ritual over against other actions as if the meaninglessness of ritual is its meaning. Does this ambiguity point to a particular kind of belief or understanding or does it undermine all beliefs? Ian Reader's focus on sweeping may not provide tidy answers but it certainly clears the way for our reflections on these issues.

℘ ℭ

It is important, when discussing ritual and ceremony, to look not only at formal ritual performances which have set and ordained (often both in terms of the ritual and in terms of prior initiation processes) participants, ritual implementa and formulae, but also at actions that, while not overtly designated as rituals, appear to express and contain many of the implicit themes, messages and meanings of formal rituals. Our understanding of ritual as a whole can only be enhanced by paying attention to the processes and nature of ritualization itself and to the ways in which this may occur, and by looking at how actions which appear, at least on the surface, to be ordinary and everyday ones, may assume the status of rituals endowed with inner symbolic meanings. Certainly in Japan, at least, the widespread structuralization of the modes of everyday behaviour, in which such matters as sending greetings cards and bowing may be placed, by the presiding rules of social etiquette, in a formal and ritualized framework, provides ample scope for such examinations.[1] It is my intention here to pursue such an examination by looking at one activity that, on the surface, appears to be functional, practical and everyday in nature, but which often assumes a ritualized format that endows it with meanings other than the apparently practical.

Clearly in this context I am treating ritual as something which provides or creates defined codes of action that regulate and structuralize individual behaviour and action, placing them in a social context whereby the behaviour of individuals can be fitted into or co-ordinated with that of others for the purpose of shared goals or aims by the participants acting either as a communal social entity or for an implicitly understood social goal. It is irrelevant whether those goals are desired or even cared about by separate individuals; what is important is the form the action takes, and the manner in which it is done. At the same time, however, the very actions which take place, and their form itself, contains, and in theory at least should express, an inner meaning that is of value to the individual performing the action and, through that individual, to the social group as well.

In order to demonstrate these points, and to illustrate my point about the applicability of the processes of ritualization to everyday actions, and the resultant transfiguration of such actions onto a plane beyond the ordinary, I will examine the seemingly mundane activity of cleaning in Japan. No matter in what context it occurs, cleaning appears to be little more than a fairly basic, functional activity that, whatever the medium—whether a broom on the floor, or a bar of soap on the face—aims to transform the unclean into the clean. Of course, it involves far more than simply removing the unclean for, as Mary Douglas (1984) has amply demonstrated, what is classified as clean or unclean is itself a matter of great cultural and ritual significance. Consequently, cleaning itself is innately connected with ideas of restoring or establishing a sense of order in the surrounding environment. In so doing it thus signifies the preoccupations and attitudes of the social milieu in which it occurs.

In Japanese terms the apparently simple action of cleaning, whether of an external environment such as a park, or a personal one such as one's face, can incorporate a whole series of metaphors which have spiritual significance, which is, in turn, related to the conduct and nature of everyday life. This is most overtly true in the religious context and, since my own primary area of interest and research is in the world of religious behaviour and activity, the main focus of this chapter will be on ritualized cleaning processes that occur in religious environments, and the ways in which they are imbued with and express specific religious symbolisms and meanings.

I will, however, attempt to broaden my perspectives a little and try to relate what occurs in religious terms to the wider world of everyday Japanese behaviour, for I consider that the borderlines between religious and cultural actions are virtually inseparable in many respects. There are, as I shall suggest in the latter part of this chapter, many resemblances between the formalized manner in which people in overtly secular situations (housewives sweeping the area outside their homes is an example that comes readily to mind) may take part in ritual, or at least ritualized, cleaning activities and the more clearly religious forms of cleaning with which I shall begin. Housewives sweeping outside their houses are not, unlike the members of new religious groups who will be described later, taking part in explicit religious actions. They are, however, performing actions that have an identifiably ritualized (and, I would add, implicitly religious) content whose meaning and nature clearly transcends the simple act of cleaning.

Six Monks, Five Brooms and Four Leaves: Zen and the Religiosity of Work

The first year I spent in Japan, in 1981–2, was spent in Zen Buddhist temples, and perhaps my fondest memories of that year were of the autumn, when I was living at a temple in Sendai. During the autumn the morning routine was fairly constant: arise at 4:00 a.m., go to the main hall of the temple for an hour and a half of meditation and chanting, followed by a long period of *samu* (a Zen Buddhist term meaning work, the inner meaning and importance of which I shall shortly discuss).[2] In the autumn at this temple, as at many others throughout Japan, the most common and pressing *samu* was sweeping up the autumnal leaves from the temple grounds and from the graveyard. This would occupy me, and occasionally a Japanese monk also staying there, until 8:00 a.m. which was time for breakfast. The simple act of sweeping up the leaves and carefully heaping them into piles ready for burning gave me a sense of tranquillity and made me feel I was doing something useful and practical to help justify the food and accommodation the temple priest provided for me.

After my happy broom-sweeping experiences in Sendai I later stayed at a Zen temple in Kanagawa prefecture. The temple routine again involved rising at 4:00 a.m. and doing meditation for some hours, followed by a morning service and then breakfast followed by a period of *samu*. On one particular day I, along with five others, was assigned to sweep up the leaves in the garden. Being a visitor to the temple, and hence not knowing the set-up well, I was the last to get to the shed where the tools were kept and hence found myself broomless, for the temple clearly possessed only five brooms, and there were six of us. In reality, in terms of the assigned task of sweeping up the leaves, I did not need a broom for there was hardly a leaf in sight; it was, after all, late winter and those who had swept the garden on the previous day had done a thorough job. In fact I could have picked up what leaves there were by hand.

My suggestion that we might as well go in and have a cup of tea (rational enough from the stance of my British work experience) fell upon shocked ears. We were there to clean the garden and sweep the leaves during the period, which normally lasted for around forty-five minutes or so, so clean it we must, and clean it we did. In actuality we went through a rather theatrical performance of work that was as much concerned with its avoidance as with its enactment. Those with brooms found it easy to go through the motions; I, broomless, had a more uncomfortable time and was confronted with a situation that perhaps was more akin to a Zen *kōan* [enigmatic questions] than anything else. How does one sweep up the leaves without a broom when there are no leaves to sweep?

I was, however, the only one who appeared to question the logic of the operation of cleaning that which was already in a state of considerable order. As a result I came to reflect on the extent to which *samu* was not simply a functional procedure. It also made it clear to me that the importance of work, in this respect, was in the performance of an action rather than with its practical ends, and that, for those of us in the garden, or at least the lucky five with brooms, the central issue was of going through the motions, with a ritual performance that stated both to themselves and to all around that they were doing the right thing in the proper way at the correct time. Cleaning and sweeping the garden was a ritual performance and hence, as with ritual in general, its importance need not primarily, or at all, be with the external actions involved but with the inner meanings they symbolized.

The concept of work is intrinsic to the whole of Zen Buddhist thought and practice. Although Zen, as its very name implies, is centred on the practice of meditation, the life of Zen monasteries has, from the outset, incorporated various other activities as well, all of which may be seen as forms of meditation in their own right.[3] In Zen terms any activity when pursued purely and totally is the same as, indeed is no other than, meditation, and is equally a gateway to the enlightenment which is embedded in, rather than separate from, everyday life. Since, in Zen Buddhism, enlightenment also is considered to be the basic human condition and hence, logically, is a matter of the everyday, Zen has always tended to emphasize basic, ordinary and menial activities such as sweeping floors and cutting wood, as suitable activities not just to provide an alternative to seated meditation, but as forms of meditative action in their own right.

The routines and life patterns of Zen temples thus traditionally incorporate periods of work—which are treated as meditations in themselves—in which all those at the temple have to participate. In earlier ages before the onset of modern plumbing, electricity and gas, such activities included cutting and carrying wood from the mountains, and drawing water from the river, as well as other tasks, such as cleaning, which are still performed today. In performing these tasks trainees were expected to maintain the concentrated mind of the meditation hall, and to use the periods of work as a form of moving, physical meditation. Like all spiritual exercises in the Zen temple, which stress the importance of the community of monks and hence of the idea of enlightenment itself as a social as well as an individual event, work was as much social as individual. By contributing to the life of the temple, by working with one's fellows, and by improving oneself, one is considered to help and contribute to the lives of others—a social contribution that brings further benefit to the individual.

It is difficult, though, to avoid the feeling that *samu* is often work created for its own sake, a view that is especially pertinent in the case of Zen temples which do not (unlike their Christian monastic counterparts) as a rule carry out economically productive work such as growing vegetables and producing goods for trade. Such mercenary activities have never found favour in the Buddhist monastic system and have been actively proscribed in Zen monastic rules. Temples instead depend for their economic support on donations and, more importantly, on the provision of religious services and rituals, the most widespread of which in Japan is the series of rites that follow a death. As a result, work in the Zen context tends to signify something that is, in economic terms, non-productive. More often than not, in contemporary temples at least, this involves some form of cleaning of the temple grounds and environment, such as sweeping the *tatami* floors of the halls of worship, meticulously dusting the Buddhist altars, washing out the toilets and scrubbing and polishing the wooden corridors, cleaning up the graveyard and sweeping up leaves. In the year I spent at Zen temples the work I performed was invariably one or more of these activities.

Zen texts and treatises have constantly stressed the importance of such work as the grounding for enlightenment. The founder of the Sōto Zen sect (it was at temples of this sect that I stayed) in Japan, the thirteenth-century monk Dōgen, laid down guidelines for the performance of and for the manner in which the practice of cleaning should be carried out in such writings as the *Tenzō kyōkun* (rules for the temple cook), as well as in his magnum opus the *Shōbōgenzō* (the eye and treasury of the true law).[4] Yet the importance of cleaning, and of cleaning as a metaphor for enlightenment, is not limited in Dōgen's view to external performances of work, or of cleaning corridors, but relates also to the cleansing of one's personal environment.

In Dōgen's view even the most basic everyday actions, such as washing the face, took on formal, ritual significance as meditative acts. One chapter of the *Shōbōgenzō* is entitled *Senmen* ("Washing the face") and is precisely that, a treatise on how to wash the face, and the meanings of this rite. Thus he writes:[5]

> Purifying the body and mind with fragrant oil and washing away impurities is the first principle of the Buddhist Law. Thoroughly washing and annointing the body ... purifies the inside and outside. When the inside and outside are purified everything around us is purified. (Nishiyama 1983, 1)

The act of cleansing is synonymous with the true law of the Buddhas (Nishiyama 1983, 3). Indeed, Dōgen further states that "It is not merely a way of removing dirt and oil—it is the lifeblood of the Buddhas and Patriarchs" (Nishiyama 1983, 4).

After this he proceeds to give detailed instructions on how to wash the face and how to clean the teeth, showing that these processes are metaphors for cleansing the entire world, for removing impurities on all levels and attaining enlightenment. The detailed instructions form the text of a ritual of personal hygiene, a point further emphasized by Dōgen's statement that the method of washing the face has been preordained by the Buddhas and hence should be followed exactly (Nishiyama 1983, 3).

Clearly, in Dōgen's writing, as in the life of Zen temples, cleaning processes are strictly formalized and made into ritual practices with specific religious meanings that transcend the physical function of simply making place and face clean. Polishing the floor, brushing the teeth and washing the face are rituals that metaphorically polish the mind and open the way to enlightenment.

The ritualization and transformation of everyday actions into meditative disciplines is not, however, solely limited to the Zen monastic sphere. Indeed much of the contemporary literature produced by the Sōtō Zen sect for its lay members manifests a similar focus and emphasis, talking in particular about cleaning in metaphorical as well as pragmatic terms, as the following comments by Fujimoto Kōhō (1977, 22) in a recent Sōtō publication show: "Zen practice starts and finishes with cleaning. By doing excellent cleaning this in itself purifies the spirit." Fujimoto further expands on this theme by talking of the importance of developing a "cleaning spirit" (*sōji suru kokoro*) (1977, 22) and seeking a "cleaning of the spirit" (*kokoro no sōji*) (1977, 23).

The various rites associated with the ancestors (which are, of course, a major area of Buddhist concern and activity in Japan) also bring into play the idea of cleaning as a religious activity. At various points in the year, such as the equinoctial *higan* festivals, it is considered obligatory for the family to clean the graves of their dead ancestors; indeed, failure to do so may, according to commonly held folklore, cause offence to the spirits of the dead and lead to various forms of spiritual retribution.

Cleaning the family Buddhist altar (*butsudan*) at regular intervals is another action that involves filial obligation as well as the pragmatic necessity of keeping a household item free of dust. Yet such actions are, according to the popular literature that Buddhist sects in Japan produce for their members, more than just pragmatic and obligatory performances: they are religious actions that show veneration and service to one's ancestors, and as such should be performed with the "cleaning spirit" that "cleans the spirit" of the performer while bringing solace to the ancestors. This point is demonstrated by the *Shinkō jūkun* (ten articles of belief), a short treatise produced by the Sōtō sect to outline the actions and attitudes expected of good Sōtō members. The first article of the ten stresses the importance of cleaning the *butsudan* on a daily basis as an act of devotion towards the ancestors (Sōtōshūshūmuchō 1981a, 4; 1981b, 28–29). Cleaning thus, for lay people as well as monks, is more than just an everyday physical action performed out of pragmatic necessity or social need. It is a distinct and ritualized religious practice in its own right.

The Ritualization of Cleaning in the New Religions

It is not, however, Zen Buddhism alone which elevates mundane work into a spiritual practice and which transforms cleaning into a symbolic and ritual performance in Japan. Similar motifs are seen in many of the Japanese new religions as well. Members of the new religion Agonshū, for instance, regularly take part in what they term *shugyō,* a word that generally refers to religious training or austerities, but which has come to be widely used by new religions when referring to the religious practices they ask their members to perform. One of the most common forms of *shugyō* performed by Agonshū's lay members involves helping in some way at the various offices and centres of the religion. As with Zen temples, this often means cleaning, usually of the floors and corridors which, although seeming quite spotless to the outside observer, may be polished vigorously and frequently by groups of Agonshū members wearing special headbands and Agonshū jackets.

They perform the task with a joy that is evident to all around them. Members I have interviewed at Agonshū centres in Tokyo and Kyoto, affirmed that taking part—indeed being able to take part—in such voluntary religious practice brought them great happiness and helped them cultivate a sense of gratitude.[6] Gratitude is an important emotion in Japanese religious terms and is a necessary concomitant and indeed component part of the process of hardship and suffering inherent in the notion of austerities or *shugyō.*[7] In performing a task that normally might be seen as arduous and menial, such as scrubbing a floor, Agonshū members learn to see beyond its menial nature and inconveniences; by performing such *shugyō* as polishing the floor they are metaphorically "polishing their souls," a term widely used (see, for example, Hardacre 1986, 11–21) to describe the nature, structure and meaning of religious practice in the new religions.

This practice is not simply individual. Indeed, in its very nature it is, as with the cleaning practices in Zen temples, innately social as well. Without the idea of service to others the action would be simply selfish; thus one cleans the floor (or indeed performs any religious practice) not just to polish one's own soul, but for the benefit of others as well, and for the good of the community. Thus one element in religious practice, and hence in such ritualized performances of cleaning, is the notion of charity and giving to others. One of many ways in which Agonshū expresses this sense of charity is through organized cleaning activities in which a group of members dressed in Agonshū shirts and headbands bearing Agonshū slogans cleans up a public area such as a park or some similar open space. Such activities are conducted on a regular basis, and members are not only encouraged to participate in them, but also to organize their own cleaning groups. The joyous manner in which they carry out these activities not only helps Agonshū members "polish their souls" while performing acts for the public good, but also of course is intended to attract new members, presumably through the suggestion that a religion whose members can be happy in the simple task of sweeping up public parks must have something going for it!

The cleaning motif is prominent also in Tenrikyō, one of the oldest and largest of all Japanese new religions, as anyone who has visited the city of Tenri will be aware. The main Tenrikyō hall of worship is flanked on all sides by long wooden corridors, all of which are shiny and extremely well-polished. Indeed it is rare, when walking along these corridors, not to have to manoeuvre one's way around Tenrikyō members wearing special jackets emblazoned with Tenrikyō motifs and diligently polishing the smooth and seemingly spotless floorboards.

These members are performing this task voluntarily, and do so normally with the joyously positive feelings of those who do the task not because it is a job that has to be done, but because it is an action of religious practice and social service. They are performing *hinokishin*, a term and concept central to Tenrikyō meaning voluntary work or service to and for others that is simultaneously helpful in one's own development. While *hinokishin* can refer to all types of actions (for example, missionary work) done for others, one prominent expression of it is in the voluntary work members put in at Tenri centres to keep the place running smoothly and, as with the ritualized polishing activities in Tenri corridors, clean.

Again, as with Zen temples, it seems not to matter all that much whether the surface that is swept and polished actually, in purely practical terms, needs cleaning. The corridors at Tenri, because of the hordes of people who glide along them in their socks (shoes of course having been removed at the entrance) and because of the constant armies of volunteers polishing them, are rarely other than bright and clean. Behind the action of cleaning, and working in conjunction with the notions of active service to others and joyous participation in organized group and social activities, there is, as with Zen, a definitively metaphorical dimension to such ritualized cleaning, and one which relates not just to the idea of "polishing the soul," but, in Tenrikyō, to the religious interpretation of the causes and healing of illness.

Tenrikyō teaches that although the mind in origin is clean and pure, it becomes clouded because of spiritual dust (*hokori*), which settles on the mind as a result of bad deeds and thoughts. This spiritual dust gradually builds up and clouds the mind, and as this happens all manner of problems may arise, such as illness.[8] Becoming ill is a sign that the mind has been allowed to become cloudy and needs cleaning.

Thus both the solution and the prevention of illness revolve around removing this spiritual dust and stopping it from accumulating. *Hinokishin*, in which the performer learns gratitude and attains joy through selfless actions, is such a practice which metaphorically polishes the soul and cleans the dust from the mind. Often, too, as we have seen, it involves the physical action

95

of sweeping dust away. Cleaning is thus a ritualized religious practice with both pragmatic and metaphorical meanings. Tenrikyō religious literature frequently refers to the processes of cleaning and sweeping that are necessary for cleaning the mind and, like the physical action of *hinokishin*, such references often allude to the actual processes of cleaning. In a discussion of Tenrikyū's view of the nature of this dust and the ways of removing it, Tanaka Kikuo (1982) affirms the importance of constant and daily spiritual practice as a form of cleaning mechanism, and uses, as an example of the necessity of constant practice, the following metaphor from daily life:

> We can keep our rooms clean only when we clean every day. We know through our daily experiences that, if we are negligent in our cleaning, dust will pile up in the meantime until we cannot easily clear it away merely by sweeping and wiping. (Tanaka 1982, 5)

In such ways, Tanaka continues, "man can keep his mind clean only when he sweeps it every day" (1982, 28), using the power of Tenrikyō's God the Parent who serves as the broom that clears away the dust. This image of God as the broom is a common image in Tenrikyō literature, deriving originally from the *Ofudesaki*, the writings of Tenrikyō's foundress Nakayama Miki, that form the basis of Tenrikyō's scriptural and theological tradition, in which there are numerous references of the following type: "Sweeping clean people's hearts throughout the world I, God, act as a broom" (*Ofudesaki*, Part 3, Section 52, in Inoue and Eynon 1987, 45).

In such respects the actions of Tenrikyō members as they religiously and ritualistically polish the floors become externalized expressions of the religion's internal processes of sweeping the dust from the mind, and may even be seen as a manifestation of the workings of Tenrikyō's chief deity, God the Parent.

Ittōen: Cleaning the Lavatory as a Ritual Practice

In at least one case a religious group has become widely known because of its emphasis on cleaning rituals. I am referring to the utopian religious movement Ittōen, whose communal centre is located a little way out of Kyoto. The daily routine at the commune commences with a ritual period of cleaning in which members scrub, sweep and clean the precincts and buildings of their commune for around twenty minutes (Davis 1975, 292). Besides this communal cleaning rite, however, Ittōen members perform a ritual practice known as *gyōgan* (literally "seeking austerities"), and it is for this practice, which usually involves some form of cleaning, generally of lavatories, that Ittōen has become widely known. In *gyōgan* members are expected to go out and seek tasks that they may perform without reward for the benefit of members of the public.

While *gyōgan* theoretically can involve any task, in reality it largely centres on cleaning toilets. The practice of cleaning latrines was strongly advocated by Ittōen's founder Nishida Tenkō because he saw in it a way of overcoming the self and eradicating the ego. Nishida was especially strongly influenced by Zen thought, and espoused the apparently demeaning process of toilet cleaning as a means of liminalizing and depriving the practitioner of status, and hence of ego, much in the same way that Zen uses the performance of menial work activities and the traditional begging round (*takuhatsu*) (Davis 1975, 284–302).

Ittōen also runs special spiritual training sessions for outsiders in which they are expected to follow the same practices. Many of those who partici-pate in these sessions have been sent by their companies, often because they are new employees, as part of the general company training and induction processes. The participants are told to go out to various housing estates and knock on doors asking permission to clean the toilets. They are expected to persevere all day no matter what response they get and, if they are lucky, to be able to clean a few toilets. Not surprisingly, however, their requests are often unsuccessful, for many people are not particularly pleased with the implication that their toilet needs cleaning, or with the idea of letting a stranger come in the house to do it. Failure to enter houses does not mean failure in the task, however, for the very process of rejection is, as many religious organizations which send their members out on door-to-door evangelizing expeditions will affirm, a further aspect of spiritual training that tests the mettle and helps polish the soul just as does the action of cleaning itself. Ittöen members also take part in periodic cleaning campaigns on public lavatories—which have, anyway, lagged somewhat behind private ones in terms of hygiene in general (Davis 1975, 303–4).

Ittōen's focus on (or perhaps obsession with) cleaning, especially of the toilet, has been ritualized into a religious practice the focus of which is clearly—as with my Zen temple experiences—far less concerned with the efficacy of the activity in its overt manifestations (i.e. actually cleaning some-thing for utilitarian purposes) than with the internal spiritual dimensions of the task. It has also involved a very definitive process of ritualization just as the formalized structures within which cleaning practices are carried out in Zen temples, with its own ritual title *(gyōgan)*. Winston Davis has commented on Ittōen's cleaning activities with the following words: "Work itself, espe-cially the perfunctory morning cleaning routine, seems often to have more importance as a ritual than as a means of keeping up the community's property or increasing its wealth" (Davis 1975, 318).

In fact—as we have seen already—the economic dimensions of work are not of primary importance in Japanese religious situations. Work in the religious context is seen not so much as a means of enabling a temple or community to prosper, as a formalized religious practice with symbolic meanings relating to the expected goals of the religious group both in individual and social terms. Consequently, it may be ritualized to the extent that the practical effects of the performance may be secondary to the meaning of the rite itself.

Creating Good Employees: Spiritual Training and Cleaning Rituals

The use of ritualized cleaning activities as a form of spiritual training is not limited just to overtly religious organizations in Japan. The numerous ethical or moral welfare training organizations (*shuyō dantai*) which have flourished in Japan in recent years and which exhibit many of the qualities and practices of religious organizations, even while eschewing their legal form, also make use of spiritual training sessions that manifest many of the practices and concepts used in Zen temples and the new religions (Numata 1988, 227–78).

Such spiritual training sessions are, like those run by Ittōen (and also increasingly by Zen temples in Japan), often patronized by business companies who send their members to them to learn determination, discipline and obedience. Dorinne Kondo (1987, 250), in an interesting description of one such training session, which she attended, notes that "cleaning is a standard ingredient of spiritual education in Japan."[9] It is not, however, as she notes, enough to just perform the task; to have the correct attitude is equally important. Thus Kondo and her fellow participants were expected to demonstrate enthusiasm for the task, even being encouraged to chant slogans in unison as they did so (1987, 251).[10] As Kondo reports, one of these chants contained the phrase "Polish the floor! If you polish the floor your heart too will shine!" (1987, 251). When the participants came to the end of the corridor they were asked to turn round and do it all over again—an affirmation, if one were needed, of the extent to which the aims of the task itself were not primarily concerned with cleaning the corridor. I am interested to note, too, that, just as I did in the face of the apparent futility of the Zen garden cleaning cited earlier, Kondo found it hard to come to terms with the logic of the situation, and admitted to anger at what she saw as a waste of energy, although none of her fellow participants expressed similar sentiments.

Self, Others and Ritual Intent

In all the accounts I have given above of instances where the activity of cleaning has been harnessed for spiritual ends, cleaning some external object has served as a metaphor for the potentially more vital goal of polishing the soul. Although such spiritual training seeks to enhance each individual it also, at the same time, is a social activity, a point I have made earlier when talking of the new religions. In her description of the ethics retreat Kondo shows that activities were organized on a group basis, with each person being considered to belong to a particular group, with the group being responsible for the actions of each of its members (1987, 248–49). In such circumstances responsibility to others is a spur to the individual's spiritual practice.

Hence, as we have seen in the practices of Agonshū members and in the concept of *hinokishin* in Tenrikyō, acting for others is an integral part of acting for and polishing the self; it also is an intrinsic part of the creation of a sense of group cohesion, belonging and identity which provides the individual with a framework in which s/he can feel at home. The humble attitude that one should take in performing such menial tasks as cleaning helps to subliminate the ego and bring all members of the group into a feeling of community and harmony in which all strive for a communal good that is equated with the individual good—which of course helps explain why companies are so keen for their employees to go on such courses! Even the suffering that is felt in some of the more ascetic practices in the ethics retreat (and in all ascetic practices) is also a gateway to joy, for it teaches one endurance and helps one realize the importance of humility. Thus, through suffering, as with all such communal acts of voluntary work, one can develop the sense of gratitude which, as I have previously mentioned, is so important to self-development.

Community Cleaning Rites:
Obligatory Attendance and Enforced Joy

Although I have concentrated on cleaning as a ritual activity largely in religious contexts, and always with some spiritual significance, I should like to conclude by drawing attention to the ways in which communal cleaning activities may occur in the day-to-day flow of life, and to suggest that in these there may be some close parallels with the spiritual nature of cleaning.

It is hard to avoid the overt, potentially obsessive, concern with ordering the personal and spatial environment in Japan. The various acts by which people remove the dirt of the outside by removing their shoes, wiping the soles of their feet, gargling, etc. (Ohnuki-Tierney 1984, 21); the actions of shopkeepers who dutifully and regularly sweep the street before their shops, often sprinkling it also with water; and the frequency with which taxi drivers dust down their taxis while waiting for customers are but a few of the examples that one could cite.

Often such activities have a socially coercive side to them: those who have lived for any amount of time in Japan may well have shared the sense of shame and discomfort my wife and I acquired on realizing that ours was the only house in the street before which the road had not been neatly swept each morning. Occasionally such cleaning is organized on a communal basis in the area around one's house or apartment, and announced by a circular sent round to all households. At such times attendance, at least for one representative of each household, appears obligatory: failure to turn up may give rise to a general feeling amongst one's neighbours that one does not have the desired and expected sense of community.

Certainly one can be made to feel guilty about failing to attend. In February 1984 my wife and I had to inform the administrative committee in charge of the apartment block where we lived in Kōbe that we would miss the semi-annual clean-up of the grounds because of other commitments. The muttered acceptances of this apology let us know that, although they would be able to manage, our absence would cause problems. The response, as it was intended to, caused us some unease and shame. We had, after all, only recently moved in, and it was clear that our failure to attend—indeed our self-centred decision to go travelling at such a time—brought into doubt our commitment to the community living in the apartment block.

We subsequently attended, dutifully and religiously, the next communal clean-up and, as a result, spent two boring hours doing very little—the area was relatively clean, there were few fallen leaves, and the drainage ditches had unfortunately remained clear of refuse and hence did not require attention. In fact, much of the activity consisted of trying to find something to do, and in exerting energy to manifest one's enthusiasm for the task. The most enthusiastic participants even competed with each other to pick up the few bits of rubbish lying around. The committee member in overall charge kept a close eye on his watch and, when a suitable time had elapsed, he decided we could all stop.

Again, as with my earlier temple experience, it was the time spent, the fact that it had been spent with and for others, and the attitude involved that was paramount, rather than the concept of a task accomplished. Certainly the cleaning session served to impose a sense of order on the external environment in terms of making sure everything was in its correct place, but underneath this physical exterior the rite imposed a further, and probably more vital, sense of order on the social environment. Obligatory attendance itself confirms a form of order, of people and households in their correct place in social terms, performing the role that is socially expected of them. The ritual of spending a couple of hours going through the motions of sweeping and gathering up (non-existent) fallen leaves allowed us to demonstrate our commitment to be in the right place at the right time and hence to uphold and reinforce the social order of the community. The very inconvenience of the process (at 9:00 a.m. on a Sunday morning when many of the participants would have preferred to be in bed seeing off the effects of Saturday night) enabled us all to demonstrate and make a sacrifice (in time and comfort) for this end. The sacrifice itself encouraged us to demonstrate the joyous attitude that was part of the process. After all, we were (or should have been!) grateful to be able to take part and help out.

The obligatory nature of organized cleaning is found elsewhere in Japanese society. In schools, for instance, students are expected to take care of their classrooms (homerooms), sweeping the floor and tidying it up every day after school (Rohlen 1983, 179). While this is intended to make class members feel part of the social community and to develop a sense of shared responsibility it also has the practical and economic function of saving money that otherwise would have been spent on cleaning staff.

Concluding Remarks: Purity, Order and a Nice Hot Bath

I think it is reasonable to raise the question of whether we can view all such processes in which cleaning takes place in any ritualized form, from the apparently secular occurrences of periodic community clean-ups to the overtly religious discipline of *samu* in Zen temples, in a similar light. Can we thus relate the housewives taking part in their ritual street sweeping to members of new religions as they perform their *shugyō* with cloths and buckets, and to the followers of Ittōen as they clean public lavatories?

In social terms there are many common threads: cleaning as a rite serves to generate a sense of community, belonging and social identity whether in a religious institution, a school or a housing estate. It demonstrates a commitment to the social milieu, a commitment that is strengthened by the apparent futility of the action when there is seemingly so little matter out of place to deal with. In individual and social terms the prevailing attitude that should be adhered to when performing the actions (and which is equally one of the aims of the action) is the same in all cases, whether in a temple or on a housing estate: endurance, service, gratitude and joy. Moreover the manner, form and the way in which this ritual process is performed are invariably more essential than the actual practical task that is carried out.

A further common area of relationship for all such forms of cleaning—a relationship that would point to the enduring sense of ritualism and to the implicit religiosity to be found in Japanese everyday behaviour—is their concern with definition, order and purification, issues that are, of course, vital components of the Japanese religious system, and of Shintō in particular. In fact I feel that it is probably the deep Japanese religious concern (expressed most strongly in Shintō) that concepts of purity and of definition should be expressed and reinforced through action which is at the heart of the obsession that Japanese Zen temples have with ritual cleaning. Certainly I have yet to find any evidence to suggest that such an intensive focus on cleaning, in ritual and religious terms, exists at Buddhist temples outside Japan.[11] Indeed, interviews I have had with Japanese Buddhist priests who have visited other Buddhist countries frequently show that they often remark on this matter and that they are often disturbed by the fact that, in their eyes, temples in other Buddhist countries are invariably "dirty."[12]

The notions of cleanliness as hygiene (which one might consider to be the primary intent of sweeping the streets) and as a moral state of purity (which is certainly the primary intent of religious cleaning) are overlapping concepts in Japan. Commenting on the importance of "feeling clean," Emiko Ohnuki-Tierney quotes the following description, made by the pianist Nakamura Hiroko about her music teacher: "when I played for her I felt as though I had *had a nice hot bath*. Everything felt clean and marvellous" (1984, 34, italics in original). She goes on to comment:

> This clean feeling is not only personally most desirable and satisfying, as Nakamura notes, it is one of the most cherished moral values in con-temporary Japan ... the same expressions are used to describe cleanliness in the hygienic as well as the moral sense. (Ohnuki-Tierney 1984, 34)

Cleaning is a process of making definitions, of imposing order on an environment, and purifying it in accord with the prevailing social and cultural understandings of what such purification involves. In this essay I have been concerned with examining the relevance and nature of cleaning—beyond its merely pragmatic functions—in Japanese society and religion. This does not mean that discussions of the type I have engaged in concerning the everyday nature of ritual, of the ritualization of everyday practices, and of the religiosity of everyday actions, are limited to Japan. Indeed, much progress has been made in identifying and discussing the themes of implicit religiosity within ordinary life in other societies.[13] What I would add here is that the Japanese case, where we find a very strong religious emphasis on cleaning as a spiritual practice and ritual, certainly appears to affirm the point that the lines of differentiation between religion, ritual and everyday activity are rather fine. In such terms one could ask to what extent it is possible to differentiate between a broom wielded by a monk in a temple, and one wielded by a housewife in the street, either in act, attitude or presumed intent—especially when neither of them might really want to be wielding them in the first place.

Notes

* Between April 1981 and April 1982 I did research on the Sōtō Zen Buddhist sect in Japan, during which time I lived at a number of Zen temples. The observations I made during this period form the basis from which this chapter developed.

1. The large numbers of guidebooks to social etiquette which may be found at any popular bookshop in Japan are evidence of a continuing, if not expanding, importance placed on the correct performance of all manner of actions, not merely those concerned with social interaction, but also with all manner of situations that involve some form of action or reaction. For instance, I recently acquired one such compendium which, as its title, *Seikatsu no chishiki hyakka* (1990), suggests, is a veritable encyclopedia of the social knowledge that is required in every aspect of social living in Japan. It provides, with illustrations, instructions on such diverse but socially important actions as behaviour and procedures at funerals and weddings, the way to send greetings and other such cards at different times of the year, how to wrap and give presents, how to sit down properly and put on a napkin at a French restaurant and many other things (*Shufu to Seikatsusha* 1990).

2. *Samu* has a clearly ritualized format, with a set and specific place in the temple routine. The ritual motif is emphasized by the fact that the monks don clothing (*samue*) consisting of loose cotton trousers (usually grey or black), a light cotton, loose, wrap-round jacket and a cloth to cover the head, all of which are worn only for this task and which thus take on the air of a ritual uniform.

3. The Japanese word "*zen*" is the Japanese pronunciation of the Chinese ideogram *ch'an* which was used to translate the Sanskrit *dhyana*, meditation: hence Zen is (or was, in its eighth-century Chinese origins) a Buddhist movement that centred almost exclusively on the practice of meditation.

4. The most complete and accessible volume of Dōgen's writings is to be found in *Dōgen zenji zenshū* compiled and edited by Ōkubo Dōshū (1969–70, 2 vols). Besides the numerous contemporary Japanese translations of his various works that are available, a growing number of translations in various European languages, notably English, have also begun to appear.

5. I have cited the translation by Nishiyama et al. here because it is the most accessible (if not always the most textually precise) of all the available translations of the *Shōbōgenzō* and also because of my own involvement with it. During the six months I stayed at Nishiyama's temple in Sendai (the one referred to earlier in this chapter) I helped with work on several sections of this translation including the chapter cited here.

6. I base these remarks on several visits to Agonshū centres and interviews with Agonshū members during the period from February 1987 until November 1988, in Tokyo, Kyoto, and Hirakata.

7. For general discussions of the dynamics of suffering, gratitude and asceticism see Miyake (1981, 128–43) and Reader (1991, 107–33). Blacker (1975), which remains the classic work on Japanese shamanism and asceticism in Western languages, also shows the close relationship between suffering, endurance, gratitude and the spiritual awarenesses that ascetics sought and achieved.

8. My explanation here is, for reasons of space, a rather generalized and simplified account of Tenrikyō teaching, for in fact Tenrikyō differentiates between eight types of spiritual dust, each caused by a particular type of misdeed or bad thought (Tanaka 1982, 7–26). Ultimately, however, the treatment for all is the same and relates to the processes of sweeping the mind described in the chapter.

9. I should like to thank Professor Jane Bachnik of the University of North Carolina for bringing this article to my attention.

10. One notes, however, that Rohlen, in a description of another company spiritual training session held at a Zen temple, notes that his fellow workers treated the ritual period of cleaning in a manner that was less disciplined than intended. Although the priest directing operations was extremely meticulous, "his example was ignored by many of the trainees who ... lazily wandered about with rakes over their shoulders" (1973,

103

1546); proof, if proof were needed, that any ritual can be undermined by the intent and attitudes of its putative performers.

11. I base my remarks on observations at Buddhist temples I have stayed at in the following countries: Thailand, India (Burmese, Tibetan and Bhutanese Buddhist), Nepal and Sri Lanka.

12. I base this remark on interviews with numerous priests during my years (1981–2 and 1983–9) in Japan. In particular I remember six young monks from a temple in Nagano whom I interviewed in December 1981, just before they left on a trip to Indian Buddhist sites, and in March 1982 just after they had returned. Before they went they had numerous images of India, mostly connected with its position as the original home of Buddhism and as a spiritual centre. On their return the overriding first impression of all of them was that it was dirty and that even the temples were untidy and disordered. Consequently, it seemed, their notions of it as a spiritual centre were appreciably diminished.

13. I am referring in particular here to the numerous papers read at the annual Denton Hall conferences of the Network for the Study of Implicit Religion, and the research interests of the members of that organization.

References

Blacker, C. 1975. *The Catalpa Bow: A Study of Shamanistic Practices in Japan.* London: George Allen and Unwin.

Davis, W. B. 1975. "Ittōen: the Myths and Rituals of Liminality," Parts I-III. *History of Religions* 14(4): 282–321.

Douglas, M. 1984. *Purity and Danger: An Analysis of the Concepts of Pollution and Taboo.* London: Ark Paperbacks.

Fujimoto Kōhō. 1977. *Gasshō no seikatsu.* Tokyo: Sōtōshūshūmuchō.

Hardacre, H. 1986. *Kurozumikyō and the New Religions of Japan.* Princeton, NJ: Princeton University Press.

Inoue Akio, and M. Eynon. 1987. *A Study of the Ofudesaki.* Tenri: Tenrikyō Dōyūsha.

Kondo, D. 1987. "Creating an Ideal Self: Theories of Selfhood and Pedagogy at a Japanese Ethics Retreat." *Ethos* 15(5): 241–72.

Miyake Hitoshi. 1981. *Seikatsu no naka no shukyō.* Tokyo: NHK Books.

Nishiyama Kōsen, et al. trans. 1975–83. *Dōgen Zenji: Shōbōgenzō.* Tokyo: Nakayama Shobō.

Numata Kenya. 1988. *Gendai Nihon no shinshūkyō.* Osaka: Sōgensha.

Ohnuki-Tierney, Emiko. 1984. *Illness and Culture in Contemporary Japan.* Cambridge: Cambridge University Press.

Ōkubo Dōshū, ed. 1969–70. *Dōgen zenji zenshū,* 2 vols. Tokyo: Chikuma Shobō.

Reader, Ian. 1991. *Religion in Contemporary Japan.* Basingstoke: Macmillan.

Rohlen, T. P. 1973. "'Spiritual Education' in a Japanese Bank." *American Anthropologist* 75: 1542–62.

—1983. *Japan's High Schools.* Berkeley and Los Angeles: University of California.

Shufu to Seikatsusha, ed. 1990. *Seikatsu no chishiki no hyakka.* Tokyo: Shufu to Seikatsusha.

Sōtōshūshūmuchō, ed. 1981a. *Sōtōshū no nenjūgyōji.* Tokyo: Sōtōshūshūmuchō.

—1981b. *Sōtōshū hōreki.* Tokyo: Sōtōshūshūmuchō.

Tanaka Kikuo. 1982. *Dust and innen.* Tenri: Tenrikyō Overseas Mission.

INSTRUCTION AND DELIGHT:
THEME PARKS AND EDUCATION[*]

Margaret J. King

Editor's Introduction

Margaret King has studied popular culture for over twenty-five years, including writing her doctoral dissertation on "The Davy Crockett Craze: A Case Study in Popular Culture." She is now director of Cultural Studies and Analysis, a Philadelphia-based think-tank that seeks to understand the connections between cultural expression and the ways in which people, especially in business, attempt to solve problems.

Studies of ritual(s), religion(s) and culture(s) commonly concentrate on elite rather than popular expressions and interests. An interest in popular culture requires explicit indication in a way that "elite culture" rarely does. Despite a long-term interest by scholars of religion in the lived reality of religions, it is still necessary to indicate an interest in any but the elite or "authoritative" tradition by the use of terms such as "popular," "implicit" or "vernacular" religion. While many scholars interested in ritual have debated distinctions and similarities between ritual and theatre as a means of defining different kinds of performance, they have rarely considered popular entertainments in the same way or for the same purpose. Margaret King forcefully demonstrates the value of entertaining the idea that Disneyland and other theme parks might be more than "entertainment," might be educational, and might inherit and express contemporary versions of pilgrimage and other kinds of ritual behaviour. One illustration of the valuable results of King's enquiry in relation to ritual and belief is her discussion of the "anamnestic (memory assisting) response" elicited by theme parks as an aspect of the creation and maintenance of American identity and experience. The link between memory and ritual is especially significant in theories of both that assume they are representative, i.e. that they re-present past or meaningful acts, or locations (see Smith 1987, 25–26). The prevalence of words related to "signify" is indicative of many such theories. In other words, the following chapter is not included only (or even principally) in order to clarify the nature of ritual by distinguishing it from entertainment, but to invite reflection on ritual's meaningfulness, signification and educative purposes.

References

King, Margaret J. 1976. "The Davy Crockett Craze: A Case Study in Popular Culture." Department of American Studies, University of Hawaii.
Smith, Jonathan Z. 1987. *To Take Place*. Chicago: University of Chicago Press.

80 03

The lecturer who puts his students to sleep looks with a jaundiced eye on the man who keeps them bolt upright, who tries to entertain them as he teaches so as to make what is taught memorable and colorful.
William Sloan, *The Craft of Writing*, 1979

Knowledge is important, but imagination is more important than knowledge.

Albert Einstein

Experts, educators, and educatees alike agree that American education is in trouble. SAT and ACT scores have been on the decline for some years and there is widespread concern about how low they will go as well as when and why. There is also agreement that education is not going to get any better without some dramatic changes. The current popularity of such critiques as Allan Bloom's *Closing of the American Mind* and John Allen Paulos's *Innumeracy* testifies to this anxious state of affairs in the teaching arts.

The challenges to education in the information age are stern. No longer is it enough merely to inform. Education is now called upon to teach forms of judgment, discrimination, values, analytical skills, and problem-solving never before imagined as well as something even more rare: to show people of all ages how to learn. The traditional trio of classroom, textbook, and teacher is simply no longer equal to the task. Nonetheless, education continues to operate as an enclave of elite culture battling for interest and respect in a universe of mass media, high technology, and the popular arts—the ecology of everyday life. What is called for is some way of bringing into better confluence these "two cultures" that have increasingly diverged over the past century. Creatively applying the tremendous success of theme parks and related forms offers perhaps the brightest prospect for this critical integration.

In "The Death of Good Taste," a lecture sponsored by the Clemson University Architectural Foundation, Dr. Roger Rollin suggested teaching some connections between *War and Peace* and *Star Wars*. "Moreover," Rollin noted, "it would seem to make sense to provide students with some of the intellectual tools they badly need to understand their popular culture. ... And we in humanistic education bear a major responsibility for helping people maximize their cultural options..."[1]

Imports from popular culture into schools is one leading-edge development. Television and computers are just two examples, but even more pervasive are the total environments of Disneyland and Walt Disney World—the theme parks. The rich fusion of entertainment and education at the Disney parks—and related "megaparks"—has been the basis of intense debate. The spatial free association of ideas that was for so long possible only in images and words has now developed, with high technology, into a three-dimensional artform. And though a stroll through Disneyland or World happens within a planned environment, the guest can endlessly vary the journey according to mood and interest. The quality and meaning of this experience has recently become the focal point for the museum and educational "events" world, where theme parks are being considered as a design model for attracting and engaging the visitor.

For a cultural audience raised on television, with a technological rather than a traditional humanities view of the world, theme parks offer the ideal setting and inspiration for education. Many of the innovations taken for granted as part of classroom and museum education enhancements, such as multimedia events, were born at the theme parks.

Education is hailed by theme parks as a central mission. "Disneyland," says the official brochure, "combines fantasy, history, adventure, and learning." Roy Disney's summation of Walt Disney World's outlook makes a similar claim: "May Walt Disney World bring joy and inspiration and new knowledge to all who come to this happy place [where all] can laugh and play and learn together" (quoted in Pettit).

The Disney penchant for educating widely and well has always stayed several moves ahead of the priorities shift in U.S. education. Since the 1960s, the emphasis has been away from knowledge building and analytical thinking as taught through the motifs of history and literature: the linear landscape of cause and effect, motive and action, personality and destiny prescribed in the study of warfare, economics, romance, and the search for the fulfillment of empire and self. New models of intelligence based on research in problem-solving and creativity have induced a fresh new agenda of curiosity, imagination, discovery, invention, and innovation. Suddenly students are being summoned to think in new paradigms (imagining scenarios like a nuclear holocaust or the eradication of all disease), to invent new solutions ("design the tallest building possible out of paper"), and to operate interactively (solving medical problems in trouble-shooting student teams rather than simulating solo practitioners).

E. Paul Torrance and Kathy Goff, researchers in creativity education, have declared, "Many educators have not fully recognized that changes in the direction of more creative education have occurred.... Practically every curriculum reform during the last 30 years has moved education in the U.S. to be more creative in nature (Torrance and Goff 1989, 139–40).

Entertainment as Education

Walt Disney has been called "the greatest educator of the twentieth century." In this oft-quoted accolade, Max Rafferty, Superintendent of Education for the State of California, was recognizing the power of the Disney enterprise to do far more than entertain. He saw in Disney's films, television, and print, and then in the theme park, the hand and mind of a creative innovator whose power drew on the American family audience's interest in learning, an impetus that closely parallels the desire to travel and explore other worlds, eras, and minds.

This perception about the nature of education has paid off many times over. Disney's genius for educating by starting with what is already known follows a well-known precept of teaching and of popular culture alike— consumer or student-oriented teaching. As Richard Beard put it in his book on EPCOT [Experimental Prototype Community of Tomorrow], "The organization that Walt fostered is a wizard at giving people facts they enjoy and remember" (Beard 1982, 35). It would certainly be safe to say that Disney has enjoyed more influence than anyone has suspected in educating every generation of Americans since the 1930s. Certainly as the artistic director of a major multi-talented enterprise—as filmmaker, artist, businessman, and creator of the City of the Future—Disney can readily be construed as America's Dean of Applied Creativity.

In the mass media age what we learn and what our children learn is most often absorbed outside the classroom: through magazines, sports, films, computer games, rock concerts, theme parks, malls, and shopping (now the major leisure activity in the U.S.) and through the sociable interchange that goes with all these. Time allotted to reading and formal instruction, of course, lags far behind these pursuits. Without a total re-thinking and overhaul, the classroom can no longer compete with the wide wonderful world of popular culture. The "Never-Never Land" of the theme park, the stagey themed atmospheres of restaurants and malls (which have now become major socialization centers), and the drama of both large and small screen are simply far more attractive, stimulating, and engaging.

Education begins with delight, with engagement, with the ring of the familiar. Teaching aids can be traced from designs first conceived for entertainment. After their integration into home life, the stereopticon and magic lantern of the late nineteenth century, followed by the Kodachrome slide, videodisc, and video game, have all made the migration from parlor and den into the halls of academe for a "second career" in education.[2] The first breath was drawn in enjoyment, not pedagogy.

Following the same fashion, formal education is already turning to alternatives in a quest to make the classroom a "learning center" rather than a traditional library/lecture hall/museum: video-assisted instruction, part-time programs, flexible schedules, field study home learning through television and computers. From their inception, theme parks posed the groundwork for alternative (or at least supplementary) educations. Thirty years later and now more fully developed as a communications media in themselves, these alternative "academies" offer both challenges and promises to ideas about how people can be induced to explore, to learn, and to remember.

As time-honored extensions of the schoolroom, museums are naturally drawn to these advancing formats, and are emerging as a leading component in public education—sometimes complementing, sometimes being handed roles to take over from the overworked school curriculum (especially in the sciences). In Philadelphia, for example, the Franklin Institute's Futures Center, with its interactive science garden, hands-on exhibits, and heavy computer use, is one prototype of this evolution of the "museum of the future" movement.

Since the mid-1950s, the Disney Corporation has pioneered and perfected the novel art form of themeing, a total sociology and aesthetic, which has been raised to a new height with the opening of EPCOT's Future World and World Showcase in the early 1980s.[3] Although often considered simply a form of highly successful mass entertainment, the theme park (or "atmospheric park," which it has also been called) (Schickel 1968, 13) has generated an ever-widening circle of influences, ranging from town planning and historic preservation to building architecture, mall design, and merchandising to home and office decor, exhibit design, crowd management, and video- and computer-assisted education. Inspired and propelled by thematic applications of technology and the use of themed motifs in decor, the extension of set design, and flights of fancy (along archetypal routes) in symbolic and fantastic architecture, the "Disney effect" is making itself seen and felt across the cultural board. As unlikely as it may seem at first blush, the models of many contemporary notions about the way public spaces should look and feel trace back to the gateways of the Disney parks. This includes the dimensions, kinetics, textures, sounds, and other character traits of the (other) places we go to encounter the world in stylized form: the Madonna Inns, Food Courts, Donut Worlds, and Magic Time Machine Restaurants, as well as the thousands of McDonald's outlets keyed to local themes.

Themeing

Throughout nearly three and a half decades of conception, development and evolution, theme parks have exerted a surprisingly disproportionate effect on American culture—both in mainstream and avant-garde endeavors. It is even possible that, as a result of that influence, there has been no more immediately successful or more all-encompassing art form in human history. Disney's is a multi-experiential approach, melding education, entertainment, food, souvenirs, travel, and other modes to achieve its effects (Schoener 1988, 38). Consider the attendance figures of fifty million a year to Disneyland, Walt Disney World, and Tokyo Disneyland—with another eleven million expected to visit Euro Disneyland in Paris after 1992.

The ancestors of the theme park are venerable, including pilgrimage place, fair, harvest rite, royal pleasure ground, theater, science exposition, history park, world's fair, and museum. The first generation was established and matured over a thirty-year period. The spin-off progeny, the second generation, now includes such prominent features of the entertainment landscape as Knotts Berry Farm, Busch Gardens, King's Island, the "Six Flags" parks, Sea World, and Opryland. The third-generation theme park offspring are showing up in themed entertainments and exhibitions, restaurant decor, historic redesign and rehabilitation, retirement and resort communities, retail and mall design, main street restoration, and in inventive extensions of and within traditional museums such as the Futures Center.

Theme parks serve as modern museums and history parks, often following even better than museums themselves the museum mandate to "endow knowledge, incite pleasure, and stimulate curiosity" (Commission on Museums for a New Century, 1984). Through the device of themeing and its shorthand stylizations of person, place, and thing, an archive of collective memory and belief, symbol, and archetype has been created.

"Imagineering" (a Disney trademark) is the brainpower of themeing: the dynamic synthesis of right- and left-brain talents, merging creativity with technical know-how. "It is precisely in this unique combination that [we have] excelled, and in creating Epcot Center we believe [we] will achieve new dimensions and dynamics in family entertainment and learning experiences," says Marty Sklar, Vice President of Creativity Development for WED Enterprises (qouted in Beard 1982, 25).

This "bank" of popular culture has earned high interest, both inside and beyond the business of entertainment. It is an account open and available for educators of every style and subject to draw upon.

The following questions suggest themselves for a study of the interface between theme parks and education: What is being learned and taught through themed environments, and how? What is the relationship between education, entertainment, and acculturation? How can themed environments offer inspiration to schools, museums, libraries, and other formal and informal educational/enrichment programs—in their operation and mission alike? What are the issues of education and accuracy versus "promotion," with its stylistic impulses and imperatives within these environments? And must these forces necessarily be cast as conflicting ones? What are the interactions between popular culture and elite/educational/historic forms in the education process? And finally, how do theme parks educate, and to what extent has their ability to teach brought them such unprecedented successes?

An appreciation of how various publics are attracted, involved, and educated by theme parks, based on the approach of "themeing" to knowledge complexes, is generic to the innovative connections currently being sought between entertainment and education, in particular the problematic "cross-cultural encounters" between formal and informal education. (For example, in the work of George MacDonald and Stephen Alsford at the Canadian Museum of Civilization, a starring example of a new age museum.)[4] These emerging integrations offer exciting new opportunities and directions for educational institutions of all stripes for the coming century. The gathering wave of world trade, tourism, and migration lends an urgency to these opportunities they have never had before (King 1990).[5] At the same time, they construct an intellectual theme of growing importance in the world at large: the creative synthesis (or reunification) of popular culture with elite in myriad motifs, trends, subjects, and styles. As a case study, theme parks, rooted in the California and Florida prototypes, are also posing some solutions (or problem-solving frameworks) to some of the central concerns of modern civilization, both Western and international. "The parks transform formidable technology into something we can understand and look forward to enjoying," says Beard (1982, 35).

Disney's efforts have often hastened the process by which less advantaged and bookless children in the U.S. have acquired knowledge of history, lore, and myth that were previously held as a cultural monopoly by the better-off. The Disney classroom can be considered as a major acculturation on the American social scene, one that has "leveled up" millions of young by saving them from Dick and Jane banality. There is a price, of course—Disney versions of Snow White and Winnie the Pooh and Bambi may lack that poetic refinement of European verbal and graphic originals. But this issue of quality obtains in all the diffusions of education and literacy and is never applied to Disney alone.

Indeed, it can be argued that the two great popularizers of the ecological movement were Rachel Carson (*Silent Spring*, 1962) and Walt Disney. Who would deny that all attitudes toward animals, wild and tame, natural and fantastic, have been mediated by Disney for at least sixty years?

Even so, it continues to be a point of pride with many American intellectuals that they have never (and refuse to) even set foot in any of these places. Analyzing the intellectual underpinnings of theme park content offers tremendous promise for mediating the battle of taste cultures, while showing potential to carry forward the whole enterprise of integrating elite and popular culture modalities.[6]

Concern with the political and social control of Disney's versions of the world—in particular, history, has prompted a generation of criticism based on the selective perception generated by Disney's brand of Midwestern conservatism—although this style, according to his biographers, is best viewed as a conservatism without commitment. These critiques take special aim at the Disney enterprise because of its special powers over the American mind. This power is attested to by the studios' great success in attracting generation after generation to the Disney oeuvre of film, parks, and merchandising.

Critical anguish is at heart, as Michael Wallace's recent review of Walt Disney as popular historian shows, an aghast perplexity about the state of education under the incursions of popular culture. "Nowadays it often seems as if the past gets presented to popular audiences more by commercial operators pursuing profit than by museums bent on education," says Wallace, "...blurring the line between entertainment center and actual museum" (Wallace 1989, 158–80). The construction of images and ideas in the Carousel of Progress, American Adventure, and the Hall of Presidents are the sourcebooks for the study of history transformed into popular culture.

Themeing is evocative as opposed to literal. Themeing is an involving form. It makes participants out of viewers. It collapses the traditional distance between the audience and the artifact. Contrast this participatory theory of art with the Western doctrine of art as disengaged, removed, and objectified, as in the conventional art museum, where velvet ropes carefully separate viewers from the thing viewed. Kant even offers the definition of "taste" as "disinterested judgment."

The parks are born of the dramatic, playful, holistic hyperbole of the video arts as contrasted with the cool, detached, analytical mentality of print media and traditional glass-case exhibit. As McLuhan noted in the *Medium is the Massage* (1967), environments out of the past become the content of new art forms. Thus the turn-of-the-century Main Street, USA, complete with gazebo and gaslights, becomes the retrograde symbol for the high-tech parks, with the even more ancient medieval castle centered as the crown jewel and polar star. In a similar vein, Disney nature films of the 1950s came to prominence just as the country was moving out of the countryside to regroup in city and suburb.[7] Both genres have been prime movers in the public's fascination with American history and with ecological issues.

Innovating on a popular culture stage rather than in an avant-garde studio, the Disney "Imagineers" have been leading-edge instigators in researching and developing concepts in the enchanted terrain between art and science. Examples are the arts of audio-animatronics (called "animation in the round"), applications of computers to problems in communication and exhibition, new uses of video disk, electronics, and fiber optics, the remaking of historic artifacts by advanced engineering, the melding of space-age with neotraditional forms and functions, and the future-planning orientation of all park features. This innovation has a very human dimension as well. Walt Disney Seminars is a prominent player in management, marketing, and communications education and consulting, an "excellence" company at the forefront of training school, hotel, hospital, and museum executives as well as front-line workers in a variety of service industries.

In this vein is EPCOT, the Experimental Prototype Community of Tomorrow, at Walt Disney World. Originally planned as a residential community of 20,000, EPCOT combined some of the most advanced thinking in consumer science and ergonomics. Architect Peter Blake remarked in *Architectural Forum*, "Not even Corbusier at his brashest ever proposed anything so daring" (Blake 1972, 28).

History and Historiography

Just as the arts have been transformed by science, so have our shared concepts of history been put to the critical test by the "death of history." Vattimo's *The End of Modernity* asks what, at the end of the doctrine of Progress, awaits us? New doctrines are developing—not out of test-tube labs, but at "living history labs" like EPCOT's Future World, and shared symbols of designed environments like Main Street, USA, the gateways to the Disney parks East and West. Richard Francaviglia describes the importance of these recreations as symbol-places to be valued and appreciated as archetypal American experiences—especially in an age in which shared national identity has been weakened at the center and is under many pressures and, many feel, is reaching a breakdown (or meltdown) point (Francaviglia 1981, 141–56). The shared "anamnestic (memory assisting) response" elicited by the parks forms an important bond.

Part of this new tension between past and present is the sheer volume of data with which we are now faced and forced to deal; turning the massive overload of data into intelligence is a prime project for modern man, with pressure points aimed directly on the opinion leaders: our academic institutions, political advisors, and directors of informal education, including museum manager, publisher, religious spokesman, and network executive.

Everywhere there is a great need for more effective ways to organize and process information. The "knowledge clusters" of exhibits such as science (Living Seas, World of Motion, Wonders of Life), and communications (Communicore), provide a tactile, visual, and kinetic message about recent science information—as does, in a very immediate manner, the monorail, Mission to Mars, and Space Mountain. Other examples are actual scientific experimentation such as plant cloning in "The Land," which U.S. Secretary of Agriculture Richard Lyng called "the cutting edge of biotechnology" at its dedication in 1988.

The Future

Philadelphia's Franklin Institute Futures Center, opened in 1990, is a design parallel to EPCOT's Future World pavilions following the Disney Method. This $58 million project spearheads the Institute's new momentum (actually a return to its original nineteenth-century mission) toward "an active education." Momentum has been fueled by *A Nation at Risk*, the Presidential Commission's 1983 report calling for a stepped-up science education (McKenna 1989, 1).

Historian Kenneth Keniston's incisive essay, "Stranded in the Present" (Keniston 1970, 40–43), describes the alienation of youth in the transformational 1960s as a function of alienation from history—both past and future. He diagnoses this modern malady as "asynchrony," time sickness, or the psychological loss of connection between generations in an age when the present is so radically different from the past that links to the future are either eroded or invisible. What is needed, Keniston suggests, are techniques beyond simply adapting to change. We need more: to find a way to assimilate change. This much taller order calls upon more universal and eloquent responses than our artists, scientists, or historians have been asked to give us in the past. In answer to these problems in historiography and in personal and social neurosis, this technique must be capable of mediating the "anxiety of historical dislocation" that has accompanied unguided technological and social change. We are planning now for a future that will be obsolete by the time we get there. This technique resides in what Keniston calls "aesthetic outlook," the translation of history into art—one of Disney's outstanding characteristics. (Think also of the many Disney history films, costume dramas that have brought the past to life in the popular imagination.)

Theme parks offer an intelligible stability in a world where change has become the rule, not the exception—and the pace of change has accelerated at mindbending rates. In addition, as a leading intergenerational learning laboratory, they answer many of the concerns of the generation gap. Two-, three- and four-generation tour groups come away from the Magic Kingdom and EPCOT with a new bond.

Change Management

In the theme park, historical and cultural archetypes set up a framework of reassurance, creating a safety zone amid the barrage of change. Vital to our mental health is coping with the great *terra incognita* of the future (including the near future), surely an educational issue of critical importance. Disney's response is a form of effective change management operating in part on the subconscious level of audience awareness. The wide acceptance and support commanded by the realms of Disney is an indication that they are connecting on too many levels and at too many points to be a mere diversion.

What are the key topics with survival value for modern living? An audit of leading themes at Disney's worlds tells the story:

Spatial: The technology of Future World, Tomorrowland
Temporal: History, collective and personal (Adventureland, Frontierland, American Adventure, Main Street, USA, World Showcase)
Psychological: Change and mobility (Future World) in time and space (World Showcase)
Informational: Social, psychic, cross-cultural (Future World, Fantasyland, Tomorrowland, Disney/MGM Studios)

In our world where the possibility of "staying ahead" has long ago disappeared beyond reach, just to know what is going on at any given time and place is an achievement of some magnitude. We can easily identify with Holden Caulfield in Salinger's *Catcher in the Rye* on his return to the New York Natural History Museum to assure himself that the hunter and deer in the prehistoric diorama are still in position as seen on his childhood visits. We are all feeling to some extent like aliens in our own age and country. The trend in "fish-out-of-water" films like *Back to the Future* testifies to a collective identity crisis.

Theme parks both supplement and compete with museums as stabilizers in this flux of modern change. This makes them especially interesting places to re-visit after having grown up in them. The entire baby boom generation is now in the process of discovering the drama in the "before" and "after" experience and impressions. As the theme park anticipates the future and plunges us into "then," carrying us all with it, it is interesting to note that certain features must in fact be updated. Thus the once-futuristic "Flight to

115

the Moon" (Disneyland) was forced further out into the cosmos as "Mission to Mars" after the moon landing had become history. For the same reason, the "House of the Future" in Tomorrowland quickly become outmoded as one of yesterday's tomorrows. An Innovations Plaza, including a Home of the Future, is planned for EPCOT in mid-1994.

Post-EPCOT "enclaves of the future," as Alvin Toffler calls them, will have the opportunity to take a lead in futurology by "reverting" to EPCOT's original conception as residential community—a fully functioning experimental "try-out" behavioral laboratory for new hard- and software, with everything from video telephones to home computer networks to moving sidewalks, solar power, and electronic elections.

Popular Culture and Tradition

While the parks are giving us the future, they also have been exemplary in restoring to public life many of the features—and with them, values—now banished from our megacities and suburbs (King 1981).[8] Very few American cities can boast horse-drawn streetcars, outdoor cafes, boats and waterways, topiary landscaping, and a leisurely and safe pedestrian way of life. Along its now-famous River Walk, the city of San Antonio, Texas, has re-introduced walking, boating, and sidewalk dining to the heart of a major American metropolis. To this exercise in applied civic themeing, public acclamation has been resounding.

The Disney Experience continues to influence much else in America and now (with Tokyo and Paris models) international life, including the look and feel of our cities, public places, and learning environments. The universality of this tour (along with the integration of television into every aspect of daily life) is the backdrop against which all other attractions must be plotted. The contemporary "grand tour" around the global village could well be a procession from theme park to theme park as self-image crystal balls of far-flung world cultures. Given this premise, there is little practical sense in talking about museum-going, formal education, government programs, or any other communication-rich institution as independent of popular culture and its demands and effects.

Within the wraparound Circlevision or audioanimatronic theaters in Disney's Magic Kingdoms, transporting us to China, the Living Seas, prehistoric forests, or deep inside the mysteries of the human body, there is no distancing oneself from the images, movement, color, and music. These are totally enveloping experiences, sensory and mental, as close to "being there" as can be achieved without teleportation.

Popular culture works as the intermediary between history and its audience, the symbiosis of media event and artifact/architecture in which each feeds on and into the other in creative interplay. These parks are a living demonstration of how popular culture and history can be mutually reinforcing, supporting, and educational. It is never an "either/or" situation, even in the most seemingly "diametric" situations. As a case in point, in a recent issue of *American Heritage*, managing editor Richard Snow's acutely evocative essay on Disneyland attributes to his visit there at age ten a lifelong interest and career in history, calling Disney's Main Street, USA "[a] triumph of historical imagination" (Snow 1987, 22–24). Moving toward the same aesthetic of engagement are the surrogate artifacts, hands-on, and interactive exhibits now part of museum and classroom learning. Disney's sense of intuition, risk-taking, and planning had much to do with setting these wheels in motion.

Archetypes

Comparisons with "literal restoration" history sites such as Williamsburg, Greenfield Village, and Slater's Mill are unavoidable. But in fact it is Disney's imaginative reconstructions, his archetypes based on stereotypes, that have served as inspiration for the Main Street architectural revivals of the 1970s. This renaissance was institutionalized as the 1977 Main Street program pioneered by the National Trust for Historic Preservation.[9] The use of archetypes is an intriguing aspect of themeing, because while they engage the visitor by drawing on and linking up with a built-in and built-up set of images about the world, including arts, cultures, peoples, and history, they must also somehow transcend that "flashpoint" to move on into deeper instruction.

The parks are an object lesson in the popular need for a shared vision and symbols of the past as well as of other places; the need to update these visions to express the cosmology of the present; and their attractiveness as a tangible index to ideas. It is no accident that the future should play its starring role at EPCOT in the late twentieth century.

There is an especially active debate around culture parks like the World Showcase at EPCOT, the Polynesian Culture Center, and "real-life" re-creations such as Sturbridge Village. It is within such "hyper-real" environments that the education staff—curator, education director, and exhibit designer—must deliberate on how to carry this focus forward and to fruition once the audience has been effectively captured.

Romanticized and fictional evocations have long enjoyed a lofty status in novels, plays, poetry, painting, architecture, and film. In their new manifestation "in the round," they now deserve re-evaluation as important historiocultural mediators.

The archetypes within themed environments can advise as well as caution in this endeavor (the forced foreshortening of time and space in Adventureland and Frontierland are obvious instances). At a museum directors' planning meeting held at Walt Disney World, Francois Barre, Grand Halle Director at Parc La Villette science museum in Paris, described the Disney World experience as one in which visitors can "rediscover their own memories, even fantasies. They are immersed in a universe where everything was at once true and false; false because it consisted only of background and illusion, but true because it existed in everyone's heart and dreams. It was not just an amusement park, but an environment stimulating new ideas" (Schoener 1988, 39).

The problem with the past is that it must be assimilated with the psychic equipment of the present. History is unruly, rampaging, inscrutable, and inaccessible. Public education faces this problem on a vast scale on a daily routine. The task seems to be, at its source, one of communication: taking the raw materials of information and artifacts to weave them into patterns that are orderly, beautiful, engaging, true.

In any event, at whatever level, the picture windows into the past must be set on the terms of the visitor, not the educator. Walt Disney's greatest asset in this regard was his close and unwavering identification with his audience. He was always one of them and never withdrew to a position above the crowd, except perhaps in his charmingly civic conceit of reserving a private apartment for himself above the firehouse on Disneyland's Main Square.

William Thompson, in *At the Edge of History*, pinpointed the cosmic place of the theme park: "Disneyland is the technological cathedral of the 20th century, as the Gothic cathedral summed up the world in the medieval town" (21). An ironic measure of Disney's place in the American mind is the answer to the question of what man-made structure can be seen from the moon. The response is just as often "Spaceship Earth at Walt Disney World" (Buckminster Fuller's geodesic globe at the entrance of Future World) as the correct answer, which is the Great Wall of China. Of course it is understood that the universe is now far more expanded, less knowable, and more uncertain than ever, mainly because of man's efforts to control and re-create it. Theme parks are a superb response to this principle, a glowing showcase of the inside of our own minds. They are full of clues for the pursuit of what historian David Lowenthal has termed the "search for sensibility." The prime job of the modern historian ("The past is a foreign country"[10]) is the exploration of ways of seeing, thinking, and feeling that have shaped the past and are molding the present.

Engagement

Philosopher Arnold Berleant, in a book titled *The Art of Engagement*,[11] studies problems of presentation and experience in public environments. In an interview discussing his book, Berleant expresses the frustration of "museum fatigue" in this way: "No matter how interesting, I can't spend over an hour and a half in a museum. I always go home exhausted. There must be a better way to interact with collections" (personal interview, April 1989). There have to be better, less taxing ways to an exhibit-assisted education—and the key will lie in the entertainment modalities that theme parks have been affording their "guests," Disney's term for visitors, which he used advisedly. While even one hour may be considered a long time to spend in a museum (the North American average is actually close to just fifty minutes), visitors routinely spend eight hours or longer strolling, sitting, eating, riding, and otherwise enjoying theme-park environments. It is not unusual to find family or friends spending an unbroken *week* hard at play at Walt Disney World and EPCOT—and then returning home to remark how sorry they are that there wasn't time to see it all! Returning visitors are a major factor in the unbeatable attendance records (twenty-five million a year at Walt Disney World) at these places.

Theme parks must process incredible numbers of visitors per day—and at increasing rates. Recently, Walt Disney World's gates have had to close at mid-morning because of capacity conditions. But by ingenious planning and management of space, light, and noise control, they manage to avoid many of the problems museums and other exhibitors are experiencing as a result of oversubscription, especially in the intimate intensity of science "discovery centers." Of particular concern to science parks is the difficulty of controlling hands-on exhibits that require concentrated one-on-one activity—especially difficult with those who stand most to benefit from them: school groups. "These exhibits are built for one-on-one, not 3,000 on one," says Wendy Pollack at the Association of Science-Technology Centers (ASTC).

One of the problems of designing good exhibits is just this situation: the more absorbing and personal, the more difficult to access. One solution to this problem posed at the theme parks is in the "dark rides," transporting the rider on an intimate and close-up "trip" through the exhibit in two-seat trams wired for sound. These modules give a feeling of privacy and "up-close" vision while they cut to almost nothing the feeling of crowding and competition for personal space and visibility that can compromise the best-laid exhibit design. For example, in the new exhibit "Body Wars" in the Wonders of Life pavilion sponsored by MetLife at EPCOT, the audience is "shrunk" to take a "Fantastic Voyage" through the human body via film and flight simulation technology. A neighboring attraction, "Cranium Command," takes viewers on a strange tour through the workings of the brain of a twelve-year-old boy.

On the broad scale, within the sprawling megapark of indoor-outdoor "museumettes" at the Disney parks and EPCOT, visitor movement is very skillfully engineered: more so for being inobvious and invisible. The radius of walkways, paved with a rubber compound to lessen foot stress, is one strategy for sidestepping the chaos that could so easily be loosed upon these places with the wrong systems in place. The genius of the plan is that within any single theme area no "foreign" theme is allowed to intrude, reducing the "overchoice" or information overload that can plague the visitor who feels he [sic] is being offered too much at a time on too many plates—attractive as each one may be (a common complaint at World's Fairs, for example). The central medieval castle stands alone above other monuments as a navigator's point. This is more than security and crowd control. It is an aesthetic of comfort and freedom as an answer to the challenges of urban congestion. The result is a national "field of care," places charged with feeling, fondness, and connection for us all.

Evaluation

Assessment of the learning process is another vogue in which Disney, on a somewhat different front, has led the way. The lessons of the theme parks have already proven to be of unexpected but welcome assistance in addressing these problems.

In 1979 the National Science Foundation held a special symposium for science museums, at which a marketing researcher for Walt Disney World was invited to speak. The museum participants were somewhat astonished to learn Disney's annual budget for this activity—$1.5 million for visitor studies, including regular schedules for indexes from zip-code data to in-depth profiles. "At that point, museums were paying very little attention to their visitors, and a lot to their donors," says Minda Borun, Assistant Director of Programs at the Franklin Institute. "Over the past ten years, that has turned around." Now that museums increasingly depend on admissions income, the emphasis has begun to swivel considerably. Following the lead of theme parks, a consumer orientation is setting the tone for the way museums are reorienting along customer-service lines. They are asking how well their exhibits and programs are teaching and what they can do to reach more people more effectively. These are marketing questions. Museums, along with churches, university presses, orchestras, and arts councils, are learning to think like businesses—in patterns already etched by the great entertainment centers Disney founded.

The stakes for theme parks, major cultural institutions, and education alike are somewhat similar in that all are "big-ticket items" within their categories. Marketing studies show that high quality (with a learning component) can motivate people to drive farther, pay higher entry fees, plan longer, and defer other purchases. With recent price hikes at both theme parks and colleges, there seems to be no limit to what the consumer is willing to pay for such "quality" experiences.

The Greying of America

The nontraditional student is the newest target audience for higher education, and is here to stay. A glance at the demographics for the coming century should be instructive in correcting the notion that theme parks are attractive mainly to families and to school groups. With the upward trend of life expectancy, already the ratio of adults to children in museums (science, leisure time) is over three to two (Source: ASTC). Contrary to their stereotype as a child's fantasy world, the Disney parks have always hosted far more adults than children—by a ratio of over four to one. An interesting sidenote is that EPCOT reports a median age a full seven years higher than Disney World in general (Dychtwald 1988, 133). Disney World's mammoth scale, its vast acreage, and multitude of options including new mini-parks such as Pleasure Island and Typhoon Lagoon, has led many visitors to view it as an adults-only experience and to leave the children at home. Increasingly, institutions of all types will be serving an older client base. By the year 2025, the Population Reference Bureau predicts, Americans over sixty-five will outnumber teenagers by two to one (1988, 21).

The upcoming generation of older culture consumers, the baby boomers, will be the largest in history, and this is a cohort born and bred not only to continuing education in all its forms but to the theme park (where continuing education for credit is, in fact, now being offered).

Disney also offers its own brand of education. For adults (over sixteen), there are special lecture tours: "Hidden Treasures of the World Showcase," and "Gardens of the World." There are continuing education programs for credit in conjunction with Florida State University in Marketing and Communication. The Earth Shuttle Program offers class trips through EPCOT with special lesson plans. For ten to fifteen-year-olds, there are the Wonders of Walt Disney World Program specializing in arts, nature, and entertainment.

In addition, EPCOT outreach and the EPCOT Teachers' Center provide a host of resources—print and electronic—to educators and students to extend the learning curve initiated by the parks. A computer-driven exchange network for educators is up and running but looking for wider and better applications than just "teacher network." These efforts are all part of Disney's "continuing commitment to excellence in education," according to the brochure phrasing.

Presentation philosophy as taught by Disney, together with the whole cadre of themeing means and motifs, can flex to fill in the many gaps that continue to pop open between what is taught and what needs to be learned. With the era of chalk and primer already far behind, the whole panoply of popular culture—private, nonprofit, business, and public—offers itself as a rich and accessible research collection.

Properly plumbed and connected, the resources of the theme park offer exciting channels for the transformation of education into the well-rounded, interactive, and integrated adventure it must become in modern life.

Notes

* The author wishes to thank Professor Reuel Denney for his generous assistance in reading and commenting on this chapter.

1. Roger Rollin, "The Death of Good Taste." Revised version of a public lecture sponsored by the Clemson University Architectural Foundation, Clemson, SC, 1987.

2. Rod Murray, Director of the Office of Academic Computing, made this observation in his Nov. 1989 progress report to the Thomas Jefferson University Medical College (Philadelphia) based on the university archival collection.

3. Disney has been particularly instrumental as a "translator" of European children's literature into American plots and images (as can be seen in Fantasyland) to the extent that many Americans believe these tales to be original Disney creations. Disney's creation and recycling of American heroes is another key study: see Margaret J. King, "The Davy Crockett Craze: A Case Study in Popular Culture." Doctoral dissertation, Dept. of American Studies, University of Hawaii, 1976.

4. See for example "The Museum as Hypermedium," "Museums as Bridges to the Global Village," "Museums in the Marketplace," "EPCOT Centre in Museological Perspective," and "The Canadian Museum of Civilization: A Museum for the Global Village" (1987–89).

5. See also M. King, "The Theme Park Experience," World Futures Society special issue, *Tomorrow's Museums* (Washington, DC) Nov./Dec. 1991: 24–31.

6. The director of a cultural museum reported to me that he visited the Bishop Museum of ethnology in Honolulu while he shunned the Polynesian Culture Center, the largest single attraction in the islands, and the main source of popular impressions and beliefs about Polynesia. He came home without ever experiencing the most important source of ideas on his museum's subject area!

7. See Reuel Denney's new Introduction to the reissue of *The Astonished Muse* (New Brunswick, NJ: Transaction Publishers, 1989), for his discussion of animals in American civilization. "In the cinematic media, no one has paid greater attention to animals—first in cartoons and later in natural form—than Walt Disney" (lvii).

8. See also William F. Whyte on the destruction of inner-city pedestrian values.

9. Richard Francaviglia discusses this topic in "After Walt Disney: The Role of Historic Image-Building in the Preservation and Revitalization of Main Street U.S.A.," paper presented at the annual meeting of the Organization of American Historians, St Louis, MO, Apr. 1989.

10. See J. P. Hartley, *The Go-Between* (Penguin, 1999 [1953]).
11. A condensed version appears as a chapter, "Experience and Theory in Aesthetics," in *Possibility of the Aesthetic Experience*, ed. M. H. Mitias (Dordrecht, Netherlands: Martinus Nijheff, 1986).

References

Beard, Richard. 1982. *Epcot Center: Creating the New World of Tomorrow*. New York: Harry Abrams.

Berleant, Arnold. 1991. *The Art of Engagement*. Philadelphia: Temple University Press.

Blake, Peter. 1972. "The Lessons of the Parks." *Architectural Forum* (June): 28.

Bloom, Allan. 1987. *Closing of the American Mind*. New York: Simon and Schuster.

Carson, Rachel. 1962. *Silent Spring*. New York: Houghton-Mifflin.

Commission on Museums for a New Century. 1984. *Museums for a New Century*. Washington, D.C.: American Association of Museums.

Dychtwald, Ken. 1988. *Age Wave: The Challenges and Opportunities of an Aging America*. Los Angeles: Tarcher.

Francaviglia, Richard. 1981. "Main Street, U.S.A.: A Comparison/Contrast of Streetscapes in Disneyland and Walt Disney World." *Journal of Popular Culture*. Summer: 141–56.

Keniston, Kenneth. 1976. "Stranded in the Present." In *Varieties of Psychohistory*, ed. George M. Kren and Leon H. Rappaport, 251–56. New York: Springer.

King, Margaret J. 1981. "Disneyland and Walt Disney World: Traditional Values in Futuristic Form." *Journal of Popular Culture*. Summer: 116–40.

—1990. "Theme Park Thesis." *Museum News*. Sept.–Oct.: 60–62.

—1991. "Disneyfication: Some Pros and Cons of Theme Parks." *Museum* (Paris: ICOM-JUNESCO). Winter: 6–8.

McKenna, Brian. 1989. "The Franklin Institute: Selling the Future." *Philadelphia City Paper* 231 (Jan. 13–20): 1.

McLuhan, Marshall. 1967. *The Medium is the Massage*. Harmondsworth: Penguin.

Paulos, John Allen. 1988. *Innumeracy: Mathematical Illiteracy and its Consequences*. New York: Hill & Wang.

Petit, Robert B. 1986. "Disney Theme Parks as Shrines of the American Civil Religion." Popular Culture Association annual meeting, Atlanta, GA.

Schickel, Richard. 1968. *The Disney Version*. New York: Simon & Schuster.

Schoener, Allan. 1988. "Can Museums Learn from Mickey and Friends?" *New York Times* (Oct. 30): 38–39.

Snow, Richard. 1987. "Disney Coast to Coast." *American Heritage* (Feb./Mar.): 22–24.

Thompson, William. 1971. *At the Edge of History*. New York: Harper & Row.

Toffler, Alvin. *A Future Shock*. London: Pan Books.

Torrance, E. Paul, and Kathy Goff. 1989. "A Quiet Revolution." *Journal of Creative Behavior* 23.2: 139–40.

Vattimo, Gianni. 1988. *The End of Modernity: Nihilism and Hermeneutics in Postmodern Culture*. Cambridge: Polity Press.

Wallace, Michael. 1989. "Mickey Mouse History: Portraying the Past at Disney World." In *History Museums in the United States*, ed. Warren Leon and Roy Rosenzweig, 158–80. Urbana: University of Illinois Press.

Whyte, William. 1990. *City: Rediscovering the Center*. New York: Anchor Books.

PROBLEMATIZING PERFORMANCE

Edward L. Schieffelin

Editor's Introduction

Edward Schieffelin is Emeritus Professor of Anthropology at University College London. His research interests could be described as being about both outer and inner dimensions of ritual and belief. He has researched and published not only on "ritual and performance" but also on ethnopyschology and emotions. He is also engaged by other contested relationships and encounters, for example those between NGOs, politicians, missions, resource extraction companies and tropical forest peoples of Papua New Guinea.

While previous chapters have already introduced questions about the relationship between ritual and other kinds of performance, Schieffelin's chapter is devoted to such matters. However, it is not only details about actions and how they are practised or enacted that are discussed here. Schieffelin is interested in the notion of performance itself as it has been used in social-science debates and in broader, conventional western understandings. In particular, relationships between "performer" and "audience" or between "performers" and "participants" is at the centre of this problematizing of the notion of performance. Do performers deceive (intentionally or otherwise) those who observe and are, perhaps, acted upon by what performers do? At what point and in what ways might performers present reality to other people? Are rituals and other acts "simply" representative or do they present actual realities? What if an actor or ritualist "merely" acts their part, let alone acts with intent to deceive or cast an illusion, rather than sincerely believing in that which they present or articulate? Schieffelin is insistent that the social construction of reality is centrally implicated in performances and that the kind of issues raised by performance, performers and participants deserve more sustained consideration in academia. In this, the authors and works referred to in this chapter will be of enormous value.

ℰℭ

Introduction

In the last ten or fifteen years anthropologists interested in cultural perfor-mances (religious rituals, political pageants, folk entertainments, curing ceremonies, spirit seances and so on) have moved increasingly away from studying them as systems of representations (symbolic transformations, cul-tural texts) to looking at them as processes of practice and performance. In part this reflects a growing dissatisfaction with purely symbolic approaches to understanding material like rituals, which seem to be curiously robbed of life and power when distanced in discussions concerned largely with mean-ing. "Performance" deals with actions more than text: with habits of the body more than structures of symbols, with illocutionary rather than propositional force, with the social construction of reality rather than its representation.

Performance is also concerned with something that anthropologists have always found hard to characterize theoretically: the creation of presence. Performances, whether ritual or dramatic, create and make present realities vivid enough to beguile, amuse or terrify. And through these presences, they alter moods, social relations, bodily dispositions and states of mind.

As is not unusual with a new direction in anthropology, there is a ten-dency for us to head enthusiastically in pursuit without carefully considering fundamental epistemological issues. What precisely (if that is possible) do we mean by "performance," where does the concept come from, and what bag-gage—as well as benefit—does its usage bring to the discipline?

"Performance" in Social Science

The notion of "performance" has been used in essentially two ways in social science. The first refers to particular "symbolic" or "aesthetic" activities, such as ritual or theatrical and folk artistic activities, which are enacted as inten-tional expressive productions in established local genres. "Performance" in this usage refers to bounded, intentionally produced enactments which are (usually) marked and set off from ordinary activities, and which call attention to themselves as particular productions with special purposes or qualities for the people who observe or perform them.

Following this view, Bauman (1986) characterizes performance as a display of expressive competence or virtuosity by one or more performers addressed to an audience. Such performances aim to evoke an imaginative reality or an intensification of experience among the spectators, and bring about an altered awareness of their situation and/or a sense of emotional release. "Performance" in this usage refers to the particular kind of performative event treated as an aesthetic whole in a larger social context. Studies of this focus on the structure of such events, the means by which they are carried out (or have their effect), and their relation to social context.

The second usage of "performance" in social science is associated with the work of Erving Goffman (Goffman 1959) and the symbolic interactionist school. The focus here is not on a type of event but rather on performativity itself: the expressive processes of strategic impression management and structured improvisation through which human beings normally articulate their purposes, situations and relationships in everyday social life. Here the notion of performance converges with implications of theories of practice, a topic we will return to in due course. The point to be made here is that both of these anthropological usages of "performance" (or "performativity") draw their inspiration and conceptual terminology from the western notions of theatrical performance: either specific cultural genres such as rituals are seen as analogous to theatrical performances, or everyday activities can be seen as brought off through expressive processes analogous to those by which imaginative realities are produced on the stage.

Before exploring the limitations of extending such theatrical concepts into anthropology, it is useful to expand a bit on what I see as the value, indeed the enormous power and potential, of the notion of "performance" in our discipline. I believe there is something fundamentally performative about human being-in-the-world. As Goffman has suggested (1959), human intentionality, culture and social reality are fundamentally articulated in the world through performative activity. When human beings come into the presence of one another, they do so expressively, establishing consensus on who they are and what their situation is about through voice, gesture, facial expression, bodily posture and action. Common values or at least working agreements about social identity and purpose are established between people not so much through rational discourse as through complex and subtle expressive manoeuvres that create an atmosphere of trust and a sense of mutual expectations.

Carried to the extreme, it would not be too much to say that without living human bodily expressivity, conversation and social presence, there would be no culture and no society. The ponderous social institutions and mighty political and economic forces of late capitalism which weigh so heavily upon us are, like illusions of maya, without any reality except in so far as they or their effects are actually and continually engaged and emergent in human discourse, practice and activity in the world: generated in what human beings say and do. It is because human sociality continues in moment-by-moment existence only as human purposes and practices are performatively articulated in the world that performance is (or should be) of fundamental interest to anthropology.

Performance as Contingent Process

Performance (of either kind above) is often thought of as characterized by conscious intent. In a recent work Humphrey and Laidlaw (1994) differentiate between "ritualization" and performance as distinct modalities of action on this basis. "Ritualization" in their formulation refers not to a type of event but to the attitude of consciousness with which it is carried out. In particular the "ritual" attitude refers to a mode of consciousness in which "acts are felt by those who perform them to be external to their intention": a person submits to ritual activity in such a way as to "remove the sovereignty of herself as agent" (1994, 96), experiencing herself or himself rather in the manner of the object or the vehicle of the pre-ordained acts she or he performs. The person carries out (or rather undergoes) her or his own enactments in the mode of automatic habitual practice with little ego-involvement.

Humphrey and Laidlaw explicitly exclude "performance" from their discussion of "ritualization," considering it to be quintessentially an activity involving conscious purposiveness and self-direction (1994, 10). In so doing, they exclude perhaps three-quarters of those activities that anthropologists have traditionally considered as rituals (1994, 10).[1] Susanna Rostas (1998) seeks a middle ground by attempting to co-ordinate a notion of performance with Humphrey and Laidlaw's "ritualization." She associates performance (or performativity) with the "extra energy" or expressivity one puts into an act to raise its meaning to something more than its ordinary significance in everyday practice—giving it a non-conventional, "creative" edge, and enhancing (or changing) its significance or using it as a vehicle for meaning. As with Humphrey and Laidlaw, performativity essentially entails intention: "the deployment of consciously formulated strategies. It implies individuality ... [and] it can be seen as creative" (Rostas, 1998).

I should mention, at this point, that I am uneasy with both of these formulations. In the first place I am uneasy with a differentiation of human activity that turns primarily on privileging the performers' internal state of mind or mode of consciousness (ego-involvement or personal intention) and downplays their interaction with others. This is not to say that a person's internal attitude is not important (indeed it can largely determine the meaning of the interaction), but, as Rostas notes, it is almost impossible, in practice, to separate ritualized from performative aspects of human action on this basis. Moreover, while the role personal intentions play in performative action can be highly important, it is by no means clear that it ultimately differentiates "performance" from "ritualized" action (as formulated above). Indeed one can question whether "performance" or "performative" action necessarily entails conscious intention at all. This may be clarified through one of Rostas's examples:

> Take washing up: this is precisely the kind of action that is done ritual-istically; it is done frequently, usually in the same way, with attention but not conscious intention, other than that of getting the dishes clean, which has become an embodied, habitual activity. If someone carries out this action rather more dramatically ... with expansive movements and rather amusingly or angrily, for example, then we might want to classify this as "performance," and look more closely at the performa-tivity, the non-conventionality of the act. (Rostas, 1998)

Now it may be that the furrowed brow and/or the clattering and banging of the dishes in the sink constitute a conscious and intentional display of emotion by the dish washer, but is there really a necessity for this? It may simply be that he or she is upset or elated and this is the way the washing gets done when the washer is in-the-world-feeling fully, without entailing any expressive intent or even awareness of self-revelatory behaviour. If this is the case, it cannot be "performance" (by the criteria of intention). But neither would it seem to be "ritualization" (though Humphrey and Laidlaw do not really deal with the question of the status of a ritualized act that might be performed unwillingly or exuberantly by the actor whose actions it authors). However, the expressed emotion in the washing up is tangible and readily analysable in performative terms (a Goffman-type exercise), as Rostas points out. What this example really reveals, I would suggest, is the expressivity (and hence performativity) inherent in any human activity in everyday life, which renders our actions communicative and effective to others in our situations whether we mean them to be or not. We are, in effect, more performative than we intend, and we are in good measure "submitted to" our performativity as part of our active being-in-the-world.[2]

Every act has an expressive dimension: it reveals something (and accomplishes something) about the actor and the situation. It is "read" by other participants. We act both for ourselves and in the eyes of our beholders. The issue here is not that our expressivity is not entirely under our control, but rather that it (also) belongs to the situation. If we strive for expressive control in everyday life and in special "performance" situations, this is *ipso facto* part of our act of participation in the situation and our contribution to its determination, process and outcome—whether or not what others see us to be doing (or revealing) is what we intend them to see.

It follows from this that any performance (indeed any performative activity) is inherently a contingent process. In some part this resides in the socio-historical circumstances in which it takes place and to which it relates. But, for the participants and their observers, a great deal of contingency resides in whether the performance itself is "properly carried out," whether it "works." Everything (in ritual no less than theatre), from the observance of the correct procedures to the resonance of the symbolism, the heightening of emotion, the sense of transformation, all depend on whether the performers and other participants can "bring it off." It is always possible the performance may fail. Thus "performance" is always inherently *interactive*, and fundamentally *risky*.[3] Amongst the various people involved (who often have different agendas) there is always something aesthetically and/or practically at stake, and something can always go wrong (Schieffelin 1995).

The burden of success or failure in a cultural performance is usually laid on the central actors, but the real location of this problem (and of the meaning of the terms "actor," "spectator," "participant") is the *relationship* between the central performers and others in the situation. In western theatrical performance, this is the relationship between actors and audience. We will return to this important issue shortly.

Finally, a performance is always something accomplished: it is an achievement in the world. This is reflected in the borrowing of the term in sports or business discourse, such as, "Jones performed well in sales this month"[4] or "Smith's poor performance cost Enfield the game." Here the connotations of "performance" move somewhat beyond the domain of expressive culture, but preserve its presentational resonances by carrying a connotation of "making a showing" which is accountable to the evaluation of others. We are talking here not only about the achievement in bringing such a performance off successfully, but also about the accomplishment of the work it was meant to do.

Performance and Text

The character of performance as accomplishment, together with its interactive quality and element of risk, make it easy to differentiate it from the notion of "text." Although some scholars have written as though performance could be treated as a form of text, in my view performance can never be text, and its unique strategic properties are destroyed when it is considered as, or reduced to, text. To be sure, performances share some qualities with texts. They have beginnings, middles and ends, they have internal structure, may refer to themselves, etc. But it is precisely the performativity of performance for which there is no analogue in text. Unlike text, performances are ephemeral. They create their effects and then are gone—leaving their reverberations (fresh insights, reconstituted selves, new statuses, altered realities) behind them. Performances are a living social activity, by necessity assertive, strategic and not fully predictable. While they refer to the past and plunge towards the future, they exist only in the present. Texts are changeless and enduring. One may return to the same text for a new reading, but a performance which one goes to see again is not the same as yesterday's. While texts and performances may be produced out of one another, this is very different from saying they are reducible to one another. Text can never be "duplicated" in performance, and performance is not reducible to text (whether script, directors' notes or ethnographic description). Still, ethnographic accounts can usefully attend to (and meditate upon) those particular properties of performances through which they produce their various modes of social reality and articulate the human world.

Performance and Practice

Much of what we have just said about performances has been said by anthropologists of "practices"—and the relationship is a close one. The term "practice" focuses on that aspect of human life and activity which is structured largely through unquestioned, unthought habit, through which human beings normally carry out the business of living both in everyday life and in important strategic situations. Practices have an internal "logic" of their own, which provides the strategic rationality or purposive orderliness of "the way things are done" in most ordinary cultural activity. Collectively, practices form the shape of the unthought behavioural regularities of a cultural world, which Bourdieu has called the habitus (Bourdieu 1977). Practices can be said to emerge from this ground of habitude in the form of structured or "regulated" improvisations when people deal with the situations in which they are involved in customary practical ways. Practices always emerge as improvisations because situations and the people that participate in them are always only analogous to each other; they are never exactly the same (Bourdieu 1977, 83).

The relation between performance and practice turns on this moment of improvisation: performance embodies the *expressive dimension of the strategic articulation of practice*. The italicized expression here could stand as our definition of performativity itself. It is manifest in the expressive aspect of the "way" something is done on a particular occasion: the particular orchestration of the pacing, tension, evocation, emphasis, mode of participation, etc., in the way a practice (at that moment) is "practised," that is, "brought off." It gives the particular improvisation of a practice in a particular situation its particular turn of significance and efficacy for oneself and others at the time—in the moment where habitude becomes action.

Thus performativity is located at the creative, *improvisatory* edge of practice in the moment it is carried out—though everything that comes across is not necessarily consciously intended.

We could go on—but it should again be clear that the concepts "performance"/"performativity" have the potential to open a considerable domain for anthropological exploration of the way that cultures actively construct their realities. It should also be clear that whether regarded as contingent self-presentation or expressive edge of practice, the process of performance, the power of performativity, turns crucially on its interactive edge, and hence on the nature of the relationship between "performers" and others in the situation to whom the performance is directed, or (in the West) "the audience." And here, at least in conventional anthropology, we encounter a significant epistemological stumbling block: the popular western notion of theatre.

The Theatrical Relation between Performer and Spectator in Social Science

For most middle-class western academics with average experience of attending theatrical performances, the notion of live performance conjures up an image of actors on a stage. Fundamental to this image is the division between (relatively active) performers and (relatively passive, but emotionally responsive) audience. In Euro-American (basically Aristotelian) tradition this divide is also a metaphysical, even ontological, one between a world of spectators which is real and a world conjured up by performers which is not, or more precisely, which has another kind of reality: a virtual or imaginary one. Schechner summarizes the basic idea with his remark: "acting means make-believe, illusion, lying ... In America we say someone's 'only acting' when we detect the seams between the performance and the non-acting surround" (Schechner 1982, 63). Although we appreciate the power and message of performance illusion, and admire the skill with which it is done, it necessarily remains for us a simulacrum.

While this traditional western concept of the performance–audience relationship can easily be shown to vary across cultures, theatre traditions and historical time, and while both the western mainstream and avant-garde theatres have consistently experimented with different ways of constructing and deconstructing the relationship, this conventional notion of the theatrical relationship between "performers" and "audience" is still with us. What I am concerned with here is that this set of ideas about the relationships entailed in performance carries hidden moral and epistemological judgements, when transported into anthropology, that tend to undermine our ethnographic intent.

According to the popular conception, the acceptance of theatrical illusion is enjoyable in the way it enthrals an audience or takes them out of their everyday lives. But this also makes it fundamentally unsettling. Actors may be brilliant virtuosos, capable of astonishing or moving us profoundly; but in their very virtuosity they are weavers of illusion and deceit. Thus, in a philosophical tradition like the Euro-American which is deeply concerned with locating and establishing truth, and in a religious tradition which is concerned with individual moral integrity and empowerment in relation to an invisible sacred reality, the status and efficacy of these illusory productions are unavoidably problematic. Laurel Kendall (1995, 19) outlines the moral and epistemological dilemma that western theatrical convention lays upon the study of performative ethnographic materials as follows:

> Our students inevitably ask us if we "believe" in the powers of the shamans we have studied, or if the spirits are "really" there. The question discomforts insofar as it implies, on the one hand, that the ethnographer [might] follow Castaneda's (1968) leap beyond the pale of professional credulity, or on the other, that acknowledgments of simulation make charlatans of one's informants.

Such a question (and also the dilemma posed in answering it) is a product of, and is driven by, western assumptions about theatre as illusion and acting as a form of inauthenticity. Kendall does not attempt to resolve this dilemma, and I will only pose it here.

Beyond these problems of truth status, and what to believe about the "presences" emergent in performance, lie the issues of manipulation and vulnerability, knowledge and power. Conventional experience in a western theatre would suggest that performers and audience must maintain quite different modes of consciousness for the performance to work. Actors in a western theatrical event must never lose sight of the broader theatrical context of the event. They are conscious not only of what they are doing in relation to each other, but also that they are performing before an audience. The audience's awareness (if all goes well) narrows its focus to the imagined situation presented, excluding awareness that the characters are performers, and/or of itself as an audience. It is this forgetfulness of the context, partly voluntary on the part of the audience, but in good part compelled by the quality of the performance, that constitutes so-called "suspension of disbelief" and enables the activity of the players to assert itself as an emergent reality, vivid and alive. This vividness is emergent from the interaction between performers and audience and (as every performer knows) is fraught with risk. And it is the product of a profound manipulation. The performers, being professionals (or virtuosos), know what they are doing. The manipulation is rationally conceived, intentional and carefully prepared. The audience (by convention) opens itself to being led by the performance and is drawn in and beguiled. To the extent that this beguilement is play and entertainment the situation is benign. But it need not be so. Where the audience is hood-winked and betrayed, or aroused to political consciousness and action by a performance, the issues of the power of illusion, of truth and deception, become increasingly urgent. There is a dormant unease about the potential for this kind of performative manipulation embedded in the conventional western notion about the relationship between performers and audience, and it is hard to still. It drives Laurel Kendall's students' questions: "do the spirits really appear at a shaman's performances?"

It is also endemic to Goffman's theoretical extension of theatrical models into social science (Goffman 1959; 1967). Goffman often writes as if the whole process of impression management in social interaction is a matter of rational calculation and individuals consciously manipulating their situations. All social life, by this implication, becomes a matter of performative illusions and strategic manipulations. Or at least it is easy for people steeped in popular conceptions of theatrical performance to read his theatrical ter-minology and discussion in this way. Goffman rarely carries his analysis forward to deal with the more philosophical question anthropology is ultimately concerned with here: what the relationship is between strategic impression management and the social construction of reality. Rather, the built-in issues of truth and deceit, reality vs imaginary, become the episte-mological blocks on which theory couched in these sorts of theatrical metaphor stumbles.[5]

My point is that these popular assumptions about the nature of the relationship between theatre audience and performers in conventional western theatre form probably the most problematic part of the extension of theatre metaphors and performative ways of thinking into social science theory. Is social life merely a tissue of illusions skilfully woven by us all? Where are the truth and efficacy in ritual located? The fact of the matter is that these issues are in large part an artefact of the way the relation between performers and audience is conventionally (if naively) conceived. As such they have become problematic issues that plague not only western episte-mologies but ethnographic understanding. It is fundamental that we find a way to resolve them if we are to come to some understanding of the role performativity plays in the social construction of human reality.

Theatre people, to their credit (and for their own reasons), have problem-atized and creatively experimented with this relationship for some time. Brecht encouraged actors to avoid enthralling their audiences in an imagina-tive reality, but to display or demonstrate what they were doing in a didactic mode so that the audience remained at an intellectual distance from the action, never forgetting they were watching a performance and able to focus on the message it modelled. At the opposite extreme, Schechner in his pro-duction of *Dionysis in 69* worked for a collapse of aesthetic distance to the point of encouraging a degree of sexual participation between audience and performers.

The simplest lesson for anthropology is that the exact nature of the performative relationship between the central performers and the other participants (including spectators) in a cultural event cannot be assumed analytically, but must be investigated ethnographically. In Papua New Guinea, where I have done my fieldwork, the relationship between dancers and spectators in the Gisalo ceremony of the Kaluli people was not at all like that between audience and performers in a western theatre. In Gisalo, the dancers sing nostalgic songs about the lands and rivers of their audience's community. Members of the audience are moved so deeply they burst into tears and then, becoming enraged, they leap up and burn the dancers on the shoulder blades with the resin torches used to light the performance (Schieffelin 1976, 21–25). Indeed, this remarkable response could be interpreted as virtually necessary to the performance, since if the audience is not moved and the tension between performers and audience does not rise to the pitch of violence, the ceremony falls apart and is abandoned in the middle of the night. In any case, after a successful performance, the dancers pay compensation to those whom they made weep. I should point out that the spectators' response is not a Durkheimian "conventional display of ritually appropriate sentiment." It is real grief and rage that are evoked. The ceremony is taken by the participants more in the manner of a deliberate provocation than of a moving performance in the western sense. The performers are held accountable for the painful emotions they evoke—and the retaliation upon them (and the compensation they must pay) return that account—as well as those emotions being an indication of the beauty and effectiveness of the performance. The dancers and song composers, for their part, certainly see it that way and are extremely pleased if they have managed to provoke numbers of the spectators to tears, despite the consequences to themselves. It is not unusual for aesthetically provoked emotion in New Guinea to be taken as deserving compensation whether or not those who provoke it are conceived to be deliberately and calculatedly causing the feelings evoked.[6]

Another kind of "audience–performer" relationship is visible in spirit seances. Kaluli spirit seances in Papua New Guinea were highly entertaining, even thrilling events, but they could only ethnocentrically be called performances in a western sense (see Schieffelin 1985; 1996). This is because, in seance, the issue is not performative illusion but the exact opposite: it is the presence of spirits. If anything, it is the spirits themselves who perform.

Kaluli spectators know very well that spirit seances can be faked and keep a sharp eye for signs of "performing" or, as they see it, deception. Spirits in seance cured illness and revealed the identity of witches, both of which were activities of considerable (even life-and-death) social and political consequence, and people did not fool around with them. It was essential that the characters who spoke through the medium were really spirits and not the performance tricks of someone who was trying to con his listeners. A "performance" in the western sense was precisely what speaking with the spirits through a medium was not and could not be. It had more of the character of a telephone conversation. Kaluli themselves likened it to speaking with someone over two-way radio. To describe the Kaluli seance as a performance in the popular western sense would be to violate its ethnographic nature.

Closer to western experience, the members of the Word of Life Movement, a Protestant evangelical sect studied by Simon Coleman (1996), base their practice of worship on the belief that sacred language (the words of scripture or speaking in tongues) contains concrete sacred power. They see the visual and physical changes in the world effected by these words as a testament to the presence of God. Sacred words act as autonomous physical sources of power. Speaking such words is an illocutionary act that creates what it pronounces. Before building their temple, members of the sect held a service in which they walked over the building site speaking tongues into the ground to saturate it with divine power. The subsequent rise of the building could be seen as a concrete manifestation of the power of this sacred language. The point here is this dramatic service at the site could not be seen as a performance in a western sense either: the performative action of speaking the power into the ground is misunderstood if it is taken as metaphorical or symbolic action. Rather the force is illocutionary and instrumental. To the members of the sect, this act of saturating the ground with the divine word was more akin to spreading fertilizer to render a field productive than to laying a cornerstone to inaugurate a construction.

Clearly there are significant problems with extending the conventional western conception of the relation between performers and audience into anthropological discussions of rituals and other cultural performances. Yet understanding the precise nature of this relationship in a performance event is fundamental to understanding the structure and character of the event itself. Where western assumptions align the relation between performer and spectator with relations like signifier/signified, text/reader, illusion/reality, deceit/authenticity, activity/passivity, manipulative/straightforward, they conceal important moral and epistemological judgements that undermine anthropological discussion which makes use of western performance ideas in an unexamined way. It is for this reason that it is important to make the relationship between the participants and others in performative events a central subject of ethnographic investigation.

Performance and the Social Construction of Reality

It is not only for the sake of ethnographic accuracy that it is important to problematize the relationship between performers and participants. More importantly for anthropology, these relationships need careful investigation —both in formal performances and in everyday life—because it is within these relationships that the fundamental epistemological and ontological relations of any society are likely to be implicated and worked out: because this is the creative edge where reality is socially constructed. If this is so, we may entertain the hypothesis that just as western notions about the relationship between performer and spectator convey fundamental (western) assumptions about the nature of action in ordinary situations, so the same may be true for people of other cultures (or historical epochs; cf. Foucault 1973), though their assumptions and the implications that flow from them may be quite different.

We may return to the Kaluli Gisalo ceremony to illustrate. When Kaluli are moved by a performance to the point of becoming enraged and attacking the dancer, they are not confusing performative evocation with reality but rather taking it as provocation. That is, they privilege the actual psychological and social effects of the poetic act over its purely aesthetic and representational qualities, and the process of social reciprocation over (what we would call) the suspension of disbelief. In this way poetic evocation (an act of aesthetic performance) is held to be morally consequential and the performers are held accountable.[7] For traditional Kaluli, playing with these volatile edges was the "stuff of theatre": what their performances were all about. At the same time it had important implications for understanding their everyday modes of moral determination, which was grounded in a sense of reciprocal practice rather than a sense of good and evil or a set of sacredly given rules or norms. In short, investigation of the structure of the performer–participant relationship in Kaluli ceremonies reveals a particular structure in the way their cultural values are aligned within their performative processes, and suggests interesting lines of further enquiry into their mode of socially constructing their reality.

Conclusions

The fundamental assertion underlying this chapter is that any ethnography of performance is inherently addressing the issue of the social construction of reality, and that, in fact, performativity is not only endemic to human being-in-the-world but fundamental to the process of constructing a human reality. However, the nature of the relationship—both moral and epistemological—between performers and participants is not specified prior to this process, but rather constituted within it (as experimental theatre people have known all along).

The central issue of performativity, whether in ritual performance, theatrical entertainment or the social articulation of ordinary human situations, is the imaginative creation of a human world. The creation of human realities entails ontological issues, and these need to be explored ethnographically rather than a priori assumed. It is time for anthropologists to include this task once again in greater depth if they are to elucidate more clearly the processes entailed when human beings construct a human world.

Notes

1. Humphrey and Laidlaw characterize these sorts of ritual as "ritualized religious performances of a quasi-theatrical kind" (1994, 10), adding "whose success and failure is of the essence" (1994, 10). They thus appreciate the contingent and risky nature of performance. "Ritualization" is in theory free of contingency, since it is simply the doing of the act (or the act doing itself through the person) rather than its manner of conduct, outcome or result that is important.

2. This would be true even of the most routine activity. What the performance of ordinary, mindless washing-up activity expresses is an ongoingness in life, the low-profile, apparent performative neutrality of familiar convention which forms the background of any situation. Depending on what is happening in the lives of the participants, it may also constitute an "escape" from the complexities of the rest of the situation, or an abdication of responsibility in an apparent fulfilment of it. Conversely such activity may represent the numbing of self in a stifled life, or a refuge in familiar activity, or many other things. But such activity is always placed in some context—though perhaps in very low performative profile—in relation to the ongoing situation.

3. See Wulff (1998) for a comparable point.

4. Cf. also Rapport (1998) on the performance of "selling."

5. Indeed one might observe that the western theatre convention stands in a sort of convenient analogy to fieldwork. Rituals and other cultural activities are easy to see as akin to theatre not only in their substantive resemblances to theatrical performances, but in the way anthropologists usually find themselves positioned in relation to such events in an audience-like observer role.

6. For an early observation that aesthetically provoked emotionality is due compensation in Papua New Guinea, see Read (1955). For a detailed discussion of the emotional economy of Gisalo performance, see Schieffelin (1976). For an exegesis of the aesthetics of Kaluli music and poetic evocation, see Feld (1990).

7. The situation is in some ways analogous to an occasion when a national state arrests (or shuts down) a theatre troupe for "subversive" or "politically provocative" or "immoral" performances. For the powers that be, the effects of such theatre are socially real and powerful enough for the performance to be taken as political action rather than entertainment.

References

Bauman, Richard. 1986. *Story, Performance, Event.* Cambridge: Cambridge University Press.

Bourdieu, Pierre. 1977. *Outline of a Theory of Practice.* New York: Cambridge University Press.

Castaneda, Carlos. 1968. *The Teachings of Don Juan: A Yaqui Way of Knowledge.* Berkeley, CA: University of California Press.

Coleman, Simon. 1996. "Words as Things: Language, Ritual and Aesthetics in Christian Evangelism." Paper presented to social anthropology seminar, University College London.

Feld, Steven. 1990. *Sound and Sentiment: Birds, Weeping, Poetics and Song in Kaluli Expression.* Philadelphia: University of Pennsylvania Press.

Foucault, Michel. 1973. *The Order of Things.* New York: Vintage Books.

Goffman, Erving. 1959. *The Presentation of Self in Everyday Life.* Garden City, NY: Doubleday Anchor.

—1967. *Interaction Ritual.* New York: Doubleday Anchor.

Humphrey, C., and J. Laidlaw. 1994. *The Archetypal Actions of Ritual.* Oxford: Clarendon Press.

Kendall, Laurel. 1995. "Initiating Performance: The Story of Chini, a Korean Shaman." In *The Performance of Healing*, ed. C. Laderman and M. Roseman, 17–58. London: Routledge.

Rapport, Nigel. 1998. "Hard Sell: Commercial Performance and the Narration of the Self." In *Ritual, Performance, Media*, ed. F. Hughes-Freeland, 177–93. London: Routledge.

Read, Kenneth. 1955. "Morality and the Concept of the Person among the Gahuku-Gama." *Oceania* 25: 233–82.

Rostas, Susanna. 1998. "From Ritualization to Performativity: The Concheros of Mexico." In *Ritual, Performance, Media*, ed. F. Hughes-Freeland, 85–103. London: Routledge.

Schechner, Richard. 1982. "Collective Reflexivity: Restoration of Behavior." In *The Crack in the Mirror: Reflexive Perspectives in Anthropology*, ed. J. Ruby. Philadelphia: University of Pennsylvania Press.

Schieffelin, E. L. 1976. *The Sorrow of the Lonely and the Burning of the Dancers.* New York: St. Martin's Press.

—1985. "Performance and the Cultural Construction of Reality." *American Ethnologist* 12(4): 707–24.

—1995. "On Failure and Performance." In *The Performance of Healing*, ed. C. Laderman and M. Roseman. London: Routledge.

—1996. "Evil Spirit Sickness, the Christian Disease." *Culture, Medicine and Psychiatry* 20: 1–39.

Wulff, Helena. 1998. "Perspectives towards Ballet Performance: Exploring, Repairing and Maintaining Frames." In *Ritual, Performance, Memory*, ed. F. Hughes-Freeland, 104–20. London: Routledge.

INTRODUCTION

Peter Stallybrass and Allon White

Editor's Introduction

Peter Stallybrass is Professor of English at the University of Pennsylvania, where he mainly teaches Renaissance and Cultural Studies, and is interested in theories of the body and of transgression. He co-edits the University of Pennsylvania Press's *New Cultural Studies*. Allon White, who died in 1988 aged thirty-eight, was one of the most important literary and cultural critics of his generation. In addition to the work from which the following chapter is drawn, *The Politics and Poetics of Transgression* (1986), he also wrote *Carnival, Hysteria, and Writing* (1993).

Previous chapters have made good use of theorists—such as Bauman, Bourdieu, Foucault—alongside ethnographers and those whose specific interest is ritual, performance and/or theatre. The following chapter brings the work of the literary theorist Mikhail Bakhtin (1895–1975) into dialogue with a variety of anthropologists and other theorists. It considers "carnival as one instance of a generalized economy of transgression and of the recoding of high/low relations across the whole social structure. The symbolic categories of grotesque realism which Bakhtin located can be rediscovered as a governing dynamic of the body, the household, the city, the nation-state—indeed a vast range of interconnected domains."

Bakhtin's influence has been increasingly important in a number of academic disciplines (e.g. Bhabha 1994). While it is his theorization of carnival, the carnivalesque, and the "grotesque body" (1987) that are most important here, his discussion of dialogue (1981) and metaphor and other speech-acts (1986) might make similarly important contributions to reflections on ritual.

References

Bakhtin, Mikhail. 1981. *The Dialogic Imagination*. Austin: University of Texas Press.
—1986. *Speech, Genres, and Other Late Essays*. Austin: University of Texas Press.
—1987. *Rabelais and his World*. Bloomington: Indiana University Press.
Bhabha, Homi K. 1994. "The Postcolonial and the Postmodern: The Question of Agency." In *The Location of Culture*, 171–97. London: Routledge.
Stallybrass, Peter, and Allon White. 1986. *The Politics and Poetics of Transgression*. London: Methuen.
White, Allon. 1993. *Carnival, Hysteria, and Writing*. Oxford: Oxford University Press.

ᎭᎤ ᏣᎡ

Amongst the many remarkable things to be found in Ernst Robert Curtius's *European Literature and the Latin Middle Ages* is an account of how the idea of "the Classic author" was originally derived from ancient taxation categories. In a chapter discussing the idea of model authors and the attendant notion of canon-formation, Curtius explains how tax-bands, a social division of citizens according to property qualifications under the constitutions of Servius, were adopted by Aulus Gellius as a way of designating the prestige and rank of writers. Citizens of the first taxation category, the top rank, came to be known as "*classici*." This development in the generic terminology of antiquity (Gellius fli. *c.* 123–*c.* 165) subsequently had an enduring influence on the European system of hierarchizing authors and works. It separated out a distinct elite set (the *classici*) from the commonality (the *proletarius*) and used this as a model for literary discriminations. Curtius remarks:

> But it was not until very late, and then only in a single instance, that the name *classicus* appears: in Aulus Gellius (*Noctes Atticae*, XIX, 8, 15... The thing to do is to follow the usage of a model author: "e cohorte illa dumtaxat antiquiore vel oratorum aliquis vel poetarum, id est classicus adsiduusque aliquis scnptor, non proletarius"; "some one of the orators or poets, who at least belongs to the older band, that is, a first class tax-paying author, not a proletarian"... The *proletarius*, whom Gellius mentions by way of comparison, belongs to *no* tax class. When Sainte-Beuve, in 1850, discussed the question What is a Classic?, he paraphrased this passage in Gellius: "un écrivain de valeur et de marque, un écrivain qui compte, qui a du bien au soleil, et qui n'est pas confondu dans la foule des prolétaires." (Curtius 1953, 249–50)

And Curtius adds wryly "What a titbit for a Marxist sociology of literature!"

It was not Curtius's inclination to follow up his own remark and indeed we can detect a certain amused astonishment when he realizes where his investigations have finally led him. From the first it seems that the ranking of types of author was modelled upon social rank according to property classifications and this interrelation was still being actively invoked in the nineteenth century. In recent times we have been inclined to forget this ancient and enduring link between social rank and the organizing of authors and works, including literary genres, although for the major part of European history it was a natural assumption for readers and writers alike. Ian Jack noted that precisely this habit of ranking "kinds in a hierarchy analogous to that of the state" has led to a contemporary distrust, particularly of Renaissance categories:

> Just as the social hierarchy was traced from the prince through the nobility down to the common people, so the realm of Poetry had its own "degrees," from Epic, the Prince of all the kinds, down to the lowest species of all, "from Homer to the *Anthologia,* from Virgil to Martial and Owen's Epigrams... that is from the top to the bottom of all poetry." (Jack 1942, 4)

It is the contention of the present book that cultural categories of high and low, social and aesthetic, like those mentioned above but also those of the physical body and geographical space, are never entirely separable. The ranking of literary genres or authors in a hierarchy analogous to social classes is a particularly clear example of a much broader and more complex cultural process whereby the human body, psychic forms, geographical space and the social formation are all constructed within interrelating and dependent hierarchies of high and low. This book is an attempt to map some of these interlinked hierarchies on the terrain of literary and cultural history. More particularly it attends both to the formation of these hierarchies and to the processes through which the low troubles the high. The high/low opposition in each of our four symbolic domains—psychic forms, the human body, geographical space and the social order—is a fundamental basis to mechanisms of ordering and sense-making in European cultures. Divisions and discriminations in one domain are continually structured, legitimated and dissolved by reference to the vertical symbolic hierarchy which operates in the other three domains. Cultures "think themselves" in the most immediate and affective ways through the combined symbolisms of these four hierarchies. Furthermore (and this is where the title of the book comes in) transgressing the rules of hierarchy and order in any one of the domains may have major consequences in the others.

Although there are all sorts of subtle degrees and gradations in a culture it is striking that the extremes of high and low have a special and often powerful symbolic charge. Thus, in the example given above from Curtius,

Gellius (as also Cicero and Arnobius) immediately fixes upon the top and bottom, the *classicus* and the *proletarius*, even though the system has five different grades within it. This does not necessarily militate against subtlety since "above" and "below" may be inscribed within a minutely discriminatory system of classification, but it does foster a simplifying binaryism of high and low *within which* further classification will be made. In other words the vertical extremities frame all further discursive elaborations. If we can grasp the system of extremes which encode the body, the social order, psychic form and spatial location, we thereby lay bare a major framework of discourse within which any further "redress of balance" or judicious qualification must take place.

In our study therefore we have focused upon the symbolic extremities of the exalted and the base. We have followed the instruction of Boethius— "Look to the highest of the heights of heaven"—and we have also plumbed the depths of social classification, the lower bodily stratum, the sewers, the underworld—what one might call the rock bottom of symbolic form. We have tried to see how high discourses, with their lofty style, exalted aims and sublime ends, are structured in relation to the debasements and degradations of low discourse. We have tried to see how each extremity structures the other, depends upon and invades the other in certain historical moments, to carry political charge through aesthetic and moral polarities. Indeed, the oppositions, interpenetrations and transgressions of high and low bear such an enormous weight of cultural organization that one marvels at the sheer labour of transcoding, displacement and partition involved in the elaborate networks of *super* and *sub-* in our cultural history.

It would be wrong to imply that "high" and "low" in this context are equal and symmetrical terms. When we talk of high discourses—literature, philosophy, statecraft, the languages of the Church and the University—and contrast them to the low discourses of a peasantry, the urban poor, sub-cultures, marginals, the lumpen proletariat, colonized peoples, we already have two "highs" and two "lows." History seen from above and history seen from below are irreducibly different and they consequently impose radically different perspectives on the question of hierarchy.

Indeed they may and often do possess quite different symbolic hierarchies but because the higher discourses are normally associated with the most powerful socio-economic groups existing at the centre of cultural power, it is they which generally gain the authority to designate what is to be taken as high and low in the society. This is what Raymond Williams calls the "inherent dominative mode" and it has the prestige and the access to power which enables it to create the dominant definitions of superior and inferior. Of course the "low" (defined as such by the high precisely to confirm itself as "high") may well see things differently and attempt to impose a counterview through an inverted hierarchy.

There is a growing body of research devoted to the topic of hierarchy inversion, of "world upside down" (WUD), and we have much to say about this in the following pages. However, the politics of hierarchy inversion as a ritual strategy on the part of subordinate groups is not our principal theme. We have chosen to concentrate rather on the contradictory nature of symbolic hierarchies within the dominant constructions of literature, the body and the social formation.

The primary site of contradiction, the site of conflicting desires and mutually incompatible representation, is undoubtedly the "low." Again and again we find a striking ambivalence to the representations of the lower strata (of the body, of literature, of society, of place) in which they are both reviled and desired. Repugnance and fascination are the twin poles of the process in which a *political* imperative to reject and eliminate the debasing "low" conflicts powerfully and unpredictably with a desire for this Other. Edward Said in his work on *Orientalism*—the myth of the Middle East constructed by Europe to legitimate its own authority—has convincingly shown this operative ambivalence in action. In political terms Orientalism

> ... depends for its strategy on [a] flexible *positional* superiority, which puts the Westerner in a whole series of possible relationships with the Orient without ever losing him the upper hand.

But at the same time Said notices that

> European culture gained in strength and identity by setting itself off against the Orient as a sort of ... underground self. (Said 1979, 3, 7)

"An underground self with the upper hand." This curious, almost oxymoronic, formulation captures a nexus of power and desire which regularly reappears in the ideological construction of the low-Other. It is not only a phenomenon of colonial and neo-colonial representation. We find the same constitutive ambivalence around the slum and the domestic servant in the nineteenth century; around the disposal of "waste" products in the city (though not in pre-Renaissance rural culture); around the carnival festivity of popular culture; around the symbolically base and abject animals like the pig and the rat. These are the subjects of specific chapters which follow in which we explore the contradictory and unstable representation of low-Others.

A recurrent pattern emerges: the "top" attempts to reject and eliminate the "bottom" for reasons of prestige and status, only to discover, not only that it is in some way frequently dependent upon that low-Other (in the classic way that Hegel describes in the master–slave section of the *Phenomenology*), but also that the top *includes* that low symbolically, as a primary eroticized constituent of its own fantasy life. The result is a mobile, conflictual fusion of power, fear and desire in the construction of subjectivity: a psychological dependence upon precisely those Others which are being rigorously opposed and excluded at the social level. It is for this reason that what is *socially* peripheral is so frequently *symbolically* central (like long hair in the 1960s). The low-Other is despised and denied at the level of political organization and social being whilst it is instrumentally constitutive of the shared imaginary repertoires of the dominant culture. This is evidenced by the history of the representation of "low" entertainment and the carnivalesque, to which we now turn.

From Carnival to Transgression

> The new historian, the genealogist, will know what to make of this masquerade. He will not be too serious to enjoy it; on the contrary, he will push the masquerade to its limits and prepare the great carnival of time where masks are constantly reappearing. Genealogy is history in the form of a concerted carnival. (Foucault 1977, 160–61)

> In the world of carnival the awareness of the people's immortality is combined with the realisation that established authority and truth are relative. (Bakhtin 1968, 10)

There is now a large and increasing body of writing which sees carnival not simply as a ritual feature of European culture but as a *mode of understanding*, a positivity, a cultural analytic. How is it that a festive ritual now virtually eliminated from most of the popular culture of Europe has gained such prominence as an epistemological category? Is there a connection between the fact of its elimination as a physical practice and its self-conscious emergence in the artistic and academic discourses of our time? For both Michel Foucault in the passage cited above and for Mikhail Bakhtin in his seminal study *Rabelais and his World*, the Nietzscheian study of history leads to the ideal of carnival. Everywhere in literary and cultural studies today we see carnival emerging as a model, as an ideal and as an analytic category in a way that, at first sight, seems puzzling.

Undoubtedly it was the translation of Mikhail Bakhtin's monumental study of Rabelais and the carnivalesque which initially catalysed the interest of Western scholars (albeit slowly—the book was only translated into English in 1968) around the notion of carnival, marking it out as a site of special interest for the analysis of literature and symbolic practices. Since the 1970s there has been an increasing number of literary and historical studies devoted to the topic. In 1978 Krystyna Pomorska could write with every justification that "Mikhail Bakhtin is today one of the most popular, if not the most popular, figures in the domain of humanistic studies" (Pomorska 1978, 379). More recently Tony Bennett averred that Bakhtin's study of Rabelais should hold an exemplary place in materialist cultural criticism (Bennett 1979, 90–92). This is surely correct: *Rabelais and his World* is ostensibly a scholarly study of Rabelais's popular sources in carnivalesque folk-culture which shows how indebted Rabelais is to the popular, non-literary, "low" folk humour of the French Renaissance. His intention in the study was self-consciously iconoclastic.

> No dogma, no authoritarianism, no narrow-minded seriousness can coexist with Rabelaisian images; these images are opposed to all that is finished and polished, to all pomposity, to every ready-made solution in the sphere of thought and world outlook. (Bakhtin 1968, 3)

Naturally this reading of Rabelais has not gone unchallenged by conventionally learned scholars (Screech 1979, 1–14, 479; also 1984, 11–13, but in this latter article, "Homage to Rabelais," Screech is much closer in spirit to Bakhtin than in the earlier book). But although Bakhtin is deeply concerned to elucidate the sources of Rabelais's work, the main importance of his study is its broad development of the "carnivalesque" into a potent, populist, critical inversion of *all* official words and hierarchies in a way that has implications far beyond the specific realm of Rabelais studies. Carnival, for Bakhtin, is both a populist utopian vision of the world seen from below and a festive critique, through the inversion of hierarchy, of the "high" culture:

> As opposed to the official feast, one might say that carnival celebrates temporary liberation from the prevailing truth of the established order; it marks the suspension of all hierarchical rank, privileges, norms and prohibitions. Carnival was the true feast of time, the feast of becoming, change and renewal. It was hostile to all that was immortalized and complete. (Bakhtin 1968, 109)

Carnival in its widest, most general sense embraced ritual spectacles such as fairs, popular feasts and wakes, processions and competitions (Burke 1978, 178–204), comic shows, mummery and dancing, open-air amusement with costumes and masks, giants, dwarfs, monsters, trained animals and so forth; it included comic verbal compositions (oral and written) such as parodies, travesties and vulgar farce; and it included various genres of "Billingsgate," by which Bakhtin designated curses, oaths, slang, humour, popular tricks and jokes, scatalogical forms, in fact all the "low" and "dirty" sorts of folk humour. Carnival is presented by Bakhtin as a world of topsy-turvy, of heteroglot exuberance, of ceaseless overrunning and excess where all is mixed, hybrid, ritually degraded and defiled.

If there is a principle to this hotch-potch it resides in the spirit of carnivalesque laughter itself, to which Bakhtin ascribes great importance:

Let us say a few initial words about the complex nature of carnival-esque laughter. It is, first of all, a festive laughter. Therefore it is not an individual reaction to some isolated "comic" event. Carnival laughter is the laughter of all the people. Second, it is universal in scope; it is directed at all and everyone, including the carnival's participants. The entire world is seen in its droll aspect, in its gay relativity. Third, this laughter is ambivalent: it is gay, triumphant, and at the same time mocking, deriding. It asserts and denies, it buries and revives. Such is the laughter of the carnival. (Bakhtin 1968, 11–12)

Carnival laughter, then, has a vulgar, "earthy" quality to it. With its oaths and profanities, its abusive language and its mocking words it was profoundly ambivalent. Whilst it humiliated and mortified it also revived and renewed. For Bakhtin ritual defilements went along with reinvigoration such that "it was precisely this ambivalent abuse which determined the genre of speech in carnival intercourse" (Bakhtin 1968, 16). The "coarse" and familiar speech of the fair and the marketplace provided a complex vital repertoire of speech patterns excluded from official discourse which could be used for parody, subversive humour and inversion. "Laughter degrades and materialises" (Bakhtin 1968, 20). Fundamental to the corporeal, collective nature of carnival laughter is what Bakhtin terms "grotesque realism." Grotesque realism uses the material body—flesh conceptualized as corpulent excess—to represent cosmic, social, topographical and linguistic elements of the world. Thus already in Bakhtin there is the germinal notion of *transcodings* and *displacements* effected between the high/low image of the physical body and other social domains. Grotesque realism images the human body as multiple, bulging, over- or under-sized, protuberant and incomplete. The openings and orifices of this carnival body are emphasized, not its closure and finish. It is an image of impure corporeal bulk with its orifices (mouth, flared nostrils, anus) yawning wide and its lower regions (belly, legs, feet, buttocks and genitals) given priority over its upper regions (head, "spirit," reason).

Bakhtin is self-consciously utopian and lyrical about carnival and grotesque realism. "The leading themes of these images of bodily life are fertility, growth and a brimming-over abundance. Manifestations of this life refer not to the isolated biological individual, not to the private, egoistic, 'economic man,' but to the collective ancestral body of all the people" (Bakhtin 1968, 19). To complete the image of grotesque realism one must add that it is always in process, it is always *becoming*, it is a mobile and hybrid creature, disproportionate, exorbitant, outgrowing all limits, obscenely decentred and off-balance, a figural and symbolic resource for parodic exaggeration and inversion. All these grotesque qualities have a positive force in Bakhtin. It was only after the Renaissance, according to Bakhtin, that the principles of grotesque realism were subjected to a monologic reading. Stigmatized as the vulgar practices of a superstitious and crude populace, the carnivalesque was prettified, incorporated into commercial or civic display or regarded as a purely negative phenomenon. Bakhtin's optimistic populism is at its most insistent (and problematic) in those passages where he emphasizes the positivity of the grotesque bodily element.

The grotesque body was traditionally presented, Bakhtin argues,

> not in a private, egotistic form, severed from the other spheres of life, but as something universal, representing all the people. As such it is opposed to the severance from the material and bodily roots of the world; it makes no pretense to renunciation of the earthy, or independence of the earthy and body. We repeat: the body and bodily life have here a cosmic and at the same time an all-people's character; this is not the body and its physiology in the modern sense of these words, because it is not individualised. The material bodily principle is contained not in the biological individual, not in the bourgeois ego, but in the people, a people who are continually growing and renewed. This is why all that is bodily becomes grandiose, exaggerated, immeasurable. (Bakhtin 1968, 19)

It is difficult to disentangle the generous but willed idealism from the descriptively accurate in passages like these. Bakhtin constantly shifts between prescriptive and descriptive categories in his work. In this passage the cosmic populism, which seems to us rather wishful and finally unusable as an analytic tool, assorts with an acute perception about the historically variable nature of the body-image. In this latter respect recent thinking has largely confirmed Bakhtin's insistence on the relation between body-image, social context and collective identity. "The whole concept of body image boundaries has implicit in it the idea of the structuring of one's relations with others" (Fisher and Cleveland 1958, 206), and in the 1972 edition of the *International Encyclopaedia of the Social Sciences* Fisher writes:

> The investigation of body-image phenomena has become a vigorous enterprise ... Speaking broadly, one may say there is an emphatic need to ascertain the principal axes underlying the organization of the body image ... There is also a need to examine the relationships between body attitudes and socialization modes in different cultures. There is evidence in the anthropological literature that body attitudes may differ radically in relation to cultural context. (Fisher 1972, 116)

It is a major premise of Bakhtin's work that this is so. Moreover, body-images "speak" social relations and values with particular force.

In Bakhtin's schema grotesque realism in pre-capitalist Europe fulfilled three functions at once: it provided an image-ideal of and for popular community as an heterogeneous and boundless totality; it provided an imaginary repertoire of festive and comic elements which stood over against the serious and oppressive languages of the official culture; and it provided a thoroughly materialist metaphysics whereby the grotesque "bodied forth" the cosmos, the social formation and language itself. Even linguistic rules are played up by what Bakhtin calls a *grammatica jocosa* whereby grammatical order is transgressed to reveal erotic and obscene or merely materially satisfying counter-meaning. Punning is one of the forms taken by the *grammatica jocosa*, and recently it has been argued, in Bakhtinian style, that the pun

> violates and so unveils the structure of prevailing (pre-vailing) convention; and it provokes laughter. Samuel Beckett's punning pronouncement "In the beginning was the Pun" sets pun against official Word and at the same time, as puns often do, sets free a chain of other puns. So, too, carnival sets itself up in a punning relationship with official culture and enables a plural, unfixed, comic view of the world. (Arthur 1982, 1)

Arthur is one of the many contemporary critics who has been profoundly influenced by Bakhtin's work, and even from the cursory outline which we have provided here it is possible to see some of the suggestive force of his project. Certainly the enthusiastic adoption of the "carnivalesque" as formulated by Bakhtin has resulted in articles and monographs on specific works, authors and periods far removed from Rabelais and the Renaissance. Film critic Robert Stamm writes:

> The notion of the carnivalesque, as elaborated by literary theorists like Mikhail Bakhtin and social anthropologists like Roberto da Matta is a potentially indispensable instrument for the analysis not only of literary and filmic texts but also of cultural politics in general. (Stamm 1982, 47)

However, it is striking that the most successful of these attempts to apply Bakhtin *tout court* focus upon cultures which still have a strong repertoire of carnivalesque practices, such as Latin America, or upon literatures produced in a colonial or neo-colonial context where the political difference between the dominant and subordinate culture is particularly charged. Régine Robin's study of Soviet Yiddish literature (Robin 1983) is of this sort and gains some of its strength from the extent to which Bakhtin's own work was already, in its original form, a cryptic anti-Stalinist allegory. *Rabelais and his World* pits against that "official, formalistic and logical authoritarianism whose unspoken name is Stalinism the explosive politics of the body, the erotic, the licentious and semiotic" (Eagleton 1981, 144). Robin's work on Soviet Yiddish nicely applies Bakhtin's use of the polyphonic "multi-voicedness" of Yiddish (arguably in itself already a "carnivalesque" language), the language of the oppressed Jewish minority. The rightness of this is underwritten by

Bakhtin's indirect championing of the humorous resistance of the "folk" through the darkest period of Stalinist terror.

For similar reasons Bakhtin has been used almost unchanged and unchallenged to provide readings of Latin American culture (Stamm 1982; Vilar de Kerkhoff 1983; Hill 1972; Malcuzynski 1983) and of minority culture in Canada (Goddard 1983; Thurston 1983). Eisenstein may well have drawn upon Bakhtin's ideas in the final scenes of his film *Que viva Mexico* in which macabre mockery of the Catholic ministers is effected through the use of carnival effigies (Ivanov 1976). Todorov's recent work on the colonization of the Americas (Todorov 1985) owes much to his recent critical interest in Bakhtin (Todorov 1984), and for some years now the appropriateness of Bakhtin to a study of James Joyce has been recognized. Joyce's "carnivalization" of "The King's English," his interest in and use of grotesque realism (Parrinder 1984, 16; Lodge 1982), suggested to Pomorska in the early 1960s that *Finnegans Wake* was the exemplary carnivalesque modernist work and recently Sidney Monas (1983) has gone some way to substantiating this view. In 1976 Ivanov wrote:

> One cannot help seeing the profound likeness between novelistic regularities discovered by Bakhtin and the structure of such twentieth century works as Joyce's *Ulysses* whose period of creation coincided with Bakhtin's youth: the intertwining and dialogic opposition of different speech genres; their conflict within the novel; the parodic and travestied features of the genre of the novel—all qualities which are at their fullest in *Ulysses* whose very structure is parodic, a travesty of the structure of Homer's *Odyssey*. (Ivanov 1976, 27)

The poetry of Shelley (Sales 1983), the plays of Samuel Beckett (Van Buuren 1983) and the writing of Jean-Claude Germain (Short 1983) have all been examined in recent criticism within a Bakhtinian frame and with a straightforward and unproblematical enthusiasm for his conceptual schema.

Others, however, have been more critical. Whilst almost every reader of Bakhtin admires his comprehensive and engaged generosity, his combination of festive populism and deep learning, and whilst few would deny the immediate appeal and the vitality of the notion of carnival, various writers have been sceptical of Bakhtin's overall project.

Terry Eagleton thinks that the weakness of Bakhtin's positive embrace of carnival is transparent:

> Indeed carnival is so vivaciously celebrated that the necessary political criticism is almost too obvious to make. Carnival, after all, is a *licensed* affair in every sense, a permissible rupture of hegemony, a contained popular blow-off as disturbing and relatively ineffectual as a revolutionary work of art. As Shakespeare's Olivia remarks, there is no slander in an allowed fool. (Eagleton 1981, 148)

149

Most politically thoughtful commentators wonder, like Eagleton, whether the "licensed release" of carnival is not simply a form of social control of the low by the high and therefore serves the interests of that very official culture which it apparently opposes. The classic formulation of this is in Max Gluckman's now somewhat dated *Order and Rebellion in Tribal Africa* (1963) and *Custom and Conflict* (1965) in which he asserted that while these "rites of reversal obviously include a protest against the established order ... they are intended to preserve and strengthen the established order" (Gluckman 1965, 109). Roger Sales amplifies both on this process of containment and its ambivalence:

> There were two reasons why the fizzy, dizzy carnival spirit did not nec-
> essarily undermine authority. First of all, it was licensed or sanctioned
> by the authorities themselves. They removed the stopper to stop the
> bottle being smashed altogether. The release of emotions and grievances
> made them easier to police in the long term. Second, although the
> world might appear to be turned upside down during the carnival
> season, the fact that Kings and Queens were chosen and crowned
> actually reaffirmed the *status quo*. Carnival was, however, Janus-faced.
> Falstaff is both the merry old mimic of Eastcheap and the old cor-
> ruptible who tries to undermine the authority, or rule, of the Lord Chief
> Justice. The carnival spirit, in early-nineteenth century England as well
> as in sixteenth century France, could therefore be a vehicle for social
> protest and the method for disciplining that protest. (Sales 1983, 169)

As Georges Balandier puts it succinctly in *Political Anthropology*: "The supreme ruse of power is to allow itself to be contested *ritually* in order to consolidate itself more effectively" (Balandier 1972, 41).

It actually makes little sense to fight out the issue of whether or not carnivals are *intrinsically* radical or conservative, for to do so automatically involves the false essentializing of carnivalesque transgression (White 1982, 60). The most that can be said in the abstract is that for long periods carnival may be a stable and cyclical ritual with no noticeable politically transformative effects but that, given the presence of sharpened political antagonism, it may often act as *catalyst* and *site of actual and symbolic struggle*.[1]

It is in fact striking how frequently violent social clashes apparently "coincided" with carnival. Le Roy Ladurie's *Carnival in Romans* (1981) has popularized one such incident when the 1580 festival at Romans in eastern France was turned into armed conflict and massacre. Other social historians have documented similar occurrences (Davis 1975; Burke 1978; Thompson 1972). However, to call it a "coincidence" of social revolt and carnival is deeply misleading, for as Peter Burke has pointed out, it was only in the late eighteenth and early nineteenth centuries—and then only in certain areas— that one can reasonably talk of popular politics *dissociated* from the carnivalesque at all. John Brewer has described English politics in the eighteenth century as "essentially a calendrical market," by which he designates a deliberate commingling of holiday and political events (in this case organized by the Hanoverians for conservative motives):

> Far too little attention had [sic] been paid to the emergence during the eighteenth century of a Hanoverian political calendar, designed to inculcate loyal values in the populace, and to emphasize and encourage the growth of a national political consensus. Nearly every English market town celebrated the dates which were considered the important political landmarks of the nation. They can be found in most almanacs of the period, barely distinguishable from the time-honoured dates of May Day, Plough Monday, Twelfth Night, Shrove Tuesday and the like... In the early eighteenth century, these dates, together with the occasion of the Pretender's birthday, were occasions of conflict. The year of the Jacobite Rebellion, 1715, was especially contentious, with Hanoverian Mug House clubs fighting it out in the streets with Jacobite apprentices and artisans. On October 30, frequenters of a Jacobite alehouse on Ludgate Hill were beaten up by members of the Loyal Society who were celebrating the birthday of the Prince of Wales, the future George II. A Jacobite attempt to burn William III in effigy on November 4 was thwarted by the same Whig clubmen who the next day tried to cremate effigies of the Pretender and his supporters. On 17 November further clashes ensued and two Jacobites were shot dead. (Brewer et al. 1983, 247)

Again this should act as a warning against the current tendency to essentialize carnival *and* politics. On the one hand carnival was a specific calendrical ritual: carnival proper, for instance, occurred around February each year, ineluctably followed by Lenten fasting and abstinence bound tightly to laws, structures and institutions which had briefly been denied during its reign. On the other hand carnival also refers to a mobile set of symbolic practices, images and discourses which were employed throughout social revolts and conflicts before the nineteenth century.

Recent work in the social history of carnival reveals its political dimensions to be more complex than either Bakhtin or his detractors might suspect. Bob Scribner has shown convincingly the importance of popular carnival practices in German Reformation struggles against Catholicism, particularly in the propagandistic application of ritual defilement to the Papacy; Martine Boiteux has shown the lengths to which the ecclesiastical powers were prepared to go in Rome in 1634 in order to "upstage" the regular, popular carnival with a patrician counter-festival designed, says Boiteux, to "repress, control and mutilate" the carnival of the common people. Whilst Simon Schama emphasizes the "benign license" of Dutch seventeenth-century carnival and its avoidance of Calvinist bourgeois strictures, David Kunzle has emphasized the directly political use of Dutch carnival forms in the War of the Netherlands (Scribner 1978; Boiteux 1977; Schama 1979; Kunzle 1978).

In recent social histories of England there has been a considerable debate over the interrelationship between popular culture and class conflict (Yeo and Yeo 1981; Bushaway 1982; Walvin 1978; Cunningham 1980; Thompson 1972; Malcolmson 1973; Stedman Jones 1983). Most of these studies unearth evidence of a long battle (with occasional truces) waged by the State, ecclesiastical and bourgeois authorities against popular custom. It is a battle that goes back well beyond the Renaissance but which, from the Renaissance on, produced local festivities as sites of resistance to the extension of power by the propertied and the State. Bushaway remarks:

> Custom and ceremony became a battleground in the struggle between the labouring poor and the increasingly wealthy landowners and proprietors over the defence of popular rights and the protection of a normative view of the structure of the community held by the labouring poor. (Bushaway 1982, 21–22)

This seems an altogether more accurate way of conceiving the relationship. Carnivals, fairs, popular games and festivals were very swiftly "politicized" by the very attempts made on the part of local authorities to eliminate them. The dialectic of antagonism frequently *turned* rituals into resistance at the moment of intervention by the higher powers, even when no overt oppositional element had been present before. All these issues in their historical complexity are discussed at greater length in the chapters which follow. In introducing them here we are only underscoring the banal but often ignored truth that the politics of carnival cannot be resolved outside of a close historical examination of particular conjunctures: there is no a priori revolutionary vector to carnival and transgression.

In his research on the carnivalesque Bakhtin had substantially anticipated by some thirty years main lines of development in symbolic anthropology. In his exploration of the *relational* nature of festivity, its structural inversion of, and ambivalent dependence upon, "official culture," Bakhtin set out a model of culture in which a high/low binarism had a fundamental place. Bakhtin's use of carnival centres the concept upon its "doubleness ... there is no unofficial expression without a prior official one or its possibility. Hence, in Bakhtin's analysis of carnival, the official and unofficial are locked together" (Wilson 1983, 320). Symbolic polarities of high and low, official and popular, grotesque and classical are mutually constructed and deformed in carnival. Two of the best general synopses of Bakhtin's work correctly perceive this to be the most significant aspect of *Rabelais and his World*. Ivanov (1976) links Bakhtin's discovery of the importance of binary oppositions with the work of Lévi-Strauss:

... the books by Bakhtin and Lévi-Strauss have much in common in their treatment of the functioning of oppositions in the ritual or the carnival which can be traced back historically to ritual performance. For Lévi-Strauss the chief purpose of the ritual and the myth is the discovery of an intermediate link between the members of a binary opposition: a process known as *mediation.* The structural analysis of the ambivalence inherent in the "marketplace word" and its corresponding imagery led Bakhtin to the conclusion (made independently from and prior to structural mythology) that the "carnival image strives to embrace and unite in itself both terminal points of the process of becoming or both members of the antithesis: birth–death, youth–age, top–bottom, face–lower bodily stratum, praise–abuse" [Bakhtin 1968, 238]. From this standpoint, Bakhtin scrutinized various forms of inverted relations between top and bottom "a reversal of the hierarchy of top and bottom" [Bakhtin 1968, 81] which takes place during carnival. (Ivanov 1976, 35)

The convergence of Bakhtin's thinking and that of current symbolic anthropology is highly significant. Where Ivanov points to the kinship Bakhtin shares with Lévi-Strauss and Edmund Leach (particularly Leach's essay on carnival, "Time and False Noses," 1961), Masao Yamaguchi suggests that Bakhtin's work significantly parallels that of Victor Turner, Barbara Babcock and Mary Douglas in their shared interest in cultural negations and symbolic inversions (Yamaguchi 1983). We may note, for instance, the similarity of Bakhtin's concept of carnivalesque high/low inversion to the concepts developed in *The Reversible World*, a collection of essays on anthropology and literature edited by Barbara Babcock. Although apparently unaware of Bakhtin's study she assembles a range of writing on "symbolic inversion and cultural negation" which puts carnival into a much wider perspective. She writes:

"Symbolic inversion" may be broadly defined as any act of expressive behaviour which inverts, contradicts, abrogates, or in some fashion presents an alternative to commonly held cultural codes, values and norms be they linguistic, literary or artistic, religious, social and political. (Babcock 1978, 14)

This is what we refer to in this book as "transgression" (though there is another, more complex use of the term which arises in connection with extremist practices of modern art and philosophy; these designate not just the infraction of binary structures, but movement into an absolutely negative space *beyond the structure of significance itself*). For the moment it is enough to suggest that, in our view, the current widespread adoption of the idea of carnival as an *analytic* category can only be fruitful if it is displaced into the broader concept of symbolic inversion and transgression.

This is not to deny the usefulness of the carnivalesque as a sort of "modelling," at once utopian and counter-hegemonic, whereby it is viewed, in Roberto da Matta's words, as a *privileged locus* of inversion. In his attempt to go beyond Bakhtin's nostalgic and over-optimistic view of carnival, Matta acknowledges the degree to which festivity is licensed release, but he also praises its deep modelling of a different, pleasurable and communal ideal "of the people," even if that ideal cannot immediately be acted upon. Victor Turner has similarly argued with respect to role reversal that carnival is "a moment when those being moved in accordance to a cultural script were liberated from normative demands, where they were ... betwixt and between successive lodgements in jural political systems." Carnival in this view has been defended as having a persistent *demystifying* potential (Jones 1983; Arthur 1982; Stamm 1982; Davis 1975). Even Terry Eagleton wants to salvage Bakhtin's carnivalesque by seeing it as a utopian modelling yoked to a glimpse through the ideological constructs of dominance, a "kind of fiction," a

> temporary retextualizing of the social formation that exposes its "fictive" foundations. (Eagleton 1981, 149)

In this perspective the carnivalesque becomes a resource of actions, images and roles which may be invoked both to model and legitimate desire and to "degrade all that is spiritual and abstract." "The cheerful vulgarity of the powerless is used as a weapon against the pretence and hypocrisy of the powerful" (Stamm 1982, 47). In a most engaging description of this utopian/critical role of carnival Stamm continues:

> On the positive side, carnival suggests the joyful affirmation of becoming. It is ecstatic collectivity, the superseding of the individuating principle in what Nietzsche called "the glowing life of Dionysian revellers" ... On the negative, critical side, the carnivalesque suggests a demystificatory instrument for everything in the social formation which renders such collectivity difficult of access: class hierarchy, political manipulation, sexual repression, dogmatism and paranoia. Carnival in this sense implies an attitude of creative disrespect, a radical opposition to the illegitimately powerful, to the morose and monological. (Stamm 1982, 55)

Refreshingly iconoclastic, this nevertheless resolves none of the problems raised so far concerning the politics of carnival: its nostalgia; its uncritical populism (carnival often violently abuses and demonizes *weaker*, not stronger, social groups—women, ethnic and religious minorities, those who "don't belong"—in a process of *displaced abjection*); its failure to do away with the official dominant culture, its licensed complicity.

In fact those writers and critics who remain purely within the celebratory terms of Bakhtin's formulation are unable to resolve these key dilemmas. It is only by completely shifting the grounds of the debate, by transforming the "problematic" of carnival, that these issues can be solved. It is precisely such an intervention in the current surge of Bakhtin-inspired studies which we have attempted in this book. The remainder of our introduction endeavours to sketch out a kind of political and aesthetic analysis building upon the work of Bakhtin but attempting to avoid the limitations here identified in his work. We have chosen therefore to consider carnival as one instance of a generalized economy of transgression and of the recoding of high/low relations across the whole social structure. The symbolic categories of grotesque realism which Bakhtin located can be rediscovered as a governing dynamic of the body, the household, the city, the nation-state—indeed a vast range of interconnected domains.

Marcel Détienne puts a similar notion most persuasively in *Dionysos Slain*:

> A system of thought ... is founded on a series of acts of partition whose ambiguity, here as elsewhere, is to open up the terrain of their possible transgression at the very moment when they mark off a limit. To discover the complete horizon of a society's symbolic values, it is also necessary to map out its transgressions, its deviants. (Détienne 1979, ix)

By tracking the "grotesque body" and the "low-Other" through different symbolic domains of bourgeois society since the Renaissance we can attain an unusual perspective upon its inner dynamics, the inner complicity of disgust and desire which fuels its crises of value. For the classificatory body of a culture is always double, always structured in relation to its negation, its inverse. "All symbolic inversions define a culture's lineaments at the same time as they question the usefulness and the absoluteness of its ordering" (Babcock 1978, 29). Indeed by attending to the low and the marginal we vindicate, on the terrain of European literary and cultural history, the more general anthropological assertion that the process of symbolic inversion,

> far from being a residual category of experience, is its very opposite. What is socially peripheral is often symbolically central, and if we ignore or minimize inversion and other forms of cultural negation, we often fail to understand the dynamics of symbolic processes generally. (Babcock 1978, 32)

This is a scrupulously accurate and indispensable formulation. The carnival, the circus, the gypsy, the lumpenproletariat, play a symbolic role in bourgeois culture out of all proportion to their actual social importance. The dominant features of the psycho-symbolic domain cannot be mapped one-to-one onto the social formation. Thus "work," for example, which occupied such a central place in individual and collective life, is notoriously "underrepresented" in artistic forms (Barrell 1980) but this should not be ascribed to some wilful act of ideological avoidance. Although work is "actually central" in the production and reproduction of the whole social ensemble there is no reason, beyond an irrationally vulgar Marxist one, to suppose that capitalism should be totally different from other societies in locating its most powerful *symbolic* repertoires at borders, margins and edges, rather than at the accepted centres, of the social body. Thus a writer such as Arnold Bennett, committed to a realist and sympathetically accurate account of commercial working life in the industrial Midlands, reaches out to the circus, the Burslem Wakes, a hot-air balloon ascent and a public execution for significant climaxes in the dramatic narrative of *The Old Wives' Tale.* The complex of utilitarianism, industry and calculating parsimony which were fundamental to the English bourgeoisie by the nineteenth century drew its imaginative sustenance from precisely those groups, practices and activities which it was earnestly and relentlessly working to marginalize and destroy. In chapters 3, 4 and 5, we explore the contradictory constructions of bourgeois desire to which this led in the nineteenth century—a construction of subjectivity through totally ambivalent internalizations of the city slum, the domestic servant and the carnivalesque.

At various points throughout this book we have turned to Bakhtin's vocabulary of "classical" and "grotesque" in our exploration of high/low symbolism. In Bakhtin the "classical body" denotes the inherent *form* of the high official culture and suggests that the shape and plasticity of the human body is indissociable from the shape and plasticity of discursive material and social norm in a collectivity. "No absolute borderline can be drawn between body and meaning in the sphere of culture" (Ivanov 1976, 3). Because he is at pains to hold onto the mediating role played by the body in cultural designation, Bakhtin is undeniably ambiguous in his use of the terms "classical body" and "grotesque body," yet the imprecision seems not unjustifiable. Clearly, as often as they are able, "high" languages attempt to legitimate their authority by appealing to values inherent in the classical body. Bakhtin was struck by the compelling difference between the human body as represented in popular festivity and the body as represented in classical statuary in the Renaissance. He noticed how the two forms of iconography "embodied" utterly contrary registers of being. To begin with, the classical statue was always mounted on a plinth which meant that it was elevated, static and monumental. In the one simple fact of the plinth or pedestal the classical body signalled a whole different somatic conception from that of the grotesque body which was usually multiple (Bosch, Bruegel), teeming, always already part of a throng. By contrast, the classical statue is the radiant centre of a transcendant individualism, "put on a pedestal," raised above the viewer and the commonality and anticipating passive admiration from below. We *gaze up* at the figure and wonder. We are placed by it as spectators to an instant—frozen yet apparently universal—of epic or tragic time. The presence of the statue is a problematic presence in that it immediately retroflects us to the heroic past; it is a *memento classici* for which we are the eternal late-comers, and for whom meditative imitation is the appropriate contrition. The classical statue has no openings or orifices whereas grotesque costume and masks emphasize the gaping mouth, the protuberant belly and buttocks, the feet and the genitals. In this way the grotesque body stands in opposition to the bourgeois individualist conception of the body, which finds *its* image and legitimation in the classical. The grotesque body is emphasized as a mobile, split, multiple self, a subject of pleasure in processes of exchange; and it is never closed off from either its social or ecosystemic context. The classical body on the other hand keeps its distance. In a sense it is disembodied, for it appears indifferent to a body which is "beautiful," but which is taken for granted.

Vasari's codification of Vitruvian categories, the famous list of *regola, ordine, misura, disegno* and *maniera*, is an interesting example of some of the governing principles of the classical body. Taking formal values from a purified mythologized canon of Ancient Greek and Roman authors—the "classic" with which this introduction began—the classical body was far more than an aesthetic standard or model. It structured, from the inside as it were, the characteristically "high" discourses of philosophy, statecraft, theology and law, as well as literature, as they emerged from the Renaissance. In the classical discursive body were encoded those regulated systems which were closed, homogeneous, monumental, centred and symmetrical. It began to make "parsimony" of explanation and "economy" of utterance the measure of rationality, thus institutionalizing Lenten rule as a normative epistemological standard. Gradually these protocols of the classical body came to mark out the identity of progressive rationalism itself. These are the terms of Foucault's "regimen" and Weber's "rationalization," the strong forms of functional purity which, certainly by the eighteenth century in England, led to the great age of "institutionalizing"—asylums, hospitals, schools, barracks, prisons, insurance and finance houses—which, as Foucault has suggested, embody and assure the maintenance of classical bourgeois reason. Furthermore Foucault's concentration upon the contained outsiders-who-make-the-insiders-insiders (the mad, the criminal, the sick, the unruly, the sexually transgressive) reveals just how far these outsiders are constructed by the dominant culture in terms of the grotesque body. The "grotesque" here designates the marginal, the low and the outside from the perspective of a classical body situated as high, inside and central by virtue of its very exclusions.

The grotesque body, as Bakhtin makes clear, has *its* discursive norms too: impurity (both in the sense of dirt and mixed categories), heterogeneity, masking, protuberant distension, disproportion, exorbitancy, clamour, decentred or eccentric arrangements, a focus upon gaps, orifices and symbolic filth (what Mary Douglas calls "matter out of place"), physical needs and pleasures of the "lower bodily stratum," materiality and parody. The opposition between classical and grotesque in this sense is invoked as automatically and unconsciously by Charcot in his description of the female hysteric as it is by the police spokesperson in a description of pickets or Auberon Waugh in his description of the women encamped at Greenham Common ("smelling of fish paste and bad oysters"). The grotesque physical body is invoked both defensively and offensively because it is not simply a powerful image but fundamentally constitutive of the categorical sets through which we live and make sense of the world.

The encampment of women protesters positioned on common land outside the entrance to the Cruise Missile Base near Newbury focuses many of these issues, and so powerfully, that it provides an exemplary instance. Malise Ruthven writes:

> all the women arouse a degree of hostility far in excess of any inconvenience they may cause to soldiers, policemen or residents living near the base. Shopkeepers and publicans refuse to serve them; hooligans unexpectedly join forces with the establishment and actualize the verbal insults by smearing the benders [homemade tents] with excrement and pig's blood ... This spontaneous and voluntary association of females, without formal leadership or hierarchy, seems to threaten the soldiers, the local gentry, the bourgeoisie of Newbury and even its hooligans far more than the missiles, although the latter would be a prime target in the event of nuclear war. (Ruthven 1984, 1048)

"What is socially peripheral may be symbolically central." The women at Greenham Common in their precarious and vulnerable condition by the roadside entrance to a vast military installation, "On the perimeter" as Caroline Blackwood describes it, occupy a very powerful *symbolic* domain *despite and because of* their actual social marginalization. They constitute what Edmund Leach calls an "intermediate and taboo-loaded category" and their association with excrement and pig's blood by a hostile local populace strongly attests to the fear and loathing which they have excited. They were accused, amongst other things, of having smeared the local town of Newbury with excrement. On one occasion, some soldiers as they were leaving the Base in a military coach ritually bared their backsides to the women "in a gesture that had clearly been rehearsed with parade-ground precision" (Ruthven 1984, 1048). So many of the themes of this book intersect here, where transgressions of gender, territorial boundaries, sexual preference, family and group norms are transcoded into the "grotesque body" terms of excrement, pigs and arses. We would argue that this is ascribable neither to a residual superstitious primitivism on the part of the good people of Newbury nor to trivial or accidental alignments. The women of Greenham Common are drawing (in some cases self-consciously) upon historical and political resources of mythopoetic transgression and conjuring from their antagonists not dissimilar reservoirs of material symbolism. They outrage the military establishment and the politicians by flagrantly maintaining their "low" hovels at the very door of the mighty military estate; they outrage the local ratepayers (RAGE—Ratepayers Against Greenham Encampment) by transgressing the neat boundaries of private and public property as the Levellers and the Diggers did before them, occupying common land in the name of the people. They outrage local youths by breaking the norms of women's dependence upon men and by their independent sexual stance and are visited, in consequence, with a "charivari"—a scapegoating carnivalesque ritual, usually carried out by young men against those whom they feel have broken the customs of courtship and sexual duty in the locality (Le Goff and Schmitt 1981; Desplatt 1982): charivari was a rowdy form of crowd behaviour often used against "unruly women," and here it is an overt reminder of patriarchal dominance.

The women live "on the wire," "on the perimeter," neither fully outside nor fully inside, and they have triggered powerful associative chains which connect the international issue of nuclear missiles with pigs' blood and excremental vandalism: the cosmic with the local, the topographic with the sexual. Arguably a special (in every sense) and privileged case, the Greenham Common women nevertheless reveal how the grotesque body may become a primary, highly-charged intersection and mediation of social and political forces, a sort of intensifier and displacer in the making of identity. The exorbitant contrast between the closed, monumental, classical body of the multi-million dollar American Military Complex and the open, muddy, exposed huddle of higgledy-piggledy polythene tents is a scandal to hegemonic dignity which it can scarcely sustain. It is indeed wonderful that so little can make so great a difference.

This book aims to give a number of exploratory testings from early modern and modern Europe (particularly England), by mapping domains of transgression where place, body, group identity and subjectivity interconnect. Points of antagonism, overlap and intersection between the high and the low, the classical and its "Other," provide some of the richest and most powerful symbolic dissonances in the culture. In mapping some of these spaces we illuminate the discursive sites where social classification and psychological processes are generated as conflictual complexes. It is precisely here where ideology and fantasy conjoin. The topography of realms which, *by virtue* of exclusions at the geographical, class, or somatic level, traces lines of desire and phobic contours which are produced and reproduced through one another. There is a secular magic to these displacements, and its law is the law of exclusion.

Thus the logic of identity-formation involves distinctive associations and switching between location, class and the body, and these are not imposed *upon* subject-identity from the outside; they are the core terms of an exchange network, an economy of signs, in which individuals, writers and authors are sometimes but perplexed agencies. A fundamental rule seems to be that what is excluded at the overt level of identity-formation is productive of new objects of desire. As new classificatory sets emerge with new forms of production and new social relations, so the carnivalesque and transgressive anti-structure of the emergent classical body will also change, marking out new sites of symbolic and metaphorical intensity in the ideological field. In class society where social conflict is always present these sites do not necessarily coincide with the "objective" conflict boundaries of antagonistic classes but will nevertheless function to the advantage of one social group rather than another. In Chapter 3, for example, we note how certain middle-class fantasies about the lumpenproletariat in the nineteenth century effaced the centrality of issues around the proletariat. On the other hand transgressive symbolic domains and the fetishism which attaches to them are never merely diversionary. There is no simple fit between the imaginary repertoire of transgressive desire and economic and political contradictions in the social formation, and yet the two are always deeply connected.

It is perhaps worth recapitulating the points we have made so far. By focusing upon the "taboo-laden" overlap between high and low discourse which produces the grotesque, we have tried to effect a transposition of the Bakhtinian conception of the carnivalesque into a framework which makes it analytically powerful in the study of ideological repertoires and cultural practices. If we treat the carnivalesque as an instance of a wider phenomenon of transgression we move beyond Bakhtin's troublesome *folkloric* approach to a political anthropology of *binary extremism* in class society. This transposition beyond the rather unproductive debate over whether carnivals are politically progressive or conservative, reveals that the underlying structural features of carnival operate far beyond the strict confines of popular festivity and are intrinsic to the dialectics of social classification as such. The "carnivalesque" mediates between a classical/classificatory body and its negations, its Others, what it excludes to create its identity as such. In this process discourses about the body have a privileged role, for transcodings between different levels and sectors of social and psychic reality are effected through the intensifying grid of the body. It is no accident, then, that transgressions and the attempt to control them obsessively return to somatic symbols, for these are ultimate elements of social classification itself.

Note

1. Kateryna Arthur: "The question I shall be addressing throughout my exploration of carnivalesque activity is: how can carnival be simultaneously revolutionary and law-abiding?" (Arthur 1982, 4). Terry Eagleton: "Carnival laughter is incorporating as well

as liberating, the lifting of inhibitions politically enervating as well as disruptive. Indeed from one viewpoint carnival may figure as a prime example of that mutual complicity of law and liberation, power and desire, that has become the dominant theme of contemporary post-marxist pessimism" (Eagleton 1981, 149).

References

MMB = *Mikhail Mikhailovich Bakhtin: His Circle, His Influence*. Papers presented at the International Colloquium, Queen's University, Kingston, Ontario, October 7–9, 1983.

Arthur, K. 1982. "Bakhtin, Kristeva and Carnival." Unpublished dissertation, Melbourne.

Babcock, B. 1978. *The Reversible World: Symbolic Inversion in Art and Society*. Ithaca, NY: Cornell University Press.

Bakhtin, M. M. 1968. *Rabelais and his World*. Trans. H. Iswolsky. Cambridge, MA: MIT Press.

Balandier, George. 1972. *Political Anthropology*. Harmondsworth: Penguin.

Barrell, J. 1980. *The Dark Side of the Landscape: The Rural Poor in English Painting*. Cambridge: Cambridge University Press.

Bennett, T. 1979. *Formalism and Marxism*. London: Methuen.

Blackwood, C. 1984. *On the Perimeter*. London: Fontana; London: Heinemann.

Boiteux, M. 1977. "Carnaval annexé: essai de lecture d'une fête romaine." *Annales* 32.2: 356–77.

Brewer, J., N. McKendrick, and J. H. Plumb. 1983. *The Birth of a Consumer Society: The Commercialization of Eighteenth-century England*. London: Hutchinson.

Burke, P. 1978. *Popular Culture in Early Modern Europe*. London: Temple Smith.

Bushaway, B. 1982. *By Rite: Custom, Ceremony and Community in England 1700–1880*. Studies in Popular Culture. London: Junction Books.

Cunningham, H. 1980. *Leisure in the Industrial Revolution*. London: Croom Helm.

Curtius, E. R. 1953. *European Literature and the Latin Middle Ages*. London: Routledge & Kegan Paul.

Davis, N. Z. 1975. *Society and Culture in Early Modern France*. Stanford: Stanford University Press.

Desplatt, C. 1982. *Charivaris en Gascogne: La 'Morale des Peuples' du XVI au XX Siècle*. Paris: Bibliothèque Berger-Levrault.

Détienne, M. 1979. *Dionysos Slain*. Trans. M. Mueller and L. Mueller. Baltimore: Johns Hopkins University Press.

Douglas, M. 1966. *Purity and Danger*. London: Routledge & Kegan Paul.

Eagleton, T. 1981. *Walter Benjamin: Towards a Revolutionary Criticism*. London: Verso.

Fisher, S. 1972. "Body Image." In *International Encyclopedia of the Social Sciences*, 2nd ed., ed. D. Sills, vol. 2, 113–16. New York: Collier-Macmillan.

Fisher, S., and S. E. Cleveland. 1958. *Body Image and Personality*. Princeton: Van Nostrand.

Foucault, M. 1977. *Language/Counter-memory/Practice*. Ed. D. F. Bouchard. Trans. D. F. Bouchard and S. Simon. Ithaca, NY: Cornell University Press.

Gluckman, M. 1963. *Order and Rebellion in Tribal Africa: Collected Essays with an Autobiographical Introduction*. London: Cohen.

—1965. *Custom and Conflict in Africa*. Oxford: Blackwell.

Goddard, B. 1983. "World of Wonders." In MMB, 51–59.

Hill, E. 1972. *The Trinidad Carnival*. Austin: University of Texas Press.

Ivanov, V. V. 1976. "The Significance of Bakhtin's Ideas on Sign, Utterance and Dialogue for Modern Semiotics." In *Papers on Poetics and Semiotics* 4. Tel Aviv: The Israeli Institute for Poetics and Semiotics, Tel-Aviv University.

Jack, I. 1942. *Augustan Satire: Intention and Idiom in English Poetry 1660–1750*. Oxford: Clarendon Press.

Jones, A. R. 1983. "Inside the Outsider: Nashe's 'Unfortunate Traveller' and Bakhtin's Polyphonic Novel." *English Literary History* 50(1): 61–82.

Kunzle, D. 1978. "World Upside Down: Iconography of a European Broadsheet Type." In *The Reversible World*, ed. B. Babcock, 39–94. Ithaca, NY: Cornell University Press.

Le Goff, J., and J.-C. Schmitt, eds. 1981. *Le Charivari*. Paris, The Hague and New York: Mouton.

Le Roy Ladurie, E. 1981. *Carnival in Romans*. Trans. M. Feeney. Harmondsworth: Penguin.

Leach, E. 1961. "Time and False Noses." In *Rethinking Anthropology*, ed. E. Leach, 132–36. Monograph/Social Anthropology 22. London: Athlone Press.

Lodge, D. 1982. "Double Discourses: Joyce and Bakhtin." *James Joyce Broadsheet* 11.

Malcolmson, R. W. 1973. *Popular Recreations in English Society 1700–1850*. Cambridge: Cambridge University Press.

Malcuzynski, M.-P. 1983. "Mikhail Bakhtin and Contemporary Narrative Theory." *University of Ottawa Quarterly* [special issue on Bakhtin] 53(1): 51–65.

Monas, S. 1983. "Finnegans Walk: Carnival, Polyphony and Chronotope." In MMB.

Parrinder, P. 1984. *James Joyce*. Cambridge: Cambridge University Press.

Pomorska, K. 1978. "Mikhail Bakhtin and his Verbal Universe." *Poetics and Theory of Literature* 3: 379–86.

Robin, R. 1983. "La literature yiddish soviétique: minorité nationale / polyphonisme." In MMB.

Ruthven, M. 1984. "Cassandras at Camp." *Times Literary Supplement* 21 (Sept.): 1048a.

Said, E. 1979. *Orientalism*. New York: Vintage Books.

—1984. *The World, the Text and the Critic*. London: Faber & Faber.

Sales, R. 1983. *English Literature in History 1780-1830: Pastoral and Politics*. London: Hutchinson.

Schama, S. 1979. "The Unruly Realm: Appetite and Restraint in Seventeenth-century Holland." *Daedalus* 108.3: 103–23.

Screech, M. A. 1979. *Rabelais*. London: Duckworth.

—1984. "Homage to Rabelais." *London Review of Books* 6: 17.

Scribner, R. 1978. "Reformation, Carnival and the World Turned Upside-down." *Social History* III, 3: 303–29.

Short, J. 1983. "Le carnivalesque dans le théâtre de Jean-Claude Germain." In MMB.

Stamm, R. 1982. "On the Carnivalesque." *Wedge* 1: 47–55.

Stedman Jones, G. 1983. *Languages of Class*. Cambridge: Cambridge University Press.

Thompson, E. P. 1972. "'Rough Music': le charivari anglais." *Annales ESC* 27(2): 285–312.

Thurston, J. 1983. "The Carnival Comes to/from Vancouver Island." In MMB, 256–68.

Todorov, T. 1984. "Mikhail Bakhtin: The Dialogic Principle." In *Theory and History of Literature* 13. Trans. W. Godzich. Minneapolis: University of Minnesota Press.

—1985. *The Conquest of America*. Trans. R. Howard. New York: Harper Collophon.

Van Buuren, M. 1983. "Carnival in the Theatre of Samuel Beckett" [abstract]. In MMB, 28.

Vilar de Kerkhoff, A. M. 1983. "Echoes of Bakhtin's Dialogic Principle in Puerto Rican Prose Fiction." In MMB.

Walvin, J. 1978. *Leisure and Society 1830–1950*. London: Longman.

Weber, E. 1979. *Peasants into Frenchmen: The Modernization of Rural France 1870–1914*. London: Chatto and Windus.

White, A. 1982. "Pigs and Pierrots: Politics of Transgression in Modern Fiction." *Raritan* (New Brunswick, NJ) 2(2) (Fall): 51–70.

Wilson, R. 1983. "Carnival and Play." In MMB, 318–21.

Yamaguchi, M. 1983. "Bakhtin and Symbolic Anthropology." In MMB, 323–39.

Yeo, E., and S. Yeo, eds. 1981. *Popular Culture and Class Conflict*. Brighton: Harvester.

Ritual as Communication: A Study of African Christian Communities in the Bijlmer District of Amsterdam

Gerrie ter Haar

Editor's Introduction

Gerrie ter Haar is Professor of Religion, Human Rights and Social Change at the Institute of Social Studies in The Hague, The Netherlands, and Deputy Secretary-General of the International Association for the History of Religions. Her teaching, research and publications focus largely on Africa and the African diaspora, and she is also interested in human rights, development, globalization and the notion of diaspora.

The chief argument of this chapter is that rituals are a primary mode of religious communication in the context of religious and cultural pluralism. This is illustrated with particular reference to African diaspora communities in the Netherlands. Ter Haar demonstrates that Christians of African origin make significant use of ritual behaviour to communicate with one another about matters of significance to them, especially as they construct and maintain identities and communities. Within that framework ter Haar discusses rituals performed for particular purposes (purification, dedication, foot-washing, and life-crises such as birth, puberty, marriage and death). She not only applies the classic work of Arnold van Gennep (1975) and Victor Turner (1969) to the rituals and communities of interest, but tests the classification of ritual processes and phases, especially liminality and *communitas*, against the need to agree an identity in a more-or-less "hostile and unstable environment." For all the pluralism of global modernity, African Christians in Europe are likely to be seen first and foremost as Africans (outsiders/others/different) rather than Christians (insiders/us/identical) in distinction to their self-perception which reverses such labelling and identifications.

163

The study of ritual and its relation to belief is greatly aided by a realistic assessment of the effects of specific behaviours among particular communities. The role of "tradition" (and understandings of what that might mean) within these rhetorics and practices of identity is also significant. Ter Haar's notion that ritual behaviour is a mode of communication within groups is worth considering in relation to other groups, contexts and theoretical approaches.

References

Gennep, Arnold van. 1975. *The Rites of Passage*. Chicago: University of Chicago Press.
Turner, V. W. 1969. *The Ritual Process: Structure and Anti-structure*. Harmondsworth: Penguin Books.

ഇ രു

Introduction

The research group "Religious Pluralism" in the Theological Faculty of Leiden University has committed itself to investigating religious interaction in pluralistic societies, marked by the presence of a variety of religions whose adherents are living adjacent to one another.[1] This poses a basic question: given the situation of religious pluralism, how do adherents of one religion respond to adherents of a different religion and how do they articulate their relationships with them? In organizing a symposium on pluralism and identity the underlying idea was that believers of any religion living in a plural society will design and use rituals, or ritual behaviour more generally, as an instrument for inter-religious demarcation. In other words, an important function of ritual behaviour in such a context is to emphasize religious identity and thus separate different believers by drawing strict lines between them.

In this paper I will argue the opposite. I will maintain that in the case which I intend to discuss, namely ritual behaviour among African Christian communities in the southeast district of Amsterdam, the purpose and function of ritual behaviour are essentially geared not to inter-religious demarcation but to intra-religious communication. Although the former idea may be a fruitful line of approach in many present-day cases, it is not a valid starting point for assessing the meaning of ritual in the communities under discussion. This is partly due to their diaspora status and partly also to their very short history in the Netherlands. Both are factors which influence ritual behaviour in these communities in such a way that, contrary to what one might expect in a context of religious pluralism, this is first and foremost aimed at creating and maintaining internal stability. The rituals designed in this context then become symbols for intra-religious communication within the Christian tradition.[2]

In my paper I will first describe the religious microcosm of the Bijlmer district of Amsterdam, paying particular attention to the African-led[3] churches and describing three different types of ritual behaviour in one of these churches. On the basis of that I will then analyse the situation of African Christian communities in the Bijlmer. In doing so, I will make use of the insights provided by van Gennep's classic study on rites of passage[4] and look at ritual behaviour in these communities in terms of a life crisis. Rites of passage are rites which can be found in all cultures and are connected to important phases of life. They mark the transition from one phase to the other and thus help in the resolution of a life crisis. Or, as van Gennep defines it, these are "rites which accompany every change of place, state, social position and age,"[5] or indeed a transition from one state into another. Rites of passage, according to van Gennep, comprise all ceremonial patterns which accompany a passage from one situation into another or from one cosmic or social world to another.[6]

This describes well the African communities under discussion. Their rituals have been designed basically to cope with a life crisis resulting from the transition from one social world to another. As van Gennep has pointed out, such drastic changes of condition do not occur without disturbing the life of society and individuals concerned, and it is the function of rites of passage to reduce the harmful effects of that change.[7] Van Gennep's concept of "rites of passage" was designed to apply to small-scale societies or discrete social groups within a larger society. In the present text, I apply his theory to a secular situation involving large-scale social trends in order to explain the situation of African religious communities in present-day Western Europe. I am thus using existing social theory to explain the ritual behaviour under discussion in the belief that this provides the best available starting point for developing a deeper theoretical understanding of the phenomena described. Although van Gennep's theory is not applied here in its "pure" and original state, we can nevertheless still derive meaning from it when it is applied to modern times and circumstances.

I will further base myself on Victor Turner's analysis of ritual as a process.[8] His concepts of communitas and liminality,[9] which he developed on the basis of van Gennep's work on rites of passage and which he applied to both religious and secular situations,[10] shed a particular light on the meaning of ritual behaviour as presently practised among African Christian communities in the Bijlmer. The social context in which the ritual process takes place has changed, as has the nature of the life crises which many Africans face today. Nowadays such existential crises no longer affect small-scale and isolated communities, but concern communities world-wide, due to the globalization of social and economic relations. This is clearly so with people affected by the large-scale migration processes of today, such as in the case of African migrants in Europe. At the same time, much of the social setting has been influenced by a process of secularization which has reduced the meaning of rites in modern times, particularly in the Western world. But, as has been stated by others, there is no evidence that a secularized urban world has lessened the need for ritualized expression of an individual's transition from one status to the other,[11] and the same can be said of specific communities.

I will conclude my argument by showing that religious demarcation is not in the interest of the African communities in the Bijlmer (or elsewhere in Western Europe) but is a concept which favours the West.

The Religious Microcosm of the Bijlmer

In the southeast district of Amsterdam, commonly though somewhat incorrectly known as the Bijlmermeer or just "Bijlmer,"[12] we find a great variety of migrant communities, including many Africans. With almost 100,000 officially registered inhabitants,[13] the southeast district is the largest district of Amsterdam containing some minority groups large enough to deserve explicit mention in government statistics. About half of the Bijlmer population is of non-Dutch origin, the largest minority group being constituted by Surinamers.[14] Other groups explicitly mentioned in the statistics are Antillians, Turks, Moroccans (including other North Africans), and "South Europeans," including Spanish, Portuguese, Italians, Greek and (former) Yugoslavs.[15] The many West Africans living in the Bijlmer and largely of Ghanaian origin, fall within the category of "other foreigners" which in 1992 comprised slightly less than 10,000 people.[16] The number of different nationalities living together in this particular district of Amsterdam is said to be over sixty.[17] Depending on their size and substance these different groups have established their own networks which help them to survive in their new environment, which is full of difficulties. They are faced with unemployment, housing problems, and criminality at a time when the general atmosphere in the Netherlands is becoming increasingly hostile towards foreigners from the poorer parts of the world.[18]

One particular social network for many migrant communities in the Bijlmer is formed by the religious organizations, of which there were some 35 different ones in 1992.[19] Since the early 1990s the local council has become aware of the importance of these organizations in, and their contribution to, the process of social renewal of the Bijlmer.[20] Muslims and Christians of various sorts, Hindu groups and Winti adherents, can all be found in this particular district of Amsterdam.[21] The African Christian communities represent only one aspect of that kaleidoscope of religions, albeit an important one. There are at least ten different churches or church groups under African leadership in the Bijlmer, varying in size. They have all been founded by Ghanaians who constitute the largest African presence in the Bijlmer. Apart from these African-led churches, there are substantial numbers of Africans who belong to one of the Catholic churches or to other denominations such as the Seventh Day Adventists.[22] The presence of Ghanaians in the Bijlmer has received special attention from the local council which counted in 1991 an official total of some 2,500 Ghanaians here.[23] However, the total number of Ghanaians in the Bijlmer is estimated to be much higher and needs probably to be doubled.[24] To a large extent it is they who are responsible for the growth and flourishing of the Christian churches in the Amsterdam Bijlmer.

One of the major problems of all religious groups in the Bijlmer is the lack of space to worship. At the time that the Bijlmer district was built, in the 1960s, provision was made for one church building which would accommodate some of the traditional Dutch churches.[25] Almost thirty years later, a completely new picture has emerged as a result of the influx of non-Dutch people,[26] many of whom are adherents of some religion. To enable themselves to worship and fulfil their religious duties they have usually started to meet at private places, forming some sort of house congregation. With the increasing number of migrants the need for space became more and more urgent. Since 1991, therefore, representatives from different religious organizations in the Bijlmer which have no adequate meeting place have come together to discuss their space problem and find practical solutions to it.[27]

Groups which cooperate in this way include people from different faiths. They receive limited support from the local authorities. Some have come to share buildings on a temporary or permanent basis; others have been able to obtain their own space, usually at great financial cost, entirely paid by membership donations; while others are still coping with the present inadequate situation. The majority of groups are Christian, many of which have found shelter in one of the empty spaces under the multi-storey car parks, or in places such as an old shop or supermarket, or they may congregate on Sundays in one of the community houses in the Bijlmer. What they have in common is, literally, their invisibility. The only other religious building in the Bijlmer, apart from the above-mentioned church, is the Taibah mosque which was opened in 1985. It caters for a few thousand Muslim believers of different origin, particularly for Muslims from Surinam.[28]

African-led Churches in the Bijlmer

To date, the lack of space to worship on Sundays and to engage in community-building activities during the week is one of the most pressing problems for the African Christian communities in the Bijlmer.[29] If we single out the self-governing churches under African leadership as a separate category, we find at the time of writing some ten different churches of varied size,[30] all founded and led by Ghanaians, who are by far the largest single African community in the Bijlmermeer.[31] The rapid growth of their churches is a relatively new phenomenon which reflects the recent influx of Ghanaians into Dutch society. The beginning of this large-scale migration lies in the early 1980s and is connected to the political and economic changes in Ghana during that time.[32] Many of them found shelter in the Bijlmer where soon they also started to come together to satisfy their religious needs. In practice this often meant a small number of people congregating in an apartment and sitting around the kitchen table to pray together and read the Bible. The increasing numbers of participants forced most groups to look for more suitable accommodation in the sense described above. The emergence of full churches, therefore, is a very recent one, in fact a development of the last five years.

In the following I will describe one of these churches, the longest in existence and with the largest membership, the True Teachings of Christ Temple,[33] which is also the one I know best. Although there are differences in style and structure between the True Teachings of Christ Temple and other African-led churches in the Bijlmer, the general pattern of religious belief and practice is rather similar. Some outstanding features of this from a Western perspective are the belief in the power of the Spirit, the importance of prayer and fasting, the intensive use of the Bible, the role of praise-giving during worship, the public testimonies and the overall pastoral care. All these are characteristics which we also find among African Christians in Africa.[34] An additional element, which is of importance in the European context, is that all these diaspora churches see themselves as charged with the task of evangelization. In view of these similarities, the True Teachings of Christ Temple may be considered a model for African Christianity in the Netherlands.

There are also common features in the structural organization. We will normally find the congregation under the leadership of a pastor, usually male,[35] assisted by a number of church officials with varying responsibilities. A board of elders, a pastoral board and a welfare committee, as well as a financial board are among the most common structures, all made up of both men and women. Most of them are known for their choirs and accompanying bands, and for their youth activities. They run their own crèches and organize Sunday schools and other activities, depending on their accommodation. Finally, and most significantly in the context of Dutch society, every one of their churches is always full on Sundays. The latter may be seen as an indication that the growth of one church does not necessarily take place at the cost of another.[36]

The True Teachings of Christ Temple was officially founded as a church when it was registered in 1988 by the Dutch Chamber of Commerce.[37] The leader and founder of the church is Reverend Daniel Himmans-Arday, commonly known as "Brother Daniel," who comes from Accra, the capital of Ghana. In spite of his involvement with the Ghanaian migrant community in the Bijlmer his own presence in the Netherlands is not related to this latest flux of migration. It is the result of a religious experience as a young man in Ghana, when, during serious illness, he was promised recovery in a vision and received a divine call to preach the gospel overseas. "You will be well, you will travel into the other continents and bring back lost souls (who will be made equally well on the account of your testimony) into My Vineyard."[38] Following his vocation he arrived in the Netherlands in the late 1970s where during the years to follow he became involved in the lives of his fellow Ghanaians as they started to come and live in the Bijlmer. In the meantime he undertook theology studies with a Bible College in the United Kingdom which further prepared him for his task. His success as a pastor owes much to his charismatic personality which instils faith and confidence in people.[39]

Over the years the True Teachings of Christ Temple has grown from a small house congregation into a full-fledged church which is housed under one of the multi-storey car-parks that are located under the huge tower-blocks in the Bijlmer district. After experiencing several translocations, like other religious communities in the Bijlmer, in 1988 the True Teachings of Christ Temple bought this former accommodation of the Jehovah's Witnesses which could hold some 350 people. Five years later the hall has already proved far too small and an extension project is in full swing which should be completed in early 1994 and give room to some 600 people. Again, this is a trend we also find in other African-led churches, all of which have to make enormous sacrifices in order to obtain or build a place of worship.[40] The largest churches are visited by hundreds of people and have a corresponding membership. The True Teachings of Christ Temple, for example, has a membership of up to about one thousand,[41] although precise indications are difficult to obtain as the African migrant community is very mobile. All churches declare themselves explicitly open to everybody who wants to visit or participate, or be a member. In practice, though for obvious reasons membership is largely defined by Ghanaians, many other Africans, particularly Nigerians, but also Antillians and Surinamese people, as well as some Dutch, frequent these churches. As a result, the services have become increasingly bi-lingual, held in both Twi and English to enhance communication among all present.[42]

Church doctrine and practice in the True Teachings of Christ Temple are derived from what is believed to be prescribed by the Bible and therefore seen, as the name indicates, as the "true teachings" on which Christianity is based. The sermons, presented in the form of "lessons" focusing on a particular theme, are a central element in the Sunday services. As in the other churches in the Bijlmer, a connection is always made between the lessons to be taken from the Bible and the present-day situation, and a line drawn from the universal meaning it entails to its individual application. In the True Teachings of Christ Temple two sermons are normally preached, the first in Twi by the second pastor with the rank of "apostle" and simultaneously translated into English, followed by a sermon in English by the minister who elaborates further on some of the issues. The atmosphere is generally relaxed, joyful and attentive. People may come and go as they like although many will sit through the hours-long sessions of preaching, praying, reading, singing, dancing and music with ease and apparent pleasure. There is much attention for individual people's problems and ample time spent on addressing these.

Sunday worship will normally start with the latter during the "morning devotion," when some of the junior pastors, known as the "Holy Children," will lead the congregation into songs and prayer, encouraging people to put their requests before God. They wear white robes with a coloured trim, just like the pastor and the apostle. Often, the pastor himself, who is known for his spiritual gifts, will conduct special healing prayers and, if necessary, pray over individual people. As in other African-led churches, the awareness of the presence of evil as a potential threat to humankind is prevalent, and is a problem which will be openly addressed. Preventive action may be taken, for example by the use of incense in the building, as well as by using the rosary during prayers. These are practices which are unique to the True Teachings of Christ Temple and not always approved of by other congregations. The True Teachings of Christ Temple also lights candles during services, another individual characteristic which is disapproved of by some other churches.

Bible reading and the lessons to be taken from that are important aspects of the Sunday services. Christianity is preached not as a doctrine but as a way of life, with Christ as the perfect model. The leaders of the church are supposed to set an example for others by their lifestyle. Through spiritual training they prepare themselves for this responsibility. To further spiritual growth the pastors and "evangelists," a group of men and women who want to live up to the principles of the church and carry these further, engage in regular prayer and fasting. The male evangelists are called "Faith Brothers" while the women are known as "Divine Sisters." Some of their tasks during services are to ensure order, to show people their seats, to answer any queries or to provide translation if needed, and to take care of the children. Like the pastors, they can be recognized by their special dress, the Divine Sisters usually wearing blue capes and the Faith Brothers a special badge.

Ritual practice is more developed in the True Teachings of Christ Temple than in any of the other African-led churches. It appears well-adapted to the

170

needs of the congregation as related to their conditions of life in the Netherlands and, more particularly, in the Bijlmer. These are often conditions of uncertainty, anxiety and extreme concern, not knowing what tomorrow will bring. The majority of Africans in the Netherlands have come to find a job which will enable them to secure a future for themselves and their families.[43] However, they are increasingly made to feel unwelcome and many have to go underground as they are unable to legalize their presence. The church provides a place where they receive encouragement in all their endeavours by the spiritual underpinning of their lives.[44] At the same time it constitutes a community of equals where people in similar circumstances can share their experiences and lend each other practical support. That way the church provides a social network for basically marginalized people who depend on each other. Love and unity, mutual concern and understanding, compassion and solidarity are constantly stressed as important values to which every true Christian should adhere.

In the following I will give some examples of ritual behaviour in the True Teachings of Christ Temple, which involves the active participation of all ritual functionaries in the church.

Ritual Acts of Purification

Purification rituals or, more simply, ritual acts, may be performed in a number of ways. They are a symbolic expression of the awareness of the existence of evil which requires effective action to counter it. Evil forces can be warded off by calling upon the power of the good forces people believe in, that is the power of Christ or the power of the Holy Spirit. They may also seek protection by burning incense which spreads a pleasant fragrance and is therefore known in various religions as a cultic means to ward off evil forces or spirits and attract good ones. The True Teachings of Christ Temple bases the use of incense on various Biblical references, such as taken from Exodus 30 which gives prescriptions for the building of an altar for burning incense. The burning of incense is also seen as representing the prayer of good people in Christianity, as expounded in the Book of Revelations (8:3–5).

The most common and obvious symbol for purification in the True Teachings of Christ Temple, like in many religions, is the use of water. The sprinkling of holy water, that is, water that has been blessed by an ordained minister, can take place on various occasions. One such occasion is at the end of the dedication ceremony, which will be described later in more detail. In this ceremony, during which a newborn child is "committed into the capable hands of the Lord," the sprinkling of holy water onto the congregation refers to the power of God as it is expressed through water and which is believed to work miracles. Evidence for such miracles is found in passages from the Bible, for example in 2 Kings 5:13–16, which tells about the miraculous healing of Naaman, the army commander of the Syrian king. Purification and healing, the example shows, go hand in hand. The same is true for the use of water in the dedication ceremony. It is a symbolic act expressing the belief that God can heal people from whatever troubles they may have. In the context of a dedication ceremony it expresses the belief that he can also heal barrenness and use his miraculous powers to provide with children even those who may—humanly speaking—have no hope of conceiving. At the same time the sprinkling and washing with water as practised in the True Teachings of Christ Temple are meant as a symbol of love and equality in the sight of God. We find the clearest expression of that on New Year's eve, when, during a night-long service, every individual's feet are washed with water by the apostle and subsequently blessed with oil by the pastor. Purification and restoration are merging here into one final act that is to symbolize the love of God for all humankind, under all circumstances and irrespective of who and where they are.

The most common symbolic use of water, however, is through sprinkling as a simple act of purification. There is no particular time or moment during services set aside for this purpose, nor does it take place as a regular part of the weekly service. Rather different from traditional Dutch churches, much is said to depend on divine inspiration (which by definition cannot be channelled in the conventional way), while at the same time much room is left for improvisation within the broader framework of the service. The sprinkling with water may take place at the beginning of the service, before the morning devotion. One of the Holy Children goes around the church hall sprinkling water from a white plastic jar. Once the hall has been purified the necessary conditions have been created for the power of God to manifest itself during and through the prayers that will follow, conducted by the pastor. There is no set pattern, and the following is just an example.

The pastor enters the hall joined by the junior pastors. They kneel down in front of the hall, facing the congregation whose members follow their example. In the meantime the sprinkling of holy water continues. The pastor starts praying to purify the hearts and minds of everyone and to remove all evil. He calls upon the Lord to remove the evil forces which are believed to be acting against the well-being of individual people as well as of mankind as a whole. He will refer to Satan as the ultimate source of evil or otherwise express the belief in satanic powers which try to influence God's essentially good creation in a negative way. In his prayers the pastor shows an acute awareness of the fact that many people in his congregation are troubled physically or spiritually or otherwise under the pressure of forces they feel unable to control. He will therefore call upon the power of Christ and ask for "spiritual blessings" for all in order to drive Satan away. He may address Satan directly by pointing out that the church is a holy place, sanctified and dedicated to the Lord and that therefore Satan is not wanted in this area. It is a powerful prayer which is said in the knowledge that as an ordained minister the pastor is not acting in his own right but on the authority of "our Lord Jesus Christ." This challenging of Satan may have a visible effect on those who indeed feel oppressed by evil in some way. Some of the members of the congregation may fall into a state of trance and start shaking, thus showing the tumultuous effect of the prayers for healing and purification.

When the prayers are concluded, that is when Satan is believed to have been effectively removed from this area, the pastor addresses himself to the congregation. He will assure them that the Lord has purified them and warns the congregation against going into any "dark places," where Satan is believed to be active and where one can easily come under the influence of satanic powers. He emphasizes the power of prayer and how the Lord is changing man's heart that way. He will call on the believers to open their hearts and to receive the Lord. All will then say the Lord's prayer together. This may be followed by a special prayer which is first said by the pastor and repeated by the congregation which is standing up with hands raised. It may go as follows: "Unto you I commit my whole body; the forces from inside and outside have no control over me; let me walk free; because of your blood I am redeemed." Once again, the congregation may call upon the Lord to cast out evil forces, with the words "cast them out, cast them all out, I will be free." Subsequently the congregation will submit itself to God by stating that "I belong to you," and ask for his protection. "Let me proclaim your glory, I need you always; protect me and protect my family; protect my feet, my eyes, my mouth, so that everything will be in glory to your name. Help me, touch me and set me free." Often the session is ended with the Lord's prayer and what is called the "song of togetherness," Psalm 133, which is in praise of brotherly love.

The Dedication Ceremony

As in all African-led churches, the True Teachings of Christ Temple pays special attention to the children. From a very young age parents take their children to church. Babies usually stay with their mothers for whom special seats are reserved in such a way that they can easily walk in and out to look after them during the service. The older children follow Sunday school classes in a separate room but participate during part of the service. Everything is aimed at preparing the children for a Christian way of life and instilling Christian values and principles from a very young age. In that context the first time a child enters the church after birth is seen as a very special and joyful occasion which is accompanied by a special ritual, called the dedication ceremony, of which the following is a description.

The dedication of a newborn child normally takes place after three months, when the mother has recovered from giving birth and will resume church attendance. Both parents will proudly present the child to the church community to which the newborn baby will also belong from now on. They will do so in the presence of a host of relatives and friends, who are not necessarily members of the church but may just accompany the parents for this special occasion in order to share in their happiness. To mark the festivity parents and other participants are dressed in their best clothes—the parents often in white—as for a party. During the service they will be seated on the front rows of the church, with the child that is going to be dedicated to God. At the appropriate moment, which is after the service has ended but before the closing prayer, parents and child with all who have accompanied them leave the church hall to re-enter again in procession. In the meantime the church mother announces the ceremony by reciting the relevant passage from the Bible which explains the need of dedication.[45] After that she also leaves the hall while the choristers rise from their seats and start singing and the congregation may join in.

Then, the Holy Children, preceded by the apostle, enter the hall solemnly in their white robes and without shoes.[46] They kneel down at the front of the church before the altar, facing the congregation. Once they have knelt down the full parade will enter, with the parents in front, the mother carrying the baby. They are preceded by the Faith Brothers and Divine Sisters and followed by other church functionaries such as members of the welfare committee. They enter in mixed couples through the centre aisle while the choir is singing and proceed to walk around the church hall. When they are back in front the Faith Brothers turn left while the Divine Sisters turn right, after which they kneel down joining the Holy Children. The parents remain standing in the middle, in front of the centre aisle with their backs to the congregation while facing the altar. The church mother positions herself behind them and takes the baby over from the mother. The pastor opens proceedings with a short speech, followed by prayer. The apostle will read from the Bible the section which speaks of Hannah who has been longing for a child and finally has her prayers answered.[47] Then the pastor leaves the altar while the choir starts singing again. He goes around blessing every individual who has knelt in front and those seated on the front rows, who are mostly family or friends. When he is finished the choir stops singing so that the actual dedication can take place.

The apostle takes the child over from the church mother while the pastor stands in front of the parental couple who have also taken off their shoes and knelt down. The apostle, who is standing behind the parents, hands the child to the pastor who hangs his rosary around its neck. He lifts the child up in the air for everybody in the church to see, walking from one side to the other, presenting the child to the congregation. He introduces the child as a gift from God to the community. "Children of Israel," as he addresses the congregation in conformity with the Biblical base for the ceremony, "here is the gift which the Lord has given us." He then sprinkles the child three times—in the name of the Father, the Son and the Holy Spirit—with blessed water from a jar held by the Holy Head, the senior of the Holy Children. In the same way he blesses the child three times with blessed oil, applying the sign of the cross on the forehead. Finally (although this may also take place in a reversed order) he kneels down with the child to make it touch the floor with its feet, again three times in the name of the Father, the Son and the Holy Spirit. He directly addresses the child which for the first time in its life has literally set foot in the house of God, represented as the house of its Father. Although the actual wording may differ, the meaning of this act is clear: the church is introduced here as the ultimate place of security. It is presented as a place of asylum and a safe haven where she or he can always go and which will always be open to him or her even though the whole world may have abandoned the person. This is the house of God, where the power of God is believed to be present and all evil will be warded off, a place where Satan cannot enter. It is a moving and meaningful sign in an environment full of uncertainties.

At the end the pastor returns the child to the parents, pointing out once more that the newborn child is a gift from God and that they are its stewards. He impresses on them that the child has been entrusted to them by the Lord. Therefore they should take good care of it so that it will grow up in good health and prosperity. He then blesses both child and parents. Finally, he pronounces a blessing for the whole community, expressing the hope that the blessing of children may also be bestowed upon others. In doing so he may sprinkle the community with water as a symbolic act of purification and a sign of God's miraculous power and fatherly love.

All those who have knelt down will be getting up now and the thanksgiving part of the ceremony will start. The mother or both parents express their thanks to the Lord, usually introduced by a song. In doing so, and surrounded by all who have accompanied her, the mother may inform the congregation about eventual problems during pregnancy or at childbirth which were successfully overcome. She may tell about her longing for a child or her long waiting, or any other circumstance related to the newborn child. After giving this testimony there is singing and dancing to thank God. The choir and the band will contribute to the festivity which creates a party spirit throughout the hall. Finally the procession leaves the hall while still in a dancing mood. Parents and family then return to their seats in front. The whole ceremony will have lasted for about half an hour and will be concluded by the pastor with a final prayer. After that the service will be brought to an end as usual while soft drinks and cakes will be distributed among the congregation to celebrate the occasion.

The Foot-washing Ritual

Once a year, at the eve of the New Year, a special ritual is performed in the True Teachings of Christ Temple to mark the transition from the old to the new year. Following the example of Jesus as described in the New Testament the feet of every member of the church are washed and blessed with oil while the person is being prayed over. The service starts in the evening and lasts into the early morning, as a few hundred people need to be served this way. In order of arrival the individual names are written down on a list which will be worked through during the night-long service. The night is spent with singing, praying, Bible reading and preaching by the various evangelists. Tea and sandwiches are served through the night. From time to time a number of individuals' names are called out, some ten at a time, for the foot-washing ceremony. They queue up at the pastor's consultation room which they will enter barefoot. When it is their turn the faithful will enter the front room one by one for the apostle to wash their feet. To that purpose a plastic tub has been put in the room filled with water by some helpers who change it regularly. The person then enters into the tiny back room, which is the pastor's meditation room containing a small altar. This time the person steps into another little tub after which the pastor will bless his or her feet with oil making the sign of the cross. He does the same on the forehead while saying a short prayer for the person and blessing him or her. In case a person does not speak English, the language of communication used by the pastor, somebody will accompany him and translate what is said. Only when every individual has been served this way will the service be concluded. At the end of the service all the pastors and evangelists will queue up in front of the church hall to shake hands with every individual member to wish them happy New Year.

In practice this means that the service goes on for some twelve hours, during which most people will stay. In the prayers during the service regular references are made to the need to be washed anew by Jesus, and God's protection is sought against attacks from the "Evil One." The washing of the feet and the blessing with oil have symbolically prepared the congregation for the year to come. The washing has purified them from whatever evil they may have been affected by, or believe to have been affected by, while the blessing with oil is meant to provide protection against any Satanic attacks. The end of the year is seen as a particularly vulnerable period, during which Satan will try to strike a final blow. Spiritual protection, therefore, is needed more than ever.

Pluralism and Identity in the Context of the Bijlmer

I have been describing three types of ritual behaviour among African Christians in the Bijlmer as derived from the Bible and adapted to the specific conditions of modern Dutch society. At the same time, it is not surprising to note that several aspects of these ceremonies reflect the religious and cultural traditions of the peoples of Ghana, particularly the Ashanti.[48] The dedication of a newborn infant, for example, is a well-known practice in Ghana as indeed in many other parts of Africa. My main concern at the present juncture, however, is not to demonstrate the undoubted cultural precedents of ritual practices of African Christians in the Netherlands, but to demonstrate their meaning. Their meaning should not be understood by reference to the context of the past but rather by reference to the present, that is to the context in which African Christians live in the Netherlands today.

By taking this approach, we may see that the notion of demarcation is not a very helpful one. The situation in the Amsterdam Bijlmer is such that African Christians live easily with believers of other faiths, such as Islam and Hinduism, to mention two which are amply represented in the Bijlmer. There is no frequent formal interaction between the different religious communities, as they are all busy building up their communities in difficult circumstances. However, representatives meet regularly, in particular to solve a common basic problem, namely the lack of space to worship.[49] On occasion the different religious groups in the Bijlmer have also worshipped together, notably at the time of mourning the dead and other victims of the plane crash which took place on 4 October 1992.[50] In their present historical phase, it seems, the need to cooperate exceeds the need to demarcate which may develop over time. The variety of religious groups in the Bijlmer of non-Dutch origin is still increasing. All of them suffer from the prevailing political climate in Western Europe, including the Netherlands, which forces them into the margins of society. Marginalization and the problems resulting from it are the main factors which define ritual behaviour in the most recent migrant communities in the Bijlmer, notably the African ones.

One may argue that, with Western Europe moving towards an effective European Union, the need for demarcation in all spheres of life manifests itself on the side of the Europeans rather than on that of the Africans. While the inner frontiers in Europe are gradually being removed in order to further integration among various peoples, new demarcation lines are being drawn at the same time in order to exclude certain other categories. The content and tone of the recent political debate in Europe on migrants and illegal workers is a logical consequence of this policy of demarcation. Significantly, the demarcation lines are largely racially determined, so that in practice a predominantly white community is consciously separating itself from largely black communities. These remarks apply to religion in the Netherlands. One of the most recent migrant communities to have established itself in the Netherlands is black people mainly from West Africa. Many of them, as we saw, are Christians. As such they identify with the Netherlands as a basically Christian country, and particularly with the Christian communities there. In such a context, they feel little need to emphasize their own identity—often ascribed to them by others—as Africans, or specifically African Christians. They have evidently understood that this would contribute to their isolation in society rather than bring them into the mainstream of Western Christianity. Therefore, Africans in the Bijlmer tend to stress their identity as Christians and not as Africans, while their congregations do not call themselves (as others do) "African churches" but international churches. In other words, what we see in the African diaspora in Europe may well represent the beginning of a new trend in the history of African-led churches. Churches of this type became known at the beginning of the twentieth century as African independent churches (AICs), a name given to them by others. Later, they changed their name into African indigenous churches, while retaining the same acronym. Now established outside the African continent, these churches refer to themselves as international churches. By using the same acronym (AIC), but interpreting the "I" with different words, one may see how the status of African churches has changed throughout the century. The changes of name are an eloquent statement of the dynamics of this particular history.

These African-led churches are international in that they explicitly declare themselves open to non-African believers, irrespective of race or colour. In practice, however, these churches attract almost exclusively black people from various African countries, mostly from Ghana, and including people from Surinam and the Dutch Antilles. It is the Dutch Christians who, even in the context of the Bijlmer where they are living next door to African Christians, prefer to stay apart. A good example of this is provided by the Roman Catholic parish in the Bijlmer, the *Graankorrel*. African parishioners meet in a separate part of the church building for services in Twi and English every Sunday, and join the Dutch-speaking congregation in the main body of the church from time to time. The Dutch-speaking congregation, however, never goes to join the Africans for worship in their part of the church. Other Dutch Christian communities invoke various reasons for not mixing with African communities. The point is that, by its behaviour, the Dutch community in general obliges African Christians in the Netherlands to stay apart. It is ironic that for African Christians in the Netherlands the relationship with their Dutch counterparts is very important but has so far proved a greater obstacle than the forced cohabitation with other faiths. I therefore propose to examine the issue under discussion—religious pluralism and identity—not in relation to other faith groups but specifically in the context of *Christian* pluralism and identity, arguing that the demarcation lines are drawn essentially not by the African Christians in the Netherlands, but by Dutch Christian communities.

We may, therefore, consider ritual behaviour in African-led churches from that point of view. The emphasis on purification, the need to ward off evil, the sharing in the power of Christ, and the offering of a secure place in the church are all ritual underpinnings of the teachings of the church. Church teachings and doctrines are all related, in one way or another, to the day-to-day situation in which people live. There is a constant awareness that the marginalization of most Africans living in the Bijlmer, in itself already the most marginalized district of Amsterdam, can easily lead them into difficulties. Drugs, prostitution and its concomitant danger of contracting AIDS, drunkenness and theft, all social evils to be found in the conditions of a marginalized society, can easily turn from potential into real dangers for migrant communities. This is particularly true for young people who form the majority of the church members of the African-led churches. One of the most striking aspects of the True Teachings of Christ Temple, therefore, is the creation of a safe place, not just physically in the form of a church hall but, more importantly, in a ritual sense. The church constitutes a sanctified space which has been set apart as the place of the Lord and can neither be entered nor touched by Satan. Incense and holy water are means to secure the place's purity and sanctity, and to protect it against evil. Whoever enters the place under the spell of Satan will be able to rid themselves of evil by the exposure of evil spirits in this sacred area, and by calling upon the power of Christ through the Holy Spirit. The ritual is controlled by an ordained minister who is considered spiritually too strong to be affected by Satan. Rituals are performed in an orderly manner. Physical signs of spiritual presence, whether it is believed to be of a good or an evil spirit, signs of the presence of God or of Satan, are accepted as a normal effect of the ritual act that is performed and dealt with without disturbing the proceedings.

The aim of the ritual is to provide security and protection in a hostile and unstable environment. Hence the dedication ritual is particularly meaningful as it explicitly symbolizes the idea of the church as a safe haven from the moment one is born. Love and unity, brotherhood and charity, caring and sharing are constantly promoted in word and action, including in ritual action. All ritual behaviour is designed to link people together by causing them to communicate with one another, literally and symbolically. For example, a "chain of the Spirit" may be formed during or after healing prayers, when people join hands in order that they may be bound by the spiritual power. The healing referred to in the prayers is not limited to physical problems, but particularly addresses the social problems which have a disturbing effect on people, such as joblessness, homelessness, and the lack of formal identity papers. Jobs, housing, documentation problems, and so on, are all recurrent themes of prayer and preaching in church services.

Ritual in Times of Crisis

African communities like that in the True Teachings of Christ Temple are confronted with life crises which they try to solve by ritual means and which therefore may be usefully analysed with the help of van Gennep's "rites of passage" model. In the particular case which we are examining at present, the life crisis has been set in motion by some form of upheaval in the home countries in Africa: war, poverty, unemployment, lack of education, food shortages, and so on. It is this type of life crisis which has motivated or even forced people to go through a transitional cycle, comparable to those described by van Gennep. It involves people separating themselves from their home countries, arriving in unknown and insecure places where they tend to live a marginal life, while preparing for full participation in their new environment. In other words, these migrant communities are going through an important transitional phase of life which, like other "life crises" such as birth, puberty, marriage and death, require ritual or ceremonial validation. The rituals in church communities such as the True Teachings of Christ Temple accompany this new type of life crisis and help in making the transition.

Van Gennep identified a regular pattern in the rites of passage which allowed him to develop a classification by distinguishing three major phases: separation, transition and incorporation.[51] I am particularly concerned with the second phase, the phase of transition or liminality which is vital to all rites of passage and marks the most sensitive phase in the ritual process. The African communities in the Bijlmer have gone through the phase of separation and are now in the most delicate phase of their life crisis, the transitional or marginal phase, which is marked by liminality. It is this phase, elaborated upon by Turner, which is vital to their eventual successful incorporation into Dutch society. The crisis inherent in the transition from Africa to Europe has a disturbing effect on the community concerned as well as on its members as individuals. Ritual behaviour, therefore, is intended to restore the balance through spiritual empowerment, coupled with practical action to solve individual problems. Hence, we may argue, all ritual behaviour in these communities is aimed at achieving internal stability in order to overcome their liminality and prepare their members for entering the third and last phase, the phase of incorporation as an accepted part of Dutch society.

I will move to Victor Turner to explore in more detail the characteristics and consequences of the second phase, the liminal phase.[52] Characteristic of the liminal phase is the ambiguity which goes with it. Liminal persons belong neither to the community from which they have come, nor yet to a new community. Such is the case in the Bijlmer. Africans living in the Bijlmer have left their original communities in their home countries behind and—although there will continue to be links—they are not really part of these any more. Nor do they yet form part of the Western community where they have come to live. They are indeed, as Turner puts it, "betwixt and between the positions assigned and arrayed by law, custom, convention, and ceremonial."[53] Liminality, as he says, goes with marginalization and structural inferiority, with low status and structural exclusion. The issue of demarcation lines being drawn by the European community is constantly and openly addressed in their churches.

The characteristics of liminality can all be found among the African communities in Amsterdam.[54] Their marginality can be demonstrated from their social as well as their geographical position. They are concentrated in the least popular district of town where they live in the huge tower-blocks which in the 1970s–80s were left by many Dutch citizens who had come to find the living conditions of the Bijlmer intolerable. Socially the majority of Africans are equally marginalized, in the sense that most of them have unskilled jobs and relatively low wages while at the same time many are forced to live clandestinely as they lack the official papers which allow them a legitimate place in Dutch society. In other words, many of them have no recognized status in the wider society of the Netherlands, which is characteristic of their liminal situation: "the passage from lower to higher status is through a limbo of statuslessness."[55] The people concerned are aware of this and determined to turn things to their advantage during the liminal phase by moving away from their lower status towards a higher one in the Netherlands. The church communities in the Bijlmer play an important role in helping them to achieve that. They provide the institutional context for a type of ritual behaviour which is designed to help individuals make the transition from one stage to the other, from separation from an old community to incorporation into a new one.

Liminality, in given circumstances, as Turner has shown, is represented in various ways, for example by lack of possessions, passiveness or humility. Most significant, however, are the comradeship and egalitarianism which are promoted in this phase and which lead to a form of homogeneity which he has labelled "communitas." It stands for a model of society or a modality of social relationship which, according to Turner, emerges recognizably in the liminal period, representing a rather unstructured and undifferentiated community, or even communion, of equal individuals who submit together to the general authority of the ritual elders.[56] This is relevant to the case of the Bijlmer, where we can discern a similar pattern, with details varying according to the specific situation. The teachings in the various churches are clearly designed to emphasize this communitas aspect. The members of the church, although mostly coming from a specific region in Ghana, all bring their different personal backgrounds, different individual experiences and their own hopes and expectations. They gather in these churches as individual beings in-between two communities: the one of the past and the one of the future. Love, equality, and sharing; firmness and discipline are among the qualities which recur in the "lessons," as the sermons are often called, and other admonitions during church services. The authority of the church leadership is (as is normally the case in churches) generally accepted and followed, even if it is only because one cannot easily evade it. The leadership is clearly aware of the importance of promoting and cultivating communitas in these marginal communities as a prerequisite for successful integration in Dutch society. In order to do so, they need to find and develop a new identity. In the given circumstances this new identity does not lie in their being Africans, which sets them apart as a different and separate community in Dutch society, but in their being Christians, which allows them to become part of the world community or, indeed, the Western community.

Communitas, as Turner sees it, is essentially a relationship between concrete, historical, idiosyncratic individuals who are not segmentalized into roles and statuses but confront one another in the manner of Martin Buber's "I" and "Thou," that is, in a mutual relationship between total and concrete persons.[57] That is precisely what one finds in these Bijlmer communities which in doctrine and practice favour an egalitarian model that, ideally, should lead to a form of solidarity which is not based on the contrast with others. The notion of demarcation is virtually absent, as the solidarity is with the marginalized, which also comprises members of other faith groups.[58] Christianity is preached not from a dogmatic point of view, but as a way of life which also offers the best solution to practical problems. Demarcation, by emphasizing the differences among believers, offers no solution to the problems of these communities. On the other hand, stressing shared human values does help in resolving their problems in life. Basing himself on a variety of sources Turner has shown the regular connection between liminality (as defined above) on the one hand, and universal human values such as peace, harmony, comradeship and brotherhood among all men, universal justice, fertility, equality before God, health of mind and body, etcetera, on the other. Christian values, therefore, are constantly preached and practised in the African Christian communities that have emerged in the Netherlands. The need for demarcation may be identified rather in the Dutch communities which so far have found it difficult to integrate African Christians into their wider Christian community, and continue to put emphasis on the African rather than on the Christian aspect of the believers. That is, Dutch Christians use culture as a mechanism to demarcate and separate, whereas the African Christians in the diaspora take the opposite view and aspire to use their Christian faith as a means of integration into Dutch society.

Communitas is the predominant element of one particular phase in the life process, the transitional or liminal phase, and as such is not a permanent condition. The communitas that emerges during that phase is born out of a condition of crisis and may well be called a "communitas of crisis."[59] Turner makes a distinction between three different types of communitas, which represent

182

three different phases in the transitional process: an existential, a normative, and an ideological communitas as it develops over time from a rather unstructured and spontaneous into a more structured and well-governed model.[60] The Bijlmer communities can best be compared to the normative communitas model, as they find themselves in a period where they need to mobilize and organize resources and require a degree of social control among members of the congregation in pursuit of these goals. Thus, from an existential communitas, often in the form of small house congregations, they have organized themselves into a more enduring social system, more structured and with an adapted institutional context. The step to an "ideological communitas" has not yet been made but seems inevitable in the course of time.

Conclusion

My argument has, somewhat unusually, focused on the relations between two types of Christianity, of Dutch and African origin, in the context of modern Dutch religious pluralism. In doing so, I have been stressing similarities rather than differences between these two trends, for reasons I explained above. This is not to deny the meaning and influence of traditional African cosmology, as some have suggested, but to bring out the dynamic interaction between tradition and modernity of African Christianity in new circumstances. In this case, these are not the circumstances of "traditional" Africa, nor of modern Africa, but of modern Europe. The content of people's beliefs and the way they give expression to these are informed by the specific conditions of their life in respective circumstances. I have described these circumstances for Africans in the European diaspora (which are also quite different, for example, from those concerning Africans in the American diaspora), and I have looked at how "traditional" Dutch communities respond to this latest process of social change. In other words, I believe that in order to try and understand ritual behaviour among African Christian communities in the Netherlands, particularly in the Bijlmer district of Amsterdam, one should not base the argument primarily on the African situation, but on the European situation, seeking points of references in the actual situation which involves and affects both African and Dutch communities.

The need for demarcation, I have argued, is a need of white Christian communities in the Netherlands which seek to separate themselves from black Christian communities in their midst. This may not be immediately apparent due to the intellectually liberal discourse often to be found in Western Christianity which stresses the right, or even the need, for Africans to maintain their own identity. This need is also expressed in the conventional view of many scholars of religion, or theologians for that matter, who use the same argument to describe and analyse the position of African Christians.[61] The demarcation argument prevents black Christians in the Netherlands from full participation in Dutch religious life. Thus institutional power remains with the Dutch in spite of the numerically growing importance of black Christianity in the country. This is equally reflected in academic debate inasmuch as theological faculties and institutes, or other places of religious studies, neglect to give institutional status to other than the traditional religious trends in the Netherlands and make no allowances for a serious input from non-Western Christians.

In practice, this means that it is Dutch Christians, or other non-Africans, who try and define for African Christians the nature of their identity, locating this in their African-ness. This in spite of the latter's efforts to show that their identity lies first and foremost in their shared Christian-ness. Only when that has been accepted will they be able to emphasize their identity as African Christians. One may recall that the establishing of a new identity is one of the most important features of the liminal phase of the ritual process as Turner has described it. This is not different for African Christians in the Netherlands in their present phase. In this second phase of the transitional process it is more important for them to establish their identity as Christians, while in the third and last phase, that of incorporation into Dutch society, it may become more important to lay emphasis on the aspect of being African as part of their identity.[62]

For African Christian communities in the West, however, in present-day conditions, it runs against their interests to emphasize their African-ness as it helps to put up barriers rather than remove them, also considering their obvious presence as black people among whites. Instead, in their own discourse, they put great emphasis on the universal values, particularly stressing concepts of mutual love and unity, among Christians of all denominations and irrespective of race and colour, but also among all human beings, irrespective of their creed. Belief in Christ, rather than functioning as a strict line of demarcation, is stretched to encompass others who want to be part of the group, even if on an occasional or temporary basis. As such, African Christians in the Netherlands continue a religious practice characterized by openness and flexibility which is a hallmark of African religiosity in general. African religions are traditionally known for their capacity to incorporate others.[63]

Ritual behaviour in African Christian communities, I conclude, as I have described and analysed it in the context of the Bijlmer district of Amsterdam, has a predominantly communicative character which expresses itself in two major ways. The building up of internal stability as a community is one important function of it, yet it is not an inward-looking affair solely aimed at strengthening group solidarity. Ritual behaviour in the African-led churches is open and flexible in character and should be considered in relation to the circumstances of Dutch society which Africans in the Netherlands aspire to join. Ascribing demarcating qualities to their rituals means ignoring their communicative qualities. Rather than functioning as demarcation, ritual behaviour of African Christians in the case we have examined is a symbol for communication with the Dutch Christian community as they try to communicate to them their identity as Christians and their need to be incorporated into the wider Christian community in the West.

Notes

1. The present article was drafted in December 1993 and does not take account of developments after that date.
2. For definition of the terms used I refer to the discussions in the Leiden research group as reflected in the preparatory papers. See also the introduction to this volume.
3. In using the term "African-led" churches I follow the practice in the United Kingdom of referring to "black-led" churches, in order to highlight the fact that these are churches under African leadership.
4. Van Gennep 1975[7].
5. See Turner 1969, 80.
6. Van Gennep 1975, 10.
7. Van Gennep 1975, 13.
8. Turner 1969.
9. Turner 1969, 80–118.
10. E.g. to the "beat generation" and the "hippies" (Turner 1969, 99). See also the way Turner compares the American folk singer Bob Dylan to the Hindu musicians in Bengal known as Bauls (Turner 1969, 153–54).
11. Kimball 1975, xvii.
12. The southeast district of Amsterdam technically consists of three parts: the Bijlmermeer, Gaasperdam and Driemond, the largest of which is the Bijlmermeer.
13. On 1 January 1992 the total number of people in the southeast district of Amsterdam was calculated at 91,084 (Anonymous 1992c, table 162.14).
14. The total number of registered Surinamers on 1 January 1992 was 23,974 (Anonymous 1992c, table 162.14).
15. Antillians: 5599; Turks: 851; Moroccans: 1005; South Europeans: 977 (Anonymous 1992c, table 162.14).
16. The exact number is: 9603 (Anonymous 1992c, table 162.14).
17. Anonymous 1992a.
18. A sign of this is the nation-wide debate on the position of immigrants which was initiated by Frits Bolkestein, the leader of the liberal party in the Netherlands, the VVD.
19. See de Jonge (1992). This is a report commissioned by the *Stuurgroep Vernieuwing Bijlmermeer*. However, the number of religious groups is still increasing.
20. See Oomen and Palm 1994. This report will contain the results of a pilot project commissioned by the Ministry of the Interior.
21. According to the latest known figures, twenty-five Christian, five Muslim and three Hindu groups or organizations are active in the Bijlmer with a total number of some 15,000 members (de Jonge 1993).
22. For example, the so-called *All Saints Church* is a group of African Christians, mainly Ghanaians, within the Roman Catholic Church, while many Nigerians are known to

attend the Bijlmer parish of the Dutch Catholic Church (*Nederlands-Katholieke Kerk*). 75% of the congregation of the Seventh Day Adventists in the Bijlmer are African.

23. The official figure is 2337, which includes 913 people with dual nationality (Anonymous 1992b).

24. Recent research has estimated the total number of Ghanaians in the Netherlands, i.e. including non-registered ones, at 15,000, 10,000 of whom are believed to live in Amsterdam (van 't Hoff 1992).

25. These were the two main Dutch Reformed churches (the *Gereforrneerden* and *Hervormden*) and the Roman Catholic parish. Recently they moved into a new church building with the same name, *De Nieuwe Stad,* which is also used by the *Evangelische Luttherse gemeenschap,* the *Evangelische Broedergemeente,* and the Indonesian Christian community *Perki.*

26. According to the introductory guide for newcomers, published by the council of Amsterdam, every year around 10,000 non-Westerners come to live in Amsterdam. Many of these settle in the Bijlmer.

27. This circle is known as the *"Overleg Religieuze Organisaties,"* an initiative of Jan de Jonge, in his capacity of leader of the Christian-Democratic Party (CDA) in the local council.

28. De Jonge 1993. In practice there seems a tendency for different groups to worship in their own environment, if necessary outside the Bijlmer. However, this seems not to be the case on feast-days.

29. Recently the local council has presented a provisional policy paper on the issue, which seems to indicate a change in policy from passive to active involvement in solving these problems for all religious organizations, implying a recognition of their role in society, especially in the process of social renewal of the Bijlmer.

30. I cannot be more precise as the situation is one of constant change in which it is difficult to keep track of new developments. Membership varies from dozens in the smaller to hundreds of people in the larger churches.

31. In 1991 Ghanaians were officially mentioned as the largest single nationality in the southeast district of Amsterdam, after Dutch and Surinamese (Anonymous 1992a).

32. In recent years Ghana has been ruled by a military government and experienced two coups d'etat, in 1979 and 1981, by the current president, Jerry John Rawlings. See further Nimako 1993.

33. This is the official name of registration in the acts of the Chamber of Commerce. Nowadays a slightly different spelling is used, namely the *True Teachings of Christ's Temple.* In the present paper I will use the official name of registration.

34. These are well-known features of African-led churches in Africa, better known as African independent or African indigenous churches.

35. Sometimes also known under a different name or title, such as "presiding elder." One of the churches, at the time known as the *Resurrection Power Evangelistic Ministries,* was founded by a Ghanaian woman. Earlier this year she split off and started her own church which has now merged with another one.

36. See also de Jonge 1993, 10.

37. It was registered with the Chamber of Commerce on 18 April 1988 as a foundation for the formation of a church community.

38. Information about the author in Himmans 1986.

39. I am using the term "charismatic" here in its common sense as well as in the religious sense of somebody believed to be endowed with a special gift of divine origin, in this case healing.

40. For example, the extension project of the TTCT cost over fl. 650,000 which had to be raised from membership donations and personal loans. Most churches practise tithing.

41. See de Jonge 1992.
42. Twi is one of the main languages of Ghana. The majority of people from Ghana living in the Netherlands are Twi-speaking. They are mainly Ashanti coming from Kumasi or surroundings. The pastor of the TTCT, interestingly, is Ga-speaking, which is the dominant language in the Accra region.
43. This includes earlier labour migrants from North Africa, such as the Moroccans, who fall outside the scope of this paper. Apart from that, a substantial number of people from Africa have come to the Netherlands as political refugees, notably from the Horn of Africa.
44. One may refer here to Edith Turner's view of ritual as the harnessing of spiritual power, based on a re-study of her husband's (Victor Turner) work which she corrected and complemented by developing an "anthropology of experience." See Turner 1992.
45. Reference is made to Lk. 2:23 which speaks of the need to dedicate every first-born (male) to the Lord.
46. The altar and its surroundings are considered sanctified space which may not be entered with shoes. In the same line of thought, women cover their hair in church. (It may be noted, in this context, that Ghanaian women's dress usually includes matching head-scarf.)
47. 1 Samuel 1:26–28.
48. For a classic study of the Ashanti people of Ghana, see Rattray 1955.
49. See above, note 27.
50. On that Sunday an Israeli cargo plane crashed into some of the tower-blocks in the Bijlmer, killing at least an official number of forty-three people. Various joint services were held to commemorate the dead. A week after the tragedy a national service was held in the *RAI*, the largest congress hall in Amsterdam, which was broadcast live. One week later the various religious groups organized their own joint memorial service in the Bijlmer *Sportcentrum*, on 18 October 1993, a unique event in inter-religious coop-eration.
51. In English translation also referred to as stages of separation, margin or limen, and aggregation (e.g. Turner 1969, 80).
52. Turner 1969, 81ff.
53. Turner 1969, 81.
54. There are, of course, individual exceptions, but as a group the statement holds true.
55. Turner 1969, 83.
56. Turner 1969, 82ff.
57. Turner 1969, 119, 124.
58. One example is the concrete help given by the TTCT to a Turkish family which was homeless after a fire in the house. The notion of demarcation only comes in at times when Christian practices may literally get mixed with non-Christian ones, e.g. with certain traditional religious practices.
59. Cf. Turner 1969, 143.
60. Turner 1969, 120.
61. One may refer, in this context, for example to the debate at a recently held missiological congress on Africa, on 21-22 October 1993 in Heerlen, focusing on the question of inculturation, under the title: "Abide by the otherness of Africa and Africans."
62. We can observe a similar trend in other non-Western communities in Dutch society which settled there much longer ago, such as Turkish or Surinamese communities.
63. See e.g. ter Haar 1993.

References

Anonymous. 1992a. *Zuidoost in cifers, 1991.* Amsterdam: Gemeente Amsterdam, Stadsdeel Zuidoost.

—1992b. *Ghanzen in Zuidoosteen verkennend onderzoek.* Amsterdam: Stadsdeel Zuidoost.

—1992c. *Diadam 1992; statieche informatie: tabellen (1e deel).* Amsterdam: Gemeente Amsterdam, Bureau voor Onderzoek en Statistiek.

Haar, G. ter. 1993. "Gemeenschapsgodsdiensten." In *In grote lijnen: de godsdiensten van de wereld*, ed. J. Weerdenburg, 9–30. Utrecht: Universiteit Utrecht, Bureau Studium Generale.

Himmans, D. 1986. *Light on the Scriptures.* London: Oval Press.

Hoff, G. van 't. 1992. *Migratie van Ghanezen* (Unpublished report of a *leeronderzoek*, Universiteit van Amsterdam).

Jonge, J. de. 1992. *Soms was er geen plaats in de herberg: em poging tot em religieuze kaart van de Bijlmermeer.* Amsterdam: Stuurgroep Vernieuwing Bijlmermeer.

—1993. *Het wemelt bier weer van kleine luyden; scriptie ter aftsluiting van de CDA-kaderschoolleergang 1992-1993.* Amsterdam (unpublished long essay).

Kimball, S. T. 1975. "Introduction." In van Gennep 1975, v-xix.

Nimako, K. 1993. *Meuwkomers in een "gevestigde" samenleving: em analyse van de Ghanese gemeens chap in Zuidoost.* Amsterdam: Gemeente Amsterdam, Stadsdeel Zuidoost.

Oomen, M., and J. Palm. 1994. *Geloven in de Bijlmer: over de rol van religieuze groeperingen.* Amsterdam: Het Spinhuis.

Rattray, R. S. 1955 [1923]. *Ashanti.* 2nd ed. Oxford: Oxford University Press.

Turner, E. 1992. *Experiencing Ritual: A New Interpretation of African Healing.* Philadelphia: University of Pennsylvania Press.

Turner, V. W. 1969. *The Ritual Process: Structure and Anti-structure.* Harmondsworth: Penguin Books.

Van Gennep, A. 1975 [1960]. *The Rites of Passage.* 7th ed. Chicago: The University of Chicago Press.

THE RITES OF POWER

David I. Kertzer

Editor's Introduction

David Kertzer is Paul Dupee, Jr. University Professor of Social Science at Brown University, where he is also professor of both anthropology and Italian studies. Among more than twenty books and other publications, he has written significantly about the Vatican's relations with Jews. In the work from which this chapter is drawn, *Ritual, Politics, and Power* (1988), Kertzer demonstrates that much of the political life of modern nation states is made explicable in political symbols used in rituals. These must be understood not only as a deliberate manipulation of majority populations, and especially of the poorly educated masses, by political and economic elites, but as practices of all sectors of society. He writes,

> The condescending view that ritual is something that can pull the wool over the eyes of the credulous, while serving the well-informed as a tool for exploiting the ill-educated, has been around for a long time (p. 193, below).

This chapter is an important contribution to our consideration of the problematic relationship between ritual and religious belief because it clarifies yet another context of ritual behaviour, tests the definition of ritual against other kinds of activity, tests the boundaries of "religiosity" against other behaviours, and seeks clarity about the intentions of ritual performers. One particular test of all this is in relation to American national spectacles that might exemplify "civil religion." When President Nixon attempted to reform the rituals of his power he demonstrably reiterated the Protestant unease with ritual. The failure of this rationalizing reform suggests, at least, that the need for ritual is deep seated and pervasive. It also furthers earlier consideration of the communicative aspects of ritual behaviours and contributes again to reflection on questions of participation. Like actors, ritual leaders do not stand alone, and the stage and staging of rituals refuses to be limited by boundar-ies—internal or external, individual or communal—however strongly constructed. Rituals are, somehow, effective and affective.

೫ ೧

... with a flag one can do anything, even lead a people into the promised land.

Theodore Herzl[1]

One sings the Marseillaise for its words, of course, but one signs it espe-cially for the mass of emotions that it stirs in our subconscious.

Maurice Barrés (1902)[2]

After examining political rites in what may seem like a tremendous variety of people, places, and historical periods, I think it is time to ask what lessons these cases offer about the nature of political life. In trying to bury the naive notion that politics is simply the outcome of different inter-est groups competing for material resources, I want to avoid the opposite fallacy, that of portraying people as zombies imprisoned in a symbolically created universe they are powerless to change.

The fact that symbols and rites are crucial to politics does not mean that people simply view the world in the way their culture and its guiding myths dictate. What *is* crucial, though, is the fact that power must be expressed through symbolic guises. Symbolism is necessary to prop up the governing political order, but it is also essential in overthrowing it and replacing it with a different political system. Where do these new symbolic systems come from? If we are simply prisoners of the dominant symbol system, if it is the symbol system that determines our perceptions of the world, our interpretation of political life, how does change come about?

Here it is hard to resist the biological analogy. Evolution can only take place where genetic diversity exists, so that with environmental change cer-tain genes, previously rare, become increasingly common. Genetic diversity itself is produced in a population both through spontaneous innovations (mutations) and through the movement of individuals from one population to another (genetic drift). In a comparable, but by no means identical way, sym-bolic diversity exists in all societies, and the diversity is replenished through symbolic invention and through contact with other populations having other symbol systems. Our symbol system, then, is not a cage which locks us into a single view of the political world, but a melange of symbolic understandings by which we struggle, through a continuous series of negotiations, to assign meaning to events.[3]

A struggle such as this implies the existence of conflicts of interest among people. The conflicts can take place within a political framework that is itself relatively unquestioned, as when many compete to fill a limited number of available positions of power. Here the symbol system itself provides the impetus for the conflict, as well as the terms in which the conflict will be fought. There can also, however, be conflict over which symbolic under-standings are appropriate: what roles should exist, what the "issues" are, and which are worth fighting over. Part of the cultural struggle is a struggle over the dominant symbolic paradigm, the struggle for hegemony. It is a battle that never ceases, for, in Fox's words, "domination has to be constantly re-created."[4] It is the struggle of the privileged to protect their positions by fostering a particular view of people's self-interest. It is a process that in-volves defining people's identity for them. How else can people's strong devotion to such abstract entities as the nation or people's willingness to die for this unseen identity be explained?[5]

But a view of culture that does not account for interaction between our symbol system and the physical world of human activity is bound to lead to a mystical anthropology, a world without any cross-cultural regularities, one in which historical change is completely fortuitous. People's symbols, and their behavior, do change, sometimes with startling rapidity, and these changes are very much linked to external events.

One example will serve to relieve this abstract discussion: the course of British royal ritual in the nineteenth century. On the surface, these rites seem to argue for the durability of symbolism, and especially ritual, in the face of massive changes in the material world. However, the splendiferous elabora-tion of ritual that so colorfully marks the British royal family today repre-sents not a simple continuation of a long-held tradition, but a re-elaboration of old symbols to meet changing political conditions.

Throughout most of the nineteenth century, the rites surrounding the family events of British royalty were rather modest, and no one could seri-ously argue that they bound the entire population in political communion. In 1830, when William attended the funeral of his predecessor, George IV, he talked his way through most of the service and then unceremoniously walked out before it was over. His own coronation was a hurried affair, the subject of snide comments among the elite. Nor did William enjoy any more ritual glory at his own funeral. The long ceremony was tedious, and some participants laughed, gossiped, and snickered not far from the coffin. During Victoria's subsequent coronation, the clergymen, who had not rehearsed the rite, lost their place, the archbishop of Canterbury could not get the small ring on the queen's pudgy finger, and two of the trainbearers chattered away, oblivious to the ceremony.[6]

It was only in the last quarter of the nineteenth century that royal cere-monial reacquired its public magnificence, its pomp magnified for the masses. This corresponded to the monarchy's final loss of power, the rise in domestic class conflict, and the need to provide a unifying symbol for the colonies. Other sources of political power, previously in competition with the Crown for influence, were no longer threatened by the ritual elaboration of royal prestige. The nonroyal elite could whole-heartedly support the symbolic re-creation of the sacred ruler, which helped prop up the hierarchical social structure. The rites gave the people a feeling of stability, as well as a mea-sure of pride by tying them into a larger imagined tradition of greatness. To understand the power of the rites it is necessary to examine the power of the symbols; but to understand why the rites developed as they did one must look at the struggle for power that has taken place in Britain, and at who con-trols these ritual productions.[7]

If no celebratory fireworks were shot off during the dark years of the Second World War, when London prepared for German air attacks, the change in ritual action could hardly be explained by symbolic constraints. The material world does indeed impinge on the world of symbolism. Geertz argues that: "The real is as imagined as the imaginary,"[8] and it is true that we can only perceive and understand the world around us through mental processes that present the world to us in a highly limited way. But we live in a world that needn't obey our imaginings. In trying to understand in what ways it won't, we come to see the vulnerability of symbols. In highly strati-fied societies, elites must work hard to foster symbolic systems among people whose experience insidiously undermines them, for the best that elites can hope to do is shore up a predominant symbolic construction of how society should work. They can never eliminate all loose ends, all contradictions in the symbols themselves, nor all vestiges of alternative symbol systems. Frag-ments of other systems, as well as internal symbolic contradictions, are for-ever threatening to replace discredited views of the political universe.[9]

Have We Outgrown Political Ritual?

Throughout Africa, South America, and Asia, missionaries face difficult decisions about how to handle traditional rites. If they try to suppress the rites, they risk the people's wrath and undermine their own efforts to win a place in the community. On the other hand, to allow the people to continue with their alternative ritual system is to admit failure, to leave the field to the competitor. Typically, the missionaries solve this liturgical conundrum by doing what they can to insinuate their church into the celebration of pre-existing rites.

If the beleaguered missionaries occasionally feel uneasy about all this, they may take comfort from the fact that their ecclesiastical predecessors faced much the same predicament in Europe. In Russia, for example, the Shrove-tide celebration began as an indigenous holiday designed to hasten the coming of the spring, but was ultimately taken over—though never fully tamed—by the Russian Orthodox Church, which found a place for this rite of sun worship in its holy calendar.[10] In France, the priests were constantly faced with popular rites that the church could control only with the greatest difficulty. For example, through the nineteenth century, in periods of drought, the peasants of Nièvre organized processions to the Fountain of Nôtre Dame de Fauboulain to seek rain. The local priest was willing to lead the pilgrims in various prayers along the way, but he was less enthusiastic about the climax of the rite. On arrival at the fountain, each member of the procession took off a shoe, filled it with fountain water, and poured the water over the priest's head.[11] When the church, for reasons of propriety or perceived symbolic incongruity, refused to sanction such rites, popular hostility gushed forth.

Quaint stories such as this, with their benighted peasants and patronizing priests, bring to mind the common image of ritual as something that more sophisticated peoples have largely outgrown. In Malinowski's influential model, as more of nature is understood, there is less need for ritual; people replace much of magic with science. They no longer need to use rites to try to control the world around them, since science robs life of many of its mysteries.[12]

Max Gluckman concluded from his African research that ritualization of social relations is a feature of small-scale societies only.[13] Subsequently, other scholars, though recognizing the importance of political ritual to modern state societies, have clung to the notion that the value of such rites lies primarily in their appeal to the ignorant rather than to the educated, to the masses rather than to the elite.[14] Typical is Lane's claim that state rituals in the Soviet Union are targeted for those who "have been unable *fully* to develop their critical faculties." Ritual is used to overcome conflict in the Soviet Union, she claims, "in relation to the culturally more backward or immature social strata who do not perceive of inequality as a basic conflict in their society." From this, she concludes that ritual "can only successfully gloss over conflicts (or resolve ambiguities) in societies, or sectors of society, which accept their social order uncritically."[15]

The condescending view that ritual is something that can pull the wool over the eyes of the credulous, while serving the well-informed as a tool for exploiting the ill-educated, has been around for a long time. But did Reagan's trip to Bitburg have meaning only for the poorly educated? Did Carter's failure to attend Tito's funeral have no significance for the Yugoslav elite, who of course realized that this was only a ritual, not the real stuff of politics? Did the draft-card burning ceremonies have no meaning to their highly-educated participants or to the political elite who directed the Vietnam war?

Political rites are important in all societies, because political power relations are everywhere expressed and modified through symbolic means of communication. Of course, certain kinds of political rites are more important in some political contexts than others. Aronoff, for example, speculates that political rites are most common in new regimes that are dominated by a single party, as found in many African states.[16] Indeed, the creation of a new nation requires a massive effort at symbolic construction, of creating a sense of unity, of identification with a new, abstract entity, the nation. Here ritual can play a major role. Given the difficulty people with no previous conception of national identity have in making the notion symbolically real to themselves, it is not surprising that such efforts often involve creation of personified images of the state. Rites of new nations thus often revolve around the image of the heroic figure leading his people to the promised land.[17]

Conversely, the struggle of groups seeking to delegitimize the new order involves a fierce struggle over symbolism. The Ethiopian flag and ubiquitous portraits of Mengitsu, the nation's leader, are anathematized in Eritrea while they are ritually venerated in Addis Ababa. Singing a national anthem to Sri Lanka in Jaffna can be hazardous for a Tamil. If the struggle for national identity is waged in part through symbols and accompanying rites, so too is the revolutionary struggle for liberation. The true nation that is to be liberated is as much a symbolic product as the false nation that is to be dismembered.

Thus, in the new nations, it is not just the regime that is in the business of cultural management, but all players in the political scene. Insofar as the concept of the nation is problematic, the need to create rituals to bolster or destroy it is politically crucial. It is a lesson to be learned from Ireland, from the Sudan, from the efforts to create an independent Quebec or an autonomous Punjab. No matter how culturally artificial or historically serendipitous the new national entity, it must be endowed with a sacred unity and made to seem a natural social unit. Such is the case in Indonesia, with its scores of component islands extending over thousands of miles and enveloping totally unrelated peoples. Playing rather loose with history, Indonesian political leaders speak of the 350 years of colonialism that Indonesia has endured, even though the whole notion of Indonesia is a twentieth-century invention, and much of what is now included in the country was conquered by the Dutch colonialists only at the end of the eighteenth century.[18] Without rites and symbols, there are no nations.

On the Effectiveness of Political Rites

The power of the rite is based in good part on the potency of its symbols and its social context. Political rites can be spectacular failures or, more routinely, simply fail to be spectacular. Many observers over the centuries have linked the success of a political rite to the degree of popular enthusiasm it generates. Elites attempting to design effective political rites have, accordingly, been advised to design them in a way that will get people emotionally involved.

This is certainly the advice that Soviet officials have recently been getting. The success of spontaneous rites in the early post-revolutionary period, with the "chaotic enthusiasm and communal feeling" that they engendered, is compared unfavorably with today's routinized state rites.[19] One scholar cautioned that the "artificial process of imposing new customs does not evoke much enthusiasm among the population." A Russian folklore expert opined, in this regard, that "our new holidays and rites are threatened by a danger … the possibility that they will become rather desiccated and conventional, and turn into tedious bureaucratic measures."[20] "Without faith," writes Struve, "there is no rite."[21]

Although seemingly incontrovertible, this is an overly narrow view of the nature and importance of political ritual. To pursue this point, it is worth looking at a Soviet example offered by a scholar who holds this opinion. Lane chronicles the transformation of the mass rites commemorating May Day and the October revolution. What once aroused delirious popular emotions has turned into a bureaucratically organized affair that has little room for spontaneous individual involvement. "Even committed communists," she writes, "admit that the demonstration has become a 'mere ritual.'" What could be a better example of the "unimaginative uniformity" of the rites than the canned music to which the parading soldiers strut?[22]

Here, then, is the consummate case of the bureaucratized, routinized state rite. But what does it mean to say that this has degenerated into "mere ritual"? What can be made of the fact that, in spite of all the heavy-handed state management of the rite, "its sheer volume made it nevertheless impressive, not only for the foreign observers but also for the Soviet people who had turned out in great numbers to witness it with interest"?[23] In fact, the rites continue to have an important political effect, with their dramatic display of military might, the prominent place occupied by the national leadership, the sea of red flags and banners, and the venerated portraits of the founding fathers. Why else, after all, would the Soviet leaders go to so much trouble and expense each year to assure that just these effects are maintained?

People's emotional involvement in political rites is certainly a key source of their power, but there are many other emotions besides joy. As is evident in the cases of Aztec cannibalism, the Nazi salute, and the French revolutionary oath, political rites are also effective when they inspire fear. The effectiveness of rituals also depends on the cognitive messages they so effectively convey, and here too there need be no collective effervescence for the messages to be sent and received. When diplomats from eleven Western countries

195

attended a massive funeral for a dozen South Africans killed by police in December 1985, they may have felt euphoric or they may have been scared to death. Either way, their participation in the ritual sent a strong message to the South African government, to the people of South Africa, and to the people of their own countries. And whatever emotion the royal subject felt as he bowed before the king, it is clear what emotion the king was likely to feel should the subject fail to bow before him. In short, not only do we commune through ritual, we also use ritual to define our relations with others. Political rites often help to allay our fears, but they can also create anxieties that we would not otherwise have.[24]

If rites can be powerful weapons of the elite, they also represent one of the most potent weapons of the powerless. Lacking the formal organization and the material resources that help perpetuate the rule of the elite, the politically deprived need a means of defining a new collectivity. This collectivity, created through rituals and symbols, not only provides people with an identity different from that encouraged by the elite, but also serves as a means to recruit others to their side. An insurgent force that lacks its own distinctive symbolism and rites is not likely to get very far. By the same token, regimes seeking to suppress insurgent movements pay very serious attention to their opponents' rites and symbols. Thus, Ukrainian nationalists in the 1960s charged the Soviet government with "symbolcide" for its systematic efforts to erase all symbols of Ukrainian independence. Said one Ukrainian, "It is impossible to break people, to make slaves out of them, until you steal their holy days from them, and until you trample upon their temples."[25] There could be no Mau Mau movement without Mau Mau rituals, nor any popular anti-Vietnam war movement without its public rites.

Ritual, Symbols, and the Nature of Political Life

The call to place politics on a more rational basis has a long history in the West, rising to international prominence with the philosophers of the Enlightenment. In this view, there is little place for ritual in politics, for rites are the products of passion, not reasoned reflection.[26] People must be freed from their "irrational obsessions."[27] Machiavelli, in a less reforming spirit, argued that "Men in general make judgments more by appearances than by reality, for sight alone belongs to everyone, but understanding to few." Accordingly, he advised the rulers to "keep the people occupied with festivals and shows."[28] Yet, for the rationalists, it was precisely this ignorant tenacity of the masses to judge by "appearances" rather than by "reality" that had to be overcome.

With the rise of Mussolini and Hitler, Western observers again pointed fearfully to the insidious role of political rites in seducing a credulous people.

Cassirer went so far as to identify political rituals with the abdication of moral responsibility, claiming that "in all primitive societies ruled and governed by rites individual responsibility is an unknown thing."[29] The world of political rites is a world of political idolatry, and a "world with no idols," opined Light, "would not be such a bad place to live in. Illusion is a curse."[30]

But if illusion is a curse, it is a curse from which no prince's kiss will free us. There can be no politics without symbols, nor without accompanying rites. Nor can there be a political system based simply on rational principles, freed from symbolic connotations. What may be emerging is a world in which all people think that their political system and their political conceptions are rational. Gilbert and Sullivan's play *H.M.S. Pinafore* with its chorus, "Yet in spite of all temptations, to belong to other nations, he remains an Englishman, he remains an Englishman," comes especially to mind. Political allegiances flow not from culture-free judgments but from symbolically nourished conceptions of the order of the universe.[31]

Some observers have recognized this but, with Freud, envision a future in which society will have evolved to a higher, more rational plane. Bagehot put the matter more colorfully, if more ambiguously: "Royalty is a government in which the attention of the nation is concentrated on one person doing interesting actions. A Republic is a government in which the attention is divided between many, who are all doing uninteresting actions. Accordingly, so long as the human heart is strong and the human reason weak, Royalty will be strong because it appeals to diffused feeling, and Republics weak because they appeal to understanding."[32] Yet, not only will people always be influenced by their emotions, they also will never be able to make judgments independent of the symbols they use, symbols that can be powerfully conditioned through rites.

In the United States, as elsewhere, the rationalist bias remains strong, and the power of political rites is downplayed and often misunderstood. No less acute an observer than John Kenneth Galbraith, for example, in examining the quadrennial American political party conventions in 1960, seemed positively peeved that people did not all share his recognition that the rites were a vestige of the past and could not survive much longer. The convention, he wrote, "is an occasion when almost nothing happens. At the same time it is the centre of a remarkable conspiracy to prevent this elementary fact from being known." It "has lost nearly all of its original functions and gained no new ones." Indeed, for Galbraith the modern nation has little use for political rites, though the recognition of their demise prompts a nostalgic, if patronizing, note: "We have few ceremonies, few rituals in the United States with a legitimate historical base. The conventions were about the best we had. So everyone hates to see them go—or to admit that, like the cavalry charge, they have gone."[33]

Jimmy Carter, infected with this same liberal spirit, made a big show at the beginning of his presidency of shedding a number of the rites that had developed around the presidency. He eschewed the cavalcade back to the White House after his inauguration, walking back instead; he removed the gold braids from the epaulets of the White House guards, and he suppressed the flourishes that accompanied the president's every formal entrance.[34] He soon learned, though, that the power of these rites, of these symbols, was not to be trifled with. If by deritualizing the office he became "one of the people," he paid for it by being popularly perceived as lacking the charisma, the sacred aura, that presidents should have.

What could be more telling than the case of the French Revolution, whose leaders, dedicating their efforts to the elimination of superstitions and the crowning of Reason, rushed to create rites of Reason? The battle of Reason against Ignorance was fought through symbols and rites. The tricolored French flag, symbol of a nation liberated from the obfuscations and oppression of the Church and aristocracy, was created the day after the fall of the Bastille in 1789. When Napoleon was exiled to Elba in 1814, one of the first acts of the reactionary government was to restore the white flag. A year later, on his return from exile, Napoleon quickly replaced the white with the tricolor. Alas, this totemic tug-of-war continued the following year, for one of the casualties of Napoleon's defeat at Waterloo was the revolutionary flag, replaced once more with the white flag of aristocratic France. Yet, though driven underground, ritual use of the tricolored flag continued to have a powerful effect in focusing democratic political loyalties and rallying opposition to the regime. When the battle that would again overthrow the old regime was being waged in July 1830, the rebels' efforts were given a big lift when some of their colleagues stole up to the tops of Nôtre Dame and city hall and hoisted the forbidden tricolored flag. The raising of the flag did not simply announce a political change; it was one of the instruments of struggle. Its effect on the rebels, wrote one observer, was "electric."[35]

A century later, in Fascist Italy, people were bound to the regime through a panoply of rites of obeisance, from the Roman salute to the Day of Faith in 1935, when all Italians were urged to show their loyalty to the regime by giving their wedding rings to the state, to be melted down to help finance the African colonial march. The socialists and communists had been severely repressed, their leaders languishing in prisons or in exile abroad. In those dark days, what gave Mussolini's opponents in the working-class areas of northern Italy most hope, what stirred their anti-Fascist sentiments most powerfully, was the sight of the red flag, mysteriously hung each May Day from the factory smokestacks. The symbolic vehicles bearing an alternative understanding of political reality, an alternative basis of social solidarity, were kept alive amidst a fearful repression; the rites of resistance were all the anti-Fascists had left.

If Galbraith detected the disappearance of ritual in modern political life, he was looking in the wrong places or, more likely, failing to see the layers of rites in which modern political life is enveloped. This is understandable, since our own rites, our own symbols, are the most difficult to see. They seem like such natural ways of behaving, such obvious ways of representing the universe, that their symbolic nature is hidden. Here, indeed, is one of the sources of power of rites and symbols, for insofar as they become dominant they create a convincing world; they deflect attention from their contingent nature and give us confidence that we are seeing the world as it really is. It is hard to argue with a flag, especially if you do not have another flag of your own; hard to argue with a song, unless you have another anthem to sing; and hard to argue with the view of the world embodied in the funeral rites of a popular leader, a fact both Communists and Christian Democrats realized to their horror when Aldo Moro's family stole away in the night with his blood-stained body.

Notes

1. Herzl was here justifying the amount of effort he had devoted to designing a flag for a nation that did not yet exist. His remarks are quoted in Mosse (1976, 49).
2. Quoted in E. Weber (1977, 172–73).
3. Turner (1985, 154) writes of culture in this vein as "an endless series of negotiations among actors about the assignment of meaning to the acts in which they jointly participate."
4. Fox (1985, 204).
5. See Bennett (1979, 107).
6. This account is based on Cannadine (1985).
7. Bloch (1986) makes a good case for the importance of distinguishing between determinants of a ritual's content and the determinants of its political functions.
8. Geertz (1980, 136).
9. Bloch (1977; 1986), attempting to cope with this issue of the relationship between the material world and symbolic constructions that guide people's lives, argues that people have two different cognitive systems: a naturalist system tied directly to the material world and differing little from culture to culture, and a culturally variable system of symbols, such as is employed in ritual. He laments that "Unfortunately many anthropologists, fascinated as usual by the exotic, have only paid attention to the world as seen in ritual." And he goes on to conclude: "they have confounded the systems by which we know the world with the systems by which we hide it" (1977, 290). I agree with his general point that there are some important regularities in cultures around the world and that these are ultimately based in regularities of the material world. However, I find his dichotomy simplistic and unconvincing. There is no such simple division between our "everyday communication," which Bloch claims is based on direct perception of nature, and "ritual communication," which he describes in terms of "static and imaginary models of … society." Everyday understandings are highly constrained by "imaginary models" just as the material world weighs heavily in ritual communication. We do not alternate between a naturalistic perception of the universe and a

mystifying symbolic view; the natural world seeps in through our symbolic lenses, not in spite of them.

10. Lane (1981, 132).
11. Berenson (1984, 61).
12. Malinowski (1945).
13. See Gluckman (1962, 38; 1965, 261–62).
14. For some of the reasons given for the importance of ritual in communication among the illiterate, see McPhee (1977, 244).
15. Lane (1981, 26, 32). This argument is also presented in Lane (1984).
16. Aronoff (1979, 306).
17. On the need for ritualization in new states, see Apter (1963) and Verba (1965, 530).
18. Anderson (1983, 19).
19. Binns (1980, 588).
20. Struve (1968, 760).
21. Struve (1968, 763).
22. Lane (1981, 185–86).
23. Lane (1981, 186).
24. This last point was made, in a somewhat different context, by Radcliffe-Brown (1952, 148–49) in his attack on Malinowski's anxiety-reduction theory of ritual.
25. Kowalewski (1980, 102).
26. In this regard, see Fernandez's (1977, 103) comments on Locke.
27. Lipsitz (1968, 533).
28. Machiavelli is quoted in Muir (1981, 74–75).
29. Cassirer (1946, 285).
30. Light (1969, 198).
31. Borhek and Curtis (1975, 105) refer to these lines from Gilbert and Sullivan in a somewhat similar context.
32. Bagehot (1914, 107).
33. Galbraith (1960).
34. Hahn (1984, 275).
35. Agulhon (1985, 190).

References

Agulhon, Maurice. 1985. "Politics, Images and Symbols in Post-revolutionary France." In *Rites of Power*, ed. Sean Wilentz, 177–205. Philadelphia: University of Pennsylvania Press.

Anderson, Benedict. 1983. *Imagined Communities: Reflections on the Origin and Spread of Nationalism*. London: Verso.

Apter, David E. 1963. "Political Religion in the New Nations." In *Old Societies and New States*, ed. Clifford Geertz, 57–104. Glencoe: Free Press.

Aronoff, Myron J. 1979. "Ritual and Consensual Power Relations: The Israel Labor Party." In *Political Anthropology: The State of the Art*, ed. S. Lee Seaton and Henri J. M. Claessen, 275–310. The Hague: Mouton.

Bagehot, Walter. 1914. *The English Constitution*. New York: Appleton.

Bennett, W. Lance. 1975. "Political Sanctification: The Civil Religion and American Politics." *Social Science Information* 14: 79–106.

—1979. "Imitation, Ambiguity, and Drama in Political Life: Civil Religion and the Dilemmas of Public Morality." *Journal of Politics* 41: 106–33.

Berenson, Edward. 1984. *Populist Religion and Left-Wing Politics in France, 1830–1852.* Princeton: Princeton University Press.

Binns, Christopher A. 1980. "The Changing Face of Power: Revolution and Accommodation in the Development of the Soviet Ceremonial System, Part 1." *Man* 14: 585–606.

Bloch, Maurice. 1977. "The Past and the Present in the Present." *Man* 12: 278–92.

—1986. *From Blessing to Violence: History and Ideology in the Circumcision Ritual of the Merina of Madagascar.* Cambridge: Cambridge University Press.

Borhek, James T., and Richard F. Curtis. 1975. *A Sociology of Belief.* New York: Wiley.

Cannadine, David. 1985. "Splendor out of Court: Royal Spectacle and Pageantry in Modern Britain, c. 1820–1977." In *Rites of Power*, ed. Sean Wilentz, 206–43. Philadelphia: University of Pennsylvania Press.

Cassirer, Ernst. 1946. *The Myth of the State.* New Haven: Yale University Press.

Fernandez, James W. 1977. "The Performance of Ritual Metaphors." In *The Social Use of Metaphor*, ed. J. David Sapir and J. Christopher Crocker, 100–31. Philadelphia: University of Pennsylvania Press.

Fox, Richard G. 1985. *Lions of the Punjab: Culture in the Making.* Berkeley: University of California Press.

Galbraith, John Kenneth. 1960. "Conventional Signs." *The Spectator* (July 29) 205: 174–75.

Geertz, Clifford. 1980. *Negara: The Theatre State in Nineteenth-Century Bali.* Princeton: Princeton University Press.

Gluckman, Max. 1962. *Les rites de passage.* In *Essays on the Rituals of Social Relations*, ed. Max Gluckman, 1–52. Manchester: Manchester University Press.

—1965. *Politics, Law and Ritual in Tribal Society.* Oxford: Blackwell.

Hahn, Dan F. 1984. "The Rhetoric of Jimmy Carter, 1976–1980." *Presidential Studies Quarterly* 14: 265–88.

Kowalewski, David. 1980. "The Protest Uses of Symbolic Politics: The Mobilization Functions of Protester Symbolic Resources." *Social Science Quarterly* 61: 95–113.

Lane, Christel. 1981. *The Rites of Rulers.* Cambridge: Cambridge University Press.

—1984. "Legitimacy and Power in the Soviet Union through Socialist Ritual." *British Journal of Political Science* 14: 207–17.

Light, Ivan H. 1969. "The Social Construction of Uncertainty." *Berkeley Journal of Sociology* 14: 189–99.

Lipsitz, Lewis. 1968. "If, as Verba says, the State Functions as a Religion, What are We to Do then to Save our Souls?" *American Political Science Review* 62: 527–53.

Malinowski, Bronislaw. 1945. *Magic, Science, and Religion.* Glencoe: Free Press.

McPhee, Peter. 1977. "Popular Culture, Symbolism and Rural Radicalism in Nineteenth-Century France." *Journal of Peasant Studies* 5: 238–53.

Mosse, George L. 1976. "Mass Politics and the Political Liturgy of Nationalism." In *Mass Politics and the Political Liturgy of Nationalism*, ed. Eugene Kamenka, 38–54. New York: St. Martins.

Muir, Edward. 1981. *Civic Ritual in Renaissance Venice.* Princeton: Princeton University Press.

Radcliffe-Brown, A. R. 1952. *Structure and Function in Primitive Society.* Glencoe: Free Press.

Struve, Nikita. 1968. "Pseudo-religious Rites in the USSR." In *The Religious Situation, 1968*, ed. Donald R. Cutler, 757–64. Boston: Beacon.

Turner, Victor. 1985. *On the Edge of the Bush.* Tucson: University of Arizona Press.

Verba, Sidney. 1965. "Conclusion: Comparative Political Culture." In *Political Culture and Political Development*, ed. Lucian W. Pye and Sidney Verba, 512–60. Princeton: Princeton University Press.

Weber, Eugen. 1977. "Who Sang the Marseillaise?" In *The Wolf and the Lamb: Popular Culture in France*, ed. Jacques Beauroy, Marc Bertrand and Edward T. Gargan, 161–73. Saratoga, CA: Anma Libri.

Ritual Expertise in the Modern World

Susan S. Sered

Editor's Introduction

Susan Sered is the research director of the Religion, Health and Healing Initiative at the Center for the Study of World Religions at Harvard University, and Associate Professor of Anthropology at Bar Ilan University, Israel. Her work is interdisciplinary, including medical anthropology, religious studies, and gender studies. She has been particularly interested in women's religions, religiosity and religious participation or marginality—conducting fieldwork among Kurdish, Yemenite and North African Jewish women in Israel, and, in Okinawa (Japan), among the only contemporary *mainstream* religion led by women. Currently her research team is surveying American religious healing rituals and practitioners, especially in the Boston metropolitan area, among a wide range of religious and ethnic communities.

The following chapter is included not only because of its focus on women's ritual behaviour, or because it is admirable in its careful view of the gendered nature of ritual practice and discourse, but also because it attends to change. A preoccupation with "tradition" (especially when this is understood as a fixed and authoritative, if not authoritarian, elite edifice) has colluded with the rhetoric of ancestral timelessness to militate against studying ritual and change. It seems commonly accepted that rituals change people, but the contrary movement has rarely been considered. When, as discussed in Sered's work, ritual change is made visible by both gendered change and cultural change (i.e. the effect of modernity), all manner of seemingly new data emerge.

While the positioning of chapters in this Reader has been fairly random, certain patterns replicate themselves, somewhat like fractals, in succeeding discussions. Understandings of the entanglement of ritual in political and cultural struggles around and across putative elite/popular, high/low, public/individual, and other boundaries, including those of gender, ethnicity and age, play themselves out not only in ritual practice but also in academic theorizing. The question of the relationship between ritual and religious belief, then, requires this discussion of gendered relationships, roles, traditions and changes.

⁖ ⌓

A number of studies have noted the effects of modernization upon the lives of women.[1] As the traditional extended family disintegrates and wage-labor replaces reciprocity, women often lose the power that derived from their traditional social and economic expertise and from their kin- and village-based support networks.

In this chapter I ask how modernization affects women's religious lives. This question has received little attention in studies of religious change, which have looked almost exclusively at men's experiences.[2] At the time of my fieldwork, the female-oriented religious traditions of the Day Center women were deeply threatened both by modern secular culture and by the masculine, Ashkenazi religious establishment in Israel. Despite the rather vulnerable status of women's religion, the Day Center women felt that modern Israel provided them with new and meaningful opportunities for religious expression. Their interest in novel religious activities, however, was tempered by their awareness of the decline of some of their other rituals.

New Opportunities

Modernization often results in an increase of religious choices for women.

The Traditional Male Religion

In the wake of modernization, women sometimes find new opportunities to participate in what were traditionally men's rituals. The Middle Eastern women have recently begun attending synagogue and Judaica lessons—two activities that were formerly for men only. They feel that because of their new Jewish knowledge they are now better Jews, better able to carry out God's will, and better able to accumulate merit [*zechut*] on their own behalf and on behalf of their families. Their daughters have all attended school and learned how to read, and the women are proud that their daughters have access to literacy, which was once a male prerogative. In addition, there are now more and more women like Rabbanit Zohara, who have become involved

203

in public teaching that centers around written texts. This is an important innovation for Middle Eastern Jewish women; in the Old Country only men studied from books. The roles that were available in the Old Country for female religious leaders did not necessitate literacy, wide knowledge of Jewish law and history, or extensive intervillage connections (see below).

These innovations in the religious lives of the Middle Eastern Jewish women take on greater significance when examined in light of the experiences of women of other, diverse cultures. Maria Powers has found Oglala women on the Pine Ridge Reservation in South Dakota participating in rituals that had once been restricted to males: The Sun Dance, the Vision Quest, and the Sweat Lodge have opened to women.[3] Among the Aowin people of southwest Ghana, women now serve as head mediums, a role that traditionally belonged to men.[4] And in modern India, Hindu women "who stay at home often perform the morning worship [*puja*] to the deity in the home shrine, especially in the urban areas, for the hours of the modern work day do not permit men time for traditional ritualism."[5]

The Traditional Female Religion

The traditional female religious sphere may sometimes acquire new significance or prestige as women come to be seen as guardians of the old ways, as experts in the traditional religion. In a number of interviews, children of the women I studied made comments such as "My mother is closer to God than I am." "The way my mother does it [religion] is better, but I myself am not strong enough to do it like she does." Even the "modern" children and grandchildren who consider much of the old women's religion to be "superstition" acknowledge the spiritual potency of their ancestresses and turn to them for information concerning the old ways (especially during life crises). Many of the children and grandchildren do not know exactly how the old women perform the rituals. The women pray in Arabic, Kurdish, and other languages (which the younger generation does not know), and the youngsters generally do not accompany the old women to the holy tombs. The old women's sacred knowledge has come to be surrounded by an aura of mystery that was not connected to the rituals in the Old Country. Even the old women's cooking has taken on a new mystique: they proudly describe their traditional foods as needing special knowledge to prepare, "not just anyone can do it."[6]

In a variety of contexts and working on almost every continent, scholars have discovered the critical role of women in preserving the old ways. Even more interesting are the studies describing situations, remarkably similar to that of the Middle Eastern women, in which women's traditional rituals have increased in prestige. Immigrant Jewish women in England at the beginning of the century did not drastically modify their religious practices, yet "the significance of these activities ... changed. ... Formerly regarded as peripheral, they now developed as key components in the transmission of a sense of Jewish identity and attachment."[7] And in modern Turkey, the traditional ritual celebrating the birth of the Prophet Muhammed has changed significantly for men, while "the women seem to have become the repositories of spiritual values to which both women and men subscribe but which, paradoxically, only women can experience with performative immediacy because of their inferior status vis-à-vis past and present religious establishments."[8]

New Frameworks

The women of this study, by moving to Israel, have come into contact with a cultural system that is in many ways alien to both the traditional male and the traditional female religious ways. These women sometimes adopt modern rituals, subtly transforming them to make the new rituals consistent with the traditional female domain. For example, their Tu b'Shavat ritual combines new symbols and old motivations (see Chapter 1). When the Day Center women planted trees, they created a new ritual, drawing upon a traditional conception of the relationship between God and humans and modern conceptions of forest management and civic duty.[9]

One of the most important new religious arenas in which the women act is that of the Israeli Defense Forces. The women of the Day Center expand their notion of family to include every soldier serving in the Israeli Army. The first step in this expanded notion of spiritual responsibility is the feeling that they must take extra care of children and grandchildren who are soldiers. For example, one woman reprimanded her friend for wearing black and dark blue clothing. She warned her that black and dark blue are the colors of mourning, and since her friend has two grandsons in the army, she must not endanger them by wearing these colors.

The most typical prayerful petitions that the women make are that "the Messiah should come and that everything should be good for the children and especially for the soldiers and the army," or that "there should be health for all of Israel, there should be peace, all of the soldiers should return in peace, all Israel should return in *tshuva* [become religious]."

During a conversation about Rabbanit Zohara in which she was criticized for collecting money from the poor women at the Day Center, Simha said, "She [Rabbanit Zohara] just needs to say the word 'soldiers' and they all give money." According to one woman, "Every soldier is like my eye, even the Druse soldiers."[10] Comparing someone to one's eye is a fairly common expression used to indicate a close relationship. However, most of these women are oblivious to the world of politics and few have ever even seen a Druse. What this woman meant is that her self-image is as spiritual mother or guardian of the Israeli Defense Forces, and that includes everyone, even the most biologically unrelated, who serves in the army.

The Day Center rabbi is well aware of the women's feeling on this matter, and when he ends his lesson with a blessing he frequently includes a blessing for the soldiers. For example, he may ask for "salvation, rebuilding the Temple, and God's protection for the soldiers who are defending us." Falhibe tells how on Memorial Day "of course I light candles for the soldiers." The women place living soldiers into the same category as their children, and dead soldiers into the category of saints.

Just as the women claim an interdependent relationship with their dead ancestors—they guard the ancestors and the ancestors help them—they see the relationship with the soldiers as being reciprocal. As the rabbi expressed this idea, observing holidays correctly according to Jewish law protects our soldiers on the borders, and the soldiers allow us to be good Jews. In other words, by behaving in accordance with Jewish law, we persuade God to protect our soldiers. And the soldiers, by ensuring the existence of the Jewish state, allow us to be practicing, observant Jews.

The women believe that it is their duty to care for the army, and like their responsibility for fertility, this is carried out both on the practical and the spiritual plane. So, for example, when the rabbi mentions that the Tomb of the Patriarchs and Matriarchs in Hebron was not in Jewish hands until the army liberated it, all of the women murmured, "God should protect them, they should be safe" and "Amen." On the other hand, a "big *mitzvah*," according to Shula, is to go to an army base and pack weapons for the soldiers. Most if not all of the women are involved in some type of charitable activity on behalf of the soldiers. This may be buying numerous lottery tickets from the Committee for the Aid of Soldiers or frequent days spent at army bases sorting uniforms or doing whatever other jobs the army asks of them. When the women volunteer to work at the army base, they genuinely want to contribute to the state of Israel, but their actual description of their activity is "helping the soldiers, all of whom are like my own children."

The women feel great satisfaction in ritually caring for the soldiers: this is a communal activity in which all can participate, and it is one that the women believe is of the utmost importance for the survival of the Jewish people and state. If modern Zionism can tentatively be described as a "new religion," the women have adopted it most wholeheartedly.

In other societies, women have joined religions that are entirely foreign to their traditional cultures. Yung-Chung Kim, looking at the spread of both Catholic and Protestant Christianity in Korea, postulates that women especially were drawn to Christianity because it helped break down class and gender barriers, encouraged social innovations, allowed women to participate in religious ritual, provided women with opportunities for education, condemned the double standard of sexual morality, and provided a vision of an afterlife that was meaningful to women.[11] New local or native religious structures that offer women increased opportunities may be another result of modernization. In Northern Sudan, for example, the *zaar* [spirit] cult is an urban phenomenon, a mechanism for helping village women adjust to life in the city by offering them opportunities to build social networks with other women to be cured of a wide range of ailments, and to actively participate in an exciting religious ritual.[12]

Female Solidarity

Most studies that mention women's religion in developing societies stress that when the social support networks of neighbors and kin available to women in traditional rural societies break down, women may join cults or churches as a means of creating new relationships. Indeed, Erika Bourguignon suggests that the "appeal of novel religious groups may lie in the opportunity they offer for the creation of private networks of power, influence and authority in a nondomestic setting."[13]

My fieldwork among the Middle Eastern women in Jerusalem certainly bears out the connection between religious involvement and social networks. These women come together in the context of a Senior Citizens' Day Center. They are of diverse ethnic groups, and most have been housewives for many years with few opportunities to meet women other than relatives and nearby neighbors. In recent years many of their close friends have died, and their neighborhood has become partially gentrified. The Day Center provides them with an opportunity to widen their circle of female friends. Many of the women avow that they come to the Center in order to get out of the house, in order not to be alone, "because I have to do something and not sit at home alone all day."

On the other hand, the members of the Day Center can choose their own activities within a budget determined by the municipality of Jerusalem, and almost all of the activities they select are religious in nature: Judaica lessons, pilgrimage to holy tombs, and holiday celebrations. The women who attend this particular Day Center are actively seeking communal religious involvement in a nontraditional but all-female context. Whatever *intention* they may verbalize the actual *function* of their Day Center involvement is a dramatic expansion of their religious world. These elderly women have created a new type of female solidarity, but they have created it in order to pursue more active religious lives; other benefits that they receive as a result of their Center membership are byproducts. The new network that the women have created by joining the Center cannot be understood as a material mutual-aid society.

It seems to me necessary reductionism to suppose that women become involved in religious organizations because of economic or social needs. My conversations with the Middle Eastern women indicate that they join the Day Center because they are interested in expanding their *religious opportunities*—

they specifically want the Day Center to organize pilgrimages to holy tombs
—they do not request outings to public swimming pools or museums. While
not denying that there are social and sometimes economic benefits to new
female religious networks, it is neither necessary nor productive to explain
women's religiosity as a fallout of economic, social, or psychological factors.

Ritual Specialists in the Old Country

Scattered throughout a very varied literature are hints of the existence of
religious leadership roles that were available to women in the Old Country.
Few of these options continue to exist today. In the following paragraphs, I
shall review some of these roles. This review will be brief both because the
primary aim of this book is to study the religious lives of the women today
(not to reconstruct life in the Old Country) and because of the shocking
paucity of information concerning the religious lives of Jewish women in
past centuries. Most of the information concerns Kurdish Jews because the
majority of the women at the Day Center are Kurdish and because the ethnographic record of women's religious lives in Kurdistan is somewhat richer
than for other parts of Asia. Having listened to the Day Center women
reminiscing about Kurdistan, Yemen, Iraq, Iran, Turkey, and North Africa, I
would surmise that similar roles for exceptional women existed throughout
much of the Jewish diaspora.

One religious function that was available to women in the past was to be
an expert in henna (the red dye that is painted on the body for luck at a number of ritual occasions). For example, the bride in Kurdistan would attend a
women's henna party before the wedding, and at this party the women would
sing traditional songs and perform certain rituals. This ceremony has almost
completely died out in modern Israel. While today there still may be a henna
party, it will probably not be sexually segregated, secular songs will be sung,
and modern clothes will be worn. In the past this ceremony included a woman
who was a ritual specialist, an expert in henna and knowledgeable about the
correct songs and dances for a henna party. That role no longer exists.

According to Donna Shai, in Israel there are many fewer opportunities
for storytelling than there had been in Kurdistan. In Kurdistan, folksingers
were specialists who were invited to perform on family and ritual occasions
(such as weddings and funerals).[14] Yona Sabar has discovered that women in
Kurdistan had their own somewhat independent oral traditions. Their folklore contained only "echoes of the barest outlines of the Aggadic themes"
[traditional Jewish stories].[15] The role of female expert storyteller of women's
stories is another role that is no longer a viable option for exceptional
women. Rabbanit Zohara, who tells the women at least one story each week,
is literate and repeats stories that she takes from sources written by men,
not from the traditional female repertoire.

Yona Sabar describes the women's tradition of chanting dirges on the evening of the Ninth of Ab.[16] After the evening meal, several women would gather on a roof and sit in a circle around one woman who knew the dirge particularly well. She would recite it very movingly, and the women would cry and sigh. These dirges were passed down orally from mother to daughter and were never put in writing. One of the dirges entitled *"Lel-Huz"* is a mixture of Kurdish and ancient Jewish legends. Briefly, it is the history of the destruction of the Temple and the Exile personified into the stories of a young man and two young women. One of the women, by drowning in the ritual bath, escapes being raped by seven infidel men. The other woman is killed by her father-in-law as a sacrifice imposed by divine edict in order to end a drought and save the entire family. Today in Israel, while some old women may still know this dirge, on the Ninth of Ab the women of the Day Center attend synagogue and sit passively in the women's section, listening to the men's prayers and rituals. The Day Center women have accepted the standards of contemporary society as a basis of self-evaluation for what they should be doing. Instead of listening to the traditional dirges, songs, and stories that they understand and that speak to their own, female experience, they sit in synagogue listening to what is for them an inaudible, incomprehensible, male-oriented service. Leading the women's dirges on the Ninth of Ab is one more traditional female role that no longer exists.

Similarly, as Nina Katz has ably demonstrated, men and women in Yemen had different musical traditions. Women, excluded from the synagogue, did not even *hear* men's religious rituals and music. Instead, the women created their own "second world" of fantasy, storytelling, and singing. Men's music was developmental, antiphonal, without instrumental accompaniment, without a definite rhythm, based on fixed texts, religious, and sung in Hebrew or Aramaic. Women's music was repetitious, never truly antiphonal, rhythmic, usually secular, and sung in Arabic with improvised texts.[17] We can but surmise that there were certain women who were more expert at creating and remembering women's songs.

Another female religious role recorded by Brauer was that of mourner or lamenter. According to Brauer there were professional women mourners who were experts at crying and who had a repertoire of songs that made others cry.[18] The role of female professional mourner hardly exists today in modern Israel. In the Old Country, a particularly pious woman could wash female corpses in preparation for burial and sew the shrouds for either female or both male and female corpses.[19] While the task of washing female corpses of course still exists, there are now so many fewer folk rites surrounding death and burial that this job has declined both in prestige and in the amount of knowledge necessary for performing it correctly.

Women in Kurdistan wore many amulets, especially during pregnancy and childbirth.[20] Many of these amulets were written by rabbis, but others were geometric shapes embroidered on clothing. Since women did the embroidery, it is reasonable to assume that there were some women who were especially knowledgeable about amulet embroidery and who aided and instructed other women in this ritual.[21] Embroidering amulets no longer exists as a women's ritual activity among the Day Center women. The most popular amulets today are printed ones, and the only handwork that the women of the Day Center do is the knitting and crocheting that they have recently been taught by an Ashkenazi teacher at the Day Center.

In Debbi Friedhaber's excellent book about dance customs of Kurdish Jews, she mentions several occasions at which the women would get together and dance. These included the Sabbath before a wedding, Passover, childbirth and first pregnancy, Shavuot, and the first Sabbath in the month of Adar.[22] Again, it is reasonable to assume that there were certain women who were more proficient at dancing and playing the tambourine, women who knew more dances and could teach them to others. Women's autonomous dancing no longer exists in modern Israel. At weddings today, all except the oldest women dance in a style that is identical to that of the men.

Women in the Old Country were also responsible for a variety of ceremonies designed to protect their families and communities from evil spirits. For example, after a new house was built, the women would pour a bit of water and wave a cloth over each hand and say [in Kurdish], "Get out, go from here devils. Enter good spirits. You should have sons and daughters, grooms and brides."[23] When a woman would become pregnant for the first time, other women would teach her about pregnancy. These teachings included information about properly disposing of fingernail parings so as to avoid miscarriage, and other fertility advice.[24] Many charms existed for easy childbirth. Once again, because of the paucity of evidence, we can only assume that there were certain women who knew more charms than other women, women who were consulted by other women for assistance in charms to keep away evil spirits and to have easier pregnancies and childbirths.

From the limited evidence available it seems that the role of midwife was an important option for women in the Old Country who sought exceptional careers. According to Brauer, the midwife would accompany the new mother to the menstrual house. This hut, built outside of the village, was always well populated. The new mother would stay there until the end of the period of impurity.[25] We can only speculate about the women's knowledge that was passed on in the menstrual hut. The midwife was also responsible for protecting the new mother and baby from Lilith and other evil spirits. For example, the midwife would hit the new mother three times and say (in Kurdish), "Get out Lilith!"[26] The midwife was an expert in both the physiological aspects of childbirth and the religious ones. In one of the very few studies ever done on the role of midwife in a premodern society, Lois and Benjamin Paul looked at the midwife as sacred specialist in a Guatemalan

village. They found that the midwives had much in common with shamans—
evidence of divine election and ecstatic journeys. The midwives were well
respected and the role highly professionalized.[27] The traditional role of midwife is one that no longer exists in modern society. Well-trained nurses who
are called midwives work in obstetrics' wards of hospitals, but they have
neither the prolonged personal contact with the women and their families
nor the expertise in the spiritual realm that constituted the role of midwife
in small, premodern villages.

In Kurdistan, women would immerse themselves in the river following
their period of menstrual impurity. Two other women would accompany the
menstruant to the river, help her immerse, and guard her on the way home.
Again, we can only speculate as to what special ceremonies, songs, laws, and
customs the women needed to know in order to do this job properly. Today in
Israel, there are still women who work at the *mikvah* [ritual bath], supervising
the women who come to dip. However, these women are closely supervised
by the (male) rabbinate. At an interview with the woman in charge of the
mikvah in the neighborhood adjacent to the Day Center, I was told that the
mikvah attendants have weekly meetings with the rabbis in which they are
repeatedly told not to decide anything by themselves. Rather, any time the
slightest question arises, they are instructed to call the rabbi. Today, the
attendant's job is limited to checking the women to make sure that they
have prepared properly for the immersion and to watch and make sure that
the woman immerses all of her body in the ritual bath.

Vulnerability of Women's Religion

Modernization has a paradoxical effect upon women's religious lives, sometimes bringing in its wake a dramatic widening of religious opportunities and
sometimes resulting in institutionalized attacks upon women's rituals, "nor-
mativization" of male religious structures, and the denigration of women's
health and reproductive expertise. As Kurdish and other Middle Eastern
women have come to Israel and increased their knowledge of normative
Jewish rituals, there has been a concurrent decrease in women's traditions.
Brauer's book abounds with examples of women's religious and nonreligious
rituals in Kurdistan. Most numerous are the wedding and childbirth rituals.
But equally interesting are women's holidays such as Shabbat Banot [Girls'
Sabbath] on the first Sabbath in the month of Adar (approximately March).
On this day the girls would organize into groups, each with a leader, and
collect wood, sing ritual songs, and act rowdy. They used the wood to heat
bath water, and all the girls would bathe. The wood was also used for an
oven in which they made special cakes called bride cakes. Two weeks later,
on Purim night, the girls would again meet and bathe in water heated from

the wood that they had previously collected. The bathing was supposed to make them beautiful like Queen Esther. Girls and their mothers would make henna and the mothers would paint all the girls, wash them, sing to them as to a bride, and throw roses and nuts at them. This ritual complex is one of many that has totally disappeared.

The traditional female-oriented religion of the Middle Eastern women has suffered a number of direct and indirect attacks at the hands of modern, male-oriented society. The most striking example concerns holy tombs. Two of the most widespread and important rituals that *women* perform at tombs (men generally do not perform these rituals) are lighting candles on behalf of needy family members and leaving the candles to burn next to the tomb, and kissing and touching the tomb in order to establish close contact with the holy person.

At a number of tombs in Israel, the Ministry of Religion has prohibited the lighting of candles, ostensibly because of fire hazard (although most of the tombs are in solid stone buildings) and asked the male guards at the tombs to enforce this new prohibition. In addition, at one very sacred shrine (the tombs of Shimon Bar Yochai and his son Elazar in Meron) a high metal fence has been erected around the tombs. This fence prevents pilgrims (mostly women) from touching the tomb or from lighting candles next to the tomb. For women, whose traditional religion was intensely relationship-oriented both in terms of attempts to establish intimacy with deceased ancestors and in terms of rituals aimed at preserving the well-being of beloved descendants, prohibiting candle lighting and building fences around tombs must be seen as a serious affront.

Cross-culturally, this is not an isolated case.[28] A common effect of modernization is to define the male sphere as normative for the entire society. This may help explain why so many Middle Eastern women have begun participating in traditional male rituals—once the male realm is defined as normative, women may choose or be forced to abandon their traditional female practices in order to take part in the mainstream religion.

In the beginning of this chapter, whenever I pointed to widening religious opportunities for women, I in fact looked at quantity—women have more niches in the multi-layered modern religious world. However, this discussion has not adequately addressed the status and power of those niches. While it seems that with modernization women may increase their ritual repertoire, it is not clear that a quantitative increase always translates into more power (spiritual or profane) or more success at thinking about and working out ultimate concerns. In fact, a frequent effect of modernization is to change the meaning of women's rituals, from acts that are necessary for the well-being of the entire community to acts that affect only the individual women themselves. Modernization may mean that women's traditional rituals are now evaluated in light of "modern" knowledge, and modern "wisdom" often labels women's religion as irrational superstition—or even witchcraft.

Rabbis bombard the Middle Eastern women of Jerusalem with admonishments to ask a [male] rabbi or [male] scholar whenever they have questions about Jewish ritual observances. These women were not accustomed to turning to a male authority in order to properly conduct their religious lives. In the Old Country men and women did not participate jointly in most religious rituals, and women were usually in charge of female matters such as *kashrut* [food taboos], menstrual taboos, and women's mourning rituals. In modern society, much of this has been taken out of female hands.

Rituals to avert the evil eye, many of which were female rituals in the Old Country, are often no longer perceived as necessary for the well-being of the community. Young couples getting married today may permit their grandmothers to smear henna on their hands (a traditional fertility ritual), they may even enjoy the ritual as a way of strengthening ethnic identity, but this smearing is no longer seen as an absolute prerequisite for the future fertility of the couple and the well-being of the community. In the Old Country, the line between official required-by-Jewish-law observances, and folk, unofficial, not-required-by-Jewish-law rituals was all but nonexistent. It is in modern Israel that many of the traditional female rituals have come to be seen as old wives' tales.

As modern technology penetrates the traditional female reproductive sphere—a sphere that was both physical and spiritual—women may lose important specialist functions. Not only midwives, but fertility, infertility, and child health experts become replaced by modern medical personnel, and women's traditional knowledge becomes denigrated. The medicalization and resultant despiritualization of childbirth and fertility—relating to birth as a biotechnical rather than a magical-spiritual event—has, in many cases, undermined one of the most important treasuries of female religious power.

According to anthropologist Clifford Geertz, through ritual is generated the belief that religious conceptions are true and religious directives, sound.[29] For the women of this study, coming to Israel [*aliya*] resulted in both a sociological and a theological reorganization of tradition. In the face of their new, *halachic* education, the women are no longer absolutely convinced (nor interested in strengthening the belief) that their traditional religious conceptions are sound or their rituals efficacious. In addition, the increased mingling of the sexes in modern Israel has led to the disintegration of autonomous women's world-views.

Innovation and Tenacity

A new ritual created by the Day Center women (and other women similar to them) is that of throwing unlit candles at tombs of saints. The impetus for this was the prohibition on lighting candles and the metal bars put up around some of the tombs.

At certain tombs the women continue to light candles despite the signs and the guards. But at other tombs, where there is absolutely no possibility of lighting candles or touching the tomb, the women have begun throwing unlit candles through the bars of the metal grating at the tomb itself. The aim of the ritual is the same: by donating something to [the tomb of] a saint, they earn the right to request help from God. And by creating some kind of physical connection between themselves and the tomb, they strengthen the bond or relationship between living Jews (themselves) and righteous ancestors who will then be reminded to intercede with God on behalf of the women and their families. In this ritual the women show great flexibility and innovation in dealing with new situations. Together with a deep concern for sacred tradition, the women are willing to develop new religious rituals that meet their current needs. This sort of "invented tradition" is a rather typical instance of people responding to a novel situation through creating a ritual that refers to old situations.[30]

In one of the few studies investigating the religious lives of elderly Jews, Barbara Myerhoff looked at a Jewish Senior Citizen's Day Center in California. Writing about the ritual life of the center, she found that the old people "revitalized selected features of their common history to meet their present needs, adding and amending it without concern for consistency, priority, or 'authenticity.'"[31] Myerhoff noted several instances of traditional rituals consciously being changed in order to meet the current needs of the senior citizens. In particular, she described a new ritual called a "graduation-*siyum*" that was held at the end of a course in Yiddish history. A *siyum*, or completion, is traditionally held when a group of men finish studying one volume of the *Talmud*. The ceremony at this graduation-*siyum* combined elements from an American graduation and a traditional Eastern European *siyum*. The graduation-*siyum,* like all rituals, had to be convincing and appear authentic. In Myerhoff's estimation, this new ritual successfully linked two distinct realms of meaning and experience into a strong ritual drama. The new ritual transcended contradictions, fused disparate elements, glossed conflicts, and provided a sense of unity.[32] In this ritual the senior citizens "exercised their basic human prerogative, the right to indicate who they are to the world, to interpret themselves to themselves instead of allowing accident and history and reality to make that interpretation for them."[33] Ritual establishes continuity, both personal and collective, and continuity is an especially important concern for the elderly.

The parallels between the graduation-*siyum* and the new rituals performed by the women of the Day Center are important. In both instances rituals have overcome disjunction; two realms of experience have been fused into a meaningful unity. The old people combined traditional elements with modern innovations in order to form new rituals that both allowed them to establish continuity between the past and the present and to publicly say who they are. For the women of the Day Center, this meant that they managed to join together elements of modern, Zionist ritual with traditional, women's petitions (in the case of the Tu b'Shvat ritual) or to overcome modern resistance to traditional women's rituals by changing the outward form but not the inward intent of the ritual (in the case of throwing candles at tombs). These women, through their rituals, interpret themselves to the world, saying: We acknowledge that we live in modern society and respect its innovations, but we choose to interpret these new prohibitions and rituals in light of our traditional, female experience.

The domestic nature of the religious experience of Middle Eastern women means that they are in charge of many of the religious symbols and rituals that reach people at the basic or gut level of emotion and childhood memories. In particular, the role of food in religious observance should not be underestimated. Many of the second and third generation secular Israelis whom I interviewed declared that the one type of ritual that they still find meaningful is the consumption of traditional foods; the aroma of nut cookies baking, the texture of Shavuot rice pudding, the taste of the Sabbath afternoon stew are not easily eradicated. And it is women who have the specialized expertise that the preparation of these foods demands.

It may be relatively simple to convince someone that a different doctrine is "truer" or to force someone to accept a powerful ecclesiastical hierarchy. However, the myriad of rituals performed by women to protect their babies are often private, personal rituals, conducted outside of the formal, official religious structure and filled with strong emotive power. Most of the daughters and granddaughters of the Day Center women have rejected most formal and legal Jewish observances (for example, they drive on the Sabbath), yet they continue to place protective amulets beneath the mattresses of their babies' cribs. Women who may be willing to risk their hypothetical happiness in the world to come would not think of taking a gamble concerning the well-being of their children in this world.

It seems likely that because women frequently stand on the fringes and sidelines of institutionalized religion, and because women often lack access to sacred texts, they can easily absorb new rituals and discard old rituals. The Day Center women, who cannot read, describe all religious rituals as "written in the Torah." Because they in fact cannot know exactly what is written in the Torah, they do not feel a need to consult rabbinical authorities before adding new rituals, such as tree planting, to their repertoire.

A certain flexibility seems to be a common characteristic of female religiosity in patriarchal societies. For the women of Jerusalem, safeguarding the health and fertility of their descendants is a major religious concern. With the advent of western medicine, the women's traditional herbal and ritual efforts on behalf of their offspring have become less valued. However, because the women's traditional approach to health and fertility allowed for the use of very eclectic means, they have been able to reinterpret and refocus their ritual activity. Mothers and grandmothers are no longer the primary dispensers of medical care, and the old women profess that if one is sick, infertile, or about to give birth it is advisable to consult a western doctor. However, *"none of it will help if God has decreed the opposite."* Instead of providing direct medical assistance, the elderly women now devote a great deal of time, energy, and expertise to *influencing* God to grant good decrees.

Notes

1. Lourdes Beneria and Gita Sen, "Accumulation, Reproduction, and Women's Role in Economic Development: Boserup Revisited," *Signs* 7(2) (1981): 279–98; Esther Boserup, *Women's Role in Economic Development* (London: George Allen and Unwin, 1970); Leela Dube, Eleanor Leacock, and Shirley Ardener, eds., *Visibility and Power: Essays on Women in Society and Development* (Delhi: Oxford University Press, 1986).
2. Shlomo Deshen, "On Religious Change: the Situational Analysis of Symbolic Action," *Comparative Studies in Society and History* 12 (1970): 260–74; Clifford Geertz, "Ritual and Social Change: A Javanese Example," *American Anthropologist* 59(1) (1957): 32–54.
3. Marla Powers, *Oglala Women* (Chicago: University of Chicago Press, 1986), esp. 194.
4. V. Ebin, "Interpretation of Infertility: The Aowin People of SouthWest Ghana," in Carol MacCormack, ed., *Ethnography of Fertility and Birth* (London: Academic Press, 1982), 141–59.
5. Katherine K. Young, "Hinduism," in Arvind Sharma, ed., *Women in World Religions* (Albany: State University of New York Press, 1987), 59–104.
6. It is likely that as the younger generation grow older, they will become more religious and to some extent replace the old women described in this book. This is a common cultural pattern. For a study of a situation in which *elderly* people regardless of gender serve to preserve and transmit tradition see Charles Briggs, "Treasure Tales and Pedagogical Discourse in Mexicana New Mexico," *Journal of American Folklore* 98 (1985): 287–314.
7. Rickie Burman, "'She Looketh Well to the Ways of Her Household': The Changing Role of Jewish Women in Religious Life, c.1880-1930," in Gail Malmgreen, ed., *Religion in the Lives of English Women, 1760-1930* (Bloomington: Indiana University Press, 1986), 253.
8. Nancy Tapper and Richard Tapper, "The Birth of the Prophet: Ritual and Gender in Turkish Islam," *Man* 22 (1987): 69–92, esp. 87.
9. See Deshen, "On Religious Change," esp. 266.
10. The Druse are members of a sect living in the Middle East whose religion combines elements of Islam, Judaism, and Christianity. Druse have been persecuted in many of the Muslim countries in which they lived. Druse living in Israel serve in the Israeli Defense Forces.
11. Yung-Chung Kim, *Women of Korea: A History from Ancient Times to 1945* (Seoul: Ewha Woman's University Press, 1982).
12. Pamela Constantinides, "Women's Spirit Possession and Urban Adaptation in the Muslim Northern Sudan," in Patricia Caplan and Janet Bujra, eds., *Women United, Women Divided* (Bloomington: Indiana University Press, 1982), 185–205.
13. Erika Bourguignon, ed., *A World of Women* (New York: Praeger, 1980).

14. Donna Shai, "Changes in the Oral Tradition Among the Jews of Kurdistan," *Contemporary Jewry* 5(1) (Spring/Summer 1980): 2–10.
15. Yona Sabar, "Kurdistani Realia and Attitudes as Reflected in the Midrashic-Aggadic Literature of the Kurdish Jews," in *Studies in Jewish Folklore*, ed. Frank Talmage, 287–96 (Cambridge, MA: The Association of Jewish Studies, 1980).
16. Yona Sabar, "Lel-Huza: Story and History in a Cycle of Lamentations for the Ninth of Ab in the Jewish Neo-Aramaic Dialect of Zakho," *Journal of Semitic Studies* 21 (1976): 138–62.
17. Paper presented at the American Anthropological Association 70th Annual Meeting, November 1971.
18. Brauer, *Jews of Kurdistan* (Jerusalem: HaMaarav Press, 1947). For a fuller description of women as professional mourners, see Margaret Alexiou, *The Ritual Lament in Greek Tradition* (Cambridge: Cambridge University Press, 1974).
19. Brauer, *Jews of Kurdistan*, 158–61.
20. There are several sources that mention the widespread use of amulets in Kurdistan. The richly illustrated catalogue of the Israel Museum exhibition on Kurdish Jewry describes the numerous silver and embroidered amulets worn by women who believed they were in danger during pregnancy and childbirth. See the Israel Museum's *Jews of Kurdistan: Tradition, and Art*, Publication No. 216 (Summer–Winter 1981–1982).
21. While it is obviously not good scholarship to "assume" that something must have been so because it logically should have been, when studying women's history, which has almost entirely been omitted from traditional historical sources, certain scholarly liberties must be permitted.
22. Debbi Friedhaber, *From the Dance Customs of Kurdish Jews* (Jewish Dance Archives, 1974).
23. Brauer, *Jews of Kurdistan*, 61–62.
24. Ibid., 126–29.
25. Ibid., 129–33.
26. Ibid., 133–38.
27. Lois Paul and Benjamin Paul, "The Maya Midwife as Sacred Specialist: A Guatemalan Case," *American Ethnologist* 2(4) (November 1975): 707–20.
28. See, for example, Elisa Buenaventura-Posso and Susan E. Brown, "Forced Transition from Egalitarianism to Male Dominance: The Bari of Columbia," in Mona Etienne and Eleanor Leacock, eds., *Women and Colonization: Anthropological Perspectives* (New York: Praeger, 1980), 109–33.
29. Clifford Geertz, "Religion as a Cultural System," in *Anthropological Approaches to the Study of Religion*, ed. Michael Banton, 28 (London: Tavistock Publications, 1969).
30. See Eric Hobsbawm, "Introduction: Inventing Traditions," in Eric Hobsbawm and Terence Ranger, eds., *The Invention of Tradition* (Cambridge: Cambridge University Press, 1983), 1–14; Richard Handler and Jocelyn Linnekin, "Tradition, Genuine or Spurious," *Journal of American Folklore* 97 (1984): 273–90.
31. Barbara Myerhoff, *Number Our Days* (New York: E. P. Dutton, 1979), 9.
32. Ibid., 104–5.
33. Ibid., 107–8.

MEMORY, REFLEXIVITY AND BELIEF: REFLECTIONS ON THE RITUAL USE OF LANGUAGE

Carlo Severi

Editor's Introduction

Carlo Severi is Directeur d'études, Ecole des Hautes Etudes en Sciences Sociales and Directeur de Recherches, Centre National de la Recherche Scientifique, Paris. He has conducted fieldwork among the Cuna of Panama and the Western Apache in the USA, and is interested in shamanism, messianic movements, representation, otherness and cognition.

In the following chapter he explores the contested territory of the role of individuals and their memories, reflexivity, beliefs and discourses in transmitting culture within shamanic and other societies. If research has shown that stories, myths, folklore and other narrations are stable and "largely independent of the identity of their narrator," do rituals permit greater improvisation and fluidity? If so, in what sense might rituals be traditional and culture stable? Severi argues that in shamanic rituals of world transformation the ritual use of language can be used to define the nature of the ritual performer and that reflexivity appears as an external way to comment upon the nature and effectiveness of ritual action. Putatively inner (reflexivity and identity) and outer (discourse and appraisal) are reciprocally and reflexively related. His conclusion formulates a hypothesis about the linguistic elements of the nature of the relationship between ritual and belief. Precisely because doubt is an integral element of belief, and because ritual actors powerfully express the tension between belief and doubt, this question of reflexivity is an important one.

❧ ❦

In a recent article devoted to the relationship between social memory and history, Kristof Pomian (1999) has expressed, with great clarity, a traditional conception of the kind of social memory that characterizes "oral" traditions: "In a society where only an oral tradition exists, social memory is always the memory of someone. As such, it is always subjected to the destiny and arbitrary will of an individual."

Anthropologists have objected in various ways to this conception, still well alive among historians and other social scientists. One of the most common arguments opposed to this point of view runs as follows: if the social memory of these societies was so exposed to the arbitrary will of individuals, we would find the "oral" cultures in a state of incessant instability and constant disorder, and it has been repeatedly shown that this is empirically untrue. Fieldwork shows on the contrary that the transmission of cultural knowledge in oral societies is never really left to the arbitrary will of the individual. What makes a representation part of a tradition is, first of all, its form. Shared knowledge is everywhere transmitted following traditional patterns as, for instance, in the form of a story or group of stories, untiringly recounted from one generation to the other. While being subjected to constant variations, these stories appear to be sustained by a number of underlying patterns of narration (what J. Goody [1977, 1987] has called the "plots" of oral tradition) that acquire a certain stability through time, and thus preserve the general identity of a tradition. From the works of V. Propp (1972) to the present day a great number of specialists have shown, for instance, that certain narrative structures characterize European folklore. These patterns, or typical forms of narration, while tolerating a certain amount of re-invention, are far from being unstable, or entirely reducible to the will of this or that narrator. It can be remarked, on the contrary, that a typical feature of these narrative patterns is precisely to be largely independent of the identity of their narrator. In folklore, a story can be told by anyone, without losing its character or its effectiveness. One can trust or distrust this particular way to transmit knowledge, but it is indisputable that a certain form of cultural (i.e. not simply individual) memory is operating in this familiar example of an oral tradition.

However, if we are able to give a satisfactory answer to the question posed by Pomian in the case of narrative traditions, this task seems much more difficult when cultural knowledge is not formulated in narrative terms. What happens, for instance, when "cultural knowledge" is expressed in the form of ritual performances? Here, the situation is, at least at first sight, much more similar to the one described by Pomian. It is well-known that in ritual performances, and in particular in the ritual use of language (as, for instance, in chants, spells or other forms of ritual speech) individual improvisation can play an important role. If we consider, for instance, the domain of American Indian shamanistic chants, we find all sorts of very different situations, ranging from the recitation of very long and complex texts committed to memory, as is the case of the Kuna (Severi and Gomez 1983; Sherzer 1983), or the Zuni (Tedlock 1983), to the relatively free use of a set of esoteric metaphors as in the Yaminahua, Arawete, Parakana and other Amazonian traditions (Viveiros de Castro 1989; Townsley 1993; Fausto 2001), to the apparently casual emission of meaningless sounds, as among the Guajiros (Perrin 1976). Narrative structures are far from being present in all these shamanistic traditions, and even when we find them, they seldom account for the complexity, and the particular style of ritual chants. How then could we describe the kind of "cultural memory" that characterizes the transmission of ritual knowledge in these cases? How can we understand the process by which a certain number of representations become part of a tradition? How could we argue against Pomian's idea of a transmission governed by no rules, and entirely entrusted to individual free will?

A first answer to these questions has been, as in the case of folklore, of an empirical nature. An American Indian ritual chant is always the result of a learned technique of enunciation (of which parallelism is the most obvious example), even when a certain kind of improvisation is used. Almost everywhere in American Indian shamanism, improvisation is only one of the rules of the ritual game. Many anthropologists have described ritual performances where a certain equilibrium is established between what is subjected to variation and a certain number of crucial points (that we could call the *foci* of ritual performances), where improvisation plays a much less important role. To learn a shamanistic chant may not mean memorizing all the details of a particular fixed text. It would mean, rather, acquiring a certain technique of enunciation, be it a certain way to "sing," or to manipulate a certain linguistic form. As Townsley has written about the Yaminahua, "Learning to be a shaman is learning to sing, to intone the powerful chant rhythms, to carefully thread together verbal images couched in the abstruse metaphorical language of shamanic songs, and follow them" (Townsley 1993, 457).

A certain number of these forms: ritual dialogues, a particular kind of "singing" (which Tedlock has defined as a particular way "to bring stress and pitch and pause into a fixed relationship to the words" [Tedlock 1983, 234]), and a certain form *of parallelism* (a term which designates the use of a limited number of repeated formulas, constantly modified with slight variations), are very widely spread in American Indian shamanism. However, the use of a special linguistic form is not sufficient to define the *ritual use* of language. Dialogues, "singing" techniques and above all "parallelistic structures" can be used in non-ritual (for instance, narrative) situations, as the famous studies of James Lord on Serbo-Croatian epics have shown (1960). There is thus no reason to consider them as inherent to ritual communication.

Shamanistic recitations, as any other ritual performance, cannot be seen as entirely dependent on the arbitrary will of an individual (the shaman) because they are oriented by a special context of interaction and communication, which is seen as radically different from ordinary social life. For a shaman, to sing is obviously to perform an action, and all the American Indian shaman's claims of power to cure and kill rest on the idea that, while operating a certain transformation on the use of language (using a "twisted language" [Yaminahua] or "raising his words right" [Zuni], etc.) he becomes able to understand, see and name things in an exceptional way.[1] The simple, and very general fact that shamanistic recitations are seldom understood by non-specialists suffices to prove that the kind of linguistic communication involved in these cases is far from being obvious. In fact, to pose simply that a "special" form of communication exists, affirming that chants are incomprehensible because they are "understood" only by "non-human spirits" (Townsley 1993, 459) or to provide, as many ethnographers have done, for good empirical descriptions of shamanistic language and metaphors, is not a satisfying definition of the formal context which gives to ritual communication its exceptional character.

How is this special context constructed? Under what conditions does it operate? How does it influence or modify ordinary forms of communication? It is clear that, in so far as we have not found a satisfying answer to these questions, we shall not be able to provide for a good solution to the problem posed by Pomian: Whose memory is working in this context? How far goes the cultural elaboration of a ritual speech? To understand what kind of cultural memory operates in this case, one needs not only to describe the kind of linguistic technique used in shamanistic chants, but also to propose an interpretation, in formal terms, of the context which characterizes ritual communication.

In a book devoted to the study of ritual action (Houseman and Severi 1998), Houseman and I have claimed that one of the essential clues for understanding ritual communication is to study the way in which, through the establishment of a particular form of interaction, a special identity for the participants is constructed. In the example we have analysed, the Naven (a transvestite ritual of the Iatmul of Sepik, Papua New Guinea), the study of a first interaction between a mother's brother *acting as* a mother (and a wife) on the one hand and, a sister's son *acting as* a son (and a husband) on the other, has led to the analysis of a series of rites involving larger social groups where the competition between men of the maternal side and mothers of the paternal side of Ego plays a major role. One of our conclusions has been that the identity of each participant is built up within the ritual context from a series of contradictory connotations (being, for instance, at once a mother and a child, a sister's son and a wife).

This process, of symbolic transformation realized through action that we have called ritual condensation gives to the ritual context of communication a particular form, that distinguishes it from ordinary life interactions. In this paper, I would like to extend this approach, until now based almost entirely on the analysis of sequences of actions, to the study of ritual situations of a different kind, where action seems to play a less important role, and is replaced, through the recitation of chants, by a special use of language. How is it possible, in a context where only special words are used as means of intervention, to build that special definition of the identity that characterizes ritual interactions? In order to understand the particular way in which, in these cases, a context of communication typical of ritual is established, let us start by some reflections about the concept of reflexivity.

Reflexivity, Ritual and Belief

Many anthropologists have remarked that rituals have a paradoxical relationship to belief. On one side, as sequences of symbolic actions, rites have been often defined as attempts to generate a mental state of belief in a fictive, or supernatural dimension of reality. Pierre Smith (1979; 1991) has, for instance, convincingly argued that this close link to the establishment of a belief should serve to distinguish "real" rituals from other contexts of social interaction (as feasts, celebrations or dances) that only resemble them. Yet the kind of belief generated by ritual ceremonies never really seems to rule out disbelief and doubt. As Hojbjerg, Rubow and Sjorslev (1999) have rightly remarked, in daily social life rituals never fail to generate comments about themselves. This does not only mean, as every anthropologist knows, that traditional societies in Europe and elsewhere are far from being societies of believers. It means, more generally, that a reflexive attitude about religious "truth" or about the existence of supernatural beings seems to be always, or at least very often, associated with the performance of a ritual action.

Ritual action may not only aim to confirm the existence of supernatural beings. It can also challenge them, or be performed in order to test the effectiveness of their powers. If this is true, we should consider religious doubt "as a condition that sustains the existence of religious ideas and practice ... and as an essential element in the process of acquisition of religious ideas" (Hojbjerg, Rubow and Sjorslev 1999). I agree with this way to approach rituals, and would like to illustrate in this paper some aspects of reflexivity (and its relation with belief) as it appears in American Indian shamanism. In order to do so, I will consider some aspects of the Kuna shamanistic tradition.[2] However, before examining the Kuna ethnography, let me make an attempt to clarify the meaning of the notion of reflexivity as applied to ritual action and to the particular context of communication that it implies.

In fact, if we want to consider reflexivity as a universal fact (as a thing present "everywhere in the world" and as "a way to study how doubt relates to ritual action" as Hojbjerg, Rubow and Sjorslev [1999] invite us to do), we should not limit reflexivity to the mere exercise of an episodic doubt about the effectiveness of ritual performances. I think that we should go further, and try to find how far this notion can lead us in the attempt to grasp some universal facts about the nature of ritual itself. If doubt, as well as the attempt to establish a belief, is always linked to ritual contexts (and if we want to include a reference to reflexivity into the definition of ritual itself) then the study of reflexivity should lead us to explore an aspect of ritual action that has not been yet entirely understood.

A first step in this direction could be to recognize that the reflexive stance—the comment on the nature of ritual actions—is not always *exterior* to (independent from, or subsequent to) the performance of a ceremony. Actually, ritual performances can *include* reflexive aspects within their own scope. Reflexivity is there not only to make people "objectify" ritual performances, or take a reflexive stance about them in daily life. It can become a constitutive part of ritual itself. A certain way to look at ritual action *per se*, and to make inferences starting from its performance may be seen as an essential part of the basic pattern of ritual behaviour itself. As Caroline Humphrey and James Laidlaw have argued in their book on Jainism (1995), the paradigm of ritual action should not be thought of as the unambiguous expression of a common cultural background, as for example Turner suggests in his descriptions of Ndembu rituals. Neither does a ritual performance necessarily entail a close community sharing a single culture and symbolic code. The effectiveness of a ritual is not necessarily to be understood as the establishment of a symbolic consensus. It is on the contrary much more realistic to describe ritual as a context that can involve a range of more fragmented, divided and historically self-conscious social situations. For Humphrey and Laidlaw a good example of this more realistic view is provided, for instance, in the description given by the Indian-Caribbean novelist V. H. Naipaul of his return to Trinidad to attend a "Hindu" funeral rite for his sister. Naipaul describes "the plurality of social experiences which the participants brought to the funeral rite; the fragmented and overlapping cultural and ethnic identities they drew upon; their more or less conscious desire to recover, reform and reinvent their traditions."

As Humphrey and Laidlaw have remarked, "the participants were united in performance even if their notions of the meaning of the rite were both incomplete and contradictory" (Humphrey and Laidlaw 1995, 80). Ritual is not to be seen as the static illustration of a traditional "truth," but rather as the result of a number of particular inferences, of individual acts of interpretation, involving doubt, disbelief and uncertainty. The acts performed during a rite regularly appear to demand a commitment from the actor, even when the actor does not understand them. For this reason, these acts become the screen upon which a number of different, even contradictory meanings, may be projected. As Humphrey and Laidlaw put it, "ritualized acts are apprehensible, waiting to be apprehended and, possibly, given meaning" (1995, 101).

Reflexivity appears no more, in this perspective, as a "comment" on ritual effectiveness made from the point of view of daily life. It becomes rather an essential part of the way in which ritual actions are made to become meaningful for the participants of a ritual celebration. Reflexivity is, in this case, situated *within* the ritual context. We can conclude, then, that the concept of reflexivity, as it applies to ritual contexts, goes far beyond the mere existence of an attitude of scepticism toward ritual belief. A kind of reflexivity exists that can be described as a way for ritual action to represent (or comment upon or even test) itself—its effectiveness as well as its meaning. All these cases, however, while being already instances of an inclusion of reflexivity within the ritual context, have yet another point in common. They all concern the result of a ritual performance. They are *post hoc* celebrations, and can be understood as mere addenda to the performance of other rituals. I think that we could proceed even further, and identify cases where reflexivity (or a certain kind of self-representation) stands as the premise, and not as the final result of ritual action. I will argue that, in American Indian shamanism, first, the ritual use of language is one of the more effective ways to achieve the process of self-representation, which can concern the performers and the actions performed in a ritual context and, second, that reflexivity as self-representation is one of the most important ways of marking the special kind of communication that distinguishes ritual communication and makes it radically different from daily-life situations.

The case of Kuna shamanistic tradition is particularly relevant to this discussion. In this tradition there is a sharp contrast between the "vague" definition of some of the central concepts used in shamanistic discourse (such as "spirit," "soul," etc.), and the very precise instructions concerning the *act of singing* therapeutical chants (Severi 1993b). The ritual procedures required by the practice of ritual chanting are in fact always very precisely defined in this shamanistic tradition. Nonetheless, this obsessive and very accurate attention to the technical procedures to be applied in the ritual performance of a chant (the orientation "toward the east" of the chanter, the preparation of his brazier, the preliminary dialogue with the ill person etc.) always coexists with an abundant room left for doubt and disbelief. Actually, any therapeutical intervention of a specialist may be submitted to public debate, and shamans themselves are often the most supercilious judges of each other. However, in the Kuna case there is probably more than what Hojbjerg, Rubow and Sjorslev (1999) have called an "inner iconoclasm." Reflexivity is not present here only in the form of doubt. In this case, as in many American Indian "shamanistic" situations, reflexivity (as we have defined it, namely as a way for ritual action to pose the problem of the definition of its own meaning and effectiveness *within* the context of ritual communication) lies at the core of the traditional knowledge and of the belief system implied by it.

Language and Ritual Transformation

In the anthropological study of ritual symbolism, great attention has been devoted to the various ways in which language, as it is used in ritual performances, transforms the usual representation of the world, and constructs its own truth-universe. A typical way to do so in American Indian shamanism is to establish a metaphorical link, a set of analogies, or a group of "mystical" relationships between ritual objects and living beings. A splendid example of this way to proceed is to be found in the Mu-Igala, a Kuna shamanistic chant devoted to the therapy of difficult childbirth (Holmer and Wassen 1953), where the baby "coming out" from the body of the mother is progressively transformed into an hybrid being, called the "bleeding pearl" (or "bead"). Let us follow briefly the phases of this transformation. In a first moment (Holmer and Wassen 1953, 56, vv. 184–85), the body of the mother is progressively transformed into a tree. First the chant starts mentioning the "roots" of the mother's body:

> Your stems grow
> In the pure golden stratum of the earth (your) root supports you
> As far as the golden stratum of earth your root stands firmly planted ...
> The animals climb every single one of your spotted branches

This description is followed by one of the suffering mother's body as a tree bending its branches as the wind blows (Holmer and Wassen 1953, 57, vv. 186–88, 58 v. 213):

> When the north wind blows through you
> Your branches bend down with the wind, they arc reclining
> with the wind. the wind whistles through them
>
> Towards the East, your silver branches are spreading

Then, the chanter starts to refer to the mother's body as a "bleeding tree," and to the baby as a "fruit" coming out from this "tree." The chanter sings (v. 184):

> Every single one of your spotted branches emits juices,
> they drip all like blood

This series of transformations (based on the analogy mother's body–tree/and baby/fruit) is followed by another, constructed through the implicit establishment of another analogy, based on the axis fruit/pearl. In this way, after mentioning a "bleeding fruit" as a symbolic equivalent for the baby, the chant draws to a conclusion this series of symbolic transformations, and starts to mention "bleeding pearls." We can thus, later in the chant, come across statements like this one (Holmer and Wassen 1953, 59, vv. 227–28):

> Your striped necklace beads open up inside all red
> Your necklace beads are all reeking of blood

Without further referring in detail to the text of the chant, we can say that this equivalence, established between the pearl and the baby, supposes a series of (implicit or explicit) statements such as these:

> The mother is a tree
> The baby is a fruit
> The body of the mother is bleeding
> The tree is bleeding
> The fruit of the tree is bleeding
> The fruit is a ritual bead
> The bead is bleeding

By the progressive extension of this way of transferring analogical connotations to other objects and other beings, an entire transformation of the world, formulated in ritual terms, is thus symbolically achieved in Kuna shamanistic tradition. As elsewhere, the linguistic instrument of these metamorphoses is parallelism,[3] a "way to thread together verbal images," as Townsley (1993, 457) has called it, present virtually everywhere in American Indian shamanism, that Kuna shamans can practice with great virtuosity. Let me underline, however, that parallelism is not only a linguistic technique. When ritually applied to the description of the experience of an ill person, it becomes a way to construct a supernatural dimension that is thought of as a possible world, possessing an existence parallel to that of the ordinary world. In this context, for instance, for the shamanistic chant to refer to a "bleeding fruit" is to refer to the real experience of the woman giving birth to a child and simultaneously to a mythical Tree-Mother bearing fruits. I would like to show now that the same instrument, parallelism, can also be used in a reflexive way, in order to define not only the world described by the ritual language, but also the identity of the person enunciating it. I will argue that it is in this way that in the case of American Indian shamanistic practices a special context that characterizes ritual communication is established.

Let us try to get further in our analysis of the Mu-Igala. Like many other chants of the Kuna healing tradition, this chant begins with a sort of introductory part, which contains an extensive and painstaking evocation of the ritual gestures and procedures necessary for enunciating the chant. In this "introduction" we see how the shaman moves around the hut, asks his wife to prepare a meal of boiled plantains, goes and washes in the river, returns to the hut, sits next to the ceremonial brazier, starts in total silence to burn cocoa beans in the brazier, gathers the statuettes that will assist him in the rite, sits down again and begins to sing. In the Mu-Igala, this preliminary part (which Lévi-Strauss [1958] analysed to other ends in his famous essay on symbolic effectiveness) takes up a considerable share of the transcription of the chant (Holmer and Wassen 1953) and periodically alternates with an account, more usual for anyone studying shamanism, of the ups and downs of the "soul snatched away by the spirits," whose absence has triggered the illness. Let us take a look at a passage of this part of the chant:

> The midwife opens the shaman's hut's door.
> The door of the shaman's hut creaks.
> The midwife is about to go in through the shaman's door.
> The shaman is lying in his hammock, in front of her.
> The shaman's first wife is also about to lie down next to the shaman.
> The midwife approaches the shaman.
> The shaman asks: "Why have you come?"
> The shaman asks: "Why have you come to see me?"
> The midwife answers: "My patient says she feels dressed in the hot clothing of illness."
> The shaman says: "Your patient says she feels dressed in the hot clothing of illness? I too feel it."
> The shaman asks the midwife: "For how many days does your patient feel she has been wearing the hot clothing of illness?"
> The midwife answers the shaman: "For two days my patient feels she has been dressed in the hot clothing of illness."
> The shaman says: "Your patient feels she has been dressed in the hot clothing of illness for two days."
> The shaman says: "Since I have no light to see through, I shall enter the dark, secret place through you."
> The midwife moves one foot forward to walk.
> The midwife touches the ground with one foot.
> The midwife moves the other foot forward.
> The midwife is about to go out of the shaman's door.
> The midwife moves one foot forward.
> The midwife touches the ground with one foot.
> The midwife moves the other foot forward.
> The midwife is about to enter the woman's door.
> The shaman sticks one leg out of the hammock.
> The shaman gets out of the hammock.
> The shaman grabs his stick.
> The shaman goes in and out of the hut.
> The midwife moves one foot forward.
> The midwife touches the ground with her foot.
> The midwife moves the other foot forward.
> The shaman reaches the door of his hut.
> The shaman opens the hut door.

The door of the shaman's hut creaks.
When he leaves the hut, the shaman stops and looks about him, looking lost.
The shaman starts walking in the direction of the path leading to the woman's hut.
The shaman places one foot on the path leading to the woman's hut.
The shaman rests one foot on the path leading to the woman's hut.
The shaman moves the other foot forward along the path leading to the woman's hut.
The shaman is about to enter the door of the woman's hut.
They place a small golden chair underneath the sick woman's hammock.
The shaman sits on the golden chair.
They place a brazier underneath the hammock, a bowl-shaped brazier.
The shaman looks for cocoa beans.
The shaman puts the cocoa beans in the brazier bowl.
The cocoa beans are burning.
The cocoa beans give off smoke.
The smoke given off by the cocoa beans fills up the hut.

In order to understand the paradox implied by a description of this type, we must remember that what the shaman is describing in this passage (the dialogue with the midwife, the encounter with his wife, the recognition of the illness, the meeting with the sick woman, the preparation—fundamental for the rite—of the brazier) is always something that has already occurred by the time he starts chanting. In other words, if we go from a simple reading of the text to a description of the conditions of the rite, we find each time that the chanter refers to himself in the third person, a kind of *regressus ad infinitum*: a shaman, sitting next to his brazier at the foot of the hammock where the woman about to go into childbirth is lying, talking about a shaman, sitting next to his brazier, at the foot of the hammock where the woman about to go into childbirth is lying, talking about a shaman. ... and so on. Before starting to sing the chant, the chanter describes himself.

For a long time I have seen this as a relatively simple mnemonic device: as an example of a special genre of the Kuna ritual "ways of speaking" (Sherzer 1983) the Mu-Igala possesses its own conditions of enunciation. It seems natural that tradition would need to preserve not only the text, but also its "instructions for use." And the more natural way to do so is, understandably enough, to verbalize them, and just store them in the chant "before it starts" (Severi 1993b). However, I have now come to see that this interpretation only accounts for a superficial aspect of the shamanistic ritual enunciation. We have already seen that the "move" consisting in describing "someone speaking about someone preparing to speak" has a first consequence: it short-cuts time. If we keep in mind that (with minor exceptions) the only tense used in this part of the chant is the present, this will appear clearly. We have seen that the enunciator says he is approaching to the ritual seat, to the hammock, to the door etc., when he has already performed such things, and is seated, as it is required, "toward the East" and facing the sea. The immediate consequence is that what is formulated in the present tense refers here to the past. This has many effects, but one of them is particularly relevant to the definition of the enunciator. When this present-meaning-past tense meets with the real present, in other terms, when the linguistic description of the situation becomes an accurate one ("the shaman is now seated there and is saying this") we have a situation where "someone is speaking about someone speaking (now)." We should remember an essential point: it is precisely this description of the position of the speaker that characterizes, in the Kuna perspective, the "special kind of communication" that is appropriate for ritual chanting. It is only when this part has been enunciated that the journey of the spirits into the supernatural world can begin, and the chant becomes ritually effective. The simple narration of travel in the supernatural world would not be expected to have any therapeutic effect.

Why is it so? What has changed here? Actually, this definition of a speaker "speaking of himself speaking" appears to be paradoxical only as far as we do not understand that it illustrates another way to apply parallelism. The shaman is actually using the same technique that we have seen used in the text concerning the baby progressively constructed as a "bleeding fruit." That technique of transformation of a real body, or person, into a "supernatural" presence described by the chant, is here applied to the enunciator himself. This transformation is never explicitly described in the chant, as in the case of the mother "becoming a tree," or of the baby being transformed into a fruit. However, from the moment the singer starts to mention a chanter about to begin to recite his chant, from the point of view of the definition of the enunciator (well before the beginning of the narration of the shamanistic journey), an entirely new situation is established: the enunciators have become two, one being the "parallel" image of the other. There is the one who is *said to be there* (in the landscape described by the chant, preparing his travel to the underworld), and there is the one saying that he is *here* (in the hut, under the hammock where the ill person lies), chanting.

This first, elementary pattern of the process of "making the enunciator plural," attributing to the enunciator a plural nature, is not an episodic detail. On the contrary, this way to "double the presence" of the chanter illustrates only the most simple way to define a plural enunciator in the shamanistic speech. Actually, we shall see that this process of constructing a complex identity can take a much more developed form in American Indian shamanism. It could thus provide for a first answer to the question that we have posed about the ritual context of shamanistic communication: how is it possible, in a context where only words are present as means of ritual action, to build a special identity? Let us, before examining another example of a Kuna shamanistic chant, briefly describe the relational context in which this construction of a complex enunciator takes place.

Shamanistic Discourse and Ritual Speech

To summarize and discuss the recent developments of the anthropological research about American Indian, in particular Amazonian, shamanism would lead us far beyond the limits imposed to this paper. Let us focus only on one point: shamanistic "therapy" of illnesses is often in America represented as the result of a confrontation between two rival beings: the pathogenic spirit (often said to be a threatening animal such as a jaguar) and the shaman or his auxiliary spirit (represented in most cases as a plant or a vegetal spirit) who has the power to heal. This kind of ritual has long been considered mainly in terms of the supposedly widespread "general model" of Siberian shamanism. According to this model, the aim of the specialist's intervention is to "reintegrate" a "missing soul" into the body of the ill person. For this reason, the argument goes (for instance, Eliade 1974), the symbolism of the rite is based on the representation of a "cosmological voyage" undertaken in order to find the spirit who has stolen the soul.

A number of case studies (Crocker 1985; Descola 1993; Descola and Taylor 1993; Severi 1993b, 2001; Wilbert 1993; Townsley 1993; Carneiro de Cunha 1998) and elsewhere (de Sales 1991; Humphrey 1996), have shown that while this approach is undoubtedly based on indigenous discourse about shamanistic activity, it in no way accounts for the complexity of a shaman's ritual behaviour. In particular, the performative aspect of the shamanistic discourse, that is, the characteristic way whereby a series of symbolic transformations are effected through ritual speech, has often been recognized as far more important than its "narrative" aspect (Tambiah 1985; Tedlock 1983). In the light of this new perspective, the primary issue at hand is no more to interpret the basic categories of shamanistic discourse (often understood as a mere comment to cosmology) but rather to understand that which is realized through a particular use of language during the shaman's ritual intervention.

Edmund Leach wrote once that in ritual language "it is not the case that words are one thing and the rite another. The uttering of the words itself is a ritual" (Leach 1966, 407). This is certainly true in the case of American Indian shamanistic traditions. Still more recently, it has also been recognized that the main focus of ritual action in the case of shamanism is not "cosmological exploration," but rather a particular process of metamorphosis implied by the "travel pattern," as well as a symbolic predation of the evil spirit ritually enacted by the shaman. Thus, to sing in order to cure a person is, in many Amerindian traditions, to hunt the most dangerous hunter of human beings, often incarnated, as we have mentioned, by a supernatural animal (for instance, a jaguar or an anaconda).

This new perspective has, without a doubt, brought about significant progress in our knowledge of shamanistic traditions: the ritual word is seen no more as a fragment of an imaginary discourse about the nature of the universe, but as an instrument of this magic predation (Descola 1993). However, while it is surely helpful to stop considering the shaman as an isolated figure in order to appreciate his activity in relational terms as a case of "symbolic predation," the nature of the relationship which is established between the shaman and his supernatural adversary is far from being fully understood. Clearly the ritual identity which the shaman assumes cannot be seen as a simple inversion of the representation of his supernatural adversary. Indeed, in many ethnographies, the shaman appears as a highly paradoxical being, represented sometimes as the chief enemy of the evil spirit and at other times as an actual (or possible) incarnation of it. Consequently, the shaman's ritual identity may oscillate between an incarnation as a healing spirit and the threatening image of a predator (Crocker 1985; Viveiros de Castro 1991). The clearest illustration of this appears among the Jivaro, where every case of illness treated by a shaman is thought to have been caused by another shaman (Descola 1993).

Let us focus on this ambivalence. Almost everywhere in America, one point seems to be clearly established: becoming the adversary of a supernatural being in no way represents a permanent symbolic status or a stable social function. To be able "to act as an effective shaman" is a very special, temporary "state of body and mind" which must be acquired anew each time a ritual intervention is required. In order to become able to hunt the ultimate predator, the shaman must, each time, undergo a ritual transformation himself. His symbolic status is thus inherent to ritual action in two senses: it must be ritually constructed, and it can disappear once the ritual is over. It is for this reason, I suggest, that the paradoxical representation of the shaman often found in these traditions does not simply reflect an ambiguous conception of his powers. Seen from this relational point of view the shaman's ritual identity appears to be founded upon a condensation of contradictory connotations, thus revealing the characteristic complexity of a ritual relationship. It is in this perspective that the construction of the shaman's identity as a complex enunciator (of which we have seen a first example in the "introductory part" of the Mu-Igala) reveals its meaning.

Let us consider a particularly well-developed example of such a construction of the shaman's ritual identity, the *Nia Ikala*, the shamanistic chant used for the treatment of what the Kuna today call *locura*, "mental illness." The background of the ritual performance is that the supernatural Jaguar of the Sky has attacked a human being. As a consequence, the crazed person is obliged to imitate the supernatural animal, and always becomes himself or herself a dangerous predator: a "hunter of men."[4] This state of madness (*locura*) is described as an act of imitation of the spirit, progressing from occasional crises of uncontrolled actions, to a complete identification with the Jaguar and the latter's dangerous behaviour. At that point, the ill person is seen as having become a spirit him/herself. The interpretative pattern that we have outlined above would lead us to expect in this case a straight-forward confrontation between a "good" (vegetal) spirit allied with human beings and a "bad" (animal) spirit, in which the Jaguar's hunting of the ill person is countered by a further act of "magical hunting" directed against the Jaguar.

However, in Kuna tradition as in many other Amerindian cases, the situation is much more complicated. First of all, the Jaguar the shaman has to confront is not a common one. It is represented as a special being, possessing an ontological status very different from that of "everyday" jaguars. In the Kuna case, the ways in which this exceptional status of the Jaguar is represented are many. First of all, the Jaguar of the Sky always appears in shamanistic chants as a double being. It is both hunter (as a being of the forest) and singer (as a bird, a being of the sky). When it appears in the chant, he is never wholly himself: now a bird sounding like a jaguar, now a jaguar sounding like a bird. In a characteristic parallelistic way, "birds" and "jaguars" are progressively assimilated in the chant:

> 149 Hanging from an umbilical cord, the bird calls; hanging from an umbilical cord, just like a jaguar of the sky, he is calling
> 150 The bird roars; hanging from an umbilical cord, the bird roars like the jaguar
> 151 Over there, at the place of the Dark Village, the Village resounds, the Village trembles, from afar one can hear it resound, over there, at the place of the Dark Village
> 152 The jaguars of the sky move through the air

> 168 At the end of the Dark Village, clinging to an umbilical cord, the bird calls, the bird roars out; clinging to an umbilical cord, the bird calls, the bird roars: clinging to an umbilical cord, the *askokoar* bird calls, the bird roars (Severi 1993, 126–29).

A threatening incarnation of death and madness, the Jaguar of the Sky is above all defined as an animal of metamorphosis. It is precisely this partial ontological coincidence of two animal species (bird and jaguar) which represents its supernatural status. Secondly, it is always said to be an invisible being. The Jaguar of the Sky is made present only through sound, its only visual manifestations being either the blinding light of the sun, or exceptional dream images that may appear when the eyes are closed. Furthermore, its presence cannot be perceived through its own "voice," but only through the cries of other animals. When the Jaguar passes through the forest, it manifests its presence by means of a particular sequence of animal cries. A bird, a monkey, a boar, a deer will be heard by the hunter walking in the forest, but none of these animals will appear. A threatening incarnation of death and madness, the Jaguar spirit that brings illnesses to human beings is thus represented as possessing a multiple and exceptional identity. It is precisely this exceptional nature which represents its supernatural status. In order to confront this special being, the shaman must achieve a similar metamorphosis: he too must transform himself into a multiple and exceptional being. This symbolic transformation is achieved in the ritual performance through the establishment of a complex, higher-order relationship between him and the spirit. Specifically, in keeping with the definition of the Jaguar, the Kuna shaman acquires a multiple nature by acquiring a complex voice, in which a variety of different beings (even enemies) are evoked together.

We have seen that, in Kuna terms, the "madness" of the patient is interpreted from the very beginning in acoustic terms: it is seen as the presence of the "voice of the Jaguar" in the ill person's body. The crazy person "contains" the invisible jaguar, and is thereby forced to speak its language. The Kuna shaman-chanter counters this emergence of "animal speech" in a human being by means of two parallel strategies. In a first part of the recitation of his chant, he explores the way leading to the abode where the patient's missing soul is hidden. In doing so, he begins to "speak the tongue of the vegetal spirit" (the special language in which the chant is composed), thereby progressively identifying himself with a seer spirit of the forest: the trunk of the balsa wood. A simple human being no more, he thus incorporates the power to heal (and the power to see the invisible) that is normally possessed by vegetal spirits.

However, this transformation is only a first step in the ritual definition of the shaman's identity. Once the shaman has reached the supernatural "village" where the lost soul of the patient is to be found and where the evil spirits are identified and attacked, his symbolic relationship to the ill person changes radically. At this point the shaman must, through the ritual recitation of the chant, not only incarnate the vegetal spirits of the forest, but also conjure up the presence of the animal spirits who dwell in the body of the ill person he is curing. Describing the place where these evil spirits are hidden, he suddenly starts uttering a long series of the hunting cries shouted by the animals into which the Jaguar is transformed: a bird, a monkey, a boar, a deer, etc.

251 Here the *nias* ("spirits") are transformed into peccaries, the peccaries are there with their black clothes, they cry "*ya-ya-ya-ya*"
252 The peccaries are now changed into *nias*, they are transformed into *nias*, the *nias* are transformed

253 They are transformed into lords of the animals with the striped fur; above the trees the *nias* with the striped fur cry *"turku-turku"*
254 The animals with the striped fur are now changed. They are transformed into deer, the *nias* are there, at the foot of the trees, with their black clothes, with their antlers intertwined, with their great pointed antlers, they cry *"me-me"*
260 The peccaries are now changed into *nias*, they are transformed into *nias*, the *nias* are transformed
262 At the foot of the trees the *nias* cry *"tatta-tatta"*, out there, at the foot of the trees, the *nias* cry *"we-we"*
270 Into monkeys the *nias* are transformed; up there, above the trees, the *nias* cry *"ti-ti-ti-ti"*
272 Into *uli-ulika* monkeys the *nias* are transformed, they are up there, above the trees, with their black clothes, and they cry *"uli-uli"*
273 The *uli-ulika* animals are changed into *nias*, they are transformed into *nias*, the *nias* are transformed
274 Into *uma-umaka* animals the *nias* are transformed, they are up there, above the trees, with their black clothes, and they cry *"uli-uli"*
(Severi 1993, 138–40)

The shaman sings then, in this crucial part of the chant, not only as a "spirit of the forest's trees" (using their "vegetal" language), but also, and so to speak simultaneously, as an "animal" spirit. Indeed, at that point, through the sequence of animal cries that appear in the chant of the shaman, the "multiple voice" of the Jaguar of the Sky itself is made present. The shaman becomes then a novel sort of enunciator, constituted by a long series of con-notations, including both the evil and the therapeutic spirits. The reflexive use of parallelism, which characterizes the chanter that we have seen in the Mu-Igala, who starts to sing about himself singing, is only the first (and, despite appearances, crucial) step in the same process that here becomes spec-tacular of accumulating contradictory identities of the image of the enunci-ator. The shaman then becomes a complex enunciator, a figure capable of lending his voice to different invisible beings. What in the relative simple case of the Mu-Igala was a simple way to "double" the presence of the chanter, has become here, by a process that we could call a cumulative inclusion, a way of concentrating on the chanter an entire series of contra-dictory identities. From a relational point of view, we can conclude that shamanistic therapy is founded upon the symbolic opposition of two terms: the patient-as-an-animal spirit and the shaman-as-a-vegetal-spirit. However, the kind of ritual identity realized in this context is based on a process of progressive cumulation in which features characteristic of one pole of the opposition, that of the ill person-Jaguar, are gradually included in the other pole, that of the shaman-vegetal spirit. The ritual identity achieved in this way by the shaman—by symbolically manifesting the coexistence of the "cries" of different beings in his single voice—thus acquires a logical status comparable to the one attributed to the supernatural Jaguar. It subsumes a series of contradictory connotations located at different logical levels.

Figure 1. *The ritual identity achieved by the shaman*

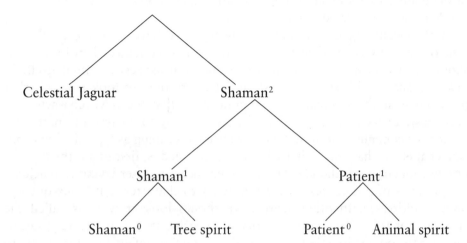

We should not forget that the only means of effecting this transformation is ritual speech. In this context, however, the spoken word is treated not only as a way of designating (and transforming, as in the case of the "bleeding pearl" in the Mu-Igala) objects in the world, but above all as a way of defining a *voice*, a complex voice indicating the exceptional nature of the speaker. Through the appearance of the animal cries within the language of the vegetal spirits, both the supernatural predator and its adversary are made present. I would like to suggest that this particular use of language, relatively independent from the meaning of the chant, is what characterizes shamanistic rituals. Language is used in this context as a way not only of conveying meaning, or as a magical way of performing a therapeutical act, but also as an acoustic mask: a reflexive means to enact the ritual identity of the speaker.

Reflexivity and the Ritual Use of Language

The study of the particular kind of reflexivity illustrated in American Indian shamanistic traditions leads to a first general conclusion concerning the "special context" which frames ritual linguistic communication: ritual enunciation always involves the metamorphosis (or definition in ritual terms) of its enunciator. We can then answer the first question that we have posed (How can we describe, in formal terms, the special context that makes ritual communication different from ordinary life?) as follows: the ritual context, illustrated here by the example of shamanistic Amerindian performances, is different from ordinary communication because it brings the pragmatic aspects of communication to the foreground, through a reflexive definition of the enunciator. It makes the enunciator a complex figure, made up by the condensation of contradictory identities.

At the beginning of this paper, however, we have also argued that, if reflexivity really is so often to be found in ritual contexts, then its analysis should also lead us to elucidate some universal aspects of ritual itself. In order to answer this second question, let us try then to look from another perspective at the context of communication that we have characterized until now. In fact, there is at least one other way to analyse the particular context of communication that we have been describing as typical of shamanistic chants. We have seen that what is transformed is, first of all, the *premise* of any spoken word, the identity of the enunciator. After trying to elucidate the premises of this context, we can now try to characterize its consequences on the addressee. In other words, we should look at what is called the "perlocutionary" effect in the theory of speech acts (Austin 1962).[5] Let us thus try to look at its relationship with the establishment of a belief, or, to be more accurate, to that particular tension between doubt and belief which seems to be typical, as we have seen, of any reflexive stance implied by ritual performances. A complete analysis of this question would no doubt require too long a development, well beyond the limits imposed by this paper. Let us then focus only on the *fictive* nature of the enunciator and the ways in which it can be interpreted. The Kuna shaman, we have argued, transcends his ordinary identity and acquires a new, complex one, which is the result of a series of metamorphoses.

We can now contrast this way of defining an enunciator with other, interactive situations where a fictive (or complex) identity is also involved. Let us consider, for instance that, at a performance of Christopher Marlowe's *Tamburlaine*, an actor, impersonating the cruel emperor, fiercely says these words:

I hold the Fates bound fast in iron chains,
And with my hand turn Fortune's wheel about
And sooner shall the sun fall from his sphere
Than Tamburlaine be slain or overcome
Draw forth thy sword thou mighty man-at-arms,
Intending but to raze my charmed skin
And Jove himself will stretch his hand from heaven
To ward the blow, and shield me safe from harm (Marlowe 1950, 11)

Let us study the appearance of the actor from a formal point of view, the same point of view we have adopted until now in our attempt to define ritual enunciation. What is typical of this situation is that, since the public, by definition takes for granted that the actor is playing the role of Tamburlaine, the identities of the acting person and that of the character he is impersonating are always *mutually exclusive*. The actor is identified either as "Tamburlaine, the emperor" (while acting), or as Mr X, the famous interpreter of the Elizabethan theatrical repertoire. The sentiments and the thoughts he expresses, and even such features of his body, as the "charmed skin" he proclaims to have, are obviously attributed to the emperor, not to the person acting as Tamburlaine. On a theatre stage, these two identities can only alternate, as mutually exclusive, because the context allows no confusion between them. The perlocutionary effect of this situation is clear: even during the most effective performance no doubt is possible about the identity of the enunciator. As we enter the theatre, we accept the kind of fiction which a performance of this kind implies.

Let us come back now to the case of the shaman, and compare it to the representation of Marlowe's drama. The first difference is of a formal nature: the shaman does not *alternate*, as the actor does, between different, mutually exclusive definitions of his identity. On the contrary, he progressively accumulates a series of non-exclusive definitions (first as the "other chanter, the one designated by the chant," then as the "vegetal spirit," and then as the deer, the monkey, the peccary etc.). His definition as an enunciator is then, like that of the actor impersonating Tamburlaine, still a complex one. But the context of communication and the kind of fiction involved here are radically different from those of the actor performing on a theatre stage.

Actually from this first formal difference (cumulating instead of alternating contradictory definitions of identity), another important difference follows that concerns the generation of a belief, the perlocutionary effect of the shamanistic performance. By cumulating on himself contradictory, yet non-exclusive and simultaneous identities (as tree, as deer, as monkey, etc.) the image of the shaman entertains a doubt about the always possible assimilation of his ordinary identity into a supernatural one. His image progressively becomes a paradoxical one, and therefore raises unanswerable questions: Is he a "vegetal" (positive) or an "animal" (negative) spirit? Is he boar, deer, monkey or jaguar? Was he really transformed into a spirit during the recitation of his chant? Will he be able, as he claims, to perform that transformation again and again? Ritual action builds a particular kind of fiction, a special context of communication, where any positive answer will imply doubt and uncertainty, and vice versa. Everybody is supposed to believe it, and yet no one can really be sure. The result of the complex definition of the enunciator, in this context, is thus always a certain kind of uncertainty. If we remember Pierre Smith's proposition, that we should consider "real" rituals only the ceremonies leading to the establishment of a belief, we can get a step further and conclude that linguistic communication becomes ritualized when a particular way to elaborate a complex image of the enunciator is made to unleash that particular tension between belief and doubt that defines a ritual-reflexive stance. The context of the ritual use of language is not defined solely by the use of any specific linguistic form, but rather by the reflexive elaboration of the image of the speaker, and by its perlocutionary effect: that particular tension between faith and doubt that characterizes any belief.

Notes

1. Since the case of women-shamans is very rare in America, I will use in this paper the masculine term he rather than she.
2. Kuna Indians live today in the San Blas archipelago of Panama. Kunaland (Tule Neka or Kuna Yala) numbers from 27,000 to 30,000 persons, who speak a language traditionally associated with the Chibcha family (Holmer 1947; 1951). A small Kuna group, which still rejects all contact with the white man, lives in the Chucunaque region of the Darien forest, near the Colombian border. Essentially, the Kuna are tropical farmers. In his brief historical survey, Stout (1947) speculates that Kuna society, one of the first to come in contact with white men after the discovery of the American continent, was "heavily stratified, and divided into four classes: leaders, nobles, citizens and slaves." Political power today is held by the *onmakket*, an assembly of all the adult males in the village, supported by a varying number of elected leaders (*sailakan*). The Kuna kinship system is bilineal, uxorilocal and founded on strict group endogamy (Howe 1976; 1986). A general survey of the Kuna literature is to be found in Kramer 1970; Chapin, Howe and Sherzer 1980; Sherzer 1983, 1990; and Severi 1993a, 1997, 2001.
3. Fox (1988) contains a wonderful group of case-studies of the use of parallelism in eastern Indonesia.
4. The kuna term is *tulekintakket*. On this point, see Severi 1993b: 49–69.
5. Austin calls perlocutionary any effect on feelings, thoughts and actions of the recipient realized through the enunciation of a speech act (Austin 1962).

References

Austin, J. A. 1962. *How to Do Things with Words*. Oxford: Oxford University Press.
Carneiro de Cunha, M. 1998. 'Pontos de vista sobre a floresta amazonica. Xamanismo e Traduçâo." *Mana-Estudos de Antropologia Social* 1998: 7–18.
Chapin, M. 1988. *Pap Ikala*. Quito: Abya Yala.
Chapin, M., J. Howe and J. Sherzer. 1980. *Cantos del congreso cuna*. Panama: Universidad de Panama.
Crocker, C. 1985. *Vital Souls*. Tucson: Arizona University Press.
de Sales, A. 1991. '*Je suis née de tes coups de tambour*', Sur le chamanisme Magar, Nepal. Paris: Société d'Ethnologie.
Descola, P. 1993. *Les lances du crépuscule*. Paris: Plon.

Descola, P., and A. C. Taylor. 1993. *La remontée de l'Amazone, L'Homme*, special issue, 126–28.

Eliade, M. 1974. *Le chamanisme et les techniques archaïques de l'extase.* Paris: Payot.

Fausto, C. 2001. *Inimigos fiéis. Historia, guerra e xamanismo na Amazonia.* Sao Paolo: Editora da Universidade de Saö Paulo.

Fox, R. 1988. *To Speak in Pairs. Essays in the Ritual Languages of Eastern Indonesia.* Cambridge: Cambridge University Press.

Goody, J. 1977. "Mémoire et apprentissage dans les sociétés avec et sans écriture. La transmission du Bagré." *L'Homme* 1977: 29–52.

—1987. *The Interface between the Oral and the Written.* Cambridge: Cambridge University Press.

Højbjerg, C., K. Rubow and I. Sjørslev. 1999. "Introductory Paper." Conference on *Religious Reflexivity. Anthropological Approaches to Ambivalent Attitudes to Religious Ideas and Practice.* Institute of Anthropology, University of Copenhagen, 15–17 September 1999.

Holmer, N. 1947. *A Critical and Comparative Grammar of the Cuna Language.* Göteborg: Etnografiska Museet.

—1951. *Cuna Crestomathy.* Göteborg: Etnografiska Museet.

Holmer, N., and H. Wassen. 1953. *The Complete Mu Ikala.* Göteborg: Etnografiska Museet.

Houseman, M., and C. Severi. 1998. *Naven, or the Other Self. A Relational Approach to Ritual Action.* Leiden-Boston-Köln: Brill.

Howe, J. 1976. "Communal Land Tenure and the Origin of Descent Groups among the San Bias Kuna." In M. W. Helms and F. O. Loveland, *Frontier Adaptations in Lower Central America.* Philadelphia: ISHI Publications.

—1986. *The Kuna Gathering.* Austin: Texas University Press.

Humphrey, C. 1996. *Shamans and Elders: Experience, Knowledge and Power among the Daur Mongols.* Oxford: Oxford University Press.

Humphrey, C., and James Laidlaw. 1995. *The Archetypal Actions of Ritual.* Oxford: Clarendon Press.

Kramer, F. 1970. *Literature among the Cuna Indians.* Göteborg: Etnografiska Museet.

Leach, E. 1966. "Ritualization in Man in Relation to Conceptual and Social Development." *Philosophical Transactions of the Royal Society of London* B, 251: 403–8.

Lévi-Strauss, C. 1958. "L'efficacité symbolique." In *Anthropologie Structurale I.* Paris: Plon.

Lord, J. 1960. *The Singer of Tales.* Cambridge, MA: Harvard University Press.

Marlowe, C. 1950. *Tamburlaine the Great.* In *Plays,* ed. Edward Thomas. London: Dent.

Perrin, M. 1976. *Le chemin des Indiens marts.* Paris: Payot.

Pomian, K. 1999. *Sur l'histoire.* Paris: Gallimard.

Propp, V. 1972. *Les racines historiques du conte de fées.* Paris: Gallimard.

Severi, C. 1993a. *La memoria rituale. Follia e immagine del bianco in una tradizione amerindiana.* Firenze: La Nuova Italia. Spanish translation, *La Memoria ritual.* Quito: Abya Yala, 1996.

—1993b. "Talking about Souls. On the Pragmatic Construction of Meaning in Kuna Ritual Language." In *Cognitive Aspects of Religious Symbolism,* ed. P. Boyer. Cambridge: Cambridge University Press.

—1997. "The Kuna Picture-Writing. A Study in Iconography and Memory." In *The Art of being Kuna. Layers of Meaning among the Kuna of Panama. Catalogue de l'exposition,* ed. M. Salvador, 245–73. Los Angeles: Fowler Museum of the University of California at Los Angeles.

—2001. "Cosmology, Crisis and Paradox. On the Image of White Spirits in Kuna Shamanistic Tradition." In *Disturbing Remains: A Comparative Inquiry into the Representation of Crisis,* ed. M. Roth and C. Salas. Los Angeles: Getty Institute for the History of Art and the Humanities.

Severi, C., and E. Gomez. 1983. "Nia Ikala. Los pueblos del camino de la locura. Texto cuna y traducción española." *Amerindia. Revue d'ethnolinguistique amérindienne* 8.

Sherzer, J. 1983. *Kuna Ways of Speaking: An Ethnographic Perspective.* Austin: University of Texas Press.

—1990. "The Grammar of Poetry and the Poetry of Magic: How to Grab a Snake in the Darién." In J. Sherzer, *Verbal Art in San Blas.* Cambridge: Cambridge University Press.

Smith, P. 1979. "Sur quelques aspects de l'organisation des rites." In *La fonction symbolique*, ed. M. Izard and P. Smith. Paris: Gallimard.

—1991. "Rite." In *Dictionnaire de l'ethnologie et de l'anthropologie.* Paris: Presses Universitaires de France.

Stout, D. 1947. *San Blas Cuna Acculturation.* New York: Viking.

Tambiah, S. J. 1985. *Culture, Thought and Social Action.* Cambridge, MA: Harvard University Press.

Tedlock, D. 1983. *The Spoken Word and the Work of Interpretation.* Philadelphia: University of Pennsylvania Press.

Townsley, G. 1993. "Song Paths: The Ways and Means of Yaminahua Shamanic Knowledge." *L'Homme* 126–128 (1993): 449–68.

Viveiros de Castro, E. 1989. *From the Enemy Point of View.* Chicago: Chicago University Press.

—1991. "Spirits of Being, Spirits of Becoming: Bororo Shamanism as Ontological Theatre." *Reviews in Anthropology* 16 (1991): 77–92.

Wilbert, J. 1993. *Mystic Endowment: Religious Ethnography of the Warao Indians.* Cambridge, MA: Harvard University Press.

Part IV

CONCLUSION: REFLECTING ON OUR CATEGORIES

CHRISTIANS AS BELIEVERS

Malcolm Ruel

Editor's Introduction

Until his retirement, Malcolm Ruel was a University Lecturer in the Department of Social Anthropology, Cambridge University. His research was mostly conducted in West and East Africa and his extensive publications are largely concerned with political anthropology and the anthropology of religion.

Much of Ruel's writing is about ritual, including most of the book from which the following chapter is taken, *Belief, Ritual and the Securing of Life: Reflexive Essays on a Bantu Religion* (1997). Although this chapter is about the peculiar emphasis laid on belief by Christians, especially Protestant Christians, and their heirs, "Westerners" of various kinds, and about the damage done by assuming the universality of this emphasis, Ruel is clear that a degree of reflexivity is commonly implicated in ritual behaviour. It is his expertise in studying and reflecting on ritual that provides Ruel with a clear view of the dynamics of Christian and modernist discourse about belief. This might have been adequately demonstrated by including his concluding discussion of four fallacies about belief. However, the whole chapter is important in detailing specificities and generalities about belief and its relationship with ritual that require consideration. Ruel's discussion of "belief" and believing provides vitally important illumination on assumptions and habits of thought and speech that may otherwise prevent understanding of and dialogue with those who do things differently.

References

Ruel, Malcolm. 1997. *Belief, Ritual and the Securing of Life: Reflexive Essays on a Bantu Religion*. Leiden: E.J. Brill.

ഇ ൚

Introduction

My argument is summed up in an early observation of Wilfred Cantwell Smith:

> The peculiarity of the place given to belief in Christian history is a monumental matter, whose importance and relative uniqueness must be appreciated. So characteristic has it been that unsuspecting Westerners have ... been liable to ask about a religious group other than their own as well, "What do they believe?" as though this were the primary question, and certainly were a legitimate one. (1978, 180. But see also Smith 1977, 1979, discussed below.)

"Unsuspecting Westerners" must of course include unsuspecting western anthropologists who, as many texts will show (e.g. Evans-Pritchard 1937, 21), give primacy to what people "believe" without fully declaring what that word means, nor recognizing, it would seem, just how rooted the concept is in our own cultural religious tradition, Christian and post-Christian, and thus how loaded any statement concerning "belief" easily becomes.

This then is one reason why an anthropologist may be excused if he moves so far from his last as to attempt, however incompetently, to sketch in outline the monumental peculiarity of Christian "belief." At a time when anthropology has turned more and more to give an account of the cognitive aspects of culture it is as well for us to be aware of the complexity of the concepts that we draw from our own culture, which have a history and contextual compulsion of their own which often ill-match the ideas and actions they are used to interpret. The need for critical reflexion becomes even greater when, as in the case of "believing," there has been a radical shift in the use of the term whilst something of its force has been retained. "Believing" in the sense of being committed to some definable set of values has become secularized, detached from Christian believing but not demoted as a concept, so that in a post-Christian, secular culture the phrase "I believe... " (e.g. in the title of Forster's essay, 1939) still gives promise of a personal statement of some significance, a declaration of moral identity.

There is here another reason why it is appropriate for an anthropologist to attempt the task of ethnographic placing, for it is part of an anthropologist's trade to look hard and long at certain key concepts and to explore how use and meaning, context and idea, are constantly engaged in an interplay in which concepts link situations while situations qualify (and thus help to define) concepts. Now "belief" is essentially a word that relates and defines: it relates people, situations and ideas; but in its turn, as I shall argue, it is also in very important ways defined by the context of its use. In this, function and meaning come almost (but never entirely) to coincide; consider, for example, the phrase "the community of believers" that runs like a thematic passacaglia through Hans Küng's *The Church* (1968). If only to keep for some short time the philosophers at bay (to whom the cognitive promise contained in the word "belief" comes, as it were, as a gift from heaven) let us assert resolutely, at least for the present, that the (Christian) concept of belief is as it does and proceed to consider it situationally and behaviourally.

I

To narrow somewhat the vastness of the topic, four periods have been selected from the history of the church in which to discuss the idea of belief and how it is involved in any definition, corporate or personal, of Christian identity. They are: (1) the critical, initial phase in which Christians, the Nazarene sect, emerged as a distinctive religious movement, a community of believers; (2) the immediately succeeding period leading to the Council of Nicea (325) that witnessed both the developing formal organization of the Church and the establishment of the orthodox creeds, sanctioned by the Church councils; (3) the Reformation and in particular Luther's reformulation of what it means to believe (i.e. to have faith); and finally, since we cannot leave ourselves out, the present period, which might be characterized as belief diffused—"beyond belief" in the phrase of one (diffusely) believing anthropologist. In this section I use the word "belief" only with its Christian reference and where at all possible I keep to this one word, assuming a sufficient continuity and overlap in meaning between "faith" and "belief" to allow "belief" to do duty for both, except where there is a particular need to distinguish them. This usage has the advantage of permitting a single word correspondence between *belief* in English, *pistis* in Greek and the root *'mn* in Hebrew; this does not imply that these words have (collectively) the same meaning nor that they have (singly) a constant meaning, only that their range of meaning is historically and semantically continuous. (On this issue my usage is radically at variance with that of Wilfred Cantwell Smith; see section III below.)

The detailed scholarly writings on the terminology of belief, *pistis*, in the New Testament books make it possible to offer a number of summary points. (I rely chiefly on Bultmann and Weiser 1961; Hatch 1917; Michel 1975; and Moule, unpublished.) In its various forms, *pistis* (belief), *pisteuo* (believe), *pistos* (faithful, trustworthy), *apistia* (unbelief), form a key and much used set of terms in the New Testament. The meaning of the word-group does not (with some qualification) depart from its general meaning, or set of meanings, in Greek, but its New Testament use also carries certain connotations derived from the fact that *pisteuo*, to believe, was the term consistently used to translate the Hebrew *he'emin,* from the root *'mn* (meaning to be true, reliable or faithful) in the Septuagint. One needs here to distinguish between the meaning of words and the religious ideas they express, for although the two may coincide, they do not always do so, and changes in meaning follow often from the development of pre-existing ideas. Thus both the original Greek use of *pisteuo* and the Hebrew term *'mn* express centrally the notion of trust or confidence. Originally the Greek word-group "denoted conduct that honoured an agreement or bond. It had a social orientation, and its use indicated misconduct by implication" (Michel 1975, 594). In classical Greek literature *pistis* means the trust that a man may place in other men, or gods; credibility, credit in business, guarantee, proof of something to be trusted. Similarly, *pisteuo* means to trust something or someone (*ibid.*). The word acquired a religious use at an early date, when to "believe" (*pisteuo*) the gods or an oracle expressed on the one hand confidence in them (their veracity or ability to promote welfare) and on the other obedience to them, an acknowledgement of their power to determine human fate. The Hebrew term *'mn* denotes even more directly a quality of relationship: it was used of the reliability or trustworthiness of a servant, a witness, a messenger, or a prophet, but it also served to characterize the relationship between God and his people, reciprocally trusted and trusting, bound by covenant to each other (Michel 1975, 595–96). In the New Testament the word *pistis* and its related forms still carry the ideas of trust and confidence. In a citation that rings reverberatively through the theology of the centuries, Paul refers to the belief (*pistis*) that Abraham had in God's promise that he would become "the father of many nations" (the story is told in Genesis 15) as an exemplar of the kind of belief (*pistis*) shared by the early Christians. As the belief (i.e. trust) of Abraham was reckoned as righteousness for him, so "Faith is to be reckoned as righteousness to us also, who believe in Him Who raised from the dead our Lord Jesus Christ, who was delivered to death for our sins and raised again to secure our justification" (Romans 4:13–24; trans. Phillips).

Yet in spite of this continuity between the Hebrew and the Greek, the Old and the New Testament, the word *pistis* does come to acquire a special twist in the apostolic writings of the New Testament. One might say that it acquires a technical use. Thus the verb *pisteuo*, to believe, is often used in the sense of to be converted, to become a Christian: "they heard the message and believed" is a formula that occurs repeatedly in the narrative of the expanding church in the Acts of the Apostles; Paul writes of "when we first believed" (Romans 13:11) in the sense of "when we were first converted;" and there are other examples. Similarly, the nominal form "believers" (either *hoi pisteuontes*, "those believing," or *hol pistol*, "those of the belief") refers to the converted, the "brothers" or the "saints" as they are also called. We should note that the word "Christian" is itself rarely used (three times in the New Testament) and then always in the context of what others—the people the Christians called unbelievers—were calling them. Finally, the noun *pistis* denotes the "belief" held collectively by the early Christians as a common conviction, a shared confidence that both distinguished and united them as a community. Paul lists these identifying features explicitly and succinctly in Ephesians 4:4–5 in which the central elements are "one Lord, one belief, one baptism."

We need to look more closely at the substance of this shared belief in the last sense above, for it is in relation to this that the concept gains added depth and range. Essentially what these early converts believed was what theologians have come to call (using another technical term) the *kerygma* or proclamation of the Christian message (Bultmann and Weiser 1961, 69; Michel 1975, 601, 605; Hatch 1917, 33–34). Now this does not mean just the teaching *of* Jesus, but rather the teaching *about* Jesus, and the crucial fact about Jesus, which summed up all the rest, was his resurrection: this fact is expressed clearly in the passage from Paul, quoted above, and throughout the epistles (and we should recall that these are the earliest Christian documents that we have; the gospels were written later). Christian *belief* now begins to part company from Hebrew *trust*. Both refer to a relationship—the confidence people have in God, and in the case of the Christians in God through Christ—but for Christians there is the added confidence or conviction about an event (the resurrection and all that that signifies) that had actually taken place. The belief is not just open-ended, oriented to what God may or can do: it is rooted firmly in what God has done, which to deny is to deny the Word of God, that is, the action of God in the world. (On this point see especially Bultmann and Weiser 1961, 82 *et seq.*) This development was to have enormous consequences for the later use of the concept for it is but a short step from *belief* as accepting as a fact (i.e. the event of the resurrection) to *belief* as asserting as a proposition. A distinction made frequently today is between "belief in" (trust in) and "belief that" (propositional belief). The distinction may clear our minds today but it confuses history, for the point about Christian belief, reiterated by theologians (e.g. Lampe 1976; Moule, unpublished), is that it was both at once.[1]

The creeds, which we must now consider, both reflect and perpetuate this particular notion of Christian belief, that concerns a person-event, not least in their reiterated verbal formula: "I believe in ... who acted thus ... ": Person + Event, the two reciprocally defining (Lampe 1976). Yet if the kernel of the creeds is the recognition of this person-event, their history is one of growing elaboration and formalization, a development that takes place in relation to the developing organization of the Christian body: the

246

shared conviction of a scattered community of Christians becomes the confirmed orthodoxy of the conciliar church.

Brief credal phrases are common in the New Testament and there are occasional longer summaries (as in the passage by Paul) when the writer evidently felt something more explicit was required. In either case they serve as summary statements of the teaching or *kerygma* concerning Christ. The formulary phrase, *Kurios Jesous*, "Jesus [is] Lord," is common and there are many variants. It is clear moreover that such phrases served as conventional declarations of religious allegiance of a symbolic kind. Thus Paul: "If with your mouth you confess *Kurios Iesous* and believe in your heart that God has raised him from the dead, you will be saved" (Romans 10:9) and in another passage (1 Corinthians 12:3) Paul contrasts this confessional formula of affirmation with its opposite, that of denial or denunciation (*Kurios Iesous* v. *Anathema Iesous*, "Cursed be Jesus"), declaring that only the former can be spoken by the Holy Spirit, i.e. that a Christian should be unable to deny Christ. There is some evidence that suspected members of the Christian sect were tested by being asked to make just such a formal denial (Lampe 1976, 54; Kelly 1972, 15) and in the gospels the story of Peter's thrice denial of Christ assumes its significance against the importance of thus "confessing Christ" in the early church (and indeed thereafter). Belief then in this context becomes a badge, a symbol, something that is explicitly affirmed where the act of affirmation has its own functional value.

Such formulary statements were not however creeds in the usual sense of extended declarations of belief. These were to develop in the period up to the fourth century. They emerged in the first place in the context of baptism and then, it would seem, began to be used as statements of the received teaching first for regional congregations and then, in a more self-consciously developed form, as the conciliar creeds prepared for and affirmed by councils representing the whole church or large sections of it. The fact that the earliest creeds were baptismal (on this all authorities are agreed) leads us to note the important post-Easter development of this rite, which acts as a ritual counterpart to the "believing" we have already spoken of as denoting conversion. Jesus's religious career was initiated by baptism from St. John the Baptist but he himself did not baptize people and (except in the case of Jesus) the baptism of St. John was specifically a "baptism of repentance" (i.e. a cleansing rite) and not an initiation. (St. John's message was similarly one of repentance, not of belief.) From the time of the early church, however, baptism came to be used to mark the transition to membership that is so characteristic of Christianity and which in this clear-cut, boundary-marking way is absent from all other world religions. Baptism and belief have parallels in other ways too, for baptism re-enacts symbolically the basic postulate of the belief: as Christ died and rose again so too (it is held) the person being baptized dies and rises again "in Christ." Baptism acts therefore not only as a rite of passage for individual Christians but also as the act by which the church, identified with the risen Christ, is perpetually re-constituted. For it should be understood that the church, although pre-figured in Christ's life, was not in fact founded until after his death and resurrection by those who "believed," i.e. accepted the *kerygma*. (On this point see Küng 1968, 70–79.) "Belief" here takes on theologically and sociologically a critical function in establishing the organic relationship between Christ, the risen Lord, and the church as the community who believe in his resurrection and in this way perpetuate it. Hence the importance of conversion (believing) as a break, a passage from the old life to the new life, a kind of resurrection, comparable for the community of believers to the passage through the Red Sea for the Israelites (the Old Testament analogue for Christian baptism). All this is implicit in Paul's "one Lord, one belief, one baptism."

In their relation to baptism the earliest creeds had a dual function: first, as part of the ritual, candidates were required to respond affirmatively to certain questions about their belief put to them; second, and by extension of the first, statements of belief in the form of a condensed, continuous declaration were used for the instruction of the candidate. (Here and throughout my account of the creeds I rely heavily on Kelly 1972.) It was the latter form that was to be adopted by the later conciliar creeds but it would seem that even before that happened their use was influenced by the recognition that the received teaching they embodied should be uniform, subject to what Irenaeus in the second century defined as a common "rule of truth," and such credal declarations grew in length and elaborateness because of this. Emerging as "a by-product of the Church's fully developed catechetical system" (Kelly 1972, 64) such creeds were in fact ancillary to the interrogatory baptismal creeds. Thus, a fourth-century treatise recalls and comments on the questions asked at baptism that date in this form from at least the second century:

> You were questioned, "Dost thou believe in God the Father almighty?" You said, "I believe," and were immersed, that is were buried. Again you were asked, "Dost thou believe in our Lord Jesus Christ and His cross?" You said, "I believe," and were immersed.
>
> Thus you were buried along with Christ; for he who is buried along with Christ rises again with Him. A third time you were asked, "Dost thou believe also in the Holy Spirit?" You said "I believe," and a third time were immersed, so that your threefold confession wiped out the manifold failings of your earlier life (*De Sacramentis* 2, 7, quoted in Kelly 1972, 37).

The triadic structure of this interrogatory form was carried over into the declaratory baptismal creeds and thence to all the later creeds.

The baptismal creeds summarized the received teaching, but their local use in the widely scattered Christian communities, headed as each was by their bishop, was subject to variation and reformulation. By the end of the third century there is evidence of certain baptismal creeds being cited to test the acceptability of the teaching of a local community, which is to say the teaching of the bishop. There was a shift here in the use of creeds that was critical. It was no longer the catechumen's belief that was at issue (and thus individual membership of the Christian community) but rather the orthodoxy of the bishop (and thus his and his congregation's valid membership of the entire Christian body). The major, decisive step was taken with the Council of Nicaea (325) when the assembled bishops were asked to accept a statement of teaching, which was set out in the form of a declaratory creed. (This was not the "Nicene creed" of the prayer books but it laid the basis for it.) A major preoccupation in the drafting of this statement was to exclude the teachings of Arius and his followers who (as it happened) had themselves drawn up a creed-like summary of their position (Kelly 1972, 206). Two hundred and eighteen out of 220 bishops attending the Council did sign their acceptance and an indication of the change in function of this the first of the conciliar creeds is the fact that the document drawn up states not only what is the received belief, but also what is not: *anathema* is pronounced on those who hold certain propositions (i.e. those held by Arius and his supporters). "Belief" now comes to define, not merely the Christian from the non-Christian, but the true Christian from the false (the true believer from the heretic). Moreover, the latter function assumes an organized authority: bishops in council and not just in their sees.

Two important circumstances are associated with the Council of Nicaea (Kelly 1972; Chadwick 1967). The first is the patronage of Constantine, who had recently adopted the Christian cause and who was concerned to bring the scattered Christian communities into some kind of common organization. Nicaea was the first of the church councils and its establishment of an overall church authority is evidenced not only by the bishops' formal acceptance of the creed but also by their agreement to a number of other liturgical and disciplinary measures (the latter concerning not least the actions of bishops). The second circumstance has already been mentioned: the teachings of Arius who, in emphasizing the absolute perfection of the Godhead, was led to accord a lower, unequal place to Christ. The Council of Nicaea did not resolve the Arian controversy (nor indeed the underlying issue of how to interpret a trinitarian God) and the fluctuating fortunes of the Arian and anti-Arian (or Nicene) camps dominated the church until the Council and creed of Constantinople (381) formulated what was to become the basic doctrine of the Trinity. Any account of this period (e.g. Chadwick 1967, chapter 9) makes it clear that, whatever the merits of the intellectual issue, community loyalties and identities were also very closely involved: the major cleavage between Greek East and Latin West; the dominance of certain key bishoprics and their sees; the fortunes of individual bishops who were promoted or ousted according to their spiritual (and human) loyalties; the relationship of the church to the foundering Roman empire; all have their part to play in the story. Out of this time and out of this general debate emerged the one doctrinal and credal point that separates the Roman from the Orthodox churches, the West from the East. This concerns the phrase *filioque*, "from the Son," which found its way into the Western creeds after the Constantinopolitan creed and has been consistently rejected by the Eastern churches. The issue bears, like Arianism, on the relative status of God the Father and the Son: the Western church, concerned for their equality of status, has come to hold that the Holy Spirit emanates equally "from the Father and from the Son" whilst the Orthodox churches hold that the phrase both is an interpolation and makes little theological sense (cf. Ware 1964, 58–60). In all these issues belief as doctrine has become embedded in the authority-structure of the church.

The conciliar creeds did not replace the baptismal creeds, nor were they intended to do so. The so-called "Athanasian" creed (composed in Latin and unrecognized as a statement of belief in the East) is really a hymn that uses the credal form (and, uniquely, embodies the anathemas also) to make an act of worship. The Apostles' Creed entered the liturgical tradition by a later and yet different route; I return to it below. Such developments in the credal form were paralleled by an ever-extending use of the creeds in the liturgy. Always important in baptism, creeds were later adopted for general use in the eucharist, first in the East (from at least the sixth century) and later in the West (formally, from the early eleventh century; Jungmann 1959, 295–98). The Orthodox, Roman, Anglican and (in lesser measure) Nonconformist churches all continue to give central place to the singing or saying of the creed in their services. The point to make here is that this performance of the creeds is as complex, symbolic and condensed an act of ritual as any other liturgical act and is consequently as much subject to the categories developed, for example, by Turner (1967) for the analysis of ritual symbolism. (On the variable meaning of the creed for different persons saying it see the chapter on the creeds in Doctrine Commission of the Church of England, 1976.)

The historical account of the creeds sketched above is that of modern scholarship, but for many years a different, more popular account of their origins was current. These stories have all the marks of a Malinowskian mythological charter and, as such, tell us something about the central place of the creeds in the ongoing life of the church. Two stories stand out, one relating to the Latin term for the creed, *symbolum*, the other to the "Apostles' Creed."

The Latin *symbolum* comes directly from the Greek *symbolon*, with the general sense of a mark, sign or token. Putting aside a number of fanciful etymologies for the word as it is applied to the creed (and we should recall that *pistis* like *symbolon* was used in Hellenistic Greek to refer to a warrant, token of trust or laissez-passer), Kelly reaches the conclusion that the Latin *symbolum* in the sense of "creed" originally referred to the baptismal interrogations—the ritual act that identified the newly admitted members of the Christian community (1972, 56–58). However, from at least the fourth century more dramatic interpretations of the word held currency. Thus Rufinus, in an account written in that century, which was to be adopted by many others later, dwells at length on the derivation of the word from the idea of a token or password:

> The Apostles realised, he says, that there were Jews going about pre-tending to be apostles of Christ, and it was important to have some token by which the preacher who was armed with the authentic apos-tolic doctrine might be recognised. The situation was analogous, he says, to one which often arises in civil wars, when the rival partisans might make the most disastrous mistakes of identity were it not that the opposing commanders hand out distinguishing emblems, or pass-words (*symbola distincta*), to their supporters: thus, if there are doubts about anyone, he is asked for his token (*interrogatus symbol urn*), and at once betrays whether he is friend or foe (Kelly 1972, 54).

Geoffrey Lampe in his own brief but still authoritative account of the creeds rehearses this story from Rufinus and, accepting its tenor rather than its historical accuracy, uses it to confirm the significance of the *symbolum*, the creed, as in origin "a sign of recognition" that differentiated the early Chris-tians from their Jewish neighbours (1976, 52–53).

The second story probably also derives its later widespread acceptance from Rufinus' telling of it, although as he narrates it it is already ancient tradition. It concerns the origin specifically of the Apostles' Creed and it held sway for something like a thousand years before coming under any seri-ous criticism in the mid fifteenth century. Scholars are in doubt about the actual origin of the present text of the Apostles' Creed. The likeliest place of origin is somewhere north of the Alps, possibly southwest France in the late sixth or seventh centuries; by the ninth century its use had become wide-spread in the Roman baptismal rite (Kelly 1972, chapter 13). The popular account is, however, much simpler, which is that on the day of Pentecost when the disciples were gathered and the Holy Spirit came upon them they then collectively composed the creed, each adding one phrase:

> Peter said "I believe in God the Father almighty...maker of heaven and earth" ... Andrew said "and in Jesus Christ His Son ... our only Lord" ... James said "who was conceived by the Holy Spirit ... born of the Virgin Mary" ... John said "suffered under Pontius Pilate ... was crucified, dead and buried" ... etc. ... (From a series of sermons, *De symbolo*, probably of the eighth century, quoted by Kelly 1972, 3.)

The story has enormous appeal, for it represents as a collective act that which distinguishes Christians as a community, and it does so on the very occasion, the day of Pentecost, when the community is represented as first coming together to assume their conscious purpose as a church.

There is no simple formula to describe what happened at the Reformation; the processes that are distinguished by that term were already in train before the period usually covered by it and they certainly continued beyond it. In describing the nature and effects of the Reformation it becomes necessary to resort to the term "faith" which, although by no means new, acquired an extra dimension of significance that gave it (like the *pisteuo* word-group before it) a quasi-technical use. Deriving from the Latin *fides* (itself cognate with the Greek *pistis*, which it normally translated in the Bible), "faith" carries by semantic origin very much the same range of meanings as did originally "belief"/*pistis*, that is, trust or confidence; and, as alternative translations of the Bible show, the two words in English often serve as synonyms, with "faith" becoming religiously the more specialized (see OED under "Belief"); the fact that "faith" has no verbal form has also produced the asymmetrical situation in which the verb "to believe" is often matched with the noun "faith." This linguistic variation is more confusing, however, than the broad semantic situation would seem to warrant. Augustine in his treatise on the creed, *De Fide et Symbolo*, uses the term faith/*fides* precisely in the sense of orthodox belief as it is expressed in the creeds, "the Catholic faith" as the received teaching of the church. We may contrast this sense with the meaning that the word more readily has in many Protestant writings, where what is at issue is less the substance of belief (although that is not unimportant) than how such belief (often expressed as the Gospel or the Word) has been subjectively appropriated. The difference between "faith" in the two senses—"the Catholic faith" and a person's own "faith"— is thus less a matter of the difference between church authority and individual reason (which anyway much exercised medieval theologians) than of the difference between belief as declaration and belief as commitment.

Luther's role in helping to effect this shift was crucial but complex. Some would see Luther as simply re-expressing the personal commitment already implicit in the Pauline explication of belief (and Paul's Epistles were of vital importance in Luther's own spiritual biography); others would see his account of belief as an appeal ultimately to unreason, a faith that is given by God's grace, no one can know how. But however one interprets Luther's life and work, a characteristic theme of both is his stress on the inward totality of Christian belief, the faith of the believer. Thus his so-momentous reaction to the spurious hawking of indulgences (the very first of the Ninety-Five Theses sets the tone by insisting that when "Jesus said 'Repent...' he meant that the whole life of believers should be one of penitence"); thus his contrast between the (external) Theology of Glory (that of the Church to

252

date) and the (inwardly experienced) Theology of the Cross (Luther's own preferred theology); thus his distinction between law, a matter of outward performance, and the Gospel, Word or Grace, that works inwardly (the point is made by one of the Heidelberg theses: "The law says 'Do this' and it is never done. Grace says 'Believe this' and everything is done"); and thus, not least, the governing principle of justification by faith, which while proffering intellectually an objective view of God's grace in fact locates faith in the intensity and totality of a person's experience of it. (On these various points see Rupp 1975; von Loewenich 1976; Rupp and Drewery 1970.) Luther stands in history not only as a thinker and a writer but also as a paradigm of the person who possesses belief by being possessed by it: such is the "faith" that comes from without but signifies a subjective transition from disorganized doubt to clarity, conviction and a certain kind of personal freedom.

Two recent representations of Luther that have something of this paradigmatic aura provide a useful bridge to the present. Erikson's psychoanalytic study (1959) grants all of Luther's theological importance (e.g. p. 250) but focuses especially on the concern Luther showed in his own biographical struggle with the intensity and expressiveness of the experience of belief. The title of the key chapter in the book, "The meaning of 'meaning it'," states the issue succinctly: as Erikson writes,

> To Luther, the preaching and the praying man, the measure in depth of the perceived presence of the Word was the reaction with a total affect which leaves no doubt that one "means it" (1959, 203).

But, as Erikson goes on to point out, what Luther had to fight to secure, comes to us as the easy convention of our age:

> [Luther's] formulations, once revolutionary, are the commonplaces of today's pulpits. They are the bases of that most inflated of all oratorical currency, credal protestations in church and lecture hall, in political propaganda and oral advertisement: the protestation, made to order of the occasion, that truth is only that which one means with one's whole being, and lives every moment. We, the heirs of Protestantism, have made convention and pretence out of the very sound of meaning it... (ibid.).

John Osborne's play (1961), which is based on Erikson's study, points to a different but related message. If—to paraphrase Erikson—we are all sincere believers now, Osborne's *Luther* hints that we should beware of being too convinced, too secure in our righteous convictions. The point is made most clearly in the two final scenes, most notably when "Martin" admits to his longstanding friend and adviser (Staupitz) that his delay under interrogation at the Diet of Worms (when his career and even his life were in jeopardy and he is said by tradition to have declared "Here I stand. I can do no other") was in fact the result of uncertainty, of his doubt. Left alone on the stage, he confesses "Oh Lord, I believe. I do believe. Only help my unbelief."

In our age then we seem to believe in belief, but with not too exclusive a conviction. This note of diffuse belief is struck quite remarkably by two books that are in their separate ways both revealing and authoritative. *The Culture of Unbelief* publishes "studies and proceedings from the First International Symposium on Belief held in Rome, March 22-27, 1969" under the sponsorship, amongst others, of the Vatican Secretariat for Non-believers, which was set up following Vatican II. The Symposium gathered a highly distinguished group of social scientists, mainly sociologists, specializing in the study of religion, without regard to their personal religious position, together with and including a number of notable churchmen. It was not, however, the intention of the Symposium to produce "dialogue"—we are told that "in a number of cases the organizers would have been hard put to identify a participant as either a 'believer' or a 'non-believer'"—but rather that of "study in preparation for dialogue" (Caporale and Grumelli 1971, ix). One must break off at this point to comment on the crucial word "unbelief": *apistia* means lack of trust or non-belief in Christ in a religious context. Thus the remark of Osborne's Luther quoted above recalls the outburst of the father of the convulsed boy in Mark 9:24, "Immediately the father of the child cried out and said, 'I believe; help my unbelief!'" There is then nothing new, or especially contemporary, in the idea of unbelief, although it has no doubt a contemporary twist. Pope Paul in his address to the Symposium certainly knew what he meant—the rejection of the Christian religion (see op. cit. 302). Yet one of the features of the Symposium is the very indeterminate value that the terms "belief" and "unbelief" come to acquire in it. Berger in his foreword refers to this "ambiguity in the definition of the problem" and notes the "rather remarkable" fact that "the theoretical position papers, each in its own way, tend to deny the very existence of the phenomenon under scrutiny [i.e. 'unbelief']" (ibid. xiii). The remark covers papers by both Luckman and Parsons but is nowhere so pertinent as in its reference to Bellah's paper, "The historical background of unbelief." Starting with an account of the Greek concept, the paper sets "belief" in an institutional, church context and associates it with "an effort to maintain authority" on the part of the church, "part of a whole hierarchical way of thinking about social control" (p. 44). Belief (which in Bellah's discussion has become very rapidly intellectualized, a matter of doctrine and dogma) is thus distinguished from religion, the former tied to an institutional (church) structure, the latter more diffusely present in shared values. Against then this narrowly defined, historical view of "belief" Bellah contrasts what he sees as an "emergent religion of humanity" (p. 50). Nevertheless, by the end of the paper he is so carried away in his enthusiasm for the latter that all distinctions have disappeared and Christians and non-Christians, belief and religion, the Church and humanity are all rolling together in a single glorious banner:

> The modern world is as alive with religious possibility as any epoch in human history. It is no longer possible to divide mankind into believers and non-believers. All believe something and the lukewarm and those of little faith are to be found inside as well as outside the churches.... Christians, along with other men, are called to build the boundaryless community, the body of man identified with the body of Christ, although all men are free to symbolize it in their own way (p. 52).

There *can* be no unbelief in such a world and the word "believe" has become so generalized as to have lost most of its content. Like Forster's "What I believe," it is a muffled (but less muted) cry.

As a book *Christian Believing* (1976) is an altogether less grandiose affair. It is the report of the Doctrine Commission of the Church of England, which was asked by the Archbishop of Canterbury to examine "the nature of the Christian faith and its expression in holy scripture and creeds." The very striking thing about the report is its lack of dogmatism, tolerance of even opposed views, concern to respect both tradition and the right to criticize and re-evaluate it. The emphasis once again is on existential belief, *believing* as the adventure of faith rather than *belief* as a body of doctrine. The most singular feature of the report is, however, the fact that over half of it consists of eight individual essays by members of the Commission, each in effect outlining his personal view of the nature of the Christian faith. The implication throughout is that each "believer" must find his own way, respecting traditional truths but respecting also other people's right to hold different views from his own. Belief as a doctrine has *almost* become the honest opinion of anyone who declares himself to be a Christian.

There is both continuity and change in the notion of belief that I have sketched above at four phases of its history: trust become conviction about an event (the "Christ-event" of history); become an initiatory declaration; become a corporately declared orthodoxy; become an inwardly organizing experience; become values common to all men (even though different). Yet throughout the concept remains central to Christianity, which is clear from the way it reflects so much of the Church's organizational and intellectual history. Moreover much of the word's meaning in non-Christian use can only be drawn from the particular significance that it has acquired in Christianity—else why attach any importance at all to having or not having beliefs? In the remainder of this essay I write Belief with a capital letter to signify this multi-layered, complex yet condensed range of use and meaning that the concept has acquired in this its long career in Christianity.

II

Negative demonstrations are always difficult and usually lengthy and for this reason I argue the comparative case only summarily. I find little evidence that there is anything equivalent to Christian Belief in other world religions although there are other comparable organizing or nodal concepts. The contrast is greatest with Judaism (as one would expect, historically and sociologically), the similarities (as one would also expect) closest with Islam. The teaching of the law, the *Torah*, stands at the centre of Judaism in a way functionally comparable—but with very different practical implications—to Belief in Christianity; and there are comparable differences in the identity-markers of the two religions. With Islam the parallel is closer: the first of the "five pillars" of Islam—witness to God and his prophet—comes close to being a credo; there is some concern for orthodoxy of belief and there are even formal creeds (although the ordinary Muslim is unlikely to know them). Islam—submission to the one God—can be identified with having a belief, *iman*; a Muslim is also a believer, *mu'min*. Yet, as these words' shared root with the Hebrew *'mn* testifies, their reference is essentially to the quality of a relationship, that of keeping faith, having trust. Correspondingly, it is less the content of belief that has become elaborated in Islam than the duties of the relationship: the practice of ritual, the following of Islamic custom, the observance of Islamic law.

Gombrich, writing about Buddhism, struggles awkwardly for two pages to find an equivalent to the verb "to believe" or "to believe in" before moving directly to the term ("best not translated at all") *dharma* (1971, 60). For Hinduism the parallels are even more indirect and fragmented.

The absence of any self-conscious credal or doctrinal component forms a commonplace observation of most, if not all, traditional or community religions. Should one attempt to distinguish for them, as one can perhaps for other world religions, any organizing concept, comparable to that of Belief in Christianity? I can answer confidently only for the two cultures I know at first-hand, and in both cases I find the question relevant and revealing. For Banyang the idea of truth (*tetup*) has a central significance, in part as an attribute of God, *Mandem*, but more particularly as a touchstone in people's relationships, where the possibility of duplicity is obsessively elaborated by Banyang witchcraft beliefs. On a less cognitive level, the Kuria category of *inyangi*, which I am forced to translate summarily as "ritual," although it means something less, and more, serves also as a touchstone ordering their own relationships (kin and generational) so as to accord with what Kuria see as the principles of natural growth. Both concepts have content but also operate functionally in the organization and determination of relationships.

III

The arguments advanced by two writers, Rodney Needham in *Belief, Language and Experience* (1972) and Wilfrid Cantwell Smith in *Belief and History* (1977) and *Faith and Belief* (1979), bear directly upon my socio-historical discussion of the notion of belief and my conclusions regarding its comparative use.

The central argument of Needham's book is that

> ...the notion of belief is not appropriate to an empirical philosophy of mind or to an exact account of human motives and conduct. Belief is not a discriminable experience, it does not constitute a natural resemblance among men, and it does not belong to "the common behaviour of mankind" (1972, 188).

None of this is in contradition to my own argument and I would want to endorse a number of his ancillary points.[2] However, my account of the situation would be different from his, giving more centrality to the particular (though vastly complex) historical and cultural circumstances associated with the notion of Belief in Christianity. It is true that Needham recognizes something of this (and for a few pages my account of *pistis* and *'mn* looks very like his: we are in fact relying upon the same basic authors) but Needham's discussion concerning the specifically Christian concept is quite considerably briefer than his discussion of the concept as treated by philosophers.

Moreover, although Needham writes of the need to treat concepts (or words) in the context of their use (e.g. p. 186), contextual considerations are notably lacking in his accounts of the way key words or concepts such as belief have been used. This applies in large issues as in small. Thus he makes much point of Evans-Pritchard's remark that "Nuer religion is ultimately an interior state" but this is one of the final sentences of a conclusion in which it is clear that Evans-Pritchard is identifying Nuer apprehension of God (Spirit) with his own:

> Though prayer and sacrifice are exterior actions, Nuer religion is ultimately an interior state. This state is externalized in rites which we can observe, but their meaning depends finally on an awareness of God and that men are dependent on him and must be resigned to his will (1965, 322).

Yet in drawing to a conclusion his discussion of the status of Nuer belief, Needham is able to summarize his enquiry thus: "We have been trying to determine how we can understand the interior state of an alien people with regard to their god" (1972, 30). The shift in meaning is quite radical: "the interior state of an alien people with regard to their god" is simply not what the book, *Nuer Religion*, is about, and whether we accept Evans-Pritchard's identification of God and *Kwoth* or not, it constitutes a contextual fact of some considerable significance. Again, the discrepancy Needham makes much of between Evans-Pritchard's noting the absence in the Nuer language of a word for belief and Crazzolara's recording of one (found also in Kiggen's dictionary) depends upon the underplaying of the obvious differences in the aims and circumstances of the respective writers. It is wholly characteristic that Needham notes in passing (in a paragraph that is worth perusing as a whole):

> The opening words of the Christian confession of faith, the Creed, define the "interior state" of the adherent by the declaration "I believe in God..." (1965, 20).

But on what grounds does he make this assertion and what is its sense as it stands? Naïvely literalist, it ignores the context and much that has been said in the pulpit about the formal act of reciting the creeds. This distorting simplification is matched by the much truncated account of Christian "belief" that stops with the New Testament and, except for a few airy waves ("centuries of dogmatic strife, theological explication, and the arduous ingenuities of translators ... accretions and giddy twists of sense"), gives no account of the later development of that notion, either in its theological or practical context.

This, of course, is to imply that Needham might do something that he is not doing and clearly does not want to do: to look specifically and contextually at his subject. If Needham ends by destroying categories, he starts by assuming that categories of this kind (i.e. universally valid classifying concepts) are really what count and that "belief" is or should be one such category. His question, "Is belief an experience?" is treated by him as a simple empirical issue of general enquiry about the natural world, and the conclusions that he reaches follow logically from the way he has posed the question. He would, I am sure, be unsatisfied by the answer that I would be tempted to give—that it was for Luther. (It was no doubt for many others as well; certainly for Evans-Pritchard, but probably for few Nuer.) My final point would be that in searching for what is common to all humanity one may well lose sight of what is highly significant for some people. Christian Belief is no less real and, in that sense, true, if it is shown to be rooted in the particularities of a certain history and culture. But I agree that, just as we should not assume that we are all Christians, neither should we assume (*pace* Bellah) that we are all believers.

The two later books by Smith, *Belief and History* and *Faith and Belief*, develop a position already sketched in his earlier *The Meaning and End of Religion*, first published in 1962. In that book he specializes the concept of "faith" to denote personal response to transcendent qualities, making this personal faith the critical, underlying feature of all religion. The central argument of the book is that such a quality of faith can be found within the major religions of the world but that it is expressed in different ways by them. Christian belief (which in this earlier book corresponds to what I have called Belief) is only one expression of faith. Smith's two later books develop this position yet further. The word "belief" he now limits in his main argument to its modern propositional sense ("the holding of certain ideas" 1979, 12) and he distinguishes this very sharply from "faith," "the fundamental religious category,"

> an engagement ... the search for conceptual clarification of man's relation to transcendence ... that human quality that has been expressed in, has been elicited, nurtured, and shaped by, the religious traditions of the world (1979, 5–6).

He seeks to show, as in the *Meaning and End of Religion*, that other world religions, Buddhism, Islam and Hinduism, can all be interpreted as expressions of faith, and goes on, inversely, to argue that belief in the propositional sense plays little or no part in them. So too in Christianity, where it is faith rather than (propositional) belief that is the important quality. (This modification to his earlier argument he notes in 1977, 39.) Accordingly, Smith documents in *Belief and History* the changes in meaning of the verb "to believe" from the end of the middle ages to the present time, where the sense has shifted from "recognizing what is true" to "proposing what is in doubt" which he describes, together with other meaning shifts, as "the drift away from faith." Furthermore, he argues somewhat startlingly that the concept of "belief" is not scriptural (the noun appears only once in the 1611 Authorized Version of the Bible whereas "faith" appears 233 times), that "believe" is used primarily because the noun "faith" lacks a verb, and (in the later book) that the correct translation of "credo" is not "I believe." But all this depends upon the limitation in meaning he has adduced for "belief."

There are many insights that Smith provides, not least in the changing meaning of the word "belief" and in his comparative comments on other world religions. On two points, however, his argument poses very grave difficulties. First, his extreme specialization of the terms "faith" and "belief," defined so as to have no overlap with each other, runs counter to almost all usage up to now. "Belief" is left as a quasi-intellectual presuppositional residue to a "faith" that has become so subjectivist and general that it is difficult to give the word any real content. It is true that this specialization is in line with what has occurred from the Reformation onwards, but it clean outruns anything that has gone before (cf. Wiebe 1979). Second, the meaning of both words is intrinsic to Smith's argument but his use of them moves between his own defined sense (which has normative implications) and a much wider, historically variable sense of his narratively descriptive passages so that one is never quite sure where they stand in relation to each other.

There is much in Smith's two books that supports my present case yet overall his conclusion is very different from mine. He is arguing for "faith" precisely what Needham denies for "belief," that it is a universal experience distinctive of all religions, or at least of all world religions. Yet, as Smith himself avows, it is a highly engaged argument, depending upon prior persuasion as to the meaningfulness of faith, and, it would seem, an equally engaged rejection of belief as an important interpretative category. My own impression is of a humane and scholarly heir to the Protestant tradition surveying the world religions with a sharp and sympathetic eye as, for example, a Buddhist might look at the same religions from a different angle, concerned to detect their underlying behavioural code, their *dharma*. As any language can with effort and ingenuity be stretched to describe any situation (although not always exactly) so can the key terms of a religion be similarly exercised, but they are not always the most appropriate terms to use, and in the stretching they lose something of their own distinctiveness. So with Smith's "faith" and "belief": "faith" has become overstretched and "belief" (the modern sense of belief) detached and disowned. It is surely very difficult to talk about the idea of Christian Belief without both of them, referring though they may do to different aspects of it, which change in emphasis through time and for different bodies of Christians.

IV

Clearly it is not possible, nor even desirable, to limit the word "belief" to its specifically Christian usage. Yet at the same time we should be clear that it has a Christian use and that this must affect its connotations in contexts other than Christian. It is surely plain naïve to pluck the word from the linguistic planisphere (the OED Guide to the Galaxy conveniently to hand) and to use it then as though it were a given, something that just happened to be around, which had incidentally been made some use of by Christians. Let me be clear: in ordinary speech there are many uses of the word "believe" that are straightforward and unambiguous. On the whole these have a relatively weak set of connotations, implying usually (of oneself) presupposition or expectation, or (of others) assumption. There are advantages, as Needham indicates, in avoiding "believe" altogether, but the word is current English and in this its weak sense it is not likely to be misunderstood. It is when the word is given a strong sense that it may well mislead: for example, when it forms part of a definition or categorization or is used in posing a problem. Here I would argue that it is almost impossible not to draw on connotations from its Christian use. Moreover, these connotations, contextually transposed, create false assumptions that then lead to fallacies. I speak of these contextually transposed assumptions as "shadow fallacies" and for the non-Christian use of the term "belief" identify four:

(1) That belief is central to all religions in the same way as it is to Christianity. That this is a fallacy is the major argument of this essay and sections I and II of the essay are concerned with its demonstration. It is, however, very easy for a Western writer to slip from talking about religion to talking about Christianity, and back again, without clear distinction. For example, Needham in considering spiritual commitment as a possible criterion of religious belief (1972, 86–89) appears to do just this: he moves from a specifically Christian view of belief as a commitment to Christ (86), then argues that other people can be similarly "committed" to particular enterprises or persons (87–88) and then concludes that there is no discriminable difference between religious and non-religious commitment (88). But it is not commitment *per se* that identifies Christianity but commitment to Christ: Christianity cannot be treated as a type-case of religious commitment; it is a specific case of a particular commitment to a claimed historical person-event. The same fallacy can be detected I think in Martin Southwold's thoughtful paper on "Religious belief." Much of Southwold's critical commentary is highly relevant to any discussion of religion but why focus the discussion on the nature of belief? And does not the framing of the question thus itself determine the kind of answer that will be obtained? Namely, that "basic religious tenets are 1) empirically indeterminate 2) axiomatic 3) symbolic, and 4) collective" (1979, 633). Christian Belief is historically and conceptually more precise in its references than this, but take belief (the shadow idea) to apply to other religions (as one might take the Judaic *torah* or a shadow extension of it) and one may well find the correspondence to be indeterminate and indirect (symbolic).

(2) That the belief of a person or a people forms the ground of his or their behaviour and can be cited therefore as a sufficient explanation for it. For an example of this fallacy I would draw on my own teaching experience. Along no doubt with many others, I regularly set my first-year students in social anthropology an essay on Zande witchcraft usually in the first few weeks of the course. One topic I commonly use runs: since Zande oracles must often give false answers, why then do Azande continue to believe in witchcraft? and, all being well, the essay that is returned duly rehearses Evans-Pritchard's situational analysis of Zande reasoning. But, not infrequently, all is not well and my (I think now misguided) weak use of "believe" is turned into a strong use: the evidence in the book for individual Zande scepticism is ignored, as is much else, to present Azande with such unalterable firmness of conviction as would make a Calvinist jealous. Nor does the matter stop there, for make belief fundamental to the behaviour of a person or a people and the issue in relation to others is then relativized. That is what

Azande believe: finish: there can be no further discussion of the substance of their belief in terms that do not bracket it off as something to do with *them* (rather than the world they experience) and thus hinder its discussion in comparative terms (i.e. what we too experience of the world). The insidiousness of this process of relativization must be emphasized. "We all have our beliefs: all peoples have their beliefs." It is a way of setting people into cultural compartments.

(3) That belief is fundamentally an interior state, a psychological condition. The fallacy once again is to transpose what some have emphasized as the inwardness of Christian belief (faith) to the non-Christian context and use of the word. I would argue that Needham does just this, to the enormous detriment of his discussion, in adopting Evans-Pritchard's assertion concerning Nuer religion and generalizing it to all belief. Yet as Alan Ryan points out (1973), over-insistence on the privacy of what goes on in people's minds distracts from the primary task of construing the sense or reality of what it is they believe, and it is one of the skills of anthropology to do precisely this by contextual explication. Is the meaning of words interior to the words? That belief was a psychological state for Luther does not imply that it must be a psychological state for everyone, or even that it was *only* that for Luther. It does not make much sense to call the belief subscribed to by the Council of Nicaea a psychological state. Southwold's criticism of Leach on the "inner psychological" aspect of belief is here much to the point (1979, 631). We should recall that the notion of "belief" gains much of its significance in Christianity from the first person use of the verb: I believe.... But anthropologists necessarily use the verb in the third person: Azande believe.... To assume that *our* presentation of their belief carries the same force as though *they* said "We believe..." is to misunderstand the semantic conjugation of the verb and to transpose Christian assumptions unwarrantably (cf. Southwold 1979, 630; Smith 1977, 52 *et seq.*).

(4) That the determination of belief is more important than the determination of the status of what it is that is the object of the belief. In Christianity to be a believer is to acknowledge an allegiance and to declare an identity: the person does not always have to be clear about the full content of his belief. The same circumstance transposed to non-Christian religions makes much less sense. To say that a people "believe" in this, that or other abstraction (witchcraft, God, spirits of the ancestors, humanism) tends to bracket off ideas that they hold about the world from the world itself, treating their "beliefs" as peculiar to them, a badge of their distinctiveness, and all knowledge of the world as our privileged monopoly. The shadow cast by the Christian respect-for-belief obscures what really it is that people see or think they see. If we are to converse with each other (and I assume that social anthropology is a kind of conversation between cultures) we need fewer such shadows, cast by the contextual transposition of inappropriate categories,

and a clearer, steadier gaze on to the world we share. Or, at least, a clearer admission as to what we think, or assume, or understand about the world we share.

Notes

1. Bultmann has suggested that this specifically Christian sense of the word *belief/pistis* is associated with a particular, and in some ways unorthodox, linguistic construction, *pistis eis* or *pisteuoeis* + Accusative (instead of *pisteuo* + *lis* Dative): "belief in" or (as one might say, using an archaic construction in English) "belief on" (Bultmann and Weiser 1961, 68–69; cf. Michel 1975, 599). Bultmann sees this construction in particular as gaining currency from its use as "missionary parlance" expressing acceptance of the person-event, the *kerygma* of Christ's life and resurrection (*ibid.* 48–49, 59, 69). But this interpretation is contentious, for at this period the Verb + Dative construction of classical Greek was already giving way to a Preposition + Accusative construction (with either *eis* or *en*) and the forms *pistis eis/en* are found with no apparent discrimination of meaning *either* between the alternative prepositions *or* between this construction and the earlier, orthodox Dative construction (Browning 1969, 42; Moule, unpublished 7; Hatch 1917, 46).
2. For example: "Anything that we might please to say, and which in common speech is usually hung on to the handy peg of 'belief' will be better said by recourse to some other word; and if we are clear about what we want to say, we shall find that it can be said clearly only by another word" (p. 229).

References

Browning, R. 1969. *Medieval and Modern Greek*. Cambridge: Cambridge University Press.

Bultmann, R., and A. Weiser. 1961. *Faith*. Bible Key Words from G. Kittel's *Theologishes Wörterbuch zum Neuen Testament*. London: Adam and Charles Black.

Caporale, R., and A. Grumelli, eds. 1971. *The Culture of Unbelief*. Berkeley: University of California Press.

Chadwick, H. 1967. *The Early Church*. The Pelican History of the Church, 1. Harmondsworth: Penguin Books.

Doctrine Commission of the Church of England. 1976. *Christian Believing*. London: SPCK.

Erikson, E. H. 1959. *Young Man Luther*. London: Faber and Faber.

Evans-Pritchard, E. E. 1937. *Witchcraft, Oracles and Magic among the Azande*. Oxford: Clarendon.

—1965. *The Nuer*. Oxford: Clarendon.

Forster, E. M. 1939. *What I Believe*. Hogarth Sixpenny Pamphlets, 1. London: Hogarth Press.

Gombrich, R. F. 1971. *Precept and Practice*. Oxford: Clarendon.

Hatch, W. H. P. 1917. *The Pauline Idea of Faith*. Harvard Theological Studies, 2. Cambridge, MA: Harvard University Press.

Jungmann, J. A. 1959. *The Mass of the Roman Rite*. Trans. from the German by E. A. Brunner and C. K. Riepe. London: Burns and Oates.

Kelly, J. N. D. 1972. *Early Christian Creed*, 3rd ed. London: Longman.

Küng, H. 1968. *The Church*. Translated from the German by R. and R. Ockenden. London: Burns and Oates.

Lampe, G. W. H. 1976. "The Origins of the Creeds." In *Christian Believing*, Doctrine Commission of the Church of England. London: SPCK.

Loewenich, W. von. 1976. *Luther's Theology of the Cross.* Belfast: Christian Journals Ltd.

Michel, O. 1975. "Faith, Persuade, Belief, Unbelief." In *The New International Dictionary of New Testament Theology*, ed. C. Brown. Exeter: Paternoster Press.

Moule, C. E. D. unpublished. "Belief and Trust in the New Testament Vocabulary." Paper given to the Cambridge "D" Society, manuscript.

Needham, R. 1972. *Belief, Language and Experience.* Oxford: Blackwell.

Osborne, J. 1961. *Luther.* London: Faber and Faber.

Rupp, E. G. 1975. "Luther and the German Reformation to 1529." In *The Reformation*, ed. G. R. Elton. The New Cambridge Modern History, 2. Cambridge: Cambridge University Press.

Rupp, E. G., and B. Drewery. 1970. *Martin Luther.* Documents of Modern History series. London: Edward Arnold.

Ryan, A. 1973. "By-ways of Belief." Review of Needham (1972). *New Society*, January 11.

Smith, W. C. 1977. *Belief and History.* Charlottesville: University Press Virginia.

—1978. [1962]. *The Meaning and End of Religion.* London: SPCK.

—1979. *Faith and Belief.* Princeton, NJ: Princeton University Press.

Southwold, M. 1979. "Religious Belief." *Man* 14(4) (December).

Turner, V. 1967. *The Forest of Symbols.* Ithaca: Cornell University Press.

Ware, T. 1964. *The Orthodox Church.* Harmondsworth: Penguin.

Wiebe, D. 1979. "The Role of 'Belief' in the Study of Religion." *Numen* 26(2): 234–49.

RITUAL REIFICATION

Catherine Bell

Editor's Introduction

Catherine Bell is Chair of the Religious Studies department at Santa Clara University and Bernard J. Hanley Professor. Her research and publications look at the role of text and rite in Chinese religion and, more broadly, the efficacy of ritual in religion generally. She is one of the most significant theorists of ritual and a vital member of the multi-disciplinary scholarly community involved in Ritual Studies. (See especially Bell 1992, 1998, 2000, 2003.)

Her chapter, which concludes this work as it does the book from which it is drawn (Bell 1997), provides an unsurpassed consideration of the uses to which the term "ritual" has been put in academia. In the process she also discusses the influence of academic theories on those who produce and lead rituals. There are, then, a whole host of entanglements involved in the consideration of ritual, rituals, ritualization, ritual behaviours, ritual meanings, and their various intersections with "belief," whatever that might mean. Reading Bell as the conclusion both to her own book and to this one, especially following Malcolm Ruel's chapter about "belief," ought to provide an important spur to the further study of ritual and to the reflexive process by which the term may be used more critically and more clearly.

References

Bell, Catherine. 1992. *Ritual Theory, Ritual Practice*. New York: Oxford University Press.
—1997. *Ritual: Perspectives and Dimensions*. Oxford: Oxford University Press.
—1998. "Performance." In *Critical Terms for Religious Studies*, ed. Mark C. Taylor. Chicago: University of Chicago Press.

—2000. "Acting Ritually: Evidence from the Social Life of Chinese Rites." In *Companion to the Sociology of Religion*, ed. Richard K. Fenn. London: Blackwell.
—2003. "Embodiment." In *Theorising Rituals*, ed. Jens Kerinath, Jan Snoek, and Michael Stausberg. Leiden: Brill.

ℰ ℭ

Discussions of ritual density and change inevitably imply that there is something essential and stable that undergoes variations according to time and place. These discussions and each of the theories of ritual outlined in Part I reify ritual, that is, assume there is a substantive phenomenon at stake, not simply an abstract analytical category. The spectrum of ritual and ritual-like activities explored in Part II appears to give little cause for inferring the substantive existence of some universal form of action best known as ritual. Nonetheless, the reification of ritual has become an important factor in our understanding of the rites around us today and even in the way we are apt to go about doing them. For this reason, the *study* of ritual as a universal mode of action has become an influential part of the context of ritual practice in contemporary Europe and America.

As Part I demonstrated, the study of ritual has gone through several historical perspectives that, in hindsight, seem to have had less to do with how people ritualize and more with how Western culture has sorted out relationships between science and religion, on the one hand, and relationships between more technologically developed cultures and more localized tribal cultures, on the other. A number of the formal theories invoked in that section were also vitally concerned with relationships between tradition and modernity, between cultural continuity and social change, between authentic and inauthentic modes of orchestrating cultural communication, and, of course, between engaging in a series of religious activities and analyzing this engagement as ritual. Such scholarship purports to identify "ritual" underlying all the permutations of form, variations of place, and changes of time that it documents and organizes. This chapter explores the ways in which scholarly study of certain types of religious and cultural practices has generated the notion of "ritual" and how, in turn, this notion has affected these religious and cultural practices.

Repudiating, Returning, Romancing

The emergence of the concept of "ritual" as an universal phenomenon that is substantively manifest in human nature, biology, or culture appears to be the result of a successive layering of scholarly and popular attitudes. These attitudes range from an early modern "repudiation" of ritual at home while finding it prevalent in so-called primitive societies, a subsequent "return" to ritual that recognized it as an important social and cross-cultural phenomenon, followed by a tendency to "romanticize" ritual by both practitioners and theorists as a key mechanism for personal and cultural transformation. The following analysis suggests that these attitudes toward ritual are intrinsic to concerted intellectual efforts to deal with the "other" in the various religious and cultural guises in which this "other" has been perceived.

People talk about the decline and repudiation of ritual in two ways: either in terms of a general stage in an embracing process of social evolution or in terms of particular historical-political situations, such as the sixteenth-century Protestant Reformation. While the latter situation is usually characterized by specific social circumstances, the first is depicted in terms of more abstract forces of rationalism, secularism, or modernization by which traditional religious communities are dramatically remade by science, pluralism, and individualism. The popular contention that ritual and religion decline in proportion to modernization has been something of a sociological truism since the mid-nineteenth century. The British philosopher Herbert Spencer (1820–1903) was probably among the first to formulate an evolutionary opposition between industrialization of modern culture and the rituals of tribal or feudal cultures, but Max Weber followed up a generation later by contrasting ritual and magic with the rationalism and "disenchantment" of modern life. For the historian Peter Burke, the nineteenth-century tendency to oppose ritual and reason was itself the product of an earlier opposition, rooted in the ethos of the Reformation, in which ritual came to be seen as artifice and mystification in contrast to the virtues of sincerity, simplicity, and directness. In this ethos, Burke argues, ritual was associated "with the shadow rather than the substance, the letter rather than the spirit, the outer husk rather than the inner kernel."[1] Emerging fields of study focused on ritual as an ideal representation of what was different from reason, what reason needed to explain and, ultimately, enlighten and transform.[2] According to Mary Douglas, among others, these attitudes led comparative studies of religion to elevate ethical Protestant-like religions in contrast to the magical ritualism of primitive, Catholic-like religions.[3]

In the second half of the twentieth century, the trend in scholarship began to swing the other way. Burke notes that people began to assume "that all societies are equally ritualised; they merely practice different rituals. If most people in industrial societies no longer go to church regularly or practice elaborate rituals of initiation, this does not mean that ritual has declined. Instead, new types of ritual—political, sporting, musical, medical, academic, and so on—have taken the place of the traditional ones."⁴ From this perspective, ritual is deemed good and healthy, humanly important, universal, and constantly concerned with what Weber, and Geertz after him, called "the Problem of Meaning."⁵ Yet this more recent attitude, embodied in the work of both Victor Turner and Clifford Geertz, continues to rely on the opposition between ritual and modernization assumed by Spencer and Weber. This time, however, the opposition casts ritual as a natural mitigator of the harsh and unwanted aspects of modern life. It is possible that sixteenth- and nineteenth-century formulations of a modern, secular repudiation of ritual may have contributed to cultural attitudes associated with a decline in ritual participation. There is certainly evidence that the more recent and positive view of ritual promoted by Turner and Geertz has been influential in people's return to ritual. In any case, it is pertinent to ask if the widespread repudiations and returns identified by the theorists have really existed.

There are many sociohistorical situations in which people reject ritual, either their own ritual traditions or those imposed on them by others. In addition to the rejection by sixteenth-century Protestant reformers of what they saw as papist idolatry and vain superstition, there are many other historical examples, including the rejection of ritual (*li*) by the ancient Taoists, the criticisms of outer ritual form in favor of inner intention by Greek and Roman philosophers, as well as Saint Paul; and a series of movements in Hinduism from the ancient Upanishadic teachers to the early-nineteenth-century Hindu reformer, Ram Mohun Roy. In most cases such criticisms were not attacks on all forms of ritual, just on certain features of pomp, mystery, rigidity, or claims for material efficacy. In the complex milieu of the Reformation, Burke points out, many different understandings of ritual were formulated and challenged. The result was not so much a general repudiation of ritual as a widespread and pluralist debate over different styles and understandings of ritual. As a consequence, he concludes, western Europeans may have become "unusually self-conscious and articulate on the subject."⁶

Typological systems as different as those of Bellah and Douglas, presented earlier, suggest that different types of social order and cultural world-view can be correlated with different styles of ritual. Yet rarely does a society have only one style or one world-view. Usually there are several different cosmological orders more or less integrated with each other but capable of tense differentiation and mutual opposition. Different parts of a society—social classes, economic strata, or ethnic groups—may hold different perspectives on ritual, or the same subgroup may have different attitudes on different occasions. Hence, any repudiation of ritual, like all ritual practice, must be seen as a very contextual thing. For example, when the most radical of the Protestant reformers, the seventeenth-century Quakers, went so far as to reject even conventional greetings as artificial "bundles of fopperies, fond ceremonies, foolish windings, turnings and crouchings with their bodies," it was in the context of a particular group distinguishing itself from others by taking ideas of inner versus outer spirituality to a new logical extreme.[7]

From this perspective, the evidence for a general, long-term historical process of repudiating ritual begun in sixteenth-century Europe becomes rather slim. It seems more likely that the century saw the emergence of alternative understandings of ritual that had close links to issues concerning the constitution of personhood, national community, and religious authority. While these clashes would not forbid the future emergence of a general consensus about ritual, the cultural pluralism amplifying the debate can make it difficult to imagine. Certainly there has been no single, smooth process of ritual atrophy in European and American culture since then. However, there has been a process in which the emerging disciplines studying religion and culture associated ritual with the primitive, tribal, and nonrational. And despite the variety of other modes of ritual surrounding them in their own societies, such theorists could convince many of a loss of ritual in modern life.

If a general repudiation of ritual in modern industrial society has been somewhat exaggerated, therefore, it is possible that the evidence for a return to ritual has also been overstated. For example, a great deal of attention has been given to the "return" of secular Jews to more demanding forms of orthodoxy. In this context, of course, the word "return" should be examined. In most cases, the people involved had never left orthodoxy; they were born and raised in secular Jewish families and communities. The fact that they are called "those who return" (*baalei teshuvah* in Hebrew) reflects the perspective of the orthodox segment of the Jewish tradition (as well as Zionist interpretations), the view from within the fold, as it were, for whom a secular Jew is a sinner and all Jews who "return" must repent for transgressing correct observance of Jewish law.[8]

The notion of return is also problematic because it rarely means simply picking up the tradition as it has been practiced in the past. Indeed, it is argued that some forms of Jewish orthodoxy to which people are said to return constitute a modern phenomenon, not a traditional one.[9] What is seized upon as tradition is usually a rather new synthesis of custom and accommodation. Many of the secular Jews who have adopted orthodoxy, for example, have no automatic place in the traditional social fabric. Institutional innovations have been necessary, including special yeshivas, synagogue programs, and the quite untraditional Manhattan outreach program for returning singles that has enrolled some 1,200 men and women. In addition, those who convert tend to embrace some aspects of tradition more than others and bring with them new needs to which the tradition must respond. This type of "return" to tradition, therefore, is clearly a force that opens the tradition to many changes. Nonetheless, Jews are embracing

269

orthodoxy in significant numbers; although some research suggests that they do not appear to offset Jews who drift away from orthodox communities.[10]

A variety of reasons have been proposed to explain this type of return to ritual. In most general terms, it is usually analyzed as a form of resistance to secularization, modernization, and, in the case of Judaism in particular, to assimilation.[11] Yet the decision to embrace orthodoxy is itself possible only in a secular society where there are various options for religious affiliation and where the whole issue is considered a matter of individual choice. Hence, if the choice of a return to orthodoxy is a form of resistance to secularism, it also reinforces some of the more central values of secularism, namely, individual choice and a plurality of options. In addition, the most statistically dominant reason for returning to orthodoxy, marriage to an orthodox spouse (by either a secular Jew or a non-Jew), suggests some ambivalence since it indicates that significant numbers of orthodox Jews are marrying outside their communities.[12] The effect of a visit to Israel is another reason commonly given for orthodox conversion, and it is testimony to the emotional impact of experiencing Judaism as a living ethnic culture. Comparably, in America and Europe today, the decision to join a highly ritualized community is often based on an interest in ethnicity as a framework for community, identity, and a sense of tradition and belonging. The sociologist Herbert Danzger finds that the formal belief system is usually less important to the newly orthodox than what Peter Berger called the "plausibility system," that is, the network of people who share the beliefs and make them appear to be a credible understanding of the true nature of things. The family is the most important component of this plausibility system, but the local community or peer group plays a decisive role as well. Identifying with this community by means of dress, residence, and lifestyle—particularly the style of interaction between men and women—can secure one a place in a high-profile, clearly demarcated community.[13]

The decision of women to embrace orthodox Judaism merits particular attention since it is a choice that would seem to fly in the face of the larger movements for women's social and personal emancipation in the twentieth century. In exploring the appeal of orthodoxy to young, middle-class, educated women, Lynn Davidman finds the "characteristic dilemmas of modern life, such as feelings of isolation, rootlessness, and confusion about gender." As a possible solution to these dilemmas, different women looked to different types of orthodox community—some that took complete control over their lives, others that encouraged them to continue living independently. Yet all of these communities honored women's roles as wives and mothers and held out to their female converts the promise of a religion that gives pride of place to a fulfilling domestic life. The primacy accorded women's domestic roles is understood in terms of the importance of a series of rituals governing food preparation and consumption, marital relations, and the observance of the Sabbath and other holidays. Orthodox women say they find in these rituals a deep recognition of their womanhood and their role in the well-being of the family.[14]

Often what is called a return to ritual may be as simple as a heightened interest in symbolism. For example, two Protestant denominations, the United Methodist Church and the Presbyterian Church (USA), recently "reclaimed," in their words, the Catholic and pre-Reformation practice of receiving a smudge of ashes in the shape of a cross on their foreheads on Ash Wednesday, the beginning of Lent, the forty-day period of preparation for Easter. The use of ashes was originally a Jewish practice, reinterpreted by Christians but rejected by Protestant reformers who looked to biblical teachings over external marks of piety. Most of the reasons given for the return to ashes appeal to an emotional resonance with this symbolic reminder of mortality and sin—and a new appreciation of the evocative power of ritual. In the words of Reverend Deborah A. McKinley, spokesperson for the Presbyterian Church (USA), people "are discovering the importance of ritual action and its ability to draw us beyond the cerebral."[15]

Reverend McKinley's comment reflects the attitude, popular since the early 1970s, that ritual is basically good for you. This is certainly the conviction of much recent scholarship, which has helped to promote and legitimate this perspective among the wider public. The post-Reformation opposition of external form and internal feeling appears displaced by a somewhat different understanding. The same is true for the early modern opposition of rational-industrial to the mystical-tribal. Ritual is now more likely to be seen as a medium of emotional, intuitive expression that is able to express the spiritual states, alternative realities, and the incipient connectedness in which individuals and communities are embedded. While ritual once stood for the status quo and the authority of the dominant social institutions, for many it has become antistructural, revolutionary, and capable of deconstructing inhuman institutions and generating alternative structures. A long-standing concern with the falsity of ritual, conveyed in the negativity of such words as "ritualistic" and "ritualism," has been replaced in many quarters with a desire for ritual as a healing experience. The older conviction that increasing modernization, rational utilitarianism, and individualism would inevitably do away with most forms of traditional ritual life has given way to a heroic championing of ritual as the way to remain human in an increasingly dehumanized world.

In 1982, Douglas argued that most scholars of religion in the postwar period were apt to overemphasize the positive and integrative aspects of religion, implicitly opposing it to modernity in the same way that theology has opposed salvation to worldliness or, in a different debate, scientific rationalism opposed the delusions of traditional religion to the progress of reason.[16] Indeed, the positive and integrative aspects of ritual action are so taken for granted that no effort is made to substantiate them. Vincent Crapanzano's conclusion that Moroccan male initiation rites cruelly traumatize a child in ways that benefit the conservatism of the social group is a rare example of a critical analysis.[17] It is dramatically outweighed by the number of studies attempting to show how initiations are good and healthy social experiences, the lack of which in modern society has resulted in profound sociocultural impoverishment. The assumptions behind this type of statement are never laid out and tested against any empirical evidence.

Since Douglas's criticism of these tendencies toward an indiscriminate affirmation of religion, the opposition of ritual and modernity has actually gone a step further and overly romanticized ritual. It is characterized by testimonies to its creative solutions to the anomie of modern society, which promise, among other things, that initiation rites can solve adolescent delinquency and that communing with the earth can rectify our ecological relationships with the environment. A variety of analyses have pushed ritual as a curative for the ills of modernity to the point where ritual appears to act independently of any sociocultural determinism. Indeed, it is set up to act almost salvifically. Aside from all the nonscholarly appeals to the roots of ritual in the "eternal wisdom of ancient peoples," there are theorists who locate ritual in pre-linguistic grammars, in the biogenetic foundation of the "reptilian brain," and in basic, cross-cultural gestures of the human body.[18] All of these views cast ritual as independent of any sociocultural context. They never implicate ritual in the emergence of modernity. Instead, ritual remains a pure, inadequately tapped human resource for ameliorating the evils of modernity—specifically, the personal and communal wholeness fractured by ethnicity, religious ideology, and areligious passivity. Tom Driver writes that "the human longing for ritual is deep," although often frustrated; he extols ritual as essentially liberating and the means of salvation for the modern world. Unable to ignore completely some of the latent contradictions in the position, however, Driver notes that Mohandas Gandhi, the spiritual leader of the Indian independence movement, and Joseph Goebbels, the director of the Nazi's "final solution" for the Jews, were both "consummate ritualist[s]."[19] Yet Driver never analyzes why ritual in the hands of Gandhi was good and in the hands of Goebbels was horrific, or how ritual in general can be so liberating if it can support both men's visions of human aspirations.

The roots of this most recent romanticization of ritual are many and complex, as are its effects. One clear result, however, is a blindness to how contemporary ritual practices are part and parcel of the modern world, often effectively promoting the very forces of modernity that such perspectives implicitly condemn.

The Emergence of "Ritual"

The twists and turns of repudiating, returning, and romancing ritual have been closely intertwined with the emergence of the very concept of ritual as a universal phenomenon accessible to formal identification and analysis. The anthropologist Talal Asad argues that modern use of the term has very specific dates attached to it. The earliest editions of the *Encyclopedia Britannica*, put out between 1771 and 1852, defined ritual as a "book directing the order and manner to be observed in performing divine service in a particular church, diocese, or the like." Even with the addition of references to the rituals of "heathens" like the ancient Romans, it is clear that ritual meant a type of prescriptive liturgical book. Similarly, the entries for "rite" indicated "the particular manner of celebrating divine service, in this or that country," for example, the Roman rite or the Eastern rite. After 1852, there were no entries for either term until 1910, by which time the meaning had clearly shifted. The brief paragraphs of the earlier editions were replaced by a long article with sections on magical elements, interpretation, change, and classification, as well as a bibliography noting the works of the early theorists discussed in Part I. For Asad, this shift is "something quite new." Ritual is "no longer a script for regulating practice, but a type of practice" found in all religions and even outside religion, involving expressive symbols intrinsic to the sense of self and workings of society.[20]

To conceive of ritual as a panhuman phenomenon rather than simply to point and gawk at the strange activities of another culture must constitute some form of progress. Yet it is also the result of a drawn-out, complex, and intrinsically political process of negotiating cultural differences and similarities. The observation of ritual commonalities between "our worship" and "their customs" was facilitated by a term, a noun, which asserted a common denominator. At the same time, however, this new commonality effectively relocated "difference." No longer the difference between "our worship" and "their customs," it became the difference between those who sufficiently transcend culture and history to perceive the universal (and scientific) in contrast to those who remain trapped in cultural and historical particularity and are therein so naturally amenable to being the object of study.

Some of the intricacies of this process of negotiating new forms of commonality and difference are preserved in the real-life vignettes of those scholars who literally mapped a frontier, marking out the borders between the newly similar and dissimilar "other." While they emerged as scholars of ritual practices, the people they studied emerged as practitioners of ritual. At one end of the spectrum of experiences and scholars that created this border, there is the story of the Third Cavalry Captain John C. Bourke's reaction to the rites of a secret Zuñi society, the Ne'wekwe (or Nehue-Cue).[21] His initial encounter with them in 1881 provoked intense nausea, which, in turn, inspired him to undertake a ten-year study of Zuñi ritual. According to the literary historian Stephen Greenblatt, who has dramatically chronicled some of the themes implicit in Bourke's work, this experience of disgust served to define what was of ethnographic interest, what was "other" (in this case, not Hebrew or Christian) and thus in need of explanation.[22]

At the other end of the "us-them" spectrum, there is the story of Frank Cushing's romantic identification with the Zuñi. An ethnologist sent by the Smithsonian in 1879 to study the Southwest Indians, he acted as Bourke's host. But in contrast to Bourke, Cushing became uncomfortable as an outside observer-scientist putting these people under a type of microscope; he wanted to learn about being Zuñi from the inside. Living with them for many years, he became fluent in their language and so comfortable with their customs that they eventually adopted him into the tribe and initiated him as a priest and war chief. Cushing claimed to think like a Zuñi. It is said that in "going native" he stopped writing about secret Zuñi myths and rituals, unwilling to publish sacred information that had been transmitted to him in confidence. There is some question, however, whether this was the real reason Cushing did not complete several of his ethnographic projects; some suggest that his reticence had less to do with idealism and more to do with sloppy work habits.[23] It is also possible that he was not as well integrated into the tribe as he thought, and his claims to think like a Zuñi may not have been perfectly echoed by the Zuñi themselves. Indeed, they appear to have been very aware of significant peculiarities about Cushing, as shown in the song they composed about him, related by Sam Gill:

> Once they made a White man into a Priest of the Bow
> he was out there with the other Bow priests
> he had black stripes on his body
> the others said their prayers from their hearts
> but he read his from a piece of paper.[24]

Aside from the contrast between prayers said from the heart and those read from the paper, the song also refers to Cushing's striped body paint. According to Gill, the Zuñi refer to paper with writing as something "striped." So it seems that Cushing's reliance on texts and writing—the instruments for the objectification of ritual and of Zuñi culture—was so distinctive that they made it his emblematic sign. In other words, as Gill tells it, they painted him up as a walking piece of writing.[25]

In the annals of ethnographic history and interpretation, many instinctive reactions of disgust or romantic attraction have been used as markers of the differences that make another culture "other," suspect, barbaric, and exotic. Such reactions, moreover, never go in just one direction. Many peoples greeted Europeans and European customs with equal reactions of disgust.

Greenblatt notes the reaction of a Native American to the European practice of "collecting and carrying around mucus in handkerchiefs."[26] Early Chinese accounts of Westerners also record many formulations of the "us-them" differences. One early Chinese visitor to the United States graphically described "the red-haired, green-eyed foreign devils with hairy faces" for his audience back home. They were, he continued, "wild and wicked, and paid no regard to the moral precepts of Confucius and the Sages; neither did they worship their ancestors, but pretended to be wiser than their fathers and grandfathers." Worse yet, men and women "were shameless enough to walk the streets arm in arm in daylight." A later Chinese visitor, more accustomed to these differences, carefully instructed his readers back home in the intricacies and repellent immodesties of that most foreign of rituals, the dinner party, where a man must be prepared to shake a strange woman's hand, offer her his arm, and even engage her in polite conversation.[27] Chinese routinely concluded that Americans had no *li*, that is, no sense of proper behavior.

Somewhere in between the extremes of Bourke's and Cushing's defining encounters with the "other" lies the well-known story of the early sociologist and ordained minister, William Robertson Smith, whose theories were discussed in Chapter 1. His career represents a more complex stage in the emergence of the notion and study of ritual. Smith's work on "totemic sacrifice" among the ancient Semitic tribes of the Sinai Desert established the role of ritual in unifying the social group. Using what he presumed was a firsthand account of "the oldest known form of Arabian sacrifice" written by a hermit named Nilus, Smith described how a tribe would tie up a camel and place it on an altar of piled stones. The head of the group would lead them in chanting around the altar three times before inflicting the first wound. Everyone rushed to drink the blood that gushed forth, after which they would all "fall on the victim with their swords, hacking off pieces of the quivering flesh and devouring them raw with such wild haste, that in the short interval between the rise of the day star ... and the disappearance of its rays before the rising sun, the entire camel, body and bones, skin, blood and entrails is wholly devoured."[28] Not unlike Bourke's experience of nausea, the brutality of this communal sacrificial meal proved its distance from modern religion; in other words, it testified to the primitiveness of the rite and hence its potential for indicating the origin and essential meaning of all communal rites. Yet even this degree of distance was threatening since it presumed some historical relationship between primitive carnage and modern worship. When Smith brought some of his critical methods of ethnographic analysis to bear on the Bible, even quite indirectly, it provoked a major conflict within the Free Church, a branch of the Church of Scotland, in which he was an ordained minister. In 1881 he was dismissed from his professorship at the Free Church Divinity College of the University of Aberdeen and put on trial in a protracted libel case known in its day as the "Robertson Smith affair."[29] The trial was essentially an accusation of heresy by conservatives reacting to the implications of his work, particularly the implication that common social forces underlie primitive *and* revealed religions.[30]

It is interesting to note that Robertson Smith himself never aired any doubts about the revealed nature of Christianity. On the contrary, he appears to have been convinced that careful and critical scholarship would only help to unfold the central revelations of the Christian scripture. His interpretation of the typical distinction of his day saw all the "lower" religions mired in the social forces that he was among the first to describe, while Christianity as the revealed truth was able to transcend such determinisms.[31] Smith's attempts to negotiate the relationship between the Bible of belief and the demands of objective scholarship were integral to the emergence of another aspect of the "us-them" boundary, the boundary distinguishing the *practice* of religion from the *study* of it. In Smith's work, this particular boundary followed from how he nearly transgressed the first one: while affirming the distinction between Christianity as revealed religion and all other religions, he also appeared to transgress it with hints of some sort of commonality— the suggestion that perhaps all acts of ritual communion shared a common origin. While such hints were too much for Smith's church, many of his colleagues and students continued to look for the origins and commonalties underlying grossly different forms of religious practice. The splits between church and academy would widen, of course, as scholars distinguished between their practices as Christian believers and their objective studies, and as the term "ritual" began to be used to talk about common forms of religious practice underlying our liturgies and their barbaric sacrifices.

Although Robertson Smith's tendency to see the ancient rite of totemic sacrifice in as primitive a light as possible did not prevent him from suggesting some modern connections, it seriously misled him in another, rather ironic way. The ancient text on which he relied for a description of this totemic sacrifice was not an authentic account of an ancient tribal ritual at all. It was, in fact, a highly dubious source, a fifth-century Christian text, *The Story of Nilus*, and a type of fictional travelogue in which a witty and sophisticated urban traveler details his hair-raising—and completely fabricated and exaggerated—adventures among stereotypically ferocious desert tribes.[32] Smith mistook this farcical tale for an objective, detached, and reliable account akin to what he himself wished to produce. Since his book laid out the first sociological theory of ritual and was the basis for much subsequent scholarship on ritual, we can wonder what it means that the study of ritual was founded on a pulp tale of primitive barbarism!

The adventures of scholars like Bourke, Cushing, and Robertson Smith along the emerging border between us and them, scholar and practitioner, and theory and data established the basis on which the term "ritual" came to denote group-oriented religious activities that are common, in fundamental ways, to all cultures and peoples.[33] At the same time, as Part I demonstrated, the concept of ritual became important to scholarly debates over how to distinguish the magical, the religious, and the rational. The effects of this simultaneous universalization and differentiation are complex. On the one hand, as the foregoing makes very clear, a focus on ritual has enabled scholars to determine the basic similarities among very different ritual practices and traditions. At the same time, however, on a more suble level, the deployment of "ritual" as a universal has also established new distinctions and borderlands, especially between those who wield such universal categories and thereby transcend their culture and those who, locked in their cultural perspectives, are the recipients of categorizations that may seem meaningless or threatening.[34]

In the end, the history of the concept of ritual suggests that the term has been primarily used to define and mediate plurality and relationships between "us and them," with the practices of "them" ranging from primitive magic to papist idolatry to the affirmation of traditional wisdom in the face of brutal modernity. Yet there is another important dimension to the emergence of these perspectives on ritual. Approaching ritual as a universal medium of symbolic expression has had significant consequences for the very practice of ritual in Europe and America. In other words, the concept of ritual has influenced how many people in these cultures go about ritualizing today. As parts of the public have come to share an awareness of the cross-cultural similarities among rituals within very different doctrinal systems, social organizations, and cosmological world-views, "ritual" has emerged for them as a more important focus of attention than the doctrines that appear so tied to particular cultures and histories. Indeed, scholarly studies of "ritual" that demonstrate the evolution and variation of ritual practices over time have been used by components of the larger public as authoritative justifications for making fresh changes in their traditional practices. As a result, the scholarly perspectives on ritual described previously have come to undermine some forms of traditional ritual authority—the authority of having been divinely mandated by God or the ancestors, the authority of seeming to be the way things have been done since time immemorial, and the authority of being the sole possession of this particular community and thus intrinsic to its particular world-view. Hence, the study of ritual practices and the emergence of "ritual" as an abstract universal have the effect of subordinating, relativizing, and ultimately undermining many aspects of ritual practice, even as they point to ritual as a powerful medium of transcultural experience.

While some observers of the current scene see social expressions of a new freedom to ritualize, others see chaotic and idiosyncratic performances that lack all authority. In actual fact, recent forms of ritualization locate their authority in rather nontraditional ways. Most common, perhaps, is an implicit appeal to the authority lodged in the abstract notion of ritual itself. Scholars, ritual inventors, and ritual participants do not usually see how scholarship has constructed this notion of ritual or the type of authority it has acquired. They think of "ritual in general" as something that has been there all along and only now discovered—no matter whether it is thought to be a social constant, a psychological necessity, or a biological determinism. As an abstraction that determines all particular rites and ceremonies, ritual itself becomes a reified construct with the authority to sanction new forms of ritualization that appeal to it as a quintessential human and social dynamic.

There are few ritual leaders and inventors these days who have not read something of the theories of Frazer, van Gennep, Eliade, Turner, or Geertz, either in an original or popularized form. Turner, in particular, by identifying a "ritual process" weaving its way through micro and macro social relations and symbol systems, has been the authority behind much American ritual invention. His books, even when only half-read, legitimize the appeal to ritual as a universal process that authenticates changes in traditional rites or empowers people to invent new ones. The ever increasing corpus of studies on ritual also functions as further testimony to the solidity of ritual as a universal phenomenon and to the legitimacy of activities done in its name. In a typical introduction to a general-audience book on the need for ritual in the modern era, the editor states:

> We take Turner's view that the "betwixt and between" times, the threshold transition times, deserve special attention as constructive "building blocks" for change, or possibly transformation and initiation to another level of consciousness. These liminal or threshold times have a power of their own for both the individual and the culture at large. ... Our book is essentially practical, applying basic ideas and patterns of initiation for several age groups.[35]

Here, the abstract patterns "identified" by Turner as common to all initiations—something that has never been proven, and strongly contested by some—are taken as intrinsically human.[36] This view of ritual gives legitimacy to the rites invented by the authors; it also interprets many different personal and cultural experiences as reflecting, and thereby further authenticating, these patterns.

Another book offering advice for creating one's own rituals uses the same logic. It states that "all cultures recognize the need to ritualize major life transitions. In 1929, anthropologist Arnold Van Gennep coined the term 'rite of passage' to describe the universal practice of ceremonializing life's major events."[37] Here the universality of the phenomenon pointed out by van Gennep is the authority behind the rites presented in the book. In a more scholarly study, the author suggests that Turner's model of pilgrimage as a transforming ritual transition should be adopted by the Roman Catholic Church as a central strategy for the pre-Cana activities meant to prepare non-Catholics for marriage in the church.[38] The authority for using this particular ritual structure is not rooted in Catholic doctrine or revelation, although the author does refer to a minor historical precedent for pilgrimage metaphors. Rather, the effective authority for using this ritual pattern is the universality accorded the ritual process described by Turner. The explicit authority vouchsafed to scholars of rituals is certainly significant and perhaps unprecedented. At various times in church deliberations over liturgial matters, the recent tendency has been to consult outside secular scholars. For modern ritualists devising ecological liturgies, crafting new age harmonies, or drumming up a fire in the belly, the taken-for-granted authority to do these things and the accompanying conviction about their efficacy lie in the abstraction "ritual" that scholars have done so much to construct.[39]

We are seeing a new "paradigm" for ritualization. Belief in ritual as a central dynamic in human affairs—as opposed to belief in a particular Christian liturgical tradition or the historical practice of Jewish law—gives ritualists the authority to ritualize creatively and even idiosyncratically. Ritual is approached as a means to create and renew community, transform human identity, and remake our most existential sense of being in the cosmos.[40] Popularized versions of the Turner-Geertz model of "the ritual process" make people expect that these rites can work as a type of social alchemy to transform good intentions into new instincts or weave the threads of raw and broken experiences into a textured fabric of connectedness to other people and things. Ritual practitioners of all kinds in Europe and America now share the sense that their rites participate in something universal. They consider what they do as fundamentally symbolic and having much in common with the equally symbolic practices of Chinese ancestral offerings, Trobriand garden magic, or Turner's accounts of Ndembu healing. And these modern practitioners can reconcile this commonality with personal commitment to the practices of a particular, if newly flexible, tradition. This is a fascinating development in the West and one that needs to be examined more closely. There is nothing inherently wrong with it, except that it is clearly not the last word on either ritualization or the concept of ritual. It is a set of attitudes that is as historically determined as the definitions laid out in the earliest editions of the *Encyclopedia Britannica*.[41] Yet, in a pragmatic sense, these recent developments may also imply that only now do we have "ritual" as such in European and American cultural life. Only now do people do various rites with a consciousness of participating in a universal phenomenon.

Just as modern theories of ritual have had a powerful effect on how people ritualize, how people ritualize profoundly affects what theorists set about to describe and explain. There is no "scientific" detachment here:

ritual theorists, experts, and participants are pulled into a complex circle of interdependence. Recognition of this interdependence makes it easier to consider how our use of the notion of ritual can influence our understanding of people who do not abstract the same experiences in the same way. In other words, our theories of ritual may do a lot to translate Confucian ancestor practices or Trobriand gardening practices into more abstract terms and models that make sense to us. But these analyses do not necessarily help us understand how these activities figure in the world-view of the Chinese or Trobrianders; they may even distort Chinese and Trobriand cultural experiences. If only now do we have "ritual" as such in European and American cultural life, then it may not be inappropriate to contend that what many Chinese and Trobrianders are doing is not "ritual."

With this historical perspective, we can be sympathetic to the critique of the anthropologist Talal Asad, who suggests that the category of ritual may not be appropriate to other, non-Christian cultural milieus, such as Islam, which involves very different "technologies of power" and "moral economies of the self." If our historically determined notion of ritual should appear to explain Islamic ritual to our satisfaction, Asad proposes, then perhaps we need to re-examine whether we have constructed categories that inadvertently tell us only what we want to know. Asad fears that Western scholarship is so powerful that it is impossible for Trobriand garden magic to survive in any form but as data for the great mills of scholarly theory. More specifically, he fears that the categories of ritual and religion will influence and even be adopted by those who would not traditionally have defined their lives in these ways.[42] While such developments may foster easier communication and shared values, they may do so by means of political subordination and substantive diminution of the diversity of human experience.

Western scholarship *is* very powerful. Its explanative power rests not only on tools of abstraction that make some things into concepts and other things into data but also on many other social activities, simultaneously economic and political, that construct a plausibility system of global proportions. Hence, it is quite possible that categories of ritual and nonritual will influence people who would define their activities differently. If scholarship on ritual as a universal construct has succeeded in creating the beginnings of a shared sense of ritual in many religious and civic practices of Euro-American culture, then we cannot dismiss the concern that such a construct can reach out to restructure practice elsewhere. We may well be in the very process of actually creating ritual as the universal phenomenon we have long taken it to be. Yet creating it has not been our intention, and does not appear to further our more self-conscious goals of understanding.

Richard Schechner concludes his study, *The Future of Ritual*, with a vision in which ritual's pairing of restraint and creativity is the best means by which human beings can avoid complete self-extinction.[43] While his romantic

evocation of ritual as a force for global good is not likely to garner the support of empiricists, this sort of vision is tied to practices that could construct as concrete a phenomenon as any empiricist might wish, by encouraging people everywhere to begin to understand their practices as cultural variations on an underlying, universal phenomenon. Certainly the construction of interpretive categories and the propensity to reify them are among the ways by which people have always shaped their world. Abstractions like freedom, human dignity, evil, or true love have had powerful and concrete effects on human affairs. A global discourse on ritual, understood as a transcultural language of the human spirit, is more likely to promote a sense of common humanity and cross-cultural respect than the view that one set of religious rites is the revealed truth itself and the idols worshiped by all other peoples must be destroyed. Yet it is clear that this discourse is being constructed not without violence, loss, and deeply rooted assumptions of cultural hegemony.

In a purely methodological vein, such concerns suggest the need for revised methodologies. The practice theories examined at the close of Chapter 3 attempt to focus on activities in such a way as to minimize the amount of preliminary selecting and framing of the data in terms of such powerful categories as ritual, religion, technology, ideology, and so on. There are also attempts to formulate elements basic to "reflexive" and "self-critical" forms of scholarly analysis.[44] There may be other alternatives as well, perhaps even a reconstructed phenomenology—a phenomenology for the post-postmodern era, so to speak—in which the scholar and the conditions of the scholarly project itself are systematically included as part of the total phenomenon under scrutiny. In any case, the links between the emergence of ritual as a category of analysis and the shifts in how people in European and American society ritualize make very clear that ritual cannot be approached as some transparent phenomenon out there in the world waiting to be analyzed and explained. It exists only in sets of complex interactions that we are just beginning to try to map.

Conclusion

The contexts in which ritual practices unfold are not like the props of painted scenery on a theatrical stage. Ritual action involves an inextricable interaction with its immediate world, often drawing it into the very activity of the rite in multiple ways. Exactly how this is done, how often, and with what stylistic features will depend on the specific cultural and social situation with its traditions, conventions, and innovations. Why some societies have more ritual than others, why ritual traditions change or do not change, and why some groups abstract and study "ritual" as some kind of universal phenomenon when others do not—these are questions of context that are at the heart of the dynamics understood as religion and culture.

The way that European and American scholars generate questions about ritual reflects and promotes basic elements of their cultural world-view. The notion of ritual has become one of the ways in which these cultures experience and understand the world. So what does this interest in ritual tell us about ourselves? Most readily, it tells us that we do not live with a seamless world-view; what we do and what we think or believe are routinely distinguished, separated out, and differently weighted. It suggests a certain drive toward transcending the particularities of place, time, and culture by means of the "higher learning" embodied in scientific, artistic, historical, and hermeneutical forms of analysis. This interest in transcending the particular suggests a fundamental drive toward world transformation and self-determination. It suggests an eagerness to find or forge spiritual-cultural commonalities among the heterogeneity of beliefs and styles in the world, but primarily in terms that extend our historical experiences as nearly universal. The hubris is not unconstructive, but it now comes face to face with a fresh set of challenges. Whether it can address and solve them is not clear, but these are the issues that ritual and the study of ritual will struggle with in the near future.

The central concern of this study has been to introduce systematically all of the issues, debates, and areas of inquiry that comprise the modern study of ritual. In most cases, this has meant raising open-ended issues, rather than presenting an authoritative consensus. Of course, the topic of ritual is not unique in this regard. Without sacrificing any of the complexity and convolutions involved in these issues, this study has also tried to impose some minimal order on them for the purpose, at least, of suggesting other orderings and contexts. If it was not clear at the beginning, it should be clear by now that "theories," "activities" and "contexts" can be only provisional frameworks. Theories and contexts affect what is seen as ritual and by whom, while those activities deemed to be ritual in turn have theoretical and contextual consequences.

In the end, "ritual" is a relatively new term that we have pressed into service to negotiate a variety of social and cultural differences, including the differentiation of scholarly objectivity and generalization as distinct from cultural particularism and parochialism. The work and hopes of many theorists and practitioners today are pinned to it, and there is no doubt that ritual has become one of the ways in which we structure and interpret our world. As an interpretive tool, it inevitably corrects a bit here and distorts a bit there, or, in terms of practice theory, it addresses problems by shifting the very terrain on which they appeared. In the future, we may have better tools with which to understand what people are doing when they bow their heads, offer incense to a deity, dance in masks in the plaza, or give a lecture on the meaning of ritual. Yet all these acts are ways of dealing with the world and its perceived forces and sources of power. The form and scope of interpretation differ, and that should not be lightly dismissed, but it cannot be amiss to see in all of these instances practices that illuminate our shared humanity.

Notes

1. Burke 1987, 223–24.
2. For an analysis of stages in the development of a "rational" project to study "religion," see Preus 1987, 3–103.
3. Douglas 1966, 18–19.
4. Burke 1987, 223.
5. Geertz 1973, 108.
6. Burke 1987, 224–28, 236.
7. Burke 1987, 233.
8. Aviad 1983, ix.
9. Heilman and Friedman 1991, 197–264; Heilman 1992, 14–39, 156–58.
10. Danzger 1989, 1–2, 328.
11. Aviad 1983, ix.
12. Danzger 1989, 328.
13. Danzger 1989, 330–31; Berger 1967, 45–51.
14. Davidman 1991, 26, 45, 192, 194. For a personal account, see Dicker 1992, 62–64.
15. Steinfels 1993, B12.
16. Douglas 1982, 2, 5.
17. Crapanzano 1981, 15–36; see Chapter 1 in this book.
18. For a discussion of these approaches, see Schechner 1995, 250–51, 253.
19. Driver 1991, 8, 33, 79, 99–101.
20. Asad 1993, 56–57. The *Oxford English Dictionary* gives a more complicated picture of the evidence that Asad deduces from the *Britannica*, probably because it includes adjectival forms as well.
21. See the excerpt from Bourke's account in Gill 1982, 39–41. Also see Bell 1992, 29.
22. Greenblatt 1982, 1–3.
23. Winters 1991, 132.
24. Gill 1985, 225.
25. Gill 1985, 225.
26. Greenblatt 1982, 3.
27. Arkush and Lee 1989, 16, 55–56.
28. Robertson Smith 1969, 338.
29. Beidelman 1974, 13–22. As Beidelman notes, the trial was technically for libel but widely understood to concern heresy (13, 17).
30. Beidelman 1974, 13–22. For another application of the myth-ritual pattern to Christianity, see James 1935, 235–60.
31. Beidelman 1974, 26, 30–51.
32. See Henninger 1955, 81–148; see Eliade 1976, 6–7.
33. Just as some anthropologists have argued that the production of texts is integral to this process of creating "ritual" as a transcultural object of study (Clifford and Marcus

1986, 1–26), so is a network of scholars defined as professionals distinguished from practitioners. See Latour (1987) and (1993).
34. Goody 1977, 25–35.
35. Mahdi 1987, ix.
36. Contested primarily on gender grounds, by Bruce Lincoln and Caroline Walker Bynum; see the discussion of the Mukanda ritual in Chapter 2.
37. Beck and Metrick 1990, i.
38. Holmes 1992, 95–113.
39. Victor Turner, Mary Douglas, Ronald Grimes—and I to a lesser extent—have all been involved in various forms of consultation as ritual experts. Grimes coined the term "ritology" to designate this form of expertise, describing the ritologist as someone concerned with assessing the effectiveness of rituals. He argues that the ritologist is just an elaboration of an internal process of assessing a rite after its completion, a process that is a common and perhaps necessary part of the ongoing dynamics by which ritual forms are interpreted, reunderstood, and renuanced. See Grimes 1990, 3–4, 9.
40. See Driver 1991.
41. For a critique of the ability of this perspective on ritual to understand practice in Islam, see Asad 1993, 55, 57, 79.
42. Asad 1993, 55, 57, 79.
43. Schechner 1993, 263.
44. Bell 1992, 5.

References

Arkush, R. David, and Leo O. Lee, eds. 1989. *Land without Ghosts: Chinese Impressions of America from the Mid-Nineteenth Century to the Present*. Berkeley: University of California Press.

Asad, Talal. 1993. *Genealogies of Religion: Discipline and Reasons of Power in Christianity and Islam*. Baltimore: Johns Hopkins University Press.

Aviad, Janet. 1983. *Return to Judaism: Religious Renewal in Israel*. Chicago: University of Chicago Press.

Beck, Renee, and Sydney B. Metrick. 1990. *The Art of Ritual: A Guide to Creating and Performing Your Own Rituals for Growth and Change*. Berkeley, CA: Celestial Arts.

Beidelman, T. O. 1974. *W. Robertson Smith and the Sociological Study of Religion*. Chicago: University of Chicago Press.

Bell, Catherine. 1992. *Ritual Theory, Ritual Practice*. New York: Oxford University Press.

Berger, Peter L. 1967. *The Sacred Canopy: Elements of a Sociological Theory of Religion*. New York: Doubleday.

Burke, Peter. 1987. "The Repudiation of Ritual in Early Modern Europe." In *The Historical Anthropology of Early Modern Italy: Essays on Perception and Communication*. Cambridge: Cambridge University Press.

Clifford, James, and George E. Marcus, eds. 1986. *Writing Culture: The Poetics and Politics of Ethnography*. Berkeley: University of California.

Crapanzano, Vincent. 1981. "Rite of Return: Circumcision in Morocco." *The Psychoanalytic Study of Society* 9: 15–36.

Danzger, M. Herbert. 1989. *Returning to Tradition: The Contemporary Revival of Orthodox Judaism*. New Haven: Yale University Press.

Davidman, Lynn. 1991. *Tradition in a Rootless World: Women Turn to Orthodox Judaism*. Berkeley: University of California Press.

Dicker, Shira. 1992. "Mikva." *Tikkun* 7, no. 6: 62–64.

Douglas, Mary. 1966. *Purity and Danger: An Analysis of Concepts of Pollution and Taboo.* New York: Praeger.

—1982. "The Effects of Modernization on Religious Change." Daedalus 111, no. 1 (Winter): 1–19.

Driver, Tom F. 1991. *The Magic of Ritual: Our Need for Liberating Rites That Transform Our Lives and Our Communities.* San Francisco: Harper Collins.

Eliade, Mircea. 1976. *Occultism, Witchcraft and Cultural Fashions: Essays in Comparative Religion.* Chicago: University of Chicago Press.

Geertz, Clifford. 1973. *The Interpretation of Culture.* New York: Basic Books.

Gill, Sam D. 1982. *Native American Religions: An Introduction.* Belmont, CA: Wadsworth.

—1985. "Nonliterate Traditions and Holy Books: Toward a New Model." In *The Holy Book in Comparative Perspective*, ed. Frederick M. Denny and Rodney L. Taylor. Columbia: University of South Carolina Press.

Goody, Jack. 1977. "Against 'Ritual': Loosely Structured Thoughts on a Loosely Defined Topic." In *Secular Ritual*, ed. Sally F. Moore and Barbara G. Myerhoff, 25–35. Amsterdam: Van Gorcum.

Greenblatt, Stephen. 1982. "Filthy Rites." *Daedalus* 111, no. 3 (Summer 1982): 1–3.

Grimes, Ronald L. 1990. *Ritual Criticism: Case Studies in Its Practice, Essays on Its Theory.* Columbia: University of South Carolina Press.

Heilman, Samuel C. 1992. *Defenders of the Faith.* New York: Schoecken.

Heilman, Samuel C., and Menachem Friedman. 1991. "Religious Fundamentalism and Religious Jews: The Case of the Haredim." In *Fundamentalism Observed*, ed. Martin E. Marty and R. Scott Appleby, 197–264. Chicago: University of Chicago Press.

Henninger, Joseph. 1955. "1st der sogenannte Nilus-Bericht eine brauchbare religions-geschichtliche Quelle?" *Anthropus* 50: 81–148.

Holmes, Paul A. 1992. "A Catechumenate for Marriage: Presacramental Preparation as Pilgrimage." *Journal of Ritual Studies* 6, no. 2 (Summer): 95–113.

James, E. O. 1935. "The Sources of Christian Ritual." In *The Labyrinth: Further Studies in the Relation between Myth and Ritual in the Ancient World*, ed. Samuel H. Hooke, 235–60. New York: Macmillan.

Latour, Bruno. 1987. *Science in Action.* Cambridge: Harvard University Press.

—1993. *We Have Never Been Modern.* Trans. Catherine Porter. Cambridge: Harvard University Press.

Mahdi, Louise Carus, Steven Foster, and Meredith Little, eds. 1987. *Betwixt and Between: Patterns of Masculine and Feminine Initiation.* LaSalle, IL: Open Court.

Preus, J. Samuel. 1987. *Explaining Religion: Criticism and Theory from Bodin to Freud.* New Haven: Yale University Press.

Robertson Smith, William. 1969 [1889]. *Lectures on the Religion of the Semites: The Fundamental Institutions.* New York: KTAV Publishing House.

Schechner, Richard. 1995. *The Future of Ritual: Writings on Culture and Performance.* London: Routledge.

Steinfels, Peter. 1993. "More Protestants Accept Ashes as Ritual for Lent." *New York Times* (February 24): B12.

Winters, Christopher, ed. 1991. *International Dictionary of Anthropologists.* New York: Garland.

INDEX OF NAMES

Agulhon, M. 200
Akiva 33
Alexander, B. 4
Al-Ghazālī, M. 5
Alsford, S. 111
Anderson, B. 200
Apter, D. E. 200
Arden, E. 72
Aristotle 131
Arius 249
Arnobius 141
Aronoff, M. 194
Arthur, K. 154, 160
Asad, T. 273, 280, 283–84
Augustine 252
Aulius Gellius 140, 142
Austin, E. 67, 71, 73–75, 236, 239
Avenarius, R. 63

Babcock, B. 153, 155
Bachnik, J. 103
Bagehot, W. 200
Bakhtin, M. 9–10, 139–62
Balandier, G. 150
Barre, F. 118
Barrell, J. 155
Barrés, M. 190
Bar-Yochai, S. 212
Bateson, G. 4
Bauman, R. 126, 139
Baumstark, A. 42
Beard, R. 108, 110–11
Beck, R. 284
Beckett, S. 148–49
Beidelman, T. O. 283
Bell, C. 4–5, 13, 265–85
Bellah, R. N. 254–55, 268
Beneria, L. 216

Bennett, T. 144–45
Berengar 44
Berenson, E. 200
Berger, P. L. 80, 254, 270
Berleant, A. 119
Beza, T. 30
Bhabha, H. 139
Binns, C. A. 200
Blacker, C. 103
Blackwood, C. 158
Blake, P. 113
Bloch, M. 7–8, 52–60, 199
Bloom, A. 106
Boas, F. 62
Boiteaux, M. 151–52
Borhek, J. T. 200
Borun, M. 120
Bosch, H. 156
Boserup, E. 216
Bourdieu, P. 4, 130, 139
Bourguignon, E. 207
Bourke, J. C. 273–76
Boyer, P. 4
Brauer, E. 209, 211
Brecht, B. 133
Brewer, J. 151
Briggs, C. 216
Brown, K. McC. 4
Brown, S. E. 217
Browning, R. 263
Bruegel, P. 156
Bücher, K. 63
Buenaventura-Posso, E. 217
Bühler, K. 73
Bultmann, R. 244, 246, 263
Burke, K. 71, 74–76
Burke, P. 145, 150, 267–69
Burman, R. 216

Index of Names

Bushaway, B. 152

Cantwell Smith, W. 243–44, 257–60, 262
Caporale, R. 254
Carneiro de Cunha, M. 230
Carson, R. 112
Carter, J. 198
Cassirer, E. 200
Casteneda, C. 132
Chadwick, H. 249
Chapin, M. 239
Charcot, J. M. 158
Cicero 28, 141
Cleveland, S. E. 147
Clifford, J. 283–84
Coleman, S. 135
Comaroff, J. 6
Commission on Museums for a New
    Century 110
Confucius 275
Constantinides, P. 216
Corbet, J. 30
Crapanzano, V. 272
Crazzolara, J. P. 258
Crocker, C. 230–31
Cunningham, H. 152
Curtis, R. F. 200
Curtius, E. R. 140–42
Cushing, F. H. 5, 274–76

da Matta, R. 148, 154
Danzger, H. 270
Davidman, L. 270
Davis, N. Z. 150, 154
Davis, W. B. 96–97
de Brosses, C. 29, 31
de Coppet, D. 4
de Sales, A. 230
Denney, R. 122
Descartes, R. 3
Descola, P. 230–31
Deshen, S. 216
Desplatt, C. 159
Détienne, M. 155
Disney, R. 107
Disney, W. 108, 112
Doctrine Commission of the Church of
    England 250, 255
Dōgen 92–93, 103
Douglas, M. 89, 153, 157, 267–68, 271–72,
    284
Drewal, M. T. 4
Driver, T. F. 272
Durkheim, E. 34–36, 62, 66–68, 77, 134
Dychtwald, K. 121
Dylan, B. 185

Eagleton, T. 148–50, 154, 160–61
Ebin, V. 216

Egeria 28
Einstein, A. 106
Eisenstein, S. M. 149
Eliade, M. 230, 278
Erasmus 31
Erikson, E. H. 253
Evans-Pritchard, E. E. 243, 257–58, 261–62

Fausto, C. 220
Feld, S. 137
Fernandez, J. W. 200
Firth, R. 71
Fisher, S. 147
Flanagan, K. 8–9, 78–86
Forster, E. M. 243, 255
Foucault, M. 136, 139, 144, 157
Fox, R. 239
Fox, R. G. 191
Francaviglia, R. 113
Frazer, J. G. 62, 64, 73, 75, 278
Freud, S. 38–39, 74, 197
Friedhaber, D. 210
Fulbright, J. 5
Fuller, B. 118

Galbraith, J. K. 197, 199
Gandhi, M. 272
Geertz, C. 4, 192, 213, 216, 268, 278–79
Germain, J.-C. 149
Gibson, T. 55
Giddens, A. 85
Gilbert, W. S. 197, 200
Gill, S. 274
Girrard, R. 52
Gluckman, M. 150, 193
Goddard, B. 149
Goebbels, J. 272
Goff, K. 108
Goffman, E. 79, 80, 126, 128, 133
Gombrich, R. F. 256
Gomez, E. 220
Goody, J. 4, 219
Greenblatt, S. 274–75
Grice, H. P. 74
Grimes, R. L. 4, 284
Grumelli, A. 254
Guss, D. M. 4

Hahn, D. F. 200
Hardacre, H. 94
Hartley, J. P. 118
Hatch, W. H. P. 244, 246, 263
Heestermann, J. C. 38
Hegel, G. W. F. 143–44
Herodotus 34
Herzl, T. 190, 199
Hill, E. 149
Himmans, D. 186
Himmans-Arday, D. 169

Hitler, A. 196
Hobsbawm, E. 217
Højbjerg, C. K. 222, 224
Holmer, N. 225–30, 239
Holmes, P. A. 284
Homer 141, 149
Hornborg, A. 11
Houseman, M. 221
Howe, J. 239
Hume, D. 29
Humphrey, C. 4, 6, 12, 127–28, 137, 223–24, 230
Huntington, R. 54

Ignatius of Loyola 43
Ingold, T. 11
Iteanu, A. 55
Ivanov, V. V. 149, 156

Jack, I. 141
Jakobson, R. 37
James, W. 63–64, 67, 74, 76
Jones, A. R. 154
Jonge, J. de 185–87
Joyce, J. 149
Jungmann, J. A. 250

Karim, W.-J. 56–59
Katz, N. 209
Kelly, J. N. D. 247–51
Kendall, L. 132–33
Keniston, K. 114
Kertzer, D. 11–12, 189–201
Kiggen, J. 258
Kim, Y.-C. 206
Kimball, K. T. 185
King, M. J. 9, 105–23
Kohler, K. 22
Kōhō, F. 93
Kohut, A. 22
Kondo, D. 98–99
Kowalewski, D. 200
Kramer, F. 239
Küng, H. 244
Kunzle, D. 152

Laidlaw, J. 4, 6, 12, 127–28, 137, 223–24
Lampe, G. W. H. 246–47, 251
Lane, C. 193, 195
Latour, B. 284
Lawson, T. 4
Le Goff, J. 159
Le Roy Ladurie, E. 150
Leach, E. 8, 54, 63, 76–77, 153, 158, 230
Lerner, B. D. 8
Lévi-Strauss, C. 8, 29, 35–36, 38–39, 41, 54, 58, 67, 152–53, 226–27
Lewis, G. 86
Light, I. H. 197

Lincoln, B. 12, 52, 284
Lipsitz, L. 200
Liturgical Commission of the Church of England 81
Lloyd, G. 70
Locke, J. 200
Lodge, D. 149
Lord, J. 220
Lowenthal, D. 118
Luckman, T. 254
Luhmann, N. 80
Luther, M. 3–5, 244, 252–54, 258, 262
Lyng, R. 114

MacDonald, G. 111
Mach, E. 63
Machiavelli, N. 196, 200
Mackenzie, C. 83
Malcolmson, R. W. 152
Malcuzynski, M.-P. 149
Malinowski, B. 8, 54–55, 61–77, 193, 200
Marlow, C. 236–37
Martial 141
Martin, D. 83
Marus, G. E. 283–84
Mauss, M. 35–36
McCauley, R. 4
McKenna, B. 114
McKinley, D. 271
McLuhan, M. 112
McPhee, P. 200
Mengistu, H. M. 194
Merton, R. K. 29
Metrick, S. B. 284
Michel, O. 244–46, 263
Middleton, C. 27–29, 44
Midgley, M. 8
Miyake, H. 103
Monas, S. 149
Moro, A. 199
Mosse, G. L. 199
Moule, C. E. D. 244, 246, 263
Munn, N. 40
Murray, R. 122
Mussard, P. 31
Mussolini, B. 196, 198
Myerhoff, B. 214

Naipaul, V. H. 223
Nakamura, H. 102
Nakayama, M. 96
Napoleon 198
Needham, R. 57, 257–58, 260–62
Neusner, J. 5
Nietzsche, F. 154
Nimako, K. 186
Nishiyama, K. 103
Nixon, R. 189
Numata, K. 98

Ohnuki-Tierney, E. 99, 102
Ōkubo D. 103
Osborne, J. 253–54

Parrinder, P. 149
Parsons, T. 254
Paul, B. 210–11
Paul, L. 210–11
Paulos, J. A. 106
Peirce, C. 74, 76
Perrin, M. 240
Pettit, R. B. 107
Phylactou, M. 55
Piaget, J. 73
Plato 67
Pollack, W. 119
Pomian, K. 219–20
Pomorska, K. 144
Powers, M. 204
Preus, J. S. 283
Propp, V. 219

Rabelais, F. 144–45
Radbertus, P. 44
Radcliffe-Brown, A. R. 200
Rafferty, M. 108
Rappaport, R. A. 4, 79
Rapport, N. 137
Rattray, R. S. 187
Rawlings, J. J. 186
Read, K. 137
Reader, I. 9, 14, 87–104
Reagon, R. 193
Robertson-Smith, W. 66, 275–77
Robin, R. 148
Rohlen, T. P. 101, 103
Rollin, R. 107
Rostas, S. 127–28
Rothenbuhler, E. W. 4
Roy, R. M. 268
Rubenstein, H. 72
Rubow, C. 222, 224
Ruel, M. 13, 242–65
Rufinus 251
Ruthven, M. 158
Ryan, A. 262

Sabar, Y. 208–9
Said, E. 143
Sales, R. 150
Salinger, J. 115
Schama, S. 151–52
Schechner, R. 4, 10, 131, 133, 280–81
Schickel, R. 109
Schieffelin, E. 10, 124–38
Schmitt, J.-C. 159
Schoener, A. 110, 118
Schriber, R. 151–52
Screech, M. A. 145

Searle, J. 74
Segal, R. A. 8
Sen, G. 216
Sered, S. S. 12, 202–17
Servius 140
Severi, C. 12–13, 218–40
Shai, D. 208
Shakespeare, W. 148, 202–17
Shelley, P. B. 149
Sherzer, J. 220, 228, 239
Short, J. 149
Sjørslev, I. 222, 224
Sklar, M. 110
Sloan, W. 106
Smith, J. Z. 4, 7, 26–50, 105
Smith, P. 222
Snow, R. 117
Sōtōshūshūmuchō 93
Southwold, M. 261–62
Spencer, H. 267–68
Spencer, J. 29
Staal, F. 4
Stallybrass, P. 10, 139–62
Stamm, R. 148–49, 154
Stanner, W. E. H. 40–41
Stedman Jones, G. 152
Stern, W. 73
Stout, D. 239
Struve, N. 200
Sullivan, A. 197, 200

Tambiah, S. J. 4, 8, 61–77, 230
Tanaka, K. 96, 103
Tapper, N. 216
Tapper, R. 216
Taylor, A. C. 230
Tedlock, D. 5, 220, 230
ter Haar, G. 11–12, 163–88
Theophrastus 28
Thomas, K. 70
Thompson, E. P. 150, 152
Thompson, W. 118
Thurston, J. 149
Tito, J. B. 193
Todorov, T. 149
Torrance, E. P. 108
Townsley, G. 220–21, 226
Turner, E. 11, 187
Turner, V. 9–11, 52, 69, 153–54, 163–88, 199, 223, 250, 268, 278–79, 284
Tylor, E. 62, 66, 73, 75

Uberoi, J. P. S. 29–30

Van Burren, M. 149
Van Gennep, A. 4, 11, 38, 52, 69, 163–88, 278
Vasari, G. 157
Vattimo, G. 113
Verba, S. 200

Vilar de Kerkhoff, A. M. 149
Virgil 141
Viveiros de Castro, E. 4, 220, 231

Walker Bynum, C. 284
Wallace, M. 112
Walvin, J. 152
Ware, T. 250
Wassen, H. 225–30
Waugh, A. 158
Weber, M. 29, 84, 157, 199, 267–68
Weiser, A. 244, 246, 263
White, A. 10, 139–62
Wiebe, D. 259
Wilbert, J. 230

Williams, R. 142
Wilson, R. 152
Wittgenstein, L. 76
Wulff, H. 137
Wundt, W. 63

Yamaguchi, M. 153
Yeo, E. 152
Yeo, S. 152
Young, K. K. 216

Zohara, R. 203–5, 208
Zuesse, E. 4
Zwingli, H. 26, 29–30

INDEX OF SUBJECTS

Actors 2, 124–38
African Indigenous (independent) Churches 178
Alterity 143–44, 155, 159, 163–88, 275, 277
Amulets 209–10, 217
Anthropology of experience 11
Arbitrariness 83
Audience(s) 10, 124–38

Beauty 72–73
Bhagavad-gita 6
Bible 5–6, 18–21, 23–24, 33, 37, 168–72, 244, 276
Bodies 139–62
Buddhism 9, 69, 87–104, 256, 259

Carnival(s) and the carnivalesque 9–10, 78, 139–62
Change 11–13, 52, 213–18, 266, 278, 280–81
Charivari 159
Children 73–74, 173
Christianity 3, 5–8, 11, 14, 18–21, 23, 26–50, 67, 78–86, 135, 151–52, 163–89, 206, 242–64, 267–68, 271, 279
Cleaning 9, 87–104
Cognition 3, 243
Communication 11–12, 163–88
Communitas 10–11, 163, 182–83
Consciousness 127
Contingency 127–29, 137
Cosmology 230

Deceit 1, 6, 85, 124, 132–35
Dialogue 139
Diaspora(s) 163–88
Disenchantment 267
Doubt 218
Druse 216
Education 10, 105–23

Efficacy 61, 71–74
Elite/high culture 9–10, 105–23, 139–62, 202
Embodiment 6
Enlightenment 3, 5, 22
Entertainment 2, 9, 78, 105–38
Etiquette 88
Expertise 12, 202–17
Expressivity and expressive actions 8, 10, 61, 127–28

Functionalism 8, 62, 66

Gender 12, 158, 202–17, 239, 270–71, 284
Gnosticism 37
Grotesque bodies and realism 139–62

Habitus 130
Hierarchy 141–43
Hinduism 6, 69, 166, 185, 204, 223, 256, 259, 268

Ideology 11, 14
Implicit religion 104, 105–23
Indigenous peoples and/or religions 5–6, 13–14, 35–36, 40, 54–61, 134–36, 166, 187, 192, 204, 206–7, 210–11, 218–40, 257, 261–62, 267, 273–74, 279–80
Individualism 18–19, 67
Individuation 3
Initiation 67
Innovation 11–13, 52, 266, 278, 213–18, 280–81
Instrumental actions 8, 10, 61
Intention 5–6, 18, 98–99, 102, 104, 126–28, 189
Inversion 154
Islam 5, 166–67, 185, 205, 256, 259, 280, 284

Jainism 6, 223
Japanese new religions 94–99
Judaism 5, 12, 14, 22–24, 148–49, 202–17,
    251, 256, 269–71, 279

Levellers and Diggers 159
Liminality 10–11, 69, 97, 163, 180–82
Linguistics and rhetoric 36–37, 71–73, 75–76,
    135, 139, 148, 164, 218–40, 272
Literacy 12
Liturgy 8, 14, 78–86, 192, 248, 279

Magic 8, 61–77, 81, 231, 267, 277, 280
Mana 35–36
Marginalization 158
Materiality 3, 21, 71, 79
Meditation 9, 87–104
Mediums and mediumship 55, 125, 134, 204,
    207
Memory 12, 105–23, 218–40
Midwives 211
Millenarianism 53
Missionaries 6, 192
Mistakes 8, 61–77, 129
Modernity and modernization 3–4, 7–8, 12, 14,
    18, 27, 29–30, 126, 183, 202–17, 266–
    67, 273, 277
Museums 109
Myth(s) 2, 7–8, 31, 39–40, 52–60, 66, 71, 218,
    220

Neurosis 38
New religions 94–99
Nonsense 32

Orality 12
Orientalism 143
Others and othering 143–44, 155, 159, 163–
    88, 275, 277

Paganism 26–28
Paying attention 33–50
Performance and performative acts 2–3, 10, 67,
    69, 124–38
Personhood 269
Pilgrimage 9, 278–79
Pittsburgh Platform 22–24
Place(s) 7, 9, 33–50, 105–23
Plausibility 80
Playfulness 86
Plural societies and pluralism 11, 80, 163–88,
    277
Politics 2, 11, 53, 125, 137, 143, 150–51, 189–
    202

Popular/low culture 9–10, 105–23, 139–62,
    202

Power 11, 150, 189–201, 280
Pragmatism 6, 8–9, 61–77, 87
Predation 231
Presence 10
Primitivism 158, 267
Private/public contrast 1–2

Quran 5

Rationality 61–77
Rebounding violence 8, 52–60
Reflexivity 12–13, 218–40, 242, 265, 281
Reification 13, 265–85
Relationality 152, 221
Religion, definitions of, 2, 5, 14, 29, 66–67, 87,
    189, 261, 269, 271, 281, 283
Renaissance 141, 146, 152
Revitalization 267–70
Rites of passage 11, 67, 81, 163–88, 202–17,
    278
Rites of reversal 150
Romanticism and romanticization 272, 280–81

Sacrality 33, 35–36, 65–66, 72–73
Sacraments 4–5, 18–21, 26–50, 248
Science 61–77
Shamans and shamanism 14, 132, 211, 218–40
Shintō 101
Sincerity 1, 5, 18
Spirituality 2–3
Superstition 30, 212
Symbolism 11, 29–30, 125, 141, 152, 155, 190

Taboo/Tabu 160, 213
Talmud 33
Taoism 268
Text, notion of 129–30
Theatre 124–38
Theme parks 9–10, 105–23
Totems and totemism 35, 67, 198
Tradition 11–13, 87, 164, 183, 192, 202–18,
    223–24, 256, 277–78
Transcendence 38, 62
Transformation 40
Transgression 139–62

Utilitarianism 67, 156

Vernacular religion 105–23
Violence 150

Witchcraft 212, 256, 261
Work 87–104, 155–56

Zen Buddhism 9, 87–104